The Secret Rulers

Books by FRED J. COOK

THE WARFARE STATE

THE FBI NOBODY KNOWS

THE CORRUPTED LAND

The Secret Rulers

CRIMINAL SYNDICATES AND HOW
THEY CONTROL THE U.S. UNDERWORLD

by

FRED J. COOK

DUELL, SLOAN AND PEARCE
New York

DUELL, SLOAN & PEARCE
AFFILIATE OF
MEREDITH PRESS

Library of Congress Catalog Card Number: 66-22237

MANUFACTURED IN THE UNITED STATES OF AMERICA FOR MEREDITH PRESS

VAN REES PRESS • NEW YORK

CONTENTS

LIST OF ILLUSTRATIONS

(following page 54)

The Secret Rulers

1

THE INFORMER

HE was a squat plug-ugly dressed like a Dapper Dan. He had features that looked as if they had been pushed in and then hacked out of New Hampshire's Great Stone Face. The nose was spatulate, with harsh downward creases framing a broad mouth and a pugnacious jaw. He stood five feet five and a half, and at 190 pounds he had a figure like a barrel, encased in a suit of charcoal gray set off by a white shirt and a light, figured summer tie. He was Joseph Valachi, about to emit the squeal heard round the underworld and dressed for stardom. His forum was the McClellan committee of the U.S. Senate, and the story he was about to tell was an insider's, worm's-eye view of the secret rulers and the invisible empire that dominate vast areas of American life.

"The underworld runs the world only the people don't know it," one of New York's most famous detectives—a man who had seen the Combination at work in its heyday—had observed a good fifteen years before. But the people still didn't know it—not in their hearts and souls, not in the very marrow of their bones, not in any deep-down sense of crediting and caring.

To the public, this business of the underworld seemed like a fantasy —like some bold, gaudy headline in the *Daily News* or the explosive play-acting in the latest cops-and-robbers television series. It somehow wasn't *real*. The events with which the headlines dealt were those of some other, never-never world of flashy molls and hard-featured guys, glamorous and picturesque, with a Damon Runyonesque flair and patois. The commuter from Scarsdale, absorbed in his daily Wall Street chore, couldn't care less. Sure, bullets sometimes flew and some character from this nether world got dumped in a gutter, un-lovely in his gore. So what? Who cared if the rats killed each other? Good riddance, wasn't it?

There was no realization of a fact of American life that had been plain for the past four decades—no understanding of the basic truth that the rats had become bloated and all-powerful rodents, rulers of an invisible empire whose boundless billions surpassed those of Detroit's motor industry. This enormous wealth spelled enormous power, as it always does. It gave the rodents in charcoal suits the resources to buy New York skyscrapers; to gain control of brokerage houses and banks; to muscle into competition in major industries, hotels and motels, steel and oil, vending machines and racetracks, dress factories and meat-packing plants.

Wherever they went, the rulers of this nether world carried with them the taint of their money and the contamination of their tactics. A proprietor didn't want their vending machines? Wreck his joint and teach him a lesson. A union was causing trouble? Buy off its business agent or murder him. A bank wasn't returning a Shylock's profit? Substitute phony paper for its good securities—loot the till and bankrupt it. Meat prices were high? Well, horses come cheap; so do dead and diseased cows. Buy the carcasses, carve them up—and sell the product as fine meat to an unsuspecting public. The profits are handsome.

These things have happened, do happen, are happening. Politicians arc also bought—and so, sometimes, are judges. The underworld that runs the world, bankrolled by its billions, becomes virtually un-touchable. And Americans, most of them, couldn't care less. Perhaps they don't care because they simply don't believe. It is easier not to believe. If one doesn't believe, it isn't necessary to do anything about it.

Into such an atmosphere of unbelief and unconcern stepped Joseph Valachi. He wasn't anybody's conception of the archangel of truth and principle. He was a thug, vicious, unrepentant. He had dealt out death to others as he would a card in a poker game, but when he drew the ace of spades himself, *his* life became precious beyond compare.

He preserved it by the only means he knew, by telling all he knew about the secret rulers of the invisible empire.

In tangled syntax, in a Brooklynese that slaughtered vowels, in a guttural voice that grated on the ear, Joe Valachi brought to life the sinister world of "button men," of "contracts" and "hits" and double crosses, of "families" that carved up and controlled the rackets of New York and the nation. He told of rites of initiation, of the oath of *omertà,* of the pledge to live by the knife and die by the knife; and he put into the language a new term which even the most knowledgeable detectives had never heard before—Cosa Nostra, "Our Thing," a name that didn't mean quite what everyone assumed it meant.

The world that Joe Valachi described was one in which, as a way of life, the double cross was matched by the *double* double cross; a world in which a man's murderer was most apt to be his best friend. Intrigue was the name of the game, and the intricate deals that were hatched threaded the national and international scene. The ties of the Cosa Nostra dons in New York to the Mafia dons in Italy were very close, and a word from Rome, passed along the chain of command, could doom a man loitering on a New York street corner. It was a way of life perhaps capsuled best in Joe Valachi's account of his masterminding the execution of Eugene Giannini, his longtime associate in evil and, incidentally, one of the Federal Bureau of Narcotics' best informers.

Giannini, a lifelong thug, possessed high connections in the secret brotherhood that Joe Valachi called Cosa Nostra, an identical twin to the Mafia. Wily, devious, as trustworthy as a stiletto, Giannini had become by the 1930's one of the principal lieutenants of Charles (Lucky) Luciano, then overlord of the New York rackets and the real brains of the American underworld. Luciano was convicted of compulsory prostitution, slapped into prison, and subsequently deported back to Italy. In exile he remained an awesome power, the brains of the international narcotics racket and a statesman of crime whose voice still rang with authority for American gangdom. When Eugene Giannini traveled to Italy, which was often, he never failed to contact and consult with his former mentor, Lucky Luciano; and when he returned to America, he would pass on the latest word from Luciano to the mob overlord with whom he had become allied, Anthony (Tony Bender) Strollo. Strollo was the czar of Greenwich

Village and the lower Manhattan waterfront; he was also the lifelong lieutenant of Vito Genovese, the sinister and power-mad figure whom Valachi was to describe as "the boss of bosses under the table."

So blessed with all the right (or wrong) connections, Eugene Giannini plunged in the early postwar era into one of the most lucrative and vicious rackets of the underworld, the importation of narcotics from the countries of the Mediterranean basin. This was the period when heroin from abroad began to flood the American market, when pushers peddled their drugs in the schoolyards of New York, when teen-agers became addicts overnight and, hopelessly hooked, turned to crime and prostitution to finance their habit. In this ignoble trafficking, Eugene Giannini played an unscrupulous and profitable role. He and a combine that he formed, bankrolled by a private treasury of some $300,000, imported heroin by the tens of kilos (a kilo is two and a half pounds) and passed it on into the underworld chain for adulteration and distribution. This activity was infinitely remunerative to an unconscionable scoundrel, but it was not without hazard. In time, it brought Eugene Giannini into conflict with the Federal Bureau of Narcotics, and Giannini, once in the bureau's toils, began to help himself by informing.

The information that he funneled to the bureau proved valuable and enabled narcotics agents to break several important cases. But Eugene Giannini could not be content with the simple double cross; he had to perfect the *double* double cross. Even while he was selling out his hoodlum pals to the bureau to save his own skin, he was polishing up a scheme to double-cross the bureau by importing a shipment of heroin on his own. For the caper, Giannini needed a go-between, and he settled on a canny ex-con whom he deemed trustworthy. He supplied the ex-con with a specially made smuggling vest, gave him money and instructions, and packed him off to Italy to complete the heroin deal. To Giannini, everything must have seemed perfectly set up. He was informing for the bureau, so the bureau wouldn't suspect him. He was smuggling heroin, so the underworld wouldn't suspect him. He had both ends perfectly played against the middle.

But there were a few elements in the equation of which Eugene Giannini remained in fatal ignorance. The most important was the simple fact that his ex-con courier was also an informer for the Federal Bureau of Narcotics. From the outset, this informer no. 2 had kept the bureau advised of the intricate plot being perfected by Eugene Giannini, its informer no. 1; and so, when a plane took off from New York's Idlewild Airport bound for Rome, it carried among its passengers not the ex-con informer no. 2, but a federal narcotics agent to whom this worthy had transferred all of Giannini's information and credentials. In Italy, the narcotics agent, posing as Giannini's ex-con courier, made contact with Giannini's brother-in-law and purchased the shipment of heroin—then sprang the trap. The howls of anguish and disillusion were quickly heard across the Atlantic.

As Joe Valachi recounted it to the McClellan committee, he got the word from Tony Bender. Answering an imperial summons, he met the thin, doleful-visaged mob boss in Rocco's Restaurant on Thompson Street.

"I sat on a table and he told me that word had come from Charlie Lucky that Giannini is an informer," Valachi testified. "So I said, 'There goes my couple of thousand that he owes me.' "

Tony Bender's reaction, Valachi said, was that it wasn't anything they had to worry about; it was up to Giannini's immediate associates to take care of him. But matters didn't work out that way.

"About a month later, Tony sent for me again," Valachi related. "This time we went down to the Gold Key Club, I met him."

The Gold Key Club was an after-hours spot in which Tony Bender held a reputed interest. On one occasion, when detectives from District Attorney Frank S. Hogan's office staged an early-morning raid on the club, they found Bender prowling in the vicinity and put the clamp on him. The gang boss was so startled by the suddenness of the grab that he evidently figured mob powers had lined him up for a "hit," and so thinking, he suffered on the spot a debilitating physical reaction that necessitated a complete change of wardrobe.

On the occasion of this second talk with Joe Valachi, however, Tony Bender suffered from no such embarrassing emotions. He was still on top, on the dealing end, and this made all the difference. He told Valachi that Giannini's associates "can't seem to find him." Then he needled Valachi.

"Gee, Joe," he said, *"you* are not thinking about the money?"

This, Valachi said, was a delicate reference to the couple of thousand dollars that Giannini owed him; it was a way of testing what weighed most with Valachi, his desire to collect his couple of thousand or his loyalty to his profession.

Valachi rose to the bait, indignant.

"They are going to start this business?" he asked Tony Bender. "Can't they find him? I will find him."

By "find," he explained, he was really volunteering to take the "contract"—not just to locate Giannini but to kill him.

For Valachi, contacting Giannini was easy. He simply returned to his restaurant and picked up the telephone. "Meet me on the corner," he said, not bothering to identify either himself or the corner. He knew, he explained, that Giannini would recognize his voice and know that by "the corner" he meant Casseldra and Westchester Avenues.

"I'll be over in the next twenty minutes," Giannini said.

He kept the date, but when he arrived, a car was trailing him that, Valachi figured, contained shadowing agents. Together, Giannini and Valachi entered the Casbah on the corner.

"What, do you have agents following you?" Valachi asked, pointing out the tail.

"Jeez, they must be watching you," Giannini told him.

"Maybe they are," Valachi agreed nonchalantly, letting the matter drop.

He left quickly, however, telling Giannini he'd call him again in a couple of days. He did—and the same thing happened. Again there was that trailing, shadowing car.

"Gee, every time I call you, you got somebody covering you," Valachi told Giannini.

"Gee, I'm surprised," Giannini said.

"Ah, let's have a drink," Valachi told him.

So they had a drink or two, and the liquor loosened Giannini's tongue. He said he had "a creeping" feeling. Valachi asked what he meant and Giannini explained: "I don't know. I feel like I'm going to be killed."

"What are you talking about?" Valachi protested, just like a loyal friend.

"That is how I feel," Giannini insisted morosely.

This obviously wouldn't do. The friend whom one is marking for murder must never be allowed to suspect that he is being marked. Valachi, determined to cheer up Giannini, called over a girl who had formerly worked for him in the Lido and introduced her to his sad friend.

"Why don't you go out and have a good time?" he asked Giannini.

The informer and double double-crosser said he was short of cash. So Valachi gave him $40 and told him: "Go ahead and enjoy yourself."

Playing the role of a generous Cupid wasn't advancing the cause of murder very fast. Joe Pagano, who was working on the problem for Valachi, scouted around and discovered that Giannini was working "at the drop" of a crap game on East 112th Street. "At the drop" means the rendezvous point to which players would report and where they would meet contact men who would ferry them to the actual site of the game.

Giannini's connection with this other underworld operation created a problem because etiquette demanded that a rubout must not jeopardize the interests of a rival racket. Valachi took the problem directly to Tony Bender. He informed the mob boss that Giannini was working for the 112th Street game run by Paulie Hamm, a disciple of another of New York's ruling "families," that of Thomas (Three-Finger Brown) Lucchese.

"I will tell the old man about that," Tony Bender said, evidently referring to Vito Genovese.

Bender cautioned Valachi not to contact him directly again, but simply to give him a telephone call at the Gold Key Club. Valachi did and got the verdict. Tony Bender said just three words. "OK on him." It was a death sentence.

As Valachi testified before the McClellan committee, he now organized a killer squad composed of Joe and Pasquale Pagano and his own nephew, Fiore Siano. He advised them to make certain, before pulling any triggers, that they had an escape route that would let them pass quickly from 112th Street to 111th. Valachi himself checked the setup. He learned, much to his annoyance, that his helpers had not run through their escape alley and insisted that they do so. Finally, everything was lined up. Giannini reported for work, loitering on the street "at the drop"; and early on the morning of September 20, 1952, Siano and the two Paganos riddled him with bullets, made their escape into 111th Street, and telephoned Valachi that they were going to take a short vacation in Newark, their signal to him that the deed had been accomplished.

When residents of the 112th Street neighborhood, aroused by the lethal racket on the street, notified police, the cops came in a hurry.

But by the time they arrived, they found an almost peaceful scene. The only figure in sight was a porter industriously swabbing down the vacant sidewalk. "Just cleaning up," the man said, but when police stooped and investigated what he was cleaning, they discovered it was blood. "Imagine that?" the man said.

Giannini's body was not discovered until some hours later, around 6 A.M. It had been dumped on the sidewalk in front of 221 East 107th Street.

In this world of the infinite double cross, there was a postscript. Joe Valachi, in testifying before the McClellan committee, had seemed almost to go out of his way to implicate his own nephew, Fiore Siano. The reason for this was that when Valachi had been sent away to prison in the narcotics case that also jailed Vito Genovese, Fiore Siano had promptly muscled in on his uncle's preserves. He took over Valachi's vending-machine business and, not content with that, he also took over Valachi's favorite girl friend. Mortally offended, Valachi groused loudly to everyone he saw about the ingratitude of his nephew, and when he took the witness stand, he lost no opportunity to stick a shiv into Siano.

According to narcotics agents, whose keen ears catch most of the rumbles from the underworld, the mob got the message. Mob leaders evidently decided that Siano's treachery was a motivating factor in Valachi's damaging squeal, and in April, 1964, Siano disappeared as if the earth had swallowed him, as, indeed, perhaps it had. He is presumed to have been murdered, as the McClellan committee later reported, and when Valachi, in prison, was informed of this official belief, he merely smiled and grunted, "Good."

The man who could smile with satisfaction at the murder of his own nephew began life in the jungle of Manhattan's East Harlem. He was one of eighteen children born into an impoverished family. His home was on 109th Street, but some of his earliest cronies were budding thugs who later formed the muscle of the notorious 107th Street mob. Valachi named some of them for the McClellan committee. There were Joseph Gagliano, known as "Pip the Blind"; Frank Callace, known as "Chick 99"; Charles (Charley Bullets) Albero; "Big Dick" Amato, and others.

With the aid of such associates, Joe Valachi became a teen-aged hood. His first caper was delightfully simple and preposterously dangerous—"crashing windows." He and his hoodlum pals would roam the city until they spotted a jewelry store with an expensive display or a department store with some costly-looking fur coats and suits in the window. Returning in the early morning hours, they would heave a brick through the window, grab as much of the merchandise as they could, and swiftly make off. They were known, Valachi told the McClellan committee proudly, as the Minutemen because they could get away so fast—in a minute or less.

Valachi always drove the car. He was an expert driver, a fact in which he took great pride. He had a special pinion gear installed, he explained, so that, in making a getaway, he could zoom up to sixty miles an hour in second gear—a remarkable automotive performance in 1922. The loot seized by the Minutemen was marketed through fences, the most prominent of whom was Vincent (Vinnie) Rao. A kingpin of the East 107th Street mob, Rao was to rise to gangland prominence as a lieutenant and later "consigliere," or high councilor, in the family of Thomas (Three-Finger Brown) Lucchese. In his dealings with Valachi and the Minutemen, however, he was something less than generous. Valachi recalled that in one notable haul, his gang made off with jewelry worth between $30,000 and $35,000, but they collected only $4,000 from their fence.

The kind of criminal activity in which Valachi engaged at this period of his development was, of course, only for suckers, the very callow and the very young. The odds were just too great. Minutemen or not, it was impossible to keep taking such risks without sooner or later running head on into a cop with a loaded gun. The inevitable finally caught up with Valachi. On one occasion he was shot in the arm by a policeman, but escaped. Another time he caught a police bullet in the back of his head; a doctor charged $2,500 to perform a sneak operation to remove the pellet; and Valachi existed for three months in a semiconscious state before he recovered. Twice, the evidence against him was too ironclad and he spent nearly four years in prison on burglary charges. This was the only time that he was to spend behind bars until, late in life, the Federal Bureau of Narcotics jailed him for his dope-peddling activities.

Out of prison, back on the street in late 1929, Valachi was at the turning point in his career—a young hood who had spent his apprenticeship in petty and foolhardy crime and was ripe for larger and more sinister endeavors. He testified that a friend of his, Dominick Petrelli,

known as "the Gap," propositioned him to join the secret brotherhood. Another friend, Bobby (Bobby Doyle) Santuccio, added a persuasive voice. He pointed out that if Valachi kept on with the cheap
thug's crimes he had been committing, he would soon get himself
killed; but, if he joined the organization, he would have backing and
a chance to prosper.

Valachi bought the deal. He still didn't know anything about Cosa
Nostra, he said, when he and Chick 99 and a couple others were
driven about ninety miles to a large private house in upstate New
York. Valachi could not recall later exactly where the house was
located, but he said there were about thirty to forty mobsters gathered
there. All were members of the Gagliano-Maranzano family, then
one of the two ruling groups of the New York underworld. They were
gathered to "make" the new recruits—that is, to admit them into the
secret, blood brotherhood.

One by one, the novitiates were ushered into the inner sanctum.
It was a large room, with a long table as its principal item of furniture.
Around the table were clustered the members of the clan. Salvatore
Maranzano, who in Valachi's words was soon to become "the boss
of all the bosses," sat on the edge of the table next to Valachi and
administered the rites of initiation.

"When I came in, I sat down and they were at the edge of the
table, it was a long table, and there was a gun and a knife on the
table," Valachi testified. ". . . I repeated some words they told me,
but I couldn't explain what he [Maranzano] meant. I could repeat
the words, but they were in Italian. . . . He went on to explain that
they lived by the gun and by the knife and you die by the gun and by
the knife . . . then, he gave me a piece of paper and I was to burn it
. . . the piece of paper is burning, and it is lighted and then in your
hand, you say—well, again, they give you the words in Italian but
I knew what it meant."

It meant, Valachi explained: "This is the way I burn if I expose
this organization."

After the oath and the paper-burning ceremony, the grim-faced
members of the brotherhood gathered closer around the table and
drew lots. This was to decide who would be Valachi's official patron,
or godfather, in the organization. Valachi's sponsor, by the luck of
the draw, turned out to be Joseph (Joe Bananas) Bonanno, who was
to become the boss of one of the five ruling families in New York

and whose disappearance by kidnaping on the eve of a federal grand jury investigation was to provide one of the more baffling mysteries of 1964.

At the time, after Bonanno had been selected as Valachi's "god-father," he pricked Valachi's finger with a needle "and he makes a little blood come out, and in other words, that is the expression, the blood relationship. It is supposed to be like brothers." The purpose, Valachi explained to the McClellan committee, was to seal in the tightest bounds of blood relationship and "family" loyalty the vital and supreme secret—that of the very existence of this evil and criminal organization.

"As to what I am telling you now," Valachi said, "I need go no further to say nothing else but this here, what I am telling you, what I am expressing to you and to the press and everybody. This is my doom. This is the promise I am breaking. Even if I talked, I should never talk about this, and I am doing so."

With this ceremony in the mob's upstate hideaway, Valachi became a button man, or a soldier, in the army of crime. This was no trifling position. A button man was not a buck private. He was more like a corporal or a sergeant, with others under his command and with ties to the higher echelons and the awesome power of the organization. It was a position and a distinction for which, according to Valachi, eager applicants in the mid-1950's were willing to pay as much as $40,000.

Once accepted as a button man, Valachi had to abide by just two main rules: he had to observe above all the oath of omertà, that pledge of inviolate secrecy; and he must never molest the wife, sister, or daughter of another member. He had, too, one supreme obligation —to kill whenever he should be given a contract, or order to kill, by his superiors. It never occurred to him or to other members of the organization to question such an order for murder, Valachi said, and in time killing became "just as natural as breathing."

Valachi insisted that the elect, the members of the clan, never called their organization "the Mafia," but the rites he described— the oath of secrecy, the blood prick, the vow to kill, to live by the knife and the gun—all were purest Mafia, transplanted with hardly a change in the trappings from the terroristic society that had dominated Sicily for centuries. Even the term "button men" is of Sicilian derivation. The Italian carabinieri originally wore large, shiny brass buttons, and they were, of course, men of authority. So the Mafia, organized along military lines, designated its members, its men of authority, as button men.

What, then, about Cosa Nostra, the term Valachi used? There is a consensus among the nation's best investigators, men with the most intimate knowledge of the underworld and its rackets, that they had never heard the name before Valachi used it. "I never heard it. I never heard it even from Joe Valachi," says one of the nation's foremost investigators. This has cast some doubt upon the validity of Valachi's story. But there is a fairly simple explanation.

Wiretaps had established that gangsters often used the term "Cosa Nostra" or "our thing." But when they did, they invariably had a specific "thing" in mind. "Our thing is having some trouble," they might say, and by this they would mean that the particular gambling or narcotic or loan-sharking racket in which they were interested had hit a snag. Chary of divulging too much over the telephone and knowing in any event that those to whom they were talking had the basic background knowledge, they would simply speak of "our thing." "But," says a top investigator, "they were talking not about the organization itself, but about the particular racket in which they were engaged at the moment." In the first great blast of publicity about the confessions of Joe Valachi, however, this rather simple use of the term "our thing" became translated into the name of the great secret society, Cosa Nostra. It was a new term. Newspapers, never having heard it before—and with good reason—were delighted, and Joe Valachi and everyone else, so the story goes, were stuck with the term Cosa Nostra.

This explanation appears to be supported by the unusual significance that is placed upon the word "our" in mob contacts and associations. That simple pronoun keys many an introduction and conveys a subtle meaning not readily apparent to an outsider. One mobster, introducing a stranger to another, may say, "He's a friend of mine." It means just that. But if the man performing the introduction should say, "He's a friend of *ours*," the meaning would be drastically altered. It would instantly be understood that the stranger was a member of the brotherhood and so the possessor of special status.

Regardless of name, the vital fact remains: the criminal organization exists. It has been called at various times the Mafia, the Unione Siciliano, the Combination, the Syndicate, and now, by Valachi at least, Cosa Nostra. The name itself is secondary. What matters is the reality of a secret organization, an invisible government of crime, its heritage and structure derived from the Sicilian Mafia with which, significantly, it maintains ties of interchangeable membership. It is not the only criminal organization in America, but it is the biggest, the most vicious, the most dangerous. It controls by far the preponderance of the rackets, and it is the only organization of its kind with ties that span the continent and extend abroad.

Investigators now agree almost unanimously about this. This much, they hold, has been firmly established. And not just by Joe Valachi.

Though the fact has not been widely publicized, Valachi is not the only member of the brotherhood to have broken the code of omertà. Both the Federal Bureau of Investigation and the Federal Bureau of Narcotics have other informers inside the criminal conspiracy, and some of them are more highly placed than Valachi was.

"We've checked out Valachi's story with our own sources," says one highly placed federal investigator, "and his story checks. It's all true. Oh, there are some things he got secondhand, some minor details on which he might be a bit off, but otherwise, for all intents and purposes, Valachi's story is accurate right down the line."

The real significance, then, of Joe Valachi as differentiated from other informers is that he got up on a public witness stand and told his story. He put it on the record in the full glare of television lights and cameras. Other informers have demanded secrecy as their best protection. But not Valachi. He had old scores to settle; he wanted to get even with Vito Genovese, the king of modern crime. And he wanted Vito Genovese to know that he, Joe Valachi, was the man who was doing all the damage.

The squeal had its origin in a cell of the Federal Penitentiary in Atlanta, Georgia, in June, 1962. Valachi and Vito Genovese had both been snared by the Federal Bureau of Narcotics in a monumental 1950 roundup of the kingpins of the drug racket. The bureau's breakthrough, powered by direct-informer testimony, had led to the capture and conviction of a whole flock of the top powers of the New York underworld. The names read like a scroll of the unprincipled elite: Vincent (Vinnie Bruno) Mauro, a top lieutenant of Tony Bender; Frank (Frankie the Bug) Caruso, another top Bender aide; John (Big John) Ormento, one of the nation's fore-

most narcotics importers; Carmine (Little Caesar) Galante, probably the most vicious enforcer of the modern mob, a man who made
the late Albert (the Lord High Executioner) Anastasia seem positively humane. And finally, of course, there had been the prize catch
of all, Vito Genovese himself.

This unsavory assortment of characters wound up in various federal prisons, but as luck would have it, Valachi and Vito Genovese
were berthed together as cell mates in Atlanta. Also incarcerated in
Atlanta at the time was Vito Agueci, a member of the Buffalo-Cana-
dian wing of the brotherhood and a follower of the district Mafia
overlord there, Stephen Maggadino. Agueci wanted to talk to Vito
Genovese; but, naturally, such was the emperor's august power,
Agueci could not approach the throne directly. He had to have a
courtier of the inner circle to intercede for him. Knowing Valachi
stood in well with Genovese, Agueci approached Valachi and asked
him to arrange for an audience.

Valachi did not like or trust Agueci, but he felt that he had to do
as Agueci requested. Otherwise, if it ever came out that he had held
back and not forwarded the request to Genovese, it might appear
that he had had something to hide. So he took Agueci's plea for an
audience to the man who, though now in prison, still wielded an
emperor's power over the affairs of crime. At first Genovese refused
to see Agueci, but later, thinking it over, he changed his mind and
listened to the tale Agueci had to tell him. Almost immediately afterwards, Valachi noticed a change in the cordial climate that had
always prevailed in his relationship with the boss.

One night shortly after this chill had set in, Genovese called Valachi and another cell mate, Ralph Wagner (not one of "ours," Valachi
said), over to his bed for a conference. Wagner, without being invited, actually sat down in the imperial presence, a breach of etiquette
that shocked Valachi who would never have thought of doing such
a thing. Choosing to ignore this lese majesty on the part of Wagner,
Genovese began to talk. He talked not openly and frankly, but in the
circumlocutions that seem to become ingrained in men who deal all
their lives in deceit and subterfuge.

It was a good thing, Genovese said, that he was a good judge of
men and knew how to evaluate a story. He could always tell when
a man was giving him the straight pitch. Then, with a glance at Valachi, he dropped the pregnant line: "You know, sometimes if I have

a barrel of apples, and one of those apples is touched [rotten], it has to be removed or it will touch the rest of the apples."

Valachi began to shake his head in protest, but Genovese held up his hand, a regal gesture that forbade dissent. With that, having spoken the lines he wanted to speak, Genovese cut off all chance of further discussion by saying, "I think I will go to sleep." He rose, grabbed Valachi's hand, remarked that they had been friends for a long time; and then, pulling Valachi close, he gave him a kiss on the cheek— as he said, for old time's sake. It was a kiss that made Valachi shudder. As he and Wagner went to their own beds, Wagner muttered in his ear, "The kiss of death." Valachi ignored him. But he could not sleep.

Terror now began to possess the soul of the squat thug to whom the slaying of others had become "as natural as breathing." He felt certain that his own number was up; that Agueci must have accused him of the heinous offense of informing—and that Genovese had believed Agueci. As he lay awake, he said, he could see Genovese lying on an opposite bed, taking "peeps to see if I was asleep." For thirty years, Valachi said, he had had such respect for Genovese that "I even stuttered when I talked to him," but now, condemned and sentenced without trial, without being able to utter a word in his own defense, he was beginning to lose some of that respect. He was also beginning desperately to try to find a way to save his own skin.

He did not dare eat for fear his food might be poisoned. He did not dare mingle with a crowd in the exercise yard, certain that, if he did, someone would stick a shiv in his back. He did not dare sleep for fear someone would stab him to death while he slept. Finally, in a frenzy of fear and desperation, he solved his problem temporarily by asking prison authorities to put him "in the hole," in solitary confinement, because he feared for his life.

From the hole he addressed a desperate appeal to Thomas (Three-Finger Brown) Lucchese. Feeling that he had been unfairly condemned without a hearing, in violation of the Cosa Nostra code designed to protect button men, Valachi appealed to Lucchese to come to Atlanta and straighten out his problem. Here is his letter:

"I'll advice you just as soon as you will receive this drop everything and come and see me don't let money stand in your way. it is of most important. don't waste one day. understand. then I will never bother you any more. when you come make sure you get in. remember don't lose any time."

Prison officials returned the letter to Valachi for rewriting, hoping to get some clue to his motivations; but Valachi, suspecting everyone, believing that Genovese's power was so great he had brought even the prison officials into the cabal against him, abandoned the entire project.

Released from the hole after a four-day confinement, Valachi quickly realized that he was in a worse predicament than ever. Though he was not yet ready to inform on anybody, he knew that, by going into the hole at his own request, he must have practically confirmed Genovese in his suspicions.

"I am a dead duck after I went into the hole . . . ," he testified to the McClellan committee afterwards. "It would be just like their seeing you go into a police station to inform. It would be exactly the same thing."

Valachi now began to disintegrate under the pressure of the death sentence that he felt certain had been passed upon him. Little incidents confirmed his worst fears and suspicions. Another convict called insults at him and tried to lure him into a fight in the prison yard; Valachi pretended not to hear. John (Johnny Dio) Dioguardi, the garment-district strong arm accused of blinding labor-columnist Victor Reisel, invited him to take a shower at a time when no one else was in the shower room; Valachi didn't go. Watching all his fellow inmates with paranoid suspicion, Valachi became convinced that a convict by the name of Joseph (Joe Beck) DiPalermo had been given the contract to do him in. And so he determined to take care of Joe Beck before Joe Beck could take care of him.

On the morning of June 22, 1962, Valachi was walking in the prison yard when he spotted, right in front of him, the figure of Joe Beck. Some construction work was being done nearby. Valachi saw a pipe, grabbed it. He leaped upon Joe Beck's back and went to work with the pipe, savagely bludgeoning the man who, he believed in his demented state, had been selected to be his own executioner.

Three times the heavy pipe rose and fell, with all the force of Valachi's squat, powerful body behind it. His victim sank to the ground, his skull crushed. Other convicts in the yard started toward Valachi. Thinking they might be in the plot to murder him, Valachi whirled upon them, waving the pipe and keeping them at a distance.

A prison guard came running and Valachi, still refusing to surrender the pipe, followed the officer meekly to the prison office. There he learned that he had murdered the wrong man—a convict named Joseph Saupp who, in height, build, and appearance, had had the misfortune to bear a close resemblance to Joe Beck.

The slaying of the wrong man was the final straw.

"Valachi," an investigator later said, "has no real remorse for anything he has done in his life, except this. Nothing crushes him more than the fact that he got the wrong guy. It really plagues him. Getting the guy who was going to get him was the one satisfaction he was willing to settle for. If he had been successful, he probably never would have talked."

Unsuccessful, Valachi apparently decided that if he was to be doomed for informing, whether he had done so or not, he might as well inform. He managed to slip a cryptic message out of prison to a New York federal narcotics agent who had questioned him at the time of his arrest and whom he respected. The agent quickly perceived that Valachi's revelations went far beyond the limited range of authority of the narcotics bureau, and the Federal Bureau of Investigation was called in. A veteran FBI agent, a man of infinite knowledge, skill, and tact, was given the chore of milking Valachi of all he knew; and for months, humoring, cajoling, pressuring a little when pressure was needed, this agent drew from Valachi the details of a lifetime spent in the nether world of crime.

At first Valachi was sequestered in the hospital wing of the Westchester County Jail, a few miles north of New York City, under the name of "Joseph DeMarco." He was questioned four days a week, for about three hours a day; he was repeatedly warned that he must tell the truth—and he was promised all the protection the federal government could give him if he did. To reassure Valachi, who knew all too well how easily the underworld can reach into a prison to perform the deed of murder, he was transferred to the Army Signal Corps base at Fort Monmouth, New Jersey, where he was placed in the stockade with whole battalions of troops surrounding him to insure his safety. Just how he lived and was guarded were matters labeled "top secret"—and, somewhat ridiculously it would seem, so they remain at this writing nearly three years later. But word of Valachi's presence at Fort Monmouth eventually leaked to the press, even as another leak from the underworld reported that a $100,000 price tag had been put on his head. So he was moved again. He had indicated a willingness to testify in public before the McClellan committee, and so it was essential in any event that he be located near the capital. On September 9, 1963, protected by security arrangements worthy of a President, he was taken from the stockade at Fort Monmouth and flown to Washington where he was placed in a private suite in a blocked-off wing of the District of Columbia jail. There he was watched over day and night by federal agents devoted to just one task—preserving his life.

The crowning paradox of the Valachi revelations is that, though they disclosed little that was entirely new, they accomplished a real breakthrough in public and official acceptance of the obvious. "This is what we have been talking about for years, but nobody would listen to us," said one well-informed New York detective. A high-ranking federal investigator put it this way: "The amount of apathy among top law-enforcement people was to me incomprehensible." This investigator points out that even after the Apalachin rally of Mafia dons in 1957, there was a stubborn tendency to insist that it couldn't be. When the Committee on Organized Crime of the National Association of Police Chiefs called for action on a national scale to cope with the interstate criminal conspiracy, there was an explosion that nearly tore the organization apart. Director J. Edgar Hoover, of the Federal Bureau of Investigation, threw all his enormous influence and prestige against the proposal, and another prominent federal law-enforcement official actually resigned from the organization in protest. About the same time, one of the great television networks did an hour-long documentary on the theme: Was there a Mafia? Was there a national syndicate of crime or was there not? And it concluded, in essence, that the whole concept was preposterous.

Yet the grim facts had been obvious for decades to anyone with the wit to see. As long ago as 1940, the Murder, Inc., probe in Brooklyn had exposed the cross-continent ramifications of underworld interests and the manner in which crime lords met and arrived at far-reaching decisions. The Brooklyn sadists of Albert Anastasia had left a trail of corpses from Maine to California; they had killed so often they couldn't even remember some of their victims; and they had done so to carry out the plans and orders of a higher, functioning criminal authority. Burton B. Turkus, the prosecutor who broke the Murder, Inc., case for the late William O'Dwyer, always insisted, on the basis of apparently unimpeachable evidence, that the real significance of Murder, Inc., lay in the fact that it was not just a local exercise in mayhem, but the enforcement arm of a national criminal syndicate.

There had been other signs and portents, each reinforcing the other. Better known to investigators than to the public was the reality of periodic gangland conventions. These gatherings brought together Mafia dons from all sections of the nation, and they were held, according to the most trusted informers, for the express purpose of reaching decisions on the future conduct of crime. Like delegates to a national political convention engaged in drafting a party platform, the Mafiosi in conclave would decide which rackets were to be de-emphasized and which promised the greatest future reward. They decided, too, on how the racket territories of the nation were to be divided and administered; they ratified the status of regional ruling dons; and, if necessary, they passed death sentences in enforcement of their decrees.

Police stumbled first upon one of these gatherings in a Cleveland hotel in 1928. In 1929, in a rally held in an Atlantic City boardwalk hotel, the actual organization of crime had been perfected and far-reaching decisions made to give the criminal purpose a suave, conservative veneer. The convention site had shifted to Chicago in 1933, and there the Mafiosi, with Prohibition about to be repealed, had made another key decision: they would switch their primary investments from the illicit liquor traffic to gambling and narcotics, the financial gushers that, ever since, have bankrolled the treasury of the underworld.

None of these conventions, however, had had the drama or carried the headline impact of the gathering in the hills of Apalachin in upstate New York on November 14, 1957. For the most part, the earlier conclaves had met and disbanded, their business transacted, before word of what had happened filtered back to investigators. Apalachin was different. It was discovered and disrupted in mid-career by Sgt. Edgar L. Croswell, of the New York State Police.

For years, Sgt. Croswell had kept a keen detective's eye upon the doings of the late Joseph Barbara, Sr., a Mafioso who had twice beaten what appeared to Croswell to be ironclad murder cases. Croswell had been convinced that Barbara's immunity was due to his

importance in the secret, sinister brotherhood of the Mafia, and so
he had kept a close watch on him and on his $150,000 hilltop man-
sion. This diligence paid off in mid-November, 1957, when Sgt.
Croswell discovered that Barbara was buying enormous quantities
of meat, making motel reservations all around the countryside, and
in other ways preparing for what obviously was to be a huge rally
of the clan.

Croswell waited until Barbara's driveway and yard were cluttered
with Cadillacs and Chrysler Imperials; then he set up a roadblock.
In panic, the Mafiosi tried to flee; and as they came down the road
into his net, Croswell rounded them up and brought them in for questioning. The industrious sergeant gathered in some sixty members of
the brotherhood, and found that they had upon them the kind of
money that talks loudly in times of trouble—more than $300,000
in cash. This time, however, the money did not talk. Sgt. Croswell
wasn't interested. He wanted the truth—and this he couldn't get.
Either the Mafiosi refused to say anything or they came up with a
favorite story to explain their presence at Apalachin. They had all,
they said, purely by chance, without any advance planning, just happened to drop in on this day of days to visit a sick friend—poor,
ailing Joseph Barbara, who, as all knew, was suffering from the
serious heart ailment that ultimately was to carry him off.

That a gaggle of the nation's toughest mobsters would flock from
New York, Cuba, Florida, Italy, California, and way stations, all
on the same day, all moved by the telepathic impulse to commiserate
with their unfortunate brother, certainly must rank as one of the
most fanciful tales of our times. The reality, clearly, was that Sgt.
Croswell had disrupted a high council of the Mafia. The stature of
some of those in attendance spoke persuasively to this effect. Among
them had been Vito Genovese, current czar of the underworld; Joe
Profaci, the "olive oil king" and don of one of New York's ruling
families; Carlo Gambino and Joseph Bonanno (Valachi's "god-
father"), two more of the ruling family chiefs; Mike Miranda, high
councilor in the Genovese wing of the empire; and flashy Big John
Ormento, boss of the 107th Street mob and a reigning narcotics king.

Others of almost equal prominence had been present, and others,
still not publicly identified to this day, had managed to escape detec-
tion. Some of the delegates at Apalachin fled into the woods; others
remained huddled for days out of sight in Joseph Barbara's cellar.

Informers later gave federal authorities a fuller picture of the size and significance of the gathering. This showed that leaders of the Chicago syndicate had participated, but had been among those who successfully dodged the spotlight. The real truth about Apalachin is that it was nearly twice as large as originally reported; it had brought together more than one hundred of the nation's leading Mafiosi.

The half-picture at the time, however, was enough to make glaring headlines. The mere fact that the Apalachin gathering had happened carried its own meed of proof. Editorial writers, such as those on the *New York Herald Tribune,* became convinced that there was an "invisible government" of crime, secret and sinister, possessed of incredible resources and paralleling in its hidden functions the legitimate government of the nation. The *Herald Trib* called loudly for action and for a time there were some stirrings, some serious attempts at prosecution. But appeals fought out in the higher courts overturned some of the major convictions, and the effort lapsed. It seemed, as the imbroglio in the National Association of Police Chiefs had demonstrated, that even high-ranking and supposedly knowledgeable law-enforcement officials were all too inclined to dismiss the idea of an "invisible government" of crime as a fantasy conjured up by journalists.

Then came Joseph Valachi. The attitudes that prevailed on some of the highest official levels before Valachi and after Valachi were perhaps best capsuled in a statement made to the *Saturday Evening Post* by William Hundley, head of the Justice Department's section on organized crime.

"Before Valachi came along," Hundley said, "we had no tangible evidence that anything like this actually existed. He's the first to talk openly and specifically about the organization. In the past we've heard that so-and-so was a 'syndicate man' and that was all. Frankly, I always thought it was a lot of hogwash. But Valachi named names. He showed us what the structure is and how it operates. . . ."

Hundley's boss at the time, Attorney General Robert F. Kennedy, was even more emphatic. Valachi's revelations, he declared, represented "the biggest intelligence breakthrough yet in combating organized crime and racketeering in the United States." In testimony before the McClellan committee and in magazine articles such as one which appeared in the *New York Times Sunday Magazine,* Kennedy spelled out in considerable detail just what had been learned and just how great was the menace.

Valachi had disclosed, he told the McClellan committee, that the national "invisible government" of crime was ruled by a commission composed of about a dozen members.

"We know," Kennedy testified, "that the commission makes major policy decisions for the organization, settles disputes among the families, and allocates territories of criminal operation within the organizations."

Kennedy also identified the members of the ruling elite. At the pinnacle, even though in prison, was Vito Genovese. The bosses of the other four New York families also sat on the commission: Joseph Profaci, Joseph Bonanno, Thomas (Three-Finger Brown) Lucchese, and Carlo Gambino. Other members of the commission were the czars of regional areas in which vital rackets flourished. The McClellan committee later produced elaborate charts, identifying these regional overlords.

The Chicago complex, a power in the organization of gangdom from the days of Al Capone and Tony Accardo, was represented by Salvatore Momo (Sam or Mooney) Giancana, the constant squire of singer Phyllis McGuire and a sometime associate of Frank Sinatra. Detroit was represented by Joseph (Mr. Joe) Zerilli, who had married Rosalie Profaci, solidifying relations with the eastern wing of the Syndicate, and who had then, with the help of Pete Licavoli and others, taken over the Detroit rackets from the infamous Purple Gang of the early 1920's.

Other major metropolitan centers supplied the remaining members of the commission: Pittsburgh, John Sebastian (Big John) La Rocca; Philadelphia, Angelo Bruno; Buffalo, Steve Maggadino; Cleveland, John T. Scalish; New England, Raymond L. S. Patriarca, whose influence was dominant in both Boston and Providence, R.I.

These were the kingpins of crime across the nation, but they were not by any means the only figures of importance. Their underbosses and consiglieri (or councilors) and lieutenants wielded enormous power. Federal agencies, Kennedy said, were pooling information on 1,100 "major racketeers" who dominated what he agreed had been "aptly described as a private government of organized crime, a government with an annual income of billions, resting on a base of human suffering and moral corrosion."

The Attorney General gave the McClellan committee some vivid insights into the sweep and extent of mob power. He noted that he had told the House and Senate in 1961 that the underworld obtained *from illegal gambling alone* a gross income of some *$7 billion annually.* Subsequent investigations, he said, had ratified that figure.

He cited the case of a former hotel in Detriot that had been taken over by the mob as headquarters for an extensive numbers operation, other types of gambling, and prostitution. The most elaborate protective devices had been installed, including a building-wide buzzer-alarm system and the spying eye of a closed-circuit television camera in the lobby. On November 9, 1962, a 100-man raiding team surrounded the onetime hotel and pulled what Kennedy called "one of the most successful raids in history." The raid was carried out so swiftly that, despite the protective devices, financial records of the hotel-racket operation were seized. These showed that this one headquarters of crime and vice had brought in a gross of $21 million a year.

"Such enormous totals are not unusual," Kennedy told the McClellan committee. "They illustrate how big a business organized crime has become."

He pointed out that records seized in one New York City numbers-game raid showed a gross profit of $6 million a year, and in three related games prosecuted in the western district of Pennsylvania, the take had been $40 million annually. "Figures of this magnitude have been found all over the country," Kennedy declared.

To get some idea of the enormous power represented by such illicit billions, note that, in many years, the entire product of Detroit's automobile industry, has borne a wholesale price tag of only $8 billion to $9 billion. The underworld, from illegal gambling alone, then, is making *an annual profit* that nearly equals the total wholesale value of every car and truck produced in America. And this is not the sum of its resources. It has additional billion-dollar sources of power in legal gambling, narcotics, loan-sharking, and other rackets. Investigators have estimated that the total annual bankroll of syndicated crime in America represents a staggering $9 billion to $11 billion.

Inevitably, such law-breaking operations entail wholesale corruption of the law. Milton R. Wessel, who headed the Attorney General's Special Group on Organized Crime after Apalachin, has estimated that a full 50 per cent of the underworld's colossal multibillion-dollar

take is spent to purchase political influence and for the corruption of
police and public officials.

Though Attorney General Kennedy made no such percentage
estimate, he told the McClellan committee that, in Texas, "a number
of public officials, including the sheriff, district attorney and police
chief of Beaumont and Port Arthur each admitted receiving substantial amounts as 'political contributions.' In one case, these amounted
to $85,000 in five years." The corruption of municipal officials had
reached such a stage, Kennedy reported, that his department was
running one hundred investigations in thirty states.

Yet the American public remains largely apathetic and the underworld goes industriously on piling up those colossal billions of dollars
that give it an insidious, corruptive power in virtually every phase of
American life. In moments of black depression, Joe Valachi realizes
all of this. "What good is what I'm telling you?" he once asked. "Nobody will listen. Nobody will believe. You know what I mean? Cosa
Nostra, it's like another government. It's too big."

Whether it's too big or not, the effort must be made to realize, to
understand. Perhaps the simplest way is to take a case history, the
story of one city that has been held in the grip of crime for most of
the past forty years—Youngstown, Ohio, widely known as "Murder
Town, USA."

2

BOMBS AWAY

THANKSGIVING DAY, 1962. It was a quiet, happy time in the household of Charles (Cadillac Charlie) Cavallaro in Youngstown, Ohio. A grape merchant, Cadillac Charlie called himself, but there were many in Youngstown who knew that his real business was not grapes, but the rackets. A heavily built man with a square, solid face, he had thinning hair, wide-set eyes, and wide, downward-slashing lips. He lived in a modest-appearing, two-story brick house at 164 Roslyn Drive, in an excellent residential neighborhood on Youngstown's North Side. The house was expensively furnished, graced with knotty pine paneling and equipped with a bar and wine cellar in the basement. In it, Cadillac Charlie lived the quiet life of a gentleman of means and a good neighbor.

Cadillac Charlie was friendly, always read to perform some neighborly service. When he backed his car out of the garage to take his sons to school or to play football in the park, neighborhood youngsters would pile in and go along. Cadillac Charlie always welcomed them. He liked kids.

In his own family there were three, a daughter Ramona, 15, and two sons, Charles Jr., 12, known as Chuckie, and Tommy, 11. The neighbors all had a special fondness for Tommy. He was a handsome boy, with bright eyes and a wide, engaging grin. All fall he had been working hard on the neighbors' yards, mowing and raking, and he had confided his motive for this industry—to earn enough money to buy his mother a Christmas present.

With the Thanksgiving holiday coming up, Cadillac Charlie came home from the grape business about 5:00 P.M. Wednesday, November 21. He drove the rented red-and-white Ford sedan straight into the garage about thirty feet in the rear of the house and left it there. All Thanksgiving Day he did not go out, but spent the time quietly with his family and made one telephone call to a sister to wish her a happy holiday.

Cadillac Charlie didn't get to bed until about two o'clock Friday morning, after watching television, and he was up at eight, puttering about the house and having breakfast with his family. About 11:30 A.M. he decided to drive down to a Front Street wholesale house, where he had the last of a load of grapes to sell and a grape bill to pay. His two sons, Tommy and Charles, went with him because they had a football practice session scheduled at Harding Field.

They walked out to the garage and opened the doors. Charlie got behind the wheel—Tommy beside him on the front seat, Charles on the far side, near the right-hand door. All was ready. Cadillac Charlie flipped the ignition switch and an instantaneous explosion rocked the neighborhood.

Mrs. Cavallaro, the former Helen Biola, ran outside with Ramona. The blast had turned the garage into a heap of rubble. The entire roof of the car had been blown up and peeled backward. The lower half of Cadillac Charlie's body had disintegrated; the upper portion had been blown into the yard.

It seemed inconceivable that anyone could have lived, yet from the mound of twisted debris came the terrified voice of a young boy, screaming in agony.

"Mommy, Mommy, help me!" the voice cried over and over.

Neighbors, rushing into the yard, found Ramona and Mrs. Cavallaro screaming and hysterical. Mrs. Cavallaro, on the verge of collapse, sobbed: "My kids need me and I can't help them."

Only one child needed her. Tommy Cavallaro, seated beside his father, had been killed instantly. Charles, on the outside of the front seat, had been trapped in the wreckage, his left hip crushed by the force of the explosion.

In such tragic fashion Youngstown paid the piper. The Cavallaro bombing was the eighty-second in a series that had rocked the city and surrounding countryside. The bombings had been going on for ten years, each one a thunderous salute to the mob's dominance of Youngstown and its environs. Yet nobody seemed to care. Each time a racket czar was killed, Youngstowners shrugged their shoulders and repeated the old refrain: "What's the difference? The only way we'll ever get rid of the rats is to have them knock each other off." The answer to such moral sophistry was delivered in definitive fashion on that morning of November 23, 1962. Not just Cadillac Charlie Cavallaro was dead, but his bright-eyed son Tommy with him. Murder, unrestrained, had claimed the innocent as well as the guilty.

Youngstown is a city of flourishing industry, of wealth and culture —yet it is a city in which, for the past forty years, the most vicious elements of the underworld have controlled politics, the police, and sometimes even the courts.

Youngstown boasts that it was the boyhood home of William Holmes McGuffey, author of the famous McGuffey's Reader; it is the home of Youngstown University, with an enrollment of more than 9,900 students; its Mill Creek Park covers 2,383 acres and contains a 36-hole public golf course and three lakes; it has its own Philharmonic Orchestra, its own Playhouse, an extensive library system, and the widely known Butler Institute of American Art—and yet it has harbored an underworld empire that takes in an estimated $4.5 million a year from the gambling rackets.

Youngstown's giant industries include Youngstown Sheet and Tube, the sixth largest steel producer in the nation, and major mills of United States and Republic Steel, the no. 1 and the no. 3 steel producers. It boasts flourishing department stores and banks, fashionable motels and nightclubs; it has a population of 166,689 and is the hub for a trading area with a population of 700,000. And yet it has remained a city in which all the wealth and power of legitimate business and allied civic organizations have exercised a puerile influence compared to the corruption fostered by the mob's $4.5 million annual gambling bankroll.

Ironically, Youngstown is a city that has made a fetish of traffic safety. One wall of the mayor's office is plastered with plaques emblematic of the city's high rating in Ohio and national safety contests —most of them won during those same ten years in which racket

czars, warring like jungle beasts for the gambling loot, were gunning
each other down—or blowing each other up by wiring dynamite sticks
to the steering columns of parked cars.

Youngstown is a city that proclaims it has 193 "well-organized
churches with excellent leadership"—yet this leadership and religious
influence has been powerless to stir the civic conscience in any effective way. The city's reputation is such that when a correspondent from
abroad dispatched a letter addressed only to "Murder Town, USA,"
it unerringly found its way to Youngstown.

Basic to the Youngstown story are the steel mills that ring the city
and largely sustain its economic prosperity. From the earliest days,
the mills have depended upon cheap, unskilled foreign labor, struggling for a foothold at the bottom of the American employment ladder.
At the time of the Cavallaro bombing, Youngstown was temporarily
under the guidance of a reform mayor, Harry N. Savasten, himself
the son of a steel worker, himself once a laborer in the mills. "Steel-
mill work used to be such a hot, dirty, dangerous job that only the
foreign born would take it," Savasten said in discussing Youngstown's
melting pot.

A breakdown of the city's population shows the early immigration's
enduring influence. According to the 1960 census, the city had 13,406
Italians of whom at least one parent had not been born in the United
States. In the same category were 7,754 Czechs; 5,546 English; 3,913
Poles; 3,736 Hungarians; and 2,936 Russians. Such figures do not
include second- and third-generation descendants and so give only
a rough indication of the heavy influx of foreign born into the Youngstown mills. According to Savasten, some 13 per cent of the city's
eligible voters in 1963 were Negroes, and the Italian voting bloc was
much heavier than that.

This racial mixture and the very nature of mill work explain much
about Youngstown. It is among just such classes, the poor and struggling foreign born, the lowly mill laborers sunk in hopeless jobs, that
the gambling rackets of the underworld have always proliferated.
Especially is this true of the numbers game, the gamble that represents
the one ray of hope for the poor and hopeless. In Youngstown, the
numbers game was known as "the bug."

The lure of the bug was irresistible to people to whom even a
few hundred dollars seemed like a fortune. They bought their daily
tickets from numbers runners, and if their number came up (usually

the winning combination is based upon the last digits of the pari-mutuel play at a given track), the winner collected at the rate of 600 to 1. Such enormous odds made the bug seem like an easy, swinging gate to fortune—except, of course, that the odds against any player's winning were even more stupendous than the rate of payout, roughly 1,000 to 1, a full 400-point advantage that always rode with the mobsters who controlled the game.

Disregarding the odds against him, the numbers addict in Youngstown, as elsewhere, poured his petty cash into the constantly losing gamble that returned millions of dollars a year to the mob. These millions, naturally, were not all clear profit. A heavy percentage frequently had to be poured back in "ice" for police protection and in "contributions" to political campaigns to insure that many elected officeholders would wink at violations of the law.

This system, one that has worked time and again throughout the nation, functioned especially well in Youngstown. By the early 1920's, the stench of corruption had become so overpowering that it inspired a crusade for reform that is still recalled by veteran residents. The leader of the campaign was one of Youngstown's most prominent and wealthy businessmen, George L. Oles.

"Oles was just unbelievably successful," one woman club worker recalled. "He was one of those businessmen who seemed to have a certain touch, and everything he tried turned to gold. He had a number of businesses in Youngstown, all fabulously successful, and he was about the last man you would expect to go into politics. But he finally became fed up with the corruption he saw all around him and decided to clean up the city.

"He ran for mayor, promising to throw out all the crooks, and everybody got whipped up and excited. He was elected by a big majority, and he went into City Hall and began to fire right and left. Oh, for a time, he really cleaned house, and everybody—that is, all the more decent people—thought it was wonderful. But it didn't last. He began to get all kinds of threats, and in a few months it was all over."

The record shows that Oles did not even serve his full two-year term. He was mayor during only one year, 1922; then he resigned. Oles is now dead, and even veteran politicians profess to be uncertain just how intimidation was accomplished. But the suspicion is that he was not only threatened, he was in some way framed or compromised—and so forced out. Whatever the method, the moral of the story was quite clear, and it has never been forgotten. When a man as wealthy and independent and well-intentioned as Oles, elected mayor by a landslide vote, could be so quickly crushed, the dominance of the rackets in their corrupt alliance with the police and politics seemed established beyond dispute.

It was to the Youngstown of the mid-1920's, already a racket haven, that Cadillac Charlie Cavallaro reported in search of fortune. Born in Agrigento, Italy, on February 2, 1902, he had sought out the land of promise by simply stowing away on a ship bound west, and when the vessel docked in New Orleans, Cadillac Charlie came blithely ashore.

There was no dispute about the deed, only about its date. Even Cadillac Charlie acknowledged that he had thumbed his nose at formalities when he crossed U.S. borders, but he always insisted that this historic occurrence had taken place on May 9, 1921. The U.S. Immigration Service contended that it had records showing Cadillac Charlie was in the Italian Army at the time he said he landed in New Orleans. The Immigration Service argued, as a result, that his illegal entry could not have taken place until sometime after 1924.

The date was important because, due to a quirk in the laws, if Cadillac Charlie had arrived before 1924, he might have been entitled to stay; if after that, he was subject to deportation. Having determined to its own satisfaction that Cadillac Charlie was deportable, the Immigration Service began in 1935 to try to banish him from the country; but in 1962, after 27 years of struggle, it still hadn't gotten anywhere. Cadillac Charlie, hiring expensive legal mouthpieces, using money and influence where it would do the most good, had kept Uncle Sam snarled up in his own courts all those years, a performance that in itself gives a good idea of the big-car lover's muscle.

The record is obscure about Cadillac Charlie's early struggles. But there isn't much question about the methods he chose or the manner in which he practiced them. His police record establishes that, by the early 1930's, he was already wheeling and dealing in the subjungle of the Youngstown underworld.

His first caper was the lucrative bootlegging racket of Prohibition days, and his first arrest in Youngstown, in 1934, was for violation of the alcohol tax laws. The charge—and this was to become a familiar refrain in the career of Cadillac Charlie—ultimately was dismissed.

There were more arrests, many more. In 1936, he was picked up on a fugitive warrant issued by the Internal Revenue Service, and in that same year he was held on a charge of blackjacking filed against him by the New York police. He seems not to have been inconvenienced by these events. In 1942 and 1943, Jefferson and Ashtabula police held him on a more serious charge, extortion, but Cadillac Charlie laughed at the extortion case as he had laughed at all the others. He was demonstrating that consistent immunity to the law that goes with power in the rackets.

In Youngstown, his base of operations was a poolroom on South Champion Street. His business was bookmaking, the numbers, and, reportedly, a share in the ever-flourishing, high-stakes, fast-roll dice game known as "barbut," a Turkish gambling innovation that Greek and Italian immigrants had introduced into Youngstown. The take from all these sources must have been fantastic. As far back as 1937, with the nation still in the throes of the Depression, Youngstown's gambling pile was reputed to mean $3 million annually to the underworld, and in lush World War II days, with steel mills running full blast around the clock, the figure soared above $5 million; some estimate as high as $8 million. Cadillac Charlie's share was more than ample to insure his indulgence in his favorite big car, but the well-loaded table at which he and others dined inevitably lured a horde of contending, lethal scavengers.

Youngstown's strategic location made the competition more than ordinarily fierce. The city is the midway point on the turnpikes, 67 miles from Pittsburgh, 66 from Cleveland. Detroit, where, according to the McClellan committee, Zerilli and the Licavolis had taken over from the Purple Gang, is only a little more than 200 miles away. Inevitably, top gangsters from all three cities, working through local affiliates, angled for ever-larger shares of the Youngstown loot.

Among these contenders, Cadillac Charlie Cavallaro made his devious, prosperous, and well-connected way. He had, of all the Youngstown hoods, the strongest ties at the top. Former Police Chief Edward J. Allen, a law-enforcement officer still remembered with affection by the better elements in Youngstown, positively linked Cavallaro with the dynasty that mattered most—with the Licavolis of Detroit and, through them, with the Mafia. Allen became convinced that Cadillac Charlie enjoyed high standing in the Mafia and that he was the only Youngstown gangster who did.

Allen himself came upon the scene only because, in the early postwar era, Youngstown once more elected a reform administration. The reformer was Charles P. Henderson, a Republican, who was elected mayor in 1948 and was kept in office until 1954. One of Henderson's first acts in attempting a cleanup of Youngstown was to seek out a tough police chief. He settled on Allen, then a police sergeant in Erie, Pennsylvania, FBI-trained and highly recommended by J. Edgar Hoover. Allen, whose determined jaw and firm-set mouth were indicative of his character, immediately began a drive to chase the hoods out of Youngstown.

He pursued bookies, closed gambling joints, and harassed racket moguls wherever he could find them. One of his principal targets was Cadillac Charlie Cavallaro. Every time Cadillac Charlie gave Allen the slightest excuse, he was nabbed and fined. Three times he was caught speeding. Twice he was arrested for blocking a sidewalk. And finally, in 1951, the city building inspector ordered his South Champion Street poolroom razed on the contention it was unsafe for human occupancy.

Such persistent harassment had some effect on the racket chiefs, but it is a testimonial to their bankroll and their endurance that it did not work any permanent miracles. The hoods had to transfer some of their more wide-open activities over the border, just outside of Youngstown, where the suddenly revivified local law could not touch them. But, according to all the evidence, not even Allen and Henderson, working in tandem, could wipe out the penchant of Youngstowners for playing the bug or gambling in a barbut game or betting on the horses. Even during Allen's regime, right inside the city, a lot of covert gambling still went on.

Allen himself was aware of the difficulties. He charged bluntly at the time that the gambling rackets had maintained their hold on Youngstown by funneling half of their enormous profits into the payoff. He even charged that the payoff money passed through the hands of a triumvirate consisting of Jasper J. (Fats) Aiello, Moosey Caputo, and Joseph DiCarlo, the latter a favorite target of the Kefauver committee.

Though Allen did his best to clear grafters out of the police force, indications are that he had little success.

"I had a man in my office the other day," Mayor Savasten said in an interview in December, 1962, "who sat there and told me about the payoffs to the police force under Allen. I'm sure Henderson never knew about it. Apparently, nobody in authority did, but it went on. Ask yourself this question: Where did all these gangsters that have been in the news in recent years come from? DiCarlo? He was here under Allen. Cavallaro? He was here. The Naples brothers? DeNiro? They were here. They were all active even when Allen was chief, and if they hadn't been making it, they wouldn't have stayed, would they?"

Most Americans are virtuously opposed to crime and corruption, at least until it becomes necessary to sacrifice some of their own pleasures and desires. Then virtue becomes an unholy burden.

This is the history of reform throughout the nation and down through the decades. The American people can stomach just so much of it, then they plump for a more easy-going way of life in which the rectitude a man professes does not have to be the rectitude he practices.

In Youngstown, history repeated itself. Six years is a long time for reform, and the strain of such sustained purity becomes in time too much for those who consider themselves relatively pure of heart. After all, what is wrong with placing a little bet? And it would be nice to be able to fix a traffic ticket, wouldn't it? Or to get authorities to wink at building violations that are not *all that* serious, but would cost a landlord some hurting cash to fix? The result of such a municipal mood was that Allen and his tough law-enforcement program became the chief issue in a heated local election; reform was scuttled; and Youngstown slid right back into its old amoral ways.

Leaders in the backsliding were some of the supposedly better elements of the town that, even during the Allen regime, refused to forego any of their pleasures. The supposed elite of the city, they participated in much of the surreptitious betting that went on during the reform administration, and they helped to keep the underworld well-heeled, strong, and flourishing by flocking to those over-the-border spas that the mob ran just out of reach of Allen's Youngstown law.

The most famous of these beyond-the-law spots was The Jungle Inn, just to the north of the Youngstown line in Trumbull County. The Inn was the special fief of Mike and John Farah. The Farahs turned The Jungle Inn into one of the swankiest gambling houses in all Ohio. The *Youngstown Vindicator,* the area's one high-quality, mass-circulation daily, growls to this day about the manner in which many of the city's elite flocked across the border to enrich the Farahs with their losses at bingo, the slot machines, roulette. The money they squandered paid the wages of crime, and in the backrooms of The Jungle Inn there gathered some of the tristate (Pennsylvania-Ohio-Michigan) area's most repulsive hoods. So evil and pervasive was the influence of the Inn that, even a generation later, its graduates continued to surface in Youngstown virtually every time crime appeared.

The career of the Inn itself was terminated in late 1949 when Governor (now U.S. Senator) Frank Lausche, calling on all the resources of state law, put a padlock on its door. But nothing could curb the gambling fever the Inn had done so much to generate. In other over-the-border oases, the heavy play continued under the suzerainty of Mike Farah, the gambling czar of Trumbull County.

The profits were so enormous that the jungle cats of the underworld were soon at each other's throats. Into their increasingly embittered warfare, they now injected a new technique—indigenous to the region and, incidentally, long favored by the Mafia of Sicily: bombing. The first of the long series of dynamitings occurred late in 1951, and other subsequent blasts punctured the last years of Allen's regime in Youngstown. These early bombings took no lives. They were terroristic, designed to convince the object of attention that he had better get in line—and stay there.

This new thunder of dynamite sticks going off all over town didn't disturb Youngstowners very much, but then, they had passed the point of caring. In a callous city reverting to the easy-going amorality of past decades, who cared if members of the underworld served each other with these explosive warnings? Not even the events of May 8, 1959, caused any deepening concern in Youngstown.

On that day a young hood named Christ Sofocleous left the apartment of a blonde divorcee with whom he had been visiting since 1:30 A.M. It was nearly noon, a fashionable hour for rising, and the happy Sofocleous seemed not to have a worry on his mind, though perhaps he should have had.

For one thing, he had turned state's evidence and helped to send three burglar companions to jail for the theft of $14,000 from a safe in a Navy commissary in Norfolk, Virginia—a deed which would hardly be popular in racket circles. For another, his blonde charmer had also captured the roving eye of Ronnie Carrabia—scion of a family from the nearby, racket-ridden suburb of Struthers, with whose members one did not lightly tangle.

Sofocleous, only thirty, had not reached the age of discretion, and so he worried neither about professional enemies nor love rivals as he walked the short distance from the girl's apartment to his car. He had parked on Park Avenue about 100 feet from St. Elizabeth's, Youngstown's largest hospital. Children were playing nearby on the sidewalk as Sofocleous opened his car door, seated himself behind the wheel, and threw on the ignition switch.

Instantly, there was a roar that shook the entire neighborhood. It was the sixty-fourth bombing in the Youngstown area, the first booby-trapped car—and the first fatality.

At the sound of the detonation, the girl, who had been having breakfast in her apartment with her four-year-old son, came running out into the street, clad only in a shortie nightgown. Sobbing and hysterical, she tried to run after the ambulance that removed Sofocleous, but neighbors came, wrapped her in a blanket, and finally got her home.

It was a miracle that the only victim had been the intended one, Christ Sofocleous. None of the playing children had been hit by the debris that showered down all around them. And the blonde and her young son, who on many mornings accompanied Sofocleous when he left the apartment, had on this day providentially remained at home.

The handwriting of future tragedy was plain, but in Youngstown few persons bothered to observe. The typical Youngstowner simply shrugged his shoulders and dismissed the Sofocleous murder as of little significance. "Who cares as long as they just knock each other off?" was repeated on every side.

In this atmosphere of indifference, the underworld stepped up the tempo. Two events dovetailed to form the background.

The first was the 1959 municipal election in Youngstown. It gave the city a new mayor, Frank R. Franko, distinguished by the fact that he was an unfrocked judge and a disbarred lawyer.

Franko, small, thin, dark haired, had been a municipal judge when he decided to run for prosecutor, and he had used the office he held to drum up support for the office he coveted. The Mahoning County Bar Association, deciding that such a dual interest was hardly appro-

priate for a judge, had filed charges against Franko. They included
the judge's indulgence in large-scale fixing of traffic tickets, especially
his own. In May, 1958, the Ohio Supreme Court had upheld the
Bar Association and had barred Franko from the practice of law for
an indefinite period.

So—and what could be more natural in Youngstown?—Franko
decided to run for mayor. He had been at various times in his career
a Republican and an independent. Now he become a Democrat, a
canny choice since the Democrats normally have a 3-1 voting edge in
Youngstown.

The scramble for the party's nomination turned into a three-way
contest in which Franko's path was smoothed by the involuntary
self-disqualification of one of his principal opponents. This worthy,
a City Councilman, was convicted of masterminding a swindle that
had filched $250,000 from insurance companies for injuries and dam-
ages in auto accidents that had never happened.

Aided by this act of political suicide, Franko won the Democratic
nomination, and in November—helped, veteran politicians insist, by
a strong following among Negro and nationality groups—the unfrocked judge and disbarred lawyer swept into City Hall.

Whether this local development had anything to do with the second
occurrence that formed the background for an unprecedented wave
of violence about to hit Youngstown is pure speculation. But it may
well have.

This second event took place far away from Youngstown, but it
affected fundamentally the events of the next few months. On December 8, 1959, some 150 Mafia dons gathered in secret session in a
suite of fifteen rented rooms in a hotel in Worcester, Massachusetts.
Their night-long conclave was later described by Attorney General
Edward J. McCormack, of Massachusetts, as a "Little Apalachin"
conference. Actually, in numbers it was even larger than the famous
Apalachin parley, and it was also more successful. This time there
was no interference by the law. This time telephone wires were kept
humming throughout the night as delegates in Worcester conferred
with emperors of the New York underworld in Manhattan. A number
of far-reaching decisions were made regarding mob rule and the
partitioning of territories. One decision, investigators later said, concerned control of the bug in Youngstown.

At the moment, the underworld hierarchy in Youngstown shaped up roughly like this:

The No. 1 man in the local rackets was reputed to be James Vincent DeNiro. After two years in Army service in World War II, DeNiro had returned to his native Youngstown and a job as clerk in a supermarket. Seeing no future in a career as a clerk, DeNiro began peddling numbers. He peddled so well that he soon struck up a partnership with Sandy Naples, and the two combined to control the bug in Youngstown. This control reportedly produced about $8,000 a day for Vince DeNiro.

The No. 2 man in the Youngstown racket world, it was generally agreed, was DeNiro's partner, Sandy Naples. Sandy had more flamboyant tastes than DeNiro. He always carried a big roll of bills. Shortly after he and DeNiro consolidated control of the bug, he bought two Cadillacs in one day—and paid for them with $14,680 in cash. Sandy had also been convicted for drug addiction; there were some reports that he was peddling heroin—and the Mafia, at Apalachin, had decided to get out of the heroin traffic because stiffer federal laws and a wave of public revulsion made it too hazardous.

Barbut supplied two other names in the top echelons of the Youngstown racket. One was Gus Leamis, proprietor of a South Avenue coffee house where a wide-open barbut game had been established for years. Another was William (Billy Sunday) Lantini, also a major barbut operator.

These were the men out front. Behind them lurked some less public but certainly potent figures. Foremost was Cadillac Charlie Cavallaro who now operated from the wings, much in the style of a Mafia elder statesman. Underworld reports kept insisting that Cadillac Charlie had a piece of this barbut game, an interest in that one. His ties to the Licavolis and the Mafia hierarchy seemed firm, and if one man in Youngstown might have been expected to know about the decisions taken at Worcester, that man almost certainly would have been Cadillac Charlie Cavallaro.

Such was the situation when, on the night of March 11, 1960, Sandy Naples made a late check of the day's business at his Center Sandwich Shop. He was interested in more than the trade in sandwiches, for the shop functioned as a bookkeeping headquarters for his numbers enterprises. Having satisfied himself that Youngstown was still gambling, Sandy gathered up a package of sandwiches (his nightly habit), got into his specially bomb-proofed sedan, and drove off to the home of his blonde girl friend, Mary Ann Vrancich. Leaving his car, tucking the sandwiches under his arm, he headed up the walk to the porch of the Vrancich home. He had almost reached it when, from either side of the porch, dark figures loomed up in the night. They carried shotguns.

Trapped, Sandy Naples reached desperately for his own rod. He managed to get it out, fired a couple of wild shots; then came the shotguns' simultaneous roar. Mary Ann Vrancich, who had just opened the door to greet Sandy, caught part of the charge; Sandy, the rest. Both died instantly.

The gunmen fled but in their haste left a memento—one of the 12-gauge shotguns they had used, a weapon that, it developed, had been stolen about a year before from a police cruiser in Canton, Ohio.

There was, of course, the usual flurry of investigation. In Sandy Naples' pockets, police found his usual wad of big bills—about $5,000 worth—and eleven heroin capsules. And that was all. They located no suspects.

In the speculation attendant upon this "putout" of the No. 2 man of the Youngstown rackets, there were reports that Sandy Naples had been trying to extend his operations from the bug and form a local combine to take over barbut. This may well have brought him into collision with other racket interests, but it probably wasn't the sole reason for his execution. For events were to show that there was a determined drive under way to change the entire face of the Youngstown underworld.

The next act was in relatively minor key. Cadillac Charlie Cavallaro had a partner in gambling ventures, a quiet little man, Joseph (Stoneface) Romano. They were said to be silent partners in a flourishing South Avenue barbut game. On the night of June 4, 1960, Stoneface Romano got a telephone call and left his apartment. He evidently kept some clandestine appointment, for it was about 1 A.M. when he returned home. As he parked the car in his garage, he became aware of strange presences in the dark and started to run up the gravel driveway toward the back door of his apartment. He didn't make it. Shotgun blasts cut him down.

Neighbors later reported that, as Stoneface fell, they heard him scream: "No more, Charlie! Please, no more!"

But the shotguns blasted again and again.

Surgeons subsequently plucked sixteen buckshot from Romano's abdomen and other pellets from his right arm and chest. Despite these perforations, he lived—and was true to his nickname of Stoneface. Not a word could police get out of him.

After the Romano shooting, there was a slight pause. A couple of lesser hoods, possible suspects in the Romano affair, died in abrupt and violent fashion, causing hardly a ripple on the Youngstown stream of consciousness. Then underworld lightning struck again— and at the very top level of the Youngstown rackets.

On the afternoon of June 10, 1961, Mike Farah, onetime potentate of The Jungle Inn, was waiting for a friend to come along for a golfing date. While he waited, he took a few practice strokes on the front lawn of his home in Warren. He was so intent on his putting that he paid no attention to a car driving slowly along the street. The first notice he had that something was wrong came when a shotgun blast cut him down.

This abrupt demise of the pharaoh of the Farah empire caused considerable anxiety. Violent and irrevocable changes were being made at the very top level of the Youngstown rackets. First Sandy Naples, then Mike Farah. Who would be next?

James Vincent DeNiro must have been asking himself that question. He had been Sandy Naples' partner, and remained untouched at the pinnacle. It didn't take a seer to guess that he might be next in line.

DeNiro was a full-cheeked, curly-haired, handsome bon vivant, the businessman-gangster in a gray flannel suit. His partnership with Sandy Naples had given him his big leg up in the rackets, and he had used the green cascade that gambling poured into his pockets to expand his operations in all directions. He became the proprietor of a wildly remunerative barbut game. He owned a used-car company, gas stations, cigar stores, wine shops, and candy stores. He controlled a company that handled most of the cigarette vending-machine business in Mahoning County. He owned Ciccro's, "The World's Most Beautiful Restaurant," on Market Street in the busy uptown section of Youngstown into which Route 7, coming off the Ohio Turnpike, funnels travelers from the East. In addition to all this, Vince DeNiro reportedly had a heavy stake (for a time at least) in the gambling casino of the plush Sans Souci Hotel in Las Vegas. From all of these sources, money showered down on James Vincent

DeNiro, the former supermarket clerk, in such engulfing tidal waves that one of his principal problems was how to spend it all. DeNiro tried. He owned six cars.

Inevitably, such is the greed of man, the impressive business holdings of Vince DeNiro, legitimate and illegitimate, aroused both envy and enmity. DeNiro began to get unmistakable warnings. A bomb went off in a home he was building for his parents, but he had just left the premises on a business errand. A second bomb attempt shortly afterwards also failed. DeNiro took the double hint. He observed extreme caution.

Wherever he drove on business appointments, he took the trouble to switch cars. If the car in which he came had been parked on the street for any length of time, he would have another car brought to drive away. He was taking no chances on exploding a couple of dynamite sticks wired to a steering column.

On the warm summer night of July 16, 1961, DeNiro drove out Market Street to Parella's Pizza Oven, two blocks from Cicero's. Robert Parella, owner of the Pizza Oven, was a close friend. So was James Modarelli, a local jeweler, whom DeNiro met in the Oven. After some discussion, the three friends worked up an appetite for a good steak dinner. As it was Sunday and Cicero's was closed, they decided to drive out to the 422 Café in nearby Warren.

DeNiro, who had parked his Thunderbird on Market Street near the Oven, observed his usual caution and left it there. He had Modarelli drive him. They made a stop at the home of DeNiro's girl friend, and DeNiro borrowed her car, a gun-metal gray Oldsmobile convertible. This he brought back and parked on Market Street across from Cicero's. Then he rejoined Modarelli and Parella for the ride out to the Warren café in Modarelli's car.

On the return trip Modarelli drove to the Pizza Oven, where Parella got into his own car and drove home. Then Modarelli chauffeured DeNiro on down Market Street and let him out behind his girl friend's gun-metal gray convertible. It was just 12:10 A.M.

Modarelli backed up a short distance and waited for a break in the flow of traffic. DeNiro got behind the wheel of his girl friend's car and turned on the ignition switch. Instantly, there was a shattering roar that shook the block.

"It was a horrible, shocking sight that I will never be able to forget," said Modarelli afterwards.

The Oldsmobile convertible was demolished. Fragments were hurled hundreds of yards, the car's hood landing on a rooftop 150 feet away. Some fifteen large store windows along the busy business block were shattered by the blast and by flying debris. DeNiro himself was blown to a pulp.

During all this blasting of gangland bodies, Mayor Franko dithered in City Hall. No one had expected him to be a crusader (after all, he had been a boyhood pal of Sandy Naples), but hardly anyone had expected him to be so publicly embarrassed by a long roll of sensational racket slayings.

With violence running riot, however, Franko's favorite reaction to a new lethal outburst was to fire his police chief and name another. Detectives bounced up to chief and back to detective like so many Yo-Yos yanked on strings from City Hall.

This procedure accomplished little beyond the further demoralization of a police department traditionally corrupt. It was obvious that the official government of Youngstown was helpless against the power of a ruthless underworld, living by its own rules and carrying out its own executions in defiance of all authority. In desperation, after the DeNiro bombing, Mayor Franko appealed to Governor Michael V. DiSalle for help, but DiSalle, though a fellow Democrat, gave the mayor the rough side of his tongue.

"It is about time that local law-enforcement officials recognize the seriousness of a situation which imperils the lives and property of decent citizens," he said. ". . . The people who have the responsibility had better throw away their powder puffs and choose weapons strong enough to drive these individuals as far away from this community as possible."

The Governor was telling Youngstown that it had the primary responsibility for cleaning up its own mess, and he was saying in effect that the "powder puff" manner in which Youngstown had treated the mob for years had produced the inevitable crisis. With a municipal election coming up in the fall of 1961, the situation seemed made to order for some paladin of reform. But they don't breed paladins these days in Youngstown. They did, however, have a Harry Savasten.

Savasten is a roly-poly man who would make a good Santa Claus. He has merry brown eyes; a round, chubby, good-humored face; and black, graying hair, now thinning at the top. Of Austrian descent, a Methodist, he comes from forebears who first worked in the steel mills, and he knows the hard road up. When he graduated from South Side High School and went off to Marietta College, his worldly resources consisted of a scholarship and $120. All the time he was in college, he worked at odd jobs; and in the summer, he worked in the steel mills. By such effort, he got his Bachelor of Arts degree.

He was employed first by Youngstown Sheet & Tube, and later, after taking courses in metallurgy, by the U.S. Steel Corporation. However, Savasten discovered that he had other ambitions. He decided, much later in life than most men make such decisions, that he wanted to become a lawyer; and so he enrolled in Youngstown University, studied nights and weekends, and in 1952 was admitted to the practice of law.

"Let's face it," said Savasten candidly, after he became mayor, "I was a poor lawyer. I had no family to give me a helping hand."

No family meant no influence in a profession and a city in which influence counts for much. Savasten, realizing that he was going to earn much less as a lawyer than he had as a metallurgist, managed to get himself appointed a bailiff in the Common Pleas Court; and between the salary this post gave him and the law fees he gradually began to pick up, he made a living for himself, his wife, and two children. But it was a living that was a long way from wealth.

This was Harry Savasten's personal situation before the election of 1961. Relatively few persons in Youngstown at the time had ever heard of Harry Savasten. Time and again, Youngstowners would tell you: "I never heard of him until he ran." Or, "I didn't know anything about him at the time." Or, "I never saw him until he was elected."

The election of Savasten has to be considered one of those flukes of politics that confound the experts. It came about primarily because few persons considered the Republican nomination for mayor a prize of any value. It was obvious that Franko, with the city Democratic machine behind him, would run for re-election. Since Youngstown normally votes Democratic by 3 to 1, sometimes by as much as 5 to 1, and since the public didn't seem to be clamoring for a change, the chances for a Republican nominee, whoever he might be, did not seem exactly bright.

Savasten, however, figured (the state of his law practice being what it was) that he had little to lose. And so one day he remarked almost casually to a friend who was a Republican leader: "What do you think about my running for mayor?" It was a new idea to Savasten's friend. He thought it over, shrugged, said: "Well, why not?"

On such a note of enthusiasm, the Savasten candidacy was launched. Savasten's opponent in the primary was a veteran party wheelhorse. Savasten won, the first indication perhaps that there were undercurrents of dissatisfaction that might be translated into votes. In the fall, Savasten ran against Franko, and these indications were confirmed. Savasten won by a little more than 4,000 votes out of nearly 60,000 cast.

The new regime came to City Hall bearing in the public mind the reform label. But Savasten was no fiery reformer. Perhaps he recognized the enormity of the task he faced; perhaps he was afraid of arousing too great expectations—and being tabbed with failure if he was unable to satisfy them. In any event, he represented the anomaly of a reformer who embraced reform, if at all, only with the utmost gingerliness.

"This has been called a reform administration," he said in December, 1962, after the Cavallaro bombing. "Well, I suppose it is if you mean by reform something different than Franko. I was against everything he was for."

One of Savasten's first and most drastic moves was to revamp the police department. He scanned the roster for a new chief, looking for a capable man with a clean record, and finally settled on short, chunky William R. Golden, a police captain with thirty-three years' service and the reputation for not accepting graft. At sixty-five, Golden was thinking only of approaching retirement and the chance to devote himself to his major love—painting. It was not easy for Savasten to persuade him to take over as chief and try to clean up the department.

Given a free hand, Golden immediately abolished the vice squad. He explained candidly that he felt it had too intimate an acquaintance with vice. In its place, he established an intelligence unit composed of fifteen detectives, many of them bright young men, new on the force, unknown even to their fellow cops.

At City Hall Savasten backed up his chief by decreeing that appointments to the force should be by merit only. The long-established custom had been for applicants to approach district political leaders; for an appropriate fee, they would be guaranteed appointment; and, inevitably, the kind who paid such secret bounties were the kind who

figured they would have multiple opportunities to get their investment back, with interest. Savasten put an end to all this.

"Look," he told one police graduating class, "you men are here
on merit, because you qualify. Not one of you has had to pay anyone
to be appointed, and what is more, if we find out any of you have
—out you go!"

Arrest figures reflected the new breeze that was sweeping through
the department. By November 1, 1962, ten months after Savasten
took office, the new intelligence squad had arrested 63 prostitutes,
raided 12 stills and made 223 arrests for liquor violations. Most significantly, it had also made 120 gambling arrests compared with only
36 for the entire department in the same period of the previous year.

But the achievement had not been easy. Both the lawless and certain elements of the law had reacted violently to the prospect of a
cleanup.

The underworld, just as it had in the days of Henderson and Allen,
moved its more wide-open activities just beyond Youngstown's borders. The first shift had been made after the DeNiro bombing, at a
time when the Franko administration was reacting sensitively to the
prospect of public outcry. Then the South Avenue barbut game had
closed, and barbut had floated off to two new locations in nearby
Struthers. Subsequently, after Savasten took office, the game moved
again, locating this time in Campbell, with Cadillac Charlie Cavallaro
rumored to be one of its heavy backers.

While the underworld was dodging the Youngstown law by flitting
beyond its jurisdiction, inside the city some elements in the established judicial system were throwing every conceivable roadblock in
the path of Golden's detectives in the pursuit and harassment of
racketeers. Golden had adopted the tactic that Allen had used before
him of bringing known gamblers and other riffraff in for questioning
on the slightest possible pretext. On occasion, the underworld responded by getting its legal mouthpieces and friendly magistrates to
spring the suspects on hastily issued writs.

"It has been tough sledding this year," Golden admitted at the end
of 1962. "We have had all sorts of writs served on us. They can be
issued by any magistrate. We had one man in here barely ten minutes,
and we had to release him before we could ask him a question. Some
of these lawyers were running around with blank writs in their pockets;

the magistrates had issued the writs to them in advance, and all they
had to do was to fill in the names."

To this secret undermining of the law by forces sworn to uphold it
was soon added the embarrassment of the continuing racket war.
Before Savasten took office, the top local hoods had been disposed of
—Sandy Naples, Mike Farah, Vince DeNiro. But the sweepout was
not yet complete; others were still to go.

On the night of June 1, 1962, Billy Naples, brother of the shot-
gunned Sandy, received a phone call at his Carlotta Avenue home.
Billy had taken over much of Sandy's bug operation; he was said to
have had a piece of the Struthers barbut action; and he was reported
to have been associated with Cadillac Charlie Cavallaro in the final
shift of the game to Campbell, then just taking place. Whether the
phone call summoned Billy to conference about some of these intricate dealings, no one will ever know; for Billy, going to a Madison
Avenue garage where he kept an old car he was using, jumped in and
flipped the switch to start the motor. Again there came that shattering
explosion with which Youngstown had become so familiar.

Still Youngstown shrugged and still the man in the street said
just another gangster, so what? But Mayor Savasten and Chief
Golden did not shrug. Billy Naples, they knew, had been just a
gangster, but what had happened to Billy Naples might well happen
to others. And so they worked hard to solve the slaying.

There were, of course, no clues—nothing beyond underworld
rumor. Detectives had to resort to the old device of bringing in for
questioning every prominent, lifelong mobster in Youngstown. Among
those they summoned was Cadillac Charlie Cavallaro.

Cadillac Charlie insisted he was in retirement. He had had some
trouble with his heart about a year before; he had to take things easy.
He had just a little business, selling grapes as a sideline, but that
was all. He didn't know anything about gambling or the rackets.
Detectives, having listened to the grapevine that pictured Cadillac
Charlie as one of the big secret backers of the barbut games, didn't
believe him.

"You may be the next, Charlie," they told him. "You better talk."
But Cadillac Charlie just kept repeating the old refrain:
"I don't know nothing. I don't know nothing."
Though police didn't get anywhere with Cadillac Charlie, they did
pick up one item of information that intrigued them. An informant

tipped them that the remaining Naples brother, Joey, was running the bug from a secret room in the basement of his home at 605 Carlotta Drive. Golden promptly obtained search warrants, and on July 24th his detectives raided the last of the Naples clan.

In the basement, they found the hideaway for which they were looking—and all kinds of evidence. The room was cluttered with a miscellany of stolen goods, the proceeds of recent burglaries. It also boasted a respectable arsenal, including a fully operative machine gun. And on a table was clinching evidence of Joey Naples' operation of the bug—slips recording numbers bets, and "rundown sheets," the master accounting forms that showed just how much business each runner had peddled during the course of a day. There were also some $3,000 in large-sized bills.

The detectives took Joey Naples and the evidence to headquarters. There they booked Joey for trial on three separate charges—receiving stolen property, illegal possession of a machine gun, and operation of a numbers game.

Joey had hardly been booked before Lt. Donald Baker got a telephone call from an anonymous underworld informant.

"You had better take good care of those bug slips," the caller told him. "The boys have a plan to steal 'em right under your noses."

After ten months in office, Harry Savasten was a deeply troubled man. He had tried to clean up the police department, to press the war on the rackets; but he had run into all kinds of roadblocks and he knew that, while his police had clamped a lid on the more wide-open operations, Youngstowners still played the bug daily or traveled to barbut games just over the border. Worse still was the casual attitude toward gambling. Even in the Mayor's own inner circle, it had been suggested that there might be some advantage in being able to wink at the right place and time.

"I have been approached," Savasten said at the time, stabbing his chest with a pointed forefinger. "A friend of mine, one of my own backers, suggested I ought to go easy and let a certain barbut game —the one that ran for years in that South Avenue coffee house— open up again. He suggested it might mean a lot to me.

"I said to him, 'Look, I've been without money for so long I wouldn't know what to do with it if I had it. Forget it! That game doesn't operate.' "

It was obvious to Savasten that, as long as gambling bankrolled the mob with some $4.5 million annually, as long as there was such utter public complacency about it, the evils that had plagued Youngstown for so many years would be perpetuated. Politics would continue to be corrupted. Police would be bribed, magistrates and the courts influenced. And gangsters would continue to war for the spoils. There would be more killings, more bombings, and sooner or later innocent people would be slaughtered along with the guilty.

Possessed by this certainty, the Mayor discussed the problem with a number of his friends among the clergy, and on October 22, 1962, he summoned a group of clergymen to an informal conference at City Hall. There, he said afterwards, he laid his cards on the table. He told the assembled clergymen that murder would continue to stalk Youngstown unless the public could be aroused about the issue, unless the public was made to realize that each man who played the bug, or bet on the horses, or rolled dice in a barbut game was financing corruption and murder. What was needed was a rousing campaign to make the people aware of the truth, and this was the kind of moral truth that could be taught best from the pulpit. The Mayor needed, and pleaded for, the clergy's help. The assembled clergymen assured Savasten they all agreed with him; they were right behind him 100 per cent. And then the meeting quietly disbanded.

Just a month later came the tragedy Savasten had feared. Cadillac Charlie Cavallaro went to his death in his booby-trapped car, and his son Tommy, one of the best-liked boys in the neighborhood, was killed with him.

Youngstown finally was shocked. The casual question, "Who cares as long as the rats knock each other off?" served no longer to whitewash the face of evil. Tommy Cavallaro was dead, and his brother Charles, though he would recover from his shattered hip, would limp the rest of his life.

At last, and for the first time, a burning indignation found expression in homes, on the streets, in letters to the Youngstown *Vindicator*.

"When innocent children are mangled and maimed, something has got to be done to stop these inhuman monsters," one man said, expressing a general sentiment.

Yet there were signs that beneath the surface, beyond the moment's reaction, not too much fundamentally had changed. Youngstowners were still gambling. Reporters for the *Vindicator* observed customers

buying race sheets and exchanging whispered words with clerks who
made some mystic notations. No betting slips were passed; it was all
word of mouth and *sub rosa,* just as it had been for months in an
effort to circumvent Golden's police. But it was still going on.

Mayor Savasten, who had not been able to rally the civic conscience in advance of the Cavallaro tragedy, acted swiftly in its aftermath. He appealed directly to Attorney General Kennedy to send
federal investigators into Youngstown, and Kennedy responded.
Teams of FBI agents poured into the city and fanned out all over the
Mahoning Valley, seeking evidence.

This unprecedented federal activity gave the underworld pause, if
only for a moment. The grapevine announced that the "boss" (nobody was naming him) had decreed a three-week moratorium on
the bug to let public indignation cool and make sure the police and
the FBI would get nowhere. Even this ukase, however, was not so
drastic as it sounded. Covert assurances were given that "regulars"
would somehow be accommodated. And three weeks after the Cavallaro murders, even a casual visitor to Youngstown could overhear
workmen, sitting at a lunch counter getting their morning's cup of
coffee, discussing a "hit" a lucky friend had made a few days before.
"There's no income tax on that money," one of them chuckled, with
relish. Not even the most callous and hideous of murders, it seemed,
could shame the soul of Youngstown or cool the appetite of its gambling addicts. Within two months, despite the activity of police and
the FBI, gambling activity in Youngstown was nearly back to normal.

The pattern of events said quite clearly that the ingrained habits
derived from forty years of gambling and lawlessness were not going
to be changed unless there was some dynamic, crusading leadership
within the city. But in Youngstown crusaders seemed to speak by
rote—and in muted tones.

Typical was the attitude of the church leaders to whom Mayor
Savasten had appealed on October 22nd. More than a month later,
this group did not even have a chairman. On November 27th, the
ministers issued a statement applauding the participation of the FBI
in the Youngstown bomb hunt and calling for a long-range program
to study the causes of community ills. "We won't be stampeded into
anything," a spokesman declared. In making this ringing declaration,
he, like all of the participating ministers and civic leaders, remained
anonymous.

On Sunday, December 2, 1962, several pastors did devote their sermons to a call for "a war against personal sin." All pointed out that the bettor who wagers 50 cents on the bug or places a $2 bet on a horse with a bookie bears a personal responsibility when the underworld murders a Tommy Cavallaro. The Rt. Rev. Msgr. Andrew Prokop at the Immaculate Heart of Mary Church called upon his parishioners to halt their contributions to gamblers "who fight over the spoils and destroy life and property for this money." In at least one sermon, certain of the churches themselves were criticized for fostering the gambling spirit that ruled Youngstown. The Rev. J. Frank Schulman, pastor of the First Unitarian Church, made pointed references to churches sponsoring bazaars "that more closely resemble Las Vegas than houses of worship."

Having said their piece in this one outburst of oratory, the ministers once more lapsed into silence. There seemed to be no indication among the clergy or the civic leaders of Youngstown of a determination to wage an unremitting campaign that alone could change their long-corrupted city. Sensing this lack on a mid-December visit to Youngstown, a reporter asked Chief Golden:

"Is there in all Youngstown one minister, one civic leader—anybody at all—who has really stood up on his hind legs and tried to arouse the people about these evils?"

The chief thought for a long moment, then said, almost unwillingly:

"Not that I know of. No name comes right away to my mind."

In this vacuum, the underworld in Youngstown went its free-swinging way, despite the brief public outcry over the Cavallaro murders, despite the presence on the scene of FBI agents and other investigators. The brashness of the mob was incredible. Two incidents illustrate its open scorn and contempt for all law and order. The first involved Chief Golden.

"I took my car down to be serviced one day," the chief recalled, "and before very long I got a call back from the serviceman. 'Did you know they've wired your car?' he asked. 'No!' I said. 'Well, they have,' he said. 'You better get a detective down here to look at it.'

"I couldn't believe it, but I sent one of my detectives over and, sure enough, he finds they had wired the ignition. They had everything there except the dynamite sticks. I suppose it was intended to scare me, to show me what they could do. When the fuse went off, it would normally make a pretty loud crack, but if it did, I didn't hear it or pay any attention to it at the time."

The chief whipped open the drawer of his desk and held up the blackened fuse and the two short lengths of wire that had attached it to his car's ignition system—graphic evidence that, in Youngstown, even the police chief continued to live only at the sufferance of the mob.

The second incident involved Joey Naples. Naples went on trial in Mahoning County Court during the very week of the Cavallaro murders. It had been decided to try him first on the charge of illegally possessing a machine gun, but the jury accepted the defense's contention and decided, for some mysterious reason, that a man could hardly be expected to know he had a machine gun in the secret room in the basement of his own home. It acquitted Naples.

This weird decision was an example of shining logic and justice compared to the remainder of the Joey Naples saga. Next, in the very aftermath of the Cavallaro murders, the State brought Joey to trial on the charge of operating a numbers game. The vital evidence consisted of the betting slips and the rundown sheets seized in the raid on Naples' basement hideaway, and these, as the trial opened, were lying on the prosecution table, ready to be offered in evidence. The defense attorney objected, and the judge decided that he would hear the legal arguments in chambers. All the lawyers trooped out of the courtroom after the judge; the bailiff went along, too. When they returned, they discovered that the prosecution table had been swept clean. Betting slips and rundown sheets had disappeared— stolen right out of the courtroom!

Despite this brazen courtroom theft, Joey Naples did not get off scot free—but only because that earlier underworld tip had alerted police.

"When we got that tip," Chief Golden recalled, "we thought that they had some plan to steal the evidence from headquarters. It never occurred to us that they would swipe it right out of the courtroom. So we had photostats made of everything, the numbers slips and the account books, and when the originals disappeared, we informed the court we had photostats. The judge let the case go to trial on that basis."

And so Joey Naples finally was convicted. He fought the verdict for a year and a half, and it was not until April, 1964, appeals exhausted, that he was sent at last to the Ohio Penitentiary. Three days before Christmas, he was freed in a legal procedure that swiftly became a state-wide scandal.

Naples' attorneys had brought an action before U.S. District Judge Mell G. Underwood, arguing that Naples' constitutional rights had been violated because the search warrant that led to the discovery of the evidence against him had been based on hearsay evidence and was therefore invalid. John F. Cianflona, an Ohio assistant attorney general, was designated to represent the forces of law and justice in the effort to keep Joey Naples in prison. When the hearing was held before Judge Underwood, however, Cianflona astonished everyone by agreeing with Naples' attorneys. This abject failure of the State to present a case gave Judge Underwood little choice. He freed Naples.

The deed made headlines throughout Ohio. The springing of Joey Naples by devious legal process seemed to the press as brazen a flexing of underworld muscle as the earlier theft of evidence right off the prosecutor's table in the open courtroom. Ohio Attorney General William Saxbe fired Cianflona because he had agreed to Naples' release instead of arguing against it. In subsequent hearings on what had happened and how and why, Saxbe suggested that some $20,000 in cash might have found its way into various hands to arrange the springing of Joey Naples, but he confessed that he had no proof. And Joey Naples remained free—evidence that, in Youngstown, even when you nab a man with a cellar full of stolen goods and a working machine gun and bug slips and account books, you really can't do very much to him, not when he's a big shot and the law has to buck the entrenched power of the mob.

What, then, is the lesson of Youngstown?

It is, quite simply, that the wages of crime are greater than the wages of virtue. And that the power of the mob can corrupt and defy the power of the law.

In Youngstown, despite Harry Savasten and Chief Golden on the local scene, despite Robert Kennedy and the best federal investigative team he could put into the field, the might of the underworld was such that gambling could run virtually uninhibited, a Joey Naples could be sprung—and murder and bombings could still be committed under the very nose of the law.

This is not to suggest that nothing has been accomplished, that there have been no gains. There have been some achievements, but at this writing there is little evidence that the backbone of mob rule in Youngstown has been seriously threatened.

The federal investigative team sent in by Kennedy sparked twin probes before a federal grand jury and a Mahoning County grand jury. A number of indictments and convictions were obtained. In June, 1963, the federal grand jury indicted seven rackets figures in Youngstown and Struthers, including four members of Struthers' powerful Carrabria family, on a variety of tax charges, including failure to file income-tax returns and conspiracy to defraud the government on excise and income taxes. Five pleaded guilty and were sentenced. In late 1963, the Mahoning County grand jury indicted eight gambling figures in connection with a numbers operation. Ronald Carrabria, one of those accused, was convicted and sentenced to a 1- to 10-year prison term in June, 1964.

These were all harassing legal actions, effective in their way, but falling short of the severe measures that would put an end to lawlessness and violence. Not even federal agents were able to solve the mystery of who had killed Cadillac Charlie Cavallaro and his son Tommy. FBI agents concentrated on a prime suspect, Dominick Moio, of Canton and Youngstown. Moio was the last man outside the Cavallaro family known to have seen Cadillac Charlie alive. He was also a prime suspect in the earlier bomb-slaying of Billy Naples. How close investigators may have been to building a case against Moio was perhaps indicated by the reaction of the mob. In September, 1963, Moio's charred body was found stuffed in the trunk of his abandoned car in a lonely strip-mine area near Canton. And investigators had another unsolved murder on their hands.

In succeeding months, the Youngstown underworld continued to demonstrate that it was not daunted by the awesome reputations of the FBI and other federal sleuths; threatened by their activities, it struck back with terror tactics. Federal investigators became highly interested in Leo (Lips) Morceri, whom they described as an enforcer of mob rule and a relative and close associate of Detroit's powerful Licavoli clan, the family with which Cadillac Charlie had once had such close ties. Federal interest in Morceri's concerns resulted in his indictment for failure to file income-tax returns for the years 1958 through 1961. This pressure by the law was promptly met by counterpressure.

On January 3, 1965, Morceri's fashionable stone mansion, nestled in an amphitheater of tree-covered slopes in Northhampton Township, a suburb of Akron, was destroyed by a bomb blast that ripped upward through the roof. The explosion and the fire that followed left the home in ruins. As Morceri and his brother Mike, and sister-in-law Ann, were all absent at the time, reportedly visiting relatives in Detroit, the violent incident was seen by investigators as a warning to "Lips" to keep his lips buttoned. He did.

Morceri went on trial in Federal court in Cleveland in February, 1965—and was acquitted. The Government's case was based on the net-worth method; that is, a demonstration that Morceri had been spending wads of money he hadn't reported for income-tax purposes. Morceri met this accusation with the defense that he had been living on $70,000 he had accumulated before he left the Ohio Penitentiary in 1957 after serving a five-year term for extortion.

With the law meeting such frustrations, Harry Savasten's rule in Youngstown was doomed. He had been at best in an unenviable spot. Tabbed in the public mind as a reformer, his inability to reform meant political death. The Cavallaro bombing, the most tragic in the long series, had occurred during his regime; and though no sensible man could argue that Savasten could have prevented it, or done more than he had to solve it, nevertheless his administration was associated with the fact and the failure. In addition, Savasten had to fight the normal 3-1 Democratic odds in Youngstown. The burden was just too much, and in the 1963 general election he was defeated by Anthony B. Flask, who had served on the Youngstown City Council for six years.

In Youngstown itself, the face of the rackets and the corruption and violence they spawned did not greatly change despite all the pressures of local and federal law. The Mahoning County grand jury, which delved into the racket picture for months, gave its findings in general terms in two presentments returned in December, 1964, and January, 1965. It estimated that the annual gambling gross of the rackets in Youngstown was still $4 million. And it wrote:

> On the basis of evidence submitted to us, it would appear that many of our citizens and many of our law-enforcement officers have little or no respect for the gambling statutes of this state, and this situation has permitted the professional gamblers to operate almost unmolested.

The jury criticized politicians who sought favors from racketeers, and it struck at "inside tips" given racketeers on police raids about to be pulled and at "accommodation arrests" made to pad the official record and make law enforcement appear active to press and public. All of this, plus a pervading public apathy, had resulted in virtually a complete breakdown of law enforcement against commercialized gambling and vice, the jury charged. It wrote further:

> The testimony has been sufficient to reflect a deplorable condition which indicates that many police officers and public officials, if not dishonest, were guilty of the utmost dereliction of their duties. . . . Crime of the stature with which we are presently confronted could not have developed without the total indifference, acquiescence or direct permissive assistance of some politicians and law-enforcement officials in Mahoning County.
>
> This Grand Jury feels that the general public of this area cannot escape their share for this blame in the breakdown of law enforcement. From testimony we have heard, we find that citizens and citizens' committees and other groups, with few exceptions, although formed and operating, have made no real effort to get in touch with any local law-enforcement body or to act as a watchdog over the activities of the various law-enforcement agencies. . . .
>
> One of the principal reasons for this laxity is the apathy of the ordinary citizen toward law enforcement. Too many "good citizens" simply do not want to get involved. . . .

Such was Youngstown, a city held in thralldom by the most vicious elements on the American landscape. And Youngstown was not alone. Its experience was being repeated across the nation.

How, one feels impelled to ask, did we ever get ourselves into such a fix? How did things ever get this way?

Joseph Valachi testifying be-
fore the Senate Permanent
Investigations Subcommittee
("McClellan Committee")—
Associated Press Wirephoto

TOP LEFT: Charles (Lucky) Luciano—*Wide World Photos.* TOP RIGHT: Vito Genovese—*Wide World Photos.* BELOW: Joe Adonis, *left,* and Solly Moretti—*Wide World Photos*

Above: Abe Reles (November 12, 1941)—*Wide World Photos.* Right: Abe (Kid Twist) Reles — *Wide World Photos*

LEFT: Harold J. Adonis—*Wide World Photos*. RIGHT: Charles (Cadillac Charlie) Cavallaro—*Wide World Photos*

Frank (The Boss) Costello
—*Wide World Photos*

ABOVE: Anthony (Tony Bender) Strollo—*Wide World Photos*
BELOW: Virginia Hill—*Wide World Photos*

ABOVE: Benjamin Siegel
(June 20, 1947) — *Wide
World Photos*. LEFT: Benjamin (Buggsy) Siegel —
Wide World Photos

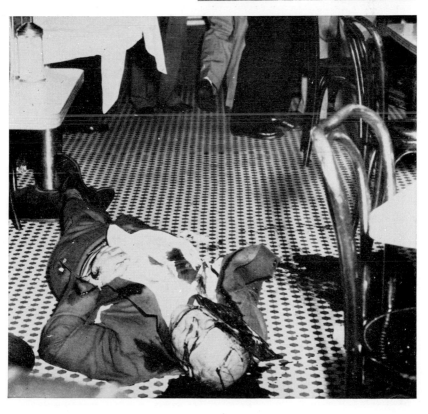

RIGHT: Willie Moretti —
Wide World Photos. BE-
LOW: Willie Moretti (Oc-
tober 4, 1951) — *Wide
World Photos*

LEFT: Anthony (Little Augie Pisano) Carfano—*Wide World Photos*
RIGHT: Janice Drake—*Wide World Photos*

Janice Drake (September 25, 1959)—*Wide World Photos*

3

HOW THE INVISIBLE
GOVERNMENT GREW

The Mafia dominated and controlled the whole social life, it had leaders and followers, it issued orders and decrees, it was to be found equally in big cities and in small centres, in factories and in rural districts, it regulated agricultural and urban rents, forced itself into every kind of business, and got its way by means of threats and intimidation or of penalties imposed by its leaders and put into execution by its officers. Its orders had the force of laws and its protection was a legal protection, more effective and secure than that which the State offers to its citizens; so that owners of property and business men insured their goods and their persons by submitting to pay the price of the insurance.

The Procurator-General of Palermo, in a report on January 19, 1931, gave this description of the power of the Mafia on the island of Sicily during the 1920's before Benito Mussolini began the purge that was to send the Mafiosi flocking by the thousands to the greener pastures of America. The structure of the Sicilian Mafia, its purposes and its power, matched as the hand the glove the invisible government of crime that Joseph Valachi was to describe to the McClellan committee in 1963. Here is a further description by the Procurator-General of Mafia methods and influence in Sicily:

The associations of the small centres ordinarily exercised jurisdiction in them, or in the adjoining communes: those of the more

55

important centres were in communication with one another and
with those in adjacent provinces, and lent one another mutual
assistance. It not infrequently occurred that in the same commune there were two Mafias, either deliberately created, spon-
taneously generated or born of some dispute over the booty,
contending for supremacy. The result of this was a bitter struggle
involving the deaths of leaders and more influential members of
the executive and of their respective families: and the mortal
conflict would continue for generations till whole families had
been extinguished. . . .

Murder was committed when a man would not obey the order
to allow himself to be robbed or to send the money demanded
either in threatening letters or after the kidnaping of some member of the family, or to wreak the Mafia's vengeance for similar
offences, or as a result of other serious disobediences or lapses,
of which the chief was that of violating the law of *omertà*—the
law of silence with regard to the criminal actions of the Mafia.

The similarity between Sicily's dread secret society and the sinister
organization that has become the binding cement of the American
underworld is apparent. The ties between the two have been demonstrated in many ways: in their virtually identical ceremonies and oaths
of allegiance, in the all-pervasive omertà that shields their every act,
in the interchangeability of membership that awards an expatriated
American Mafioso high status in Sicily and vice versa, and not least
in the international brotherhood of murder, a working arrangement
by which either wing of the enterprise will carry out a death sentence
passed by the other.

Since it is at last evident that the Mafia lies at the core of the
American criminal problem, it becomes imperative to know something
about the parent Sicilian organization and its antecedents.

The Mafia, in essence, is an outgrowth of the Middle Ages, of
some of mankind's darkest chapters, enduring and wielding a perverted and powerful influence in the modern age. Its birthplace was
Sicily, island of poverty and darkness, suppressed for some 2,000
years under a succession of ruthless conquerors. The Saracens at one
time possessed the island, only to be conquered and supplanted by
the feudalistic Normans. Germans, French, and Spanish came and
conquered in their turn, and with the Spanish, in the fourteenth century, came the Inquisition. The Holy Office and its familiars swept
across the tragic land like a swarm of locusts. Since the business of

the Holy Office was heresy, heresy was found everywhere; and the wealthier a man was, the more likely he was to be found guilty and thrown into prison, his estates and fortune the reward of the black-cowled inquisitors who had ferreted out the wayward ways of his soul. For three centuries, Sicily suffered and endured under the fami-liars of the Inquisition whom Norman Lewis has called "these psalm-singing marauders."

In *The Honored Society,* the best modern treatment of the Sicilian Mafia, Lewis adds:

> The poor man's only shield was the Mafia. Justice was not to be come by, but the association of "men of respect"—silent, per-sistent, inflexible—could at least exact a bloody retribution for the loss of a wife or daughter or the burning down of a house. It was in the school of the vendetta that the traditional character of the *mafioso* was formed. As a victim of absolute power, the common man had to learn to stomach insult or injury with appar-ent indifference, delaying vengeance until an opportunity for its consummation presented itself. The *mafioso* therefore developed a kind of self-control closely resembling the quality that the Japanese call *giri*. A true "man of respect" never weakened his position or armed his enemy in advance by outbursts of passion or of fear. When he suffered some grave injury, he made a pact with himself to be revenged, and thereafter would wait patiently and unemotionally for half a lifetime, if necessary—often on seemingly excellent terms with the man he proposed to destroy —until his moment came. . . .

The Mafia began, then, as a secret agency dedicated to avenge the downtrodden. And it became, as such secret societies tend to become, a law unto itself and an instrument of evil. For the omertà that could protect the patriot could also protect the villain, and the instrument of terror and righteous vengeance, by a mere twist of the blade, became the instrument of ruthless aggrandizement. When the cowl of the Inquisition was lifted from Sicily near the end of the eighteenth century, the Mafia remained, an institution rooted in centuries of bloodshed and custom. No longer having oppressors to fight, it became itself the oppressor.

With the advent of Garibaldi and the creation of the modern dem-ocratic Italian state, the Mafia acquired new dimensions and power. It went covertly into politics. Lawyers and doctors, leaders in every phase of community life, became bound to it by ties that could be severed only by death. Mafia support, Mafia money and intimidation, elected delegates to the Italian Parliament, and in the immediate pre-Mussolini era, at least two members of the Italian Cabinet were bound to the Mafia by indissoluble ties. With such power, the Mafia became in Sicily virtually a separate state, an independent criminal government that exacted tribute from every business, oppressed labor and kept it in servile subjection, elected mayors and local officials, and slew police chiefs who had the bad judgment to become too interested in its activities. It was, as Mussolini's Procurator-General in Palermo was to write in 1931, an invisible government superior in its power to the constituted government of the land.

Yet the Mafia remained, to the Italian people at large and to the outside world, little more than a controversial myth. This paradox of the possession of life-and-death power under the protective cloak of fantasy must be understood; for both in Italy and America one of the most effective camouflages of the secret brotherhood for generations has been ridicule and astutely inculcated disbelief. The whole concept of the Mafia, a secret and invisible government of the nether world dominating much of modern, open, and so-called civilized society, appears at first glance too fantastic for reality. The average citizen's limited imagination and experience boggle at the whole grandiose conception, and he is predisposed to attribute the entire idea of the Mafia to a myth concocted by journalists in search of sensational headlines. No popular mood could be more ideal for the Mafia's private purposes, and the Mafia itself has done its industrious and wily best to foist off on the public the real myth of journalistic concoction and fantasy.

Mussolini's Prefect of Police, Cesare Mori, who commanded the Duce's military-like campaign against the Mafia in Sicily in the latter 1920's, subsequently wrote a book in which he described the subtlety with which the Mafiosi played on the theme that the Mafia didn't even exist.

"One theory, to begin with, was simplicity itself," Mori wrote. "It denied not only the grave problem of public security, but any specifically criminal quality in the Mafia, regarding it as indistinguishable from the type of criminal agency common to all countries. Some people even went so far as to invent the slogan: 'The Mafia? ... Why Mori invented it!' The conclusion from this total negative was that there was nothing to be done, and that the desire to do anything was a libel on Sicily. . . ."

Norman Lewis, in *The Honored Society*, lay equally heavy emphasis on the Mafia's success with the tactic of disbelief. He wrote:

> In 1962, a novel on the theme of the Mafia appeared from the pen of the distinguished Sicilian author Leonardo Sciascia. Called *Il Giorna della Civetta,* it contains an interesting passage that suggests the immense success of the Mafia in preserving its secrecy, and demonstrates the use of a standard form of trickery —the attempt to pull the wool over the eyes of the inquisitive by arguing that the whole thing is hardly more than a blown up piece of newspaper sensationalism. A politician in the book has taken it upon himself to have a fatherly chat with a carabiniere officer who has dared to arrest an important citizen as being implicated in a Mafia killing.
>
> "I ask you [says the politician], is it possible to conceive of the existence of a criminal association so enormous, so well-organized, so secret, and so powerful that it can do what it likes, not only here but in the United States? . . . Very well, then, put it this way: Can you tell me of a single trial that has ever produced proof of the existence of a criminal association called the Mafia, which actually arranges for and carries out crimes? Has a single document ever been found—I mean real written evidence —any sort of proof, in fact, of a relationship between criminality and the so-called Mafia?"

Lewis added that the question must of necessity have been answered in the negative at the time Sciascia wrote, but in Sicily, as in America, the code of omertà was being broken. In 1962, the Sicilian newspaper *L'Ora* managed to get its hands on a confession obtained by police in 1937 from a Dr. Melchiorre Allegra, of Castelvetrano. The document, probably one of several similar confessions obtained during Mussolini's drive against the Mafia, had been mislaid in police files and only belatedly had come to light. It described the manner in which Dr. Allegra, a medical officer in a military hospital in Palermo in 1916, had been approached by the Mafia and propositioned into membership in the society. One fascinating aspect of the document, written in Sicily in 1937, is that it duplicates virtually detail for detail the testimony that Joe Valachi gave the McClellan committee in 1963 about the ritual of the secret brotherhood he called Cosa Nostra.

Allegra described the manner in which he was contacted and taken

to a small fruit shop where three sinister Mafia figures gathered
around a table and told him the facts of life. He wrote:

> They explained to me that they belonged to a very important
> association, which included people in every rank of society, not
> excluding the highest. All of them were called "men of respect."
> The association was what in fact was known to outsiders as
> the Mafia but was understood by most people only in a very
> vague way, because only members could be really sure of its
> existence. . . . Continuing their explanation, they told me that
> infractions of the association's rules were severely punished.
> Members were not allowed, for example, to commit thefts, but
> in certain circumstances homicide was permissible, although
> always by license of the chiefs. Breaking the rules in this case—
> that is, by taking the law into one's own hands—was punishable
> by death. . . .
> On the subject of the administrative structure, it was explained
> to me that the association was split up into "families," each one
> headed by a chief. Usually, a family was made up of small groups
> from neighboring towns or villages; if a family became too large
> for convenient administration, it was split up into units of ten,
> each with its subordinate chief. In the matter of the relationship
> between the different provinces, the rule, in the main, was in-
> dependence. However, the provincial heads kept in close touch
> with one another, and in this way an informal working interpro-
> vincial liaison was maintained. The association had powerful
> overseas offshoots in both North and South America, in Tunisia,
> and in Marseille. A chief was elected by members of his "family,"
> and he was assisted by a counsellor, who could act as his sub-
> stitute in case of his absence [Valachi's consigliere]; in matters
> of high policy, it was absolutely necessary for a chief to consult
> his counsellor before taking action. They then added that in gen-
> eral the association was not interested in politics, but that from
> time to time a "family" might decide to support the candidacy
> for Parliament of a politician whose parliamentary influence they
> could count on.

Dr. Allegra said that he listened to these disclosures with growing
apprehension. He realized that he was being told so much he had
been robbed of any choice about joining the Mafia. After what he had
been told, he could not imagine that he would ever be permitted to
leave the little fruit stand alive if he announced that he did not wish
to become a member of the brotherhood. "My one course was not

only to accept on the spot but to accept with apparent enthusiasm," he wrote.

He then described the ritual of initiation in words that virtually duplicated those of Joe Valachi a quarter of a century later.

> The tip of my middle finger was pierced by a needle, and blood was squeezed from it to soak a small paper image of a saint. The image was burned, and, holding the ashes in my hand, I was called upon to swear an oath more or less as follows: "I swear to be loyal to my brothers, never to betray them, always to aid them, and if I fail may I burn and be turned to ashes like the ashes of the image."

The Mafia entered the United States during the first wave of immigration from Southern Europe in the late 1800's. Some of the Southern Italians and Sicilians emigrating to this country were criminals departing their homeland from necessity rather than choice; and once they had settled in America, they took up where they had left off abroad, establishing new cells of the perfected criminal organization of which they had been members. Soon terror, protected by omertà, began to stalk the streets of American cities.

Two gallant American police officers whose names have now been almost forgotten were the first to oppose the brotherhood in cases that shocked the country and should have alerted the American people a half century before Kefauver to the reality and menace of the Mafia.

The first clash and exposure came in New Orleans in 1890. There a group of Mafiosi had taken over the docks and established a pattern of extortion and coercion that was later to become familiar in New York's Fulton Fish Market and along the wharves of most important eastern seacoast cities. New Orleans in 1890 had become a focal port, the major artery for the rapidly expanding fruit trade with Latin America, and the newly organized local Mafia clamped onto this lucrative traffic. No banana freighter could be unloaded without paying tribute to the firm of Antonio and Carlo Matranga, transplants from Palermo. Negro and Italian longshoremen could not work on the docks and would not lay hands on a cargo unless they had the approving nod of Matranga foremen. Dock racketeering was a common practice then as now, and the importers, never a militant lot, figured as always that it was cheaper to pay than to fight. So they paid the tribute demanded, which was passed on of course to the American consumer, and there were no complaints.

Then, as always happens in the jungle, war broke out over the loot. A series of especially gory murders made headlines in New Orleans. One Italian, his throat slashed from ear to ear, was dropped into a canal. Another, his head almost severed from his body, was found partially stuffed into his own roaring fireplace. Every week had its murders. Shotguns, bombs, daggers—all favorite weapons of the Mafia—left such a growing trail of corpses that Police Chief David Hennessey became convinced he was facing a unique crime wave.

A man of courage, integrity, and imagination, Hennessey began to probe beneath the surface. The instant he did, he ran into the blank wall of omertà, though he did not, of course, recognize it by that name. He discovered, however, to his astonishment, that not even the Italian members of his own police force could be trusted. They knew nothing, saw nothing, heard nothing. Neither did the members of the Italian community in which the atrocities had been occurring. A vast silence, mysterious and impenetrable, cloaked the deeds of murder.

Hennessey was a stubborn man. Unable to rely on his Italian detectives, he pursued his own investigation. He was warned to desist; efforts were made to bribe him. He was impervious both to threats and the lure of cash. Bit by bit, he fitted the pieces of the puzzle together until he could show the manner in which the formidable Matranga family had established suzerainty over the New Orleans docks. The action of the Provenzano brothers in trying to muscle in on this Matranga preserve had precipitated the murders, Hennessey found.

He had reached this point in his researches and had his case nearly complete, ready to submit to a grand jury, when the brotherhood decided he had become a menace to its safety. Hennessey was walking toward his home from police headquarters one evening, just a few days before he was scheduled to testify, when four figures suddenly converged upon him and opened fire from leveled shotguns. Riddled with pellets and mortally wounded, Hennessey still managed to pull his service revolver from its holster. Propping himself up on one arm, he emptied his gun at his fleeing assailants. A detective in the neighborhood, hearing the gunfire, rushed up and found his chief alone, sitting on the stoop of a house to which he had dragged himself, his gun still clutched in his fingers. As the detective knelt beside him, Hennessey's gun clattered to the sidewalk, and his head pitched forward between his knees. He muttered just one word—"Dagoes." A few hours later, unable despite desperate efforts to get out another word, he died.

The assassination of Chief Hennessey on the streets of New Orleans provided America with one of its first and most dramatic examples of omertà. Not even the killing of a courageous police chief, it seemed at first, could make witnesses give evidence. Even Hennessey's own police department did not exhibit any zeal to avenge its fallen chief. But in New Orleans at this time there was an element that was to grow steadily weaker with the years—an angry and aroused public opinion. The citizens still had the capacity for outrage, and their demands for action became so vociferous that even the police were compelled to bestir themselves.

Some of Hennessey's more loyal assistants testified before a grand jury. This initial jury was unable to obtain clinching evidence and returned a presentment, describing the nature of the criminal organization it had encountered and the wall of silence that had frustrated its efforts. "The existence of a secret organization known as the Mafia has been established beyond doubt," the jury declared. It found that this society was composed of Italians and Sicilians who had fled from their own country to avoid punishment for their crimes. And, though the jury had never heard of omertà, it reported that it had been "strangely difficult, almost impossible to discover the perpetrators of these crimes and to secure witnesses . . ."

The presentment stimulated further public outcry. Under pressure from public and press, the police were virtually forced to produce. The heat of public opinion even began to break down the protective screen of omertà. Some sixty witnesses were located, including several who had seen and could identify the four slayers, and indictments were at last returned. In all, nineteen Sicilians eventually stood trial as principals or conspirators in the murder of Chief Hennessey.

Now, as it was so often to do in the future, the Mafia went to work to demonstrate that its power was superior to that of the law. Money flowed into New Orleans. A battery of the most eminent criminal lawyers in the land, all of impeccable Anglo-Saxon antecedents, was hired to represent the defense. Every pressure known to the Mafia, including bribery and intimidation, was aimed at individual members of the jury. The result: when the trial ended, the jurors acquitted sixteen of the defendants and reported they could not decide on the guilt or innocence of the other three.

This courtroom travesty fanned the flames of public indignation. Mayor Joseph A. Shakespeare, a reformer, saw the issue in terms that hold as true today as they did then. In a report to the New Orleans Council, he declared: "A decent community cannot exist with such a society in its midst. The society must be destroyed or the community will perish. The Sicilians who come here must become American citizens and obey the law of the land, or else there is no place for them in our country."

The mayor's indignation reflected the popular mood. A mass protest meeting was called by leading citizens, with the approval of the mayor and the city's two major newspapers, the *Picayune* and the *Times-Democrat*. It began quietly enough, but passions ran too close to the surface to be kept under control and it ended by spawning an unruly mob of thousands. The impromptu army marched upon the parish prison, where the defendants had been held pending the completion of legal technicalities for their release. Deputy sheriffs at the prison, seeing that resistance was futile, took to their heels, and self-appointed execution squads searched for the accused Sicilians, found them, and dragged them out.

Two were hung from lampposts in front of the prison and then thoroughly riddled with bullets. Nine more were lined up in front of a prison wall and mowed down with rifles, pistols, and shotguns. So was the slaying of Chief Hennessey avenged.

The lynching provoked an international uproar and threatened to end diplomatic relations between Italy and the United States. Newspapers throughout the nation and much of the world discovered the name "Mafia" for the first time and catapulted it into glaring headlines. In New Orleans, the Mafia subsided for a time; it went under cover, the headlines died—and the public forgot.

Ten years later there was a reminder, this time in New York City. Immigrants from Southern Italy and Sicily had flocked to New York's Lower East Side where they crowded into tenements and lived the hard, poverty-ridden life of newcomers trying to find work and adjust to new ways. Along with the honest and industrious had come the criminal and the vicious, nurtured by two secret societies, the Camorra of Naples and the Mafia of Sicily. Disciples of each had brought with them their organizational methods and unscrupulous practices, and they soon established something of a reign of terror over New York's East Side.

Blackmail, extortion, kidnaping became common practices. The small shopkeeper was forced to pay for "protection," the father for the safety of his family. Refusal was followed by bombing or by murder, and always the darkest deeds were hidden by omertà. For those bold enough to violate the code of silence, there was the certainty of the Mafia's implacable vengeance—for a minor offense, the slit tongue; for real betrayal, the slit throat and the corpse dumped on the street.

The symbol of these depredations was the black hand. Extortion notes would be signed with a drawn dagger and the imprint of a black and bloody hand, designed to strike terror and induce acquiescence. Newspapers fastened upon the symbol and dubbed the terrorists the Black Hand Society; but actually there was no organization by that name. The black hand was merely a decorative trademark for the Camorra and the Mafia.

Lawlessness and terror on the East Side, where, incidentally, much of America's future syndicate of crime was to be born, became so serious that the New York Police Department created a special Italian squad under Lieutenant Joseph Petrosino. Petrosino had been born in the coastal town of Salerno, near Naples, and as a boy he had heard much from his parents about the Mafia and its terroristic practices. A stocky man, standing five feet eight, with a round head, a slightly pock-marked face and snapping black eyes, he developed a hatred for the Mafia that ruled his life like an obsession; he was to become the first American nemesis of the evil brotherhood and ultimately a martyr to the cause of law enforcement.

Petrosino appears to have been the first American policeman to appreciate the full scope of the Camorra and Mafia as criminally organized enterprises, capable of extending their power and vengeance across city, state, and national boundaries. Working with a small squad out of the old, rambling Metropolitan Police headquarters at 300 Mulberry Street, Petrosino began systematically to compile complete records on the Mafia and its members, the first thorough dossier of its kind in the nation. Under a variety of disguises, he personally mingled with the toughest elements in the Italian community, and at daily risk of his life gathered the information that enabled him to identify the principal Mafiosi of his day—the dock czars, brothel keepers, fish and meat market extortionists, bomb throwers.

In 1900, from information gathered among New Jersey anarchists, he tipped off Italian police to a plot to murder King Humbert. In one year, he personally made 700 arrests. Hundreds of Italians, especially Sicilians, who had entered the country illegally or neglected their naturalization procedures, were ferreted out by Petrosino and deported. The Mafia began to hate him with all the venom of which it was capable.

Petrosino himself was increasingly frustrated. He appreciated the magnitude of the criminal conspiracy he was fighting—an *organization* of crime that still appeared a doubtful myth, a product of journalistic sensationalism, to many sober citizens—and he felt balked by his inability to make others see what he saw so clearly. A second source of frustration was his inability to strike a really devastating blow at the real rulers of this criminal empire. Petrosino had identified the supreme chief of the Camorra as Enrico Alfano, alias Erricone, and the boss of the Mafia as Ignazio Lupo, known as "Lupo the Wolf." Both, however, were so well protected by their lieutenants and followers—as the rulers of the Mafia are to this day—that Petrosino could not pin directly upon them any of the hideous crimes for which they were responsible.

The New York detective finally caught up with Erricone, the Camorra czar, but there was still no local case against him. Petrosino had to settle for Erricone's deportation to Italy, where he was wanted by Italian law. Lupo the Wolf proved an even more elusive antagonist. Petrosino found it impossible to lay a hand upon the Mafia chieftain.

So stood events in the summer of 1907 when a new wave of Black Hand violence swept across New York. Petrosino found a Harlem saloonkeeper who had been forced to act as broker for the extortionists; an Italian banker, who, under threat of death, had been compelled to supply bail for the blackmailers, who of course then jumped their bonds, leaving the banker holding the bag. In August, 1907, a plucky Italian merchant, Joseph Trano, came to Petrosino and said he had received a Black Hand letter demanding $500 upon the pain of death. Petrosino praised Trano for his courage, gave him marked bills, and set a trap.

Into it walked Vincenzio Abadezza, one of Lupo the Wolf's principal henchmen. Petrosino and his detectives watched the payoff, then tailed Abadezza to find out the identities of others in the conspiracy. In the resulting roundup, Abadezza and eight others were arrested. On one of the suspects, two notebooks were found. One contained a list of some twenty names of members of the secret brotherhood; the other, the names of sixty laborers, scattered throughout the state, who were paying tribute of from one dollar to three dollars a week to the extortionists.

Petrosino, at first elated by this arrest, according to fellow detectives, was in despair when the cases came into court. Judges tended to look down their long noses in disbelief at the whole idea of an invisible government of crime, just as they do today. As a result, Abadezza drew a two-and-a-half-year prison sentence, but the others all got off with slap-on-the-wrist penalties of a few days in jail.

Discouraged by the blindness of the judiciary, Petrosino decided that the only way he could really show such educated skeptics the reality of the sinister organization he was fighting was to go to Italy and trace there the ties that bound the Mafia abroad to the Mafia in New York. Police Commissioner Theodore Bingham at first attempted to dissuade him, but finally agreed to let him carry out the plan. And so, in January, 1909, Lieutenant Petrosino sailed secretly for Italy.

Though his mission had been kept quiet for his own protection, Petrosino was a marked man. Later investigations showed that Lupo the Wolf knew of Petrosino's trip and its purpose almost as soon as the detective sailed. So a complicated, transatlantic plot was set in motion, the full details of which are not known to this day.

Petrosino, traveling incognito, was well received by Italian officials in Rome and Naples. He obtained the records of more than 600 desperate criminals known to have emigrated to America. Not content with such background information and wanting more complete, on-the-scene details, he traveled on to Palermo. There, on the evening of March 13, 1909, he dined in a restaurant on Marino Square— then set out to cross the square, walking toward the Hotel di Palma where he was staying. As Petrosino strolled along through the crowds, two men came up behind him, whipped out revolvers and pumped four bullets into his back and head. At the first shot, the Lieutenant whirled, clutching at his own revolver. He managed to get it out, to touch off one wild shot; then he crashed down dead on the pavement. The Mafia in Sicily had expunged the detective who most menaced the Mafia in New York.

Petrosino's murderers, hardly quickening their steps, simply walked away—and the wall of omertà closed behind them. Though the assassination had been witnessed by scores of pedestrians, no one had seen a thing; no one could identify the killers. Petrosino's body was shipped home, and he was given a hero's burial. But his knowledge had died with him. No one else could put together all the sinister ties and practices of the Mafia.

In death, it would seem, Lieutenant Petrosino had demonstrated his most vital thesis—the *fact* of underworld organization, the existence of a machinery so well administered and so far reaching that it could stretch across the ocean and strike down a dangerous New York detective on the streets of Palermo. Yet even this demonstration seems to have been almost completely ignored. Lieutenant Petrosino was dead—and all too soon forgotten.

Not until Mussolini and Cesare Mori conducted their relentless drive against the Mafia in the mid-1920's did some additional details about Petrosino's assassination leak out. Norman Lewis has recounted them in *The Honored Society*. Petrosino's slaying, Lewis writes, was engineered by Don Vito Cascio Ferro, who had been the head of the Sicilian Mafia for twenty-five years before Mori jailed him. Don Vito had spent part of his youth in the United States, had been active in some of the early Black Hand extortions here, and then had returned to his native Sicily where he rose to command the Mafia.

Don Vito was a man of peculiar, magnetic force. Almost completely illiterate, Lewis writes, he was nevertheless

> . . . a favorite of high society and frequented Palermo's most glittering *salons*. He was in demand to open exhibitions of water colors, he romped with dukes and duchesses in party games, he listened with reverence to famous actors giving poetry readings from Leopardi, he dressed himself fashionably in knickerbockers and Norfolk jacket to shoot thrushes in distinguished company, and he joined aristocratic carriage parties to pelt the children of the poor with cakes and sweets on All Souls' Eve. Women of gentle birth spoke of the strange magnetic force with which a room seemed charged when Don Vito was present, and he once administered a severe admonition to his barber for selling his hair clippings to a maker of amulets.

In his lifetime, Don Vito had been accused of some seventy major crimes, twenty of them homicides. He had always been acquitted. But he never made any secret of the fact that he had killed Lieutenant Petrosino. He bragged about it. Indeed, in his own version, the second gunman disappeared completely, and Don Vito alone took credit for the slaying. As he saw it, Petrosino's audacity in invading Palermo was an affront not to be ignored. On the evening of the murder, as Don Vito told the story, he was dining with a member of Parliament. During the meal, he suddenly pretended that he had forgotten an important errand at home and asked if he could borrow his host's carriage to take care of it. The host was most obliging, and so Don Vito rode to murder in the private carriage of a member of Parliament. His timing had been perfect. He came upon Petrosino crossing the square, fired the fatal shots, climbed back into the waiting carriage and returned to the home of his Parliamentary host in time to enjoy the port. "When the suspicion later fell upon Don Vito," Lewis wrote, "the friend was ready to swear in court that his guest had never left the house on the night of the killing."

The assassination of Petrosino spurred a brief, intensified campaign against Mafia chieftains in New York. Lupo the Wolf was finally jailed on a counterfeiting charge, and some of his underbosses were rounded up. But then the steam went out of the drive, owing to several factors. The Mafia itself became more circumspect, abandoning the crudity of Black Hand letters and refining its techniques of power and persuasion. As the society submerged like a submarine below the surface of life, it also stimulated a wave of propaganda, playing upon the ethnic sensibilities of New York's large Italian voting population. It was vicious and unfair, the argument went, to maintain an Italian squad; the very existence of such a squad was a libel upon the fair name of the hundreds of thousands of law-abiding Italians who had become good American citizens. Sensitive to the power of all those Italian votes, New York's politicians heeded the outcry, and Petrosino's Italian squad was quietly disbanded. With its liquidation, the nation lost its best eyes and ears; there was no one to watch, to trace, and to catalogue the fantastic growth of underworld organization and power during the next two decades.

Two major events conjoined during the 1920's to build the U.S. Mafia into the awesome power it has become. One was Mussolini's purge of the Mafia in Sicily; the other, American Prohibition.

When Il Duce gave Prefect Cesare Mori carte blanche powers to exterminate the Mafia, he started a train of events that were to send thousands of members of the secret brotherhood fleeing to the United States. Mori fought the Mafia the way a general conducts a war. He sometimes put hundreds of carabinieri into the field and fought pitched battles. He concentrated on breaking down the wall of omertà, holding his prisoners incommunicado for days and subjecting them to remorseless, continuous questioning. Mori operated on the theory that many Mafia members in the upper classes of society belonged to the evil brotherhood because they had been terrorized; that, once convinced of the power and protection of the state, they would talk and name names. He was right. They did.

Mafia suspects were rounded up by the hundreds and marched into court, chained to one another, highly polished shoes agleam, eyes fierce above their ferocious mustaches. They were herded, like so many dangerous beasts in a zoo, into great iron cages and subjected to mass trials that sometimes continued for months. Mori's methods, obviously, could be employed only in a dictatorial society; the trials were like drumhead courts-martial, a far cry from the more fair and deliberative processes of justice. But the effects at the time were dramatic. Twenty-year-old murders were solved; some 2,000 Mafiosi were tried, convicted, imprisoned. Mori proclaimed that he had exterminated the Mafia, and Mussolini trumpeted this achievement. Both were wrong.

Modern critics, made skeptical by the reappearance of the Mafia in Sicily in all its old strength once the pressure was relaxed, have been inclined to write off Mori's celebrated crusade as much sound and fury, signifying little. Norman Lewis insists that Don Vito Cascio Ferro, the slayer of Petrosino and the No. 1 man of the Sicilian Mafia, was the only really "big fish" that Mori caught. The rest, he charges, were mere gunmen and stiletto artists, the lowly of the brotherhood. The verdict may be too harsh, for Mori did round up many a powerful and influential figure, including mayors and police chiefs who had been secret members of the Mafia. It is indisputable, however, that Mori, contrary to his own belief at the time, fell far short of his intent to wipe out the top leadership. The more wily of the Mafia chieftains joined the Fascist Party, voluble in their protestations of undying fealty to Il Duce, and then they waited, biding their time until it would be safe to surface again.

Others, having less fortitude, simply fled. They decamped by the thousand, most of them heading for America where the brotherhood had such well-established branches and contacts. The fortunate who had passports entered as legal immigrants; but many others did not bother with such formalities. They simply crossed the Canadian or Mexican borders, or, like Cadillac Charlie Cavallaro, they debarked from Italian ships in American ports. However they came, their arrival was important. They swelled the army of American crime at a critical juncture.

Prohibition had transformed the underworld. It poured into the coffers of gangdom a golden cascade that gave the most vicious thugs resources the U.S. Treasury might envy. Fortunes made in the almost universal business of bootlegging transformed not only the underworld but much of American society. The nether world became overnight respectable and incredibly powerful. Previously, crime had been simply crime; now it was big business. The change occurred in a period of about five years.

When Prohibition closed saloon doors in 1920, crime in New York was the preserve of vicious slum mobs engaged in looting, dock and commercial racketeering, extortion, the lotteries, narcotics, and other nefarious enterprises. Their activities, like the earlier Black Hand extortions of the Camorra and Mafia, were relatively crude and the returns, compared to the flood that came from defying Prohibition, were relatively picayune. In this poorer and simpler world of crime, various ethnic groups operated within fairly well-defined boundaries. The Irish mobs controlled the West Side docks and waterfront; Jewish and Italian gangs, produced by the East Side ghettos, claimed the area from the tip of Manhattan up into East Harlem and the Bronx; and, across the river in Brooklyn, other Jewish and Italian conclaves in the Brownsville and South Brooklyn sections were breeding lethal rulers whose names were to become synonymous with crime across the nation for the next thirty years.

The manner in which Prohibition bankrolled crime and made it one of the nation's largest industries can best be appreciated by a look at some individual fortunes. Take, for example, a Chicago hench-man of Johnny Torrio's named Jimmy La Penna. La Penna was such an inconspicuous mobster that nobody today remembers his name, and his only significance is perhaps attributable to his limited intelligence. La Penna was so stupid that he didn't try to hide the cash he received, he simply took it to the bank—and so presented Internal

Revenue with a gilt-edged income-tax-evasion case. This one lower-echelon gangster banked a fantastic $804,676.97 in 1931; and, even in 1932, despite the Depression, the threat of the imminent end of Prohibition, and other reverses, he still managed to deposit $330,088.39.

The rewards in the executive suite of crime were, of course, even more alluring. Take the saga of William Vincent (Big Bill) Dwyer, one of the era's first crime-created millionaires. In 1920, Dwyer was just a stevedore on the Chelsea docks of Manhattan's West Side. He promptly got into the bootlegging racket, first as a hired hand, then as boss and major importer. He struck up an alliance with Owney Madden, West Side dock czar, and was soon rolling in money. The federal government subsequently charged that in 1922, just two years after his standing start as a stevedore, Dwyer had short-changed the government $100,000 on income taxes. The following year, according to the government, Dwyer failed to pay Uncle Sam $800,000. This, it must be understood, was *the amount of taxes due, not income.* And in 1924, again according to the government, Dwyer capped his previous performances by overlooking $1,200,000 in taxes. Since the income-tax rates then were far lower than they are today, Dwyer's tax delinquency record—$2 million in just two years—speaks for itself about the enormity of his actual earnings.

Dwyer was typical of his age in other respects. A master organizer, he acquired his own fleet of vessels that he stationed in Rum Row, strung out at sea just beyond territorial limits off the East Coast, and he built up his own speedboat ferrying fleet to smuggle the liquid gold ashore. Since this smuggling had to be accomplished under the very noses of the Coast Guard and police, Dwyer became an outstanding artist in bribery and corruption. Some of his feats were so brash that even his competitors admired them. One coup that no other entre-preneur of his day ever topped was Big Bill's success in bribing the entire crew of a Coast Guard cutter which he then sent steaming out to Rum Row to fetch in a cargo of 700 cases of liquor. Another Coast Guard craft was on patrol at the time and the crew of the cutter had the devil's own time convincing skeptical Rum Row skippers that they were actually in the service of Big Bill Dwyer and not Uncle Sam, as their uniforms said. Eventually, all difficulties were surmounted, the liquor was loaded and brought safely into port. The Coast Guard cutter then pulled into a dock near Canal Street, and the cases of liquor were unloaded while a contingent of police stood thirstily by, not bothering to interfere.

The flamboyance of such operations finally became too much even for the corrupted law of the 1920's. The federal government got after Dwyer, finally managed to perfect a bribery case against him, and packed him off to Atlanta Penitentiary. It was a relatively painless servitude, lasting only a little more than a year; then Big Bill was free again. He decided now, having made his stake, that it might be wise to turn legitimate. He had already introduced hockey to New York as a professional sport, and he owned the Coney Island racetrack at Cincinnati and a half interest in the Mount Royal track at Montreal. Disposing of these investments, Dwyer founded Tropical Park near Miami and became one of the major backers of the new Rockingham Park at Salem, New Hampshire. He was now a sportsman and a social figure. By March, 1936, *The New York Times* was reporting in its society notes from Miami that William Vincent Dwyer, of New York, "managing director of the Gables Racing Association" (no mention here, naturally, of Chelsea dock and bootlegging origins) had entertained at a buffet luncheon a distinguished list of society guests, headed by "Sir Graeme Sinclair-Lockhart, Bart., and Lady Lockhart."

If Big Bill Dwyer's career was symbolic of an era in its progression from dock walloper to hosting baronets on a bankroll of illicit millions, it was less typical of the enduring pattern of crime that was to emerge from the conditions of the time. Dwyer was an individualist, an opportunist; others—the leaders of the Mafia or, as it came to be called, the Unione Siciliano—were career criminals. A Dwyer or an Owney Madden might feast on Prohibition profits and then get out. But the Mafiosi would feast and feast—and never get out. That was the difference.

"Prohibition really put the Mafia in the saddle," says a veteran narcotics agent, discussing the trend of the times. "All of the gangs, of course, went into bootlegging, but the Mafia was the one organization in the underworld that already had a perfected, functioning organization stretching across state lines, across the country. It was the one outfit able to take control."

The logistics of the bootlegging operation also played into the hands of the New York-centered Mafia and helped its chieftains set a new pattern of crime across the nation. The prohibited thirst of a continent could be assuaged only by enormous quantities of smuggled liquor; and, while some of it could be brought in by land across northern and southern borders, the vast bulk had to be imported by sea, smuggled into East Coast ports, and then distributed. Millions of dollars were involved, intricate fixes, clandestine landing and hauling operations. It all required an army of men, the firmest connections, well-established lines of credit.

Since the East Coast mobs held control at the neck of the liquor bottle, so to speak, theirs was the decisive voice in determining whom they would do business with, what credit they would extend, what arrangements for payment would be made. Inevitably, they preferred to do business with their own, either members of the Mafia or gang chiefs with whom their Mafia overlords had had intimate connections. It was therefore no accident that the decade of the Roaring Twenties, which saw incredible fortunes piled up from the trafficking in smuggled and diluted liquor, also saw the proliferation across the nation of criminal mobs headed by gangsters who had received their training in crime on the streets of the Lower East Side or Brooklyn. Charles (King) Solomon emigrated from New York to Boston and became czar of the New England rackets; the Bernsteins went out to found the Purple Gang in Detroit; Johnny Torrio and Scarface Al Capone, products of the Brooklyn breeding ground, went west and subjugated all Chicago.

Trafficking in liquor and millions operated on two levels. On the lower echelons, there were the trigger-happy cutthroats; on the upper, the astute businessmen of crime. Much of the Prohibition Era featured a dichotomy between these elements. During the earlier years, the brawling of the cutthroats dominated life in the rackets. Liquor trucks on their way from East Coast ports to distribution centers were hijacked in the night by rival gangs; and, in retribution, machine guns blasted in the streets at high noon, leaving a trail of corpses from one corner of the nation to the other. Chaotic was the world of crime, and the chaos could not be indefinitely tolerated. The racketing of guns in the streets, the gaudy headlines, the interminable gang warfare—all this interfered with the quiet and orderly processes by which a profitable multibillion-dollar business should be run. It also posed a threat to the men who had already made their millions; they never knew when a blast out of the night might cut *them* down. Only in organization lay the solution of such problems and the dissipation of such evils.

The first corporate arrangements were designed to unify the interests of the major East Coast liquor importers. The heads of the various smuggling mobs got together to set up a cartel to handle purchasing and distribution of the Rum Row cargoes. Definite quotas, fixed percentages of the business, were assigned to rival mobs, and the lines of distribution to inland baronies of crime were similarly delineated. This first organization of bootleggers became known in the underworld as the Big Seven. Represented on the board of the Big Seven were these interests: the Unione in the person of Charles (Lucky) Luciano; Waxey Gordon; Madden and Dwyer; Benjamin (Buggsy) Siegel and Meyer Lansky, proprietors of the lethal Bug and Meyer mob; Louis (Lepke) Buchalter and his partner, Gurrah Shapiro; Frank Costello and Dandy Phil Kastel; Longy Zwillman, of Newark; and Charles Solomon, of Boston.

As can be seen, this combination represented a variety of ethnic mob interests. Bosses of Irish, Jewish, and Italian combines all sat on the board. Significantly, there were strong crossties and business relationships among several of these dominant outfits. Frank Costello, for example, began his rise in the rum-running profession as a disciple of Big Bill Dwyer. Lucky Luciano had a special fondness for Siegel and Lansky, whose torpedoes he sometimes used in moments of need, and he also had connections with the wily Buchalter, whose specialty was to become business extortion.

United in the Big Seven, these powers obtained virtual control over the illicit liquor traffic along the whole Atlantic Coast from Boston to Baltimore. They had less success in imposing a rule of order on the rowdy mob life of the period. Brash interlopers were always trying to cut in on the racket, and foolhardy double-crossers, not yet educated to the idea of an awesome and all-powerful syndicate of crime, were continually trying to hijack somebody else's payload. The answer to such deeds was always more gunfire, more bodies, more headlines—the kind of violent notoriety that was such a deterrent to the calm pursuit of business.

Take, for example, the career of Frankie Uale, or, as he was better known in the underworld, Frankie Yale. A loud, flashy, swaggerer who fancied tailor-made suits and diamond-studded belts, Yale was one of the underworld's more notorious killers. Chicago police, though they could never make a case against him, were convinced that he was the hood who had perforated Big Jim Colosimo in 1920, making it possible for Johnny Torrio, Frankie Yale's boyhood chum in Brooklyn, to take command of The Loop. Chicago detectives also credited Frankie with the murder of Dion O'Banion in the midst of the bouquets in his flower shop in 1924, a deed that insured the ascension of Al Capone. When not occupied with such business excursions to Chicago, Frankie Yale tended to his Brooklyn affairs as the principal over-the-river lieutenant of Joe (The Boss) Masseria, chief of the dominant Mafia family in New York at the time. His status as the Mafia's man-in-charge in Brooklyn helped to elevate Frankie Yale another notch as the Eastern lieutenant of Al Capone. In this high office, he became responsible for seeing that nothing happened to Capone's liquor trucks as they rumbled through Brooklyn streets laden with their high-proof cargoes from Rum Row offshore.

One might have thought that, with all these connections and a "diamond-studded" wardrobe, Frankie Yale would have been content with life. But one would have been wrong. Frankie's fatal flaw was a greed that knew no contentment, and so strange things began to happen, especially to Scarface Al Capone's liquor trucks. They began to be hijacked just like anybody else's liquor trucks. Scarface Al, who was never accused of being stupid, quickly figured out that this couldn't happen—and keep on happening—without the active participation of his supposed henchman, Frankie Yale.

Suspecting the double cross, Capone dispatched an undercover man to Brooklyn to investigate. The agent didn't last long—he was murdered. And Capone declared war.

About three o'clock on July 1, 1928, a quiet Sunday afternoon, Frankie Yale arrayed himself in his most resplendent finery and went on his last ride. Behind the wheel of his powerful new sedan, bullet-proof windows down to let in the air, he cruised contentedly through a quiet residential area along Brooklyn's 44th Street. He was so much at peace with the world that he didn't notice another sedan, going a little faster, coming up behind and pulling out to pass. Right alongside, the strange sedan seemed to accommodate its speed to Frankie Yale's, and at that instant, a most frightful racket broke out. It sounded as if all the automobiles in Brooklyn had started backfiring at the same instant, but Frankie Yale never heard the unseemly Sunday uproar.

The machine gun pumped its bullets unerringly, and Frankie sagged forward over the steering wheel, dead. His car, out of control, leaped the sidewalk, crashed through a low hedge, hit the stone steps of a nearby house—and dumped Frankie Yale's suddenly unlovely body into the midst of a Sunday afternoon garden party.

The slaying of Frankie Yale caused a tremendous furore. It was also the forerunner of a string of killings that seemed to bring the racket wars of the Roaring Twenties to a raging crescendo. In Chicago, Tony Lombardo, one of the more important Unione bosses, was standing on a curb in The Loop one evening when someone walked up casually behind him and riddled his spine with a .45. Al Capone was doing sanguinary battle with the George (Bugs) Moran mob, and on St. Valentine's Day, 1929, his henchmen trapped seven Moran torpedoes in a North Clark Street garage, lined them up against a wall and mowed them down with machine-gun fire in what became known as the St. Valentine's Day massacre. In New York, Legs Diamond and Dutch Schultz were blasting away at each other. There seemed no end to the carnage, and the wiser and younger brains, then just struggling to the fore in the Mafia, decided that something must be done.

The decision led to the first grand council meetings of the secret brotherhood. The first session of which authorities have record took place in a Cleveland hotel in 1928. Cleveland police stumbled upon the conclave as it was breaking up and found twenty-one Mafiosi, several of them toting guns. Strikingly enough, some of the delegates so identified at this first meeting were to turn up nearly thirty years later at Apalachin. This fact in itself tells much about the continuity of the invisible government that was then just being established.

Not very much is known about the agenda of this first Cleveland council session, but it was apparently a forerunner of the most important meeting of minds ever held by the American Mafia. This took place in the President Hotel on the Atlantic City boardwalk in late April, 1929; to it came Capi Mafiosi from all sections of the nation; and from it resulted the structure of an actually functioning invisible government.

Presiding at the Atlantic City conclave was Frank Costello. He was not yet known as the Prime Minister of crime, but he was a rising and important power as his inclusion on the board of the Big Seven rum-running syndicate already had shown. Like the departed Frankie Yale, he belonged to the family of Joe (the Boss) Masseria, and he was consigliere, or councilor, to Masseria's right-hand man, Lucky Luciano. A gangster diplomat and politician, Costello's genius for organization was already well recognized in mob circles; and so, according to later informers, he had been selected by the leaders to call all the bosses of the various gangs together for a convention to chart the future. According to some reports, Costello shelled out some $25,000 of his own money to cover expenses.

Delegates came from Chicago, New York, Detroit, Philadelphia, Boston, and other major cities. The most sinister figure in this sinister group was Scarface Al Capone, the Neapolitan strong man who had made murder a feature of everyday life in Chicago. With him was his bodyguard, Frank Cline, and his leading henchmen, Frank (The Enforcer) Nitti and Jake (Greasy Thumb) Guzik. At the other end of a mahogany table were men who were soon to be the most powerful in the American underworld: Frank Costello, Lucky Luciano, and Joe Adonis. These three were most representative of the new breed just coming to power—the businessmen of crime, intent upon ending the blatant street warfare and upon murdering, when murder was necessary, quietly and with decorum.

Since crime's masterminds forgathered along the Atlantic City boardwalk in 1929, a good deal of reliable information has leaked out concerning their deliberations and decisions. The Federal Bureau of Narcotics, after checking and cross-checking the accounts of various informants, feels assured that the Atlantic City conclave accomplished these things:

1. It perfected for the first time the outlines of a truly national crime syndicate and established its organization. Delegates supposedly took a map of the United States and carved the nation up into specific territories. Jurisdiction in each region was accorded to the Mafia chief who had proved himself most efficient in running his individual rackets. He became head of the Mafia family in his area and sat on the national board.

2. The hierarchy of crime was protected. No longer was a racket boss to be permitted to go out and slay of his own free will. Even lowly button men like Joe Valachi were not to be executed without

a hearing before the underboss or lieutenant in their particular family. On the top level, no ruler was to be violently deposed unless the governing council had adjudged him guilty of grave offenses. In effect, a system of kangaroo courts, establishing gangland's own judicial system, was provided.

3. The new organization appointed emissaries to deal with politicians and public officials on a nationwide basis. The masterminds of crime knew that they could not continue to thrive without ironclad protection, and they had learned, from their Prohibition arrangements, how secure this protection could be if appropriate amounts of money were devoted to purchasing it. According to some informants at least, the Atlantic City conferences decided to establish a multi-million-dollar fund to be used to bribe law-enforcement officials and assure the election of complaisant politicians to important offices.

4. Another lush fund was to be established—an "educational fund." The object was to further the development of promising young Italians, to guarantee them an education and the proper veneer to fit them for future executive roles in the organization of crime. This was an important decision that marked a sharp switch in mob emphasis—away from the swaggering Frankie Yale types and toward the self-effacing criminal executive of the future, well educated, suave, indistinguishable in manners and person from the millionaire businessman in the charcoal suit.

To implement these decisions, said some reports, Johnny Torrio was called back from the retirement into which he had withdrawn after his onetime henchman, Al Capone, started to blast things wide open in Chicago. Torrio, according to this version, was to act, temporarily at least, as a senior councilor and administrator to get the machinery of the new organization running.

The historic Atlantic City convention had an immediate after-effect—an incident that suggested the double cross had not been outlawed in the new rule of law and order. Al Capone, on his way home to Chicago, stopped off in Philadelphia and went to a movie. When he came out, the law was waiting for him. Just how the law knew the exact details of Capone's itinerary remains a mystery to this day. Anyway, it did, and it found Scarface Al, as usual, toting a gun. The gun-carrying charge put him away in prison for a year, the first dent in his armor of invulnerability.

During the months that Capone was deactivated, monumental

changes shook the underworld. At the Atlantic City convention, the framework of an all-powerful criminal structure had been erected, but not all the powers in gangland appreciated its advantages. As always, there was the old order that rebelled at newfangled ideas—and at any usurpation of its own prerogatives and power. And so, before the new system could begin to function, there was to be another blood bath.

4

THE PURGE OF THE GREASERS

JOE (the Boss) Masseria had led a charmed life. Or, looking at it another way, the devil had long protected him. Joe the Boss ruled the New York Mafia, then usually called the Unione Siciliano, throughout most of the decade of the twenties. He had escaped murder so many times that the legend grew he could run faster and dodge quicker than any bullet could fly. The legend, like most legends, strayed from truth. Joe the Boss could dodge only the bullets of his enemies, not those of his friends.

Joe the Boss had climbed to power in 1920 by gunning down a rival, a bootlegger named Salvatore Mauro, in a pitched battle in the middle of Chrystie Street. During his early reign, he sometimes had to fend off challenges from upstarts suffering an excess of brashness and a deficiency of discretion. One of the most ambitious of these rivals was Umberto Valenti. In the spring of 1922, Valenti decided to strike directly at the authority of Joe the Boss, and he made his intentions clear by murdering Vincent Terranova, the younger brother of Ciro Terranova, the Artichoke King, who ruled the Bronx and was a close ally of Joe the Boss.

The murder of the brother of so prized a cohort could not be ignored, and Joe the Boss planned retribution in the very shadow of Police Headquarters. In those days, the mob had established what

became known as "the curb exchange" in the streets outside headquarters. The curb exchange was the rumrunner's version of the
stock exchange. A bootlegger might become overloaded, for example, with good bourbon just when his customers all developed an
exclusive taste for Scotch. In such exigency, he would have to swap
the liquor he had for the liquor he needed; he would have to make
contact with other members of the fraternity to make his deal. So,
with a brashness that seems incredible today, the top bootleg barons
of the period had established the curb exchange along Kenmare,
Broome, Grand, and Elizabeth Streets, practically encircling headquarters; and, when disputes broke out over who had gypped whom
in a deal, they settled matters with gunfire not far from the windows
of the Police Commissioner and Chief of Detectives. Joe the Boss
had little doubt that his rival would show up at the curb exchange
to transact necessary business, so he stationed himself and two henchmen in the doorway of 194 Grand Street, only a short distance from
the southern end of headquarters.

Events worked out as Joe the Boss had foreseen—up to a point.
Early in the evening of May 8, 1922, as workmen were hurrying
home from their jobs, Umberto Valenti and a hired gun, Silva
Tagliagamba, turned out of Mott Street into Grand and began walking
toward the ambush of Joe the Boss. Masseria waited until Valenti
and Tagliagamba were in front of 190 Grand, then he nodded his
head and he and his two torpedoes popped out into the street, the
guns in their hands going off like firecrackers. Valenti and Tagliagamba fired back, and the bullets zinging along the street wounded
four passersby, two women and two men. Valenti and Tagliagamba
fled.

With the racket almost splitting the eardrums of detectives in
headquarters, the law made an appearance—and Masseria and his
helpers also took to their heels. Joe the Boss, short and heavily
built, churned around the corner of Mulberry Street into Broome,
where his agents were transacting the day's business. The boys ducked
into doorways when they saw The Boss charging by with two detectives on his heels. Joe the Boss lightened his load by tossing a .38
caliber revolver into the gutter. And while one of the pursuing
detectives stopped to repossess it, Joe the Boss sped on. He dashed
across Broome toward Kenmare Street, but here ran into Edward
Tracey, a detective sergeant, on his way to headquarters. Tracey

swerved his car directly into Masseria's path, jumped out and struck Joe the Boss over the head with a nightclub.

In the nearby headquarters, when detectives frisked Joe the Boss, they found a curious document—a gun permit signed by Justice Selah B. Strong in Supreme Court permitting him to carry a weapon anywhere he went in the state. Naturally, gun permits were not supposed to be issued to notorious criminals, but in the New York of those days and in most other parts of the country as well, a lot of strange things were happening.

There was, of course, a great scandal. But like many of that period, this quickly and conveniently died, achieving little beyond the disclosure that Joe the Boss could persuade the law to issue him a pistol permit. Other matters stemming from the ambush in the shadows of headquarters were not settled so fast.

Valenti's henchman, Tagliagamba, who had been wounded in the gun battle, held on until late June before he succumbed. The law went through the motions of charging Joe the Boss with murder, but it permitted him his liberty on bail, an indication of the law's generosity during this period to distinguished citizens of Joe the Boss's stature. Another indication was the fact that the case against Joe the Boss never came to trial. Postponement followed postponement, and Joe the Boss continued to do business as usual at his old stand.

Umberto Valenti became impatient. He had held his fire, hoping the electric chair might do his work for him; but when it became apparent the only chair Joe the Boss would ever sit in was his own upholstered one, Valenti decided he would help the law. For this high-minded mission, he picked four torpedoes who were supposed to know their business.

Joe the Boss lived with his wife and two children at 80 Second Avenue, just a few doors from the corner of Fifth Street. Shortly after noon on the hot summer day of August 9, 1922, he left his apartment, sporting a new straw hat, and turned north toward Fifth Street. Two of the torpedoes had been waiting in a black limousine parked down the street and two others in a coffee house across the way. These latter, the instant they saw Joe the Boss emerge from his home, dropped their coffee cups and ran out, one cutting behind him, the other racing ahead to cut him off.

The man in front was too eager; he opened fire too soon and Joe the Boss, alerted to his danger, sprinted into Heiney's Millinery Shop at 82 Second Avenue. The gunman followed at his heels. Fritz Heiney, the proprietor, stood petrified at the scene that now took place before his eyes.

"The man with the revolver came close to the other fellow and aimed," he said. "Just as he fired the man jumped to one side. The bullet smashed the window of my store. Then the man fired again and the fellow he aimed at ducked his head forward. The third shot made a second hole in my window."

Out of bullets, the frustrated torpedo clicked his revolver futilely a couple more times at Joe the Boss's bobbing head, then dashed out of the shop and ran with his companion to the getaway car. The car swung the corner into Fifth Street, swarming at the time with members of the International Ladies' Garment Workers' Union coming from a meeting in Beethoven Hall, half a block away. Some of the unionists tried to stop the speeding car, but the thugs who had failed to eliminate Joe the Boss were equal to pumping bullets into this massed, unarmed humanity. Their shots felled five of the workers, and two others were knocked down by the speeding car. One man subsequently died of his wounds.

Detectives, arriving belatedly, found Joe the Boss at home, sitting on the side of his bed, his feet, aching from his latest marathon with death, soaking in a pan of hot water. On his head he still wore his new straw hat—with two bullet holes in its crown.

Far from eliminating Joe the Boss, the clumsiness of Valenti's stooges had boosted him to greater status in the underworld. Squat, chunky, hard-running Joe Masseria became a living legend—the man who could outrun and outdodge bullets. Such celebrity, however, would not settle the issue between him and Umberto Valenti. Only bullets would do that, and Joe the Boss decided the next bullets would be fired from his side of the fence.

To achieve this end, Joe the Boss reasoned, he must move swiftly and nothing could serve his purpose better than a peace conference. So he sent an emissary to Valenti, suggesting that they compose their differences. The deluded Valenti, evidently thinking Joe the Boss must be winded by his bullet-dodging feat, closed his eyes and consented.

The opposing factions met in a spaghetti house on East Twelfth Street near Second Avenue on August 11, 1922. Valenti came with one retainer; Masseria, with one. What Valenti didn't know was that Joe the Boss had two more thugs in hiding outside. After breaking the bread of peace and stuffing themselves with spaghetti, the conferees adjourned to the street and took a leisurely stroll along Twelfth, walking in the direction of Second Avenue. At the corner, they halted—and Masseria's two extra guns appeared. At a signal from Joe the Boss, all his boys suddenly whipped out their barkers.

The street-corner group, so amicable a few seconds before, split and ran in all directions, guns blazing furiously. Valenti, trying to emulate Joe the Boss's agile footwork, sped diagonally across the intersection toward a waiting taxicab. One of Masseria's gunmen followed him out into the intersection, stopped, and touched off a full clip of bullets. Valenti managed to reach the taxicab and open the door. Then he pitched over backwards from the impact of the final and fatal shot.

At such hazards had Joe the Boss pulled off his coup. Valenti had been eliminated, and only Joe the Boss ruled the New York Mafia.

Though two murder charges had been brought against Joe the Boss in three months, nothing happened to him. Witnesses, confronted with the sinister power of the Mafia, suddenly lost all recollection of events, and the law, for whatever mysterious reasons, never seemed very eager to prosecute anyway. So Joe the Boss went right on running the affairs of crime.

He did make certain alterations in technique. After the Valenti shoot-down, he exhibited more circumspection. He seemed to have learned well the first lesson of a criminal boss: never get yourself out front, never attract a lot of newspaper notoriety. That's dangerous. Let others man the front-line trenches and take the rap if things go wrong; stay in the background yourself and pull the strings. Such is the prescription for immunity, longevity, and ever more millions.

Operating on this theory, Joe the Boss let it be known that he had retired and was living on his accumulated hoard. He was, of course, doing nothing of the kind. A Mafioso hardly ever retires; he pursues his career of crime to the end. And Joe the Boss was no exception to the rule.

He learned, however, to keep well in the shadows. His name no longer made newspaper headlines. Lieutenants and underbosses now

carried out his missions. In the Bronx, he still had his alliance with
Ciro Terranova. In Manhattan, Charles (Lucky) Luciano gradually
rose in status and power until he became right-hand man and principal lieutenant. Across the river in Brooklyn, there was, originally,
Frankie Yale to keep an eye on his interests; and after Frankie was
toppled from the barony, there were other lieutenants who took over:
first Anthony (Little Augie) Pisano and next, right behind him, an
even more potent figure—Joe Adonis.

With affairs of crime so well organized, with his own pinnacle so
secure against assault by the law, Joe (the Boss) Masseria ruled
with hardly a hitch until 1930. Then war broke out, a bloody conflict
that shook the underworld. It was a warfare waged on two levels:
first, the open battle of two powerful gang chieftains for control of
the New York Mafia; secondly, submerged within this visible conflict,
the secret, conspiratorial thrust of the new breed—Luciano, Costello,
Adonis—to rise, seize supreme power, and impose upon the lawless
the rule of gang law and order first drafted at Atlantic City.

At this point Joe Valachi comes back into our tale. The prize
informer of 1963 had viewed the 1930 battleground from the level
of the troops, from the limited perspective of the button man carrying out killings on assignment. He knew nothing about the Atlantic
City conclave of the previous year or the far-reaching decisions made
there; all he knew was that the forces of Joe (the Boss) Masseria
were at war with those of Salvatore Maranzano—and that he was
a soldier in the army of Maranzano.

According to Valachi, the trouble started when Joe the Boss
assigned one of his triggermen to gun down Tommy Reina, head of
a family in the Maranzano group. This deed, carried out on February
26, 1930, was to set off a succession of explosions. Valachi might be
expected to know as much as anyone about this initial act, for his
wife is the former Mildred Reina, daughter of the slain gang chief.
Yet the reasons for the Reina murder remain obscure unless it was,
as Valachi intimates, that Joe the Boss felt himself so powerful he
could take over another family at will. In any event, that is what
Joe the Boss endeavored to do, installing one of his own henchmen,
Joseph Pinzolo, as new boss of the family. The slain Reina's underboss, Thomas Gagliano, did not take kindly to this usurpation, and so
an alliance was formed between the original Reina-Gagliano troop
and the forces of Maranzano.

It was at first a secret pact. Maranzano and Gagliano wanted to gain as much advantage as they could by "sneaking." This, as Valachi explained, was a strategy of lying low, perfecting plans, and then suddenly "hitting" as many of the opposition leaders as possible before they knew what was going on or just what quarter the bullets were coming from. The desire to sneak a few murders, Valachi explained, was the principal reason he had been recruited for the Maranzano family. New faces were needed. "The idea was they figured the opposite mob wouldn't know us," he explained.

The first body sneaked was that of the unpopular Joseph Pinzolo in the late summer of 1930. According to Valachi, the murder was committed by Girolamo (Bobby Doyle) Santuccio. "I was told by Bobby Doyle himself," he testified, "that he got the break of his life. He went down to Pinzolo's office and he found him all alone and he killed him."

It was at about this point, according to Valachi, that the war of the underworld took on the broader aspects of a racial feud. Joe the Boss passed a death sentence on all Sicilians coming from the Castellemarese area. Just why he should suddenly have developed such a passionate blood-thirst for all Castellemarese is not clear, but Joseph Profaci, who was one of them and who was to become one of the gang powers of New York, assured Valachi that it was so. Castellemarese were to be eliminated wherever Joe the Boss's gunmen found them—in New York, Buffalo, Chicago, anywhere in the United States.

The Castellemarese, headed by Salvatore Maranzano, naturally reacted to this edict and decided to conduct a counterelimination program of their own. A key figure in their plans was a rollicking killer whom Valachi knew only as "Buster from Chicago." This Buster was *persona non grata* with Al Capone, a very unhealthy state in Chicago, and so he had come East, a gun for hire, and had been enlisted by Maranzano. "Buster looked like a college boy, a little over six feet, light complexion, weighed about 200 pounds," Valachi told the McClellan committee. "He also would carry a violin case." In the case, there was, of course, no violin—just a machine gun.

With Buster from Chicago bolstering the fire power of the Castellemarese, the Maranzano forces set out to sneak the top command of the Masseria group. They hoped, naturally, to sneak Joe the Boss himself, but Joe the Boss was not circulating very freely in these parlous days. The Maranzano forces decided, therefore, that their best tactic would be to keep a close watch on two of his important henchmen, Alfred Mineo and Steve Ferrigno, the latter known to Valachi under the name of Fennuci. Fennuci had an apartment at 750 Pelham Parkway in the Bronx, and Valachi was assigned the task of setting up a plant in another apartment directly across a courtyard from Fennuci's. Here Valachi, Buster from Chicago, the Doc, Nick Capuzzi, and Joe Profaci waited and watched for nearly two months.

Then, one day in early November, 1930, just as Valachi was about to enter the apartment building, a car drew up outside and Fennuci and Joe the Boss himself climbed out. They all entered the elevator together, the newcomers instantly wary and suspicious of Valachi. "Punch yours," they told him. So he punched the sixth-floor button, got off and ran downstairs to his second-floor apartment, where he told his waiting killers that Joe the Boss was visiting Fennuci. Great was the excitement. Buster, a true sharpshooter, set up a watch at the window, eager for the chance to draw a bead on Joe the Boss. Valachi began to sweat. He didn't want the killing to take place from *his* apartment.

Fortunately for both Valachi and Joe the Boss, Masseria and his henchmen didn't appear in public again that night. The next morning, to Valachi's relief, the sharpshooting squad rented another apartment in the building with an equally excellent view of the courtyard. Reinforcements poured in, including "Bobby Doyle" Santuccio, the killer of Pinzolo; and Valachi left, deciding he had fulfilled his chore as spotter and wouldn't be needed in the action that was to come. But he learned all the details afterwards, he said, from Bobby Doyle, who was ecstatic at the way things started to pop almost the moment he arrived. "I got a break," he told Valachi. "I didn't have to be around too long."

Evidently, Valachi said, there had been a big meeting of Masseria's troop in Fennuci's apartment. Valachi estimated some twenty to twenty-four hoods had gathered there. About 2:45 on the afternoon of November 5, 1930, the meeting started to break up. The troop slipped out in pairs and the watching killers let them pass, waiting for Joe the Boss to appear. But they caught no sight of Joe the Boss. Finally, with the gathering virtually disbanded, Alfred Mineo and Fennuci stepped out into the daylight.

"When these two appeared, they didn't want to gamble any more," Valachi said, describing the reactions of the killer squad. "They said, 'Let us grab what we have. Maybe Joe got out during the night,' and they shot these two, which were two bosses. They were just as important as Masseria was."

This statement probably reflects the greatest gap in Valachi's knowledge as his view was from the bottom, looking up. He had no intimate knowledge, in most instances, of the dealing in the executive suite of crime; he knew only what filtered down, what he learned by rumor and report. Mineo and Fennuci may have been important cogs in the machinery of Masseria's organization; but they weren't anywhere near as important as Joe the Boss himself or as Joe the Boss's real right arm, Lucky Luciano.

With the slaying of Mineo and Fennuci, the sneaking largely ended. The Masseria group traced the furniture that had been delivered to Valachi's Pelham Parkway apartment; they found it had been purchased by his sister and they realized that Maranzano had been behind the killings. Despite the loss of two key henchmen, Masseria, according to Valachi, put out peace feelers. Perhaps he was trying to pull another Umberto Valenti coup, or perhaps he meant it. In any event, the maneuver didn't work. Maranzano was not Valenti, and, besides, he still had a score to settle.

One of Masseria's henchmen, Joseph Catania, alias Soldier Joe Baker, had been hijacking some of Maranzano's liquor trucks. This was a serious affront, and Maranzano decreed that Soldier Joe Baker had to go. The chore of arranging for his departure was assigned to Nick Capuzzi, Salvatore (Sally Shields) Shillitani, and Buster from Chicago, with Joe Valachi as their getaway-car driver.

Maranzano's spies had discovered that Soldier Joe regularly called at an apartment on Belmont Avenue in the Bronx. They rented a lookout post down the street, but it was almost a block away, too far for any kind of accurate shooting. Joe Valachi was disgusted. He told Maranzano that, if the boys kept hanging out around the neighborhood, someone was going to spot them and Masseria's torpedoes would come in and blast them out. Joe favored action while his side still had the initiative. Maranzano backed him.

Using a couple of spring leafs from a car, Joe pried open the door of the apartment Soldier Joe Baker was in the habit of visiting. He and his troop had timed the crash-in for about a half hour before

Soldier Joe's regular calling time, but they hadn't been prepared for
the sight that met their eyes when they jimmied the door.

"So, to my amazement," Joe Valachi testified, "I crashed the
doorway, the apartment was empty and there were three painters
in there. . . . These painters wanted to give us money. They thought
we were sticking them up. We said: 'We don't want any money, just
keep painting.' "

The painters obeyed instructions. The gunmen waited. In about
half an hour, right on schedule, Soldier Joe Baker came walking
along the street.

"As soon as he made the appearance," Valachi continued, "I left
to get the car ready. In other words, to have the motor ready instead
of going down there and running down and starting the car. I left
about a minute before and I had the motor ready. Within about a
minute's time, they were right behind me. . . ."

In that minute, Soldier Joe Baker had been dispatched, shot six
times in the head and body. Though he was still alive when he
reached Fordham Hospital, he sealed his lips and died without
naming his slayers.

The liquidation of Soldier Joe, coming on top of the murders of
Pinzolo, Mineo, and Fennuci, seemed to indicate to the underworld
that Maranzano was winning the war for control of the New York
rackets. He had now at his command an army of about 600 thugs
and more were "coming over" regularly. He had also the financing
for an extensive campaign. Tom Gagliano, the boss of the Reina
family once Pinzolo had been put out of the way, had contributed
$140,000. Steve Magaddino, then as now the rackets lord of Buffalo,
contributed $5,000 a week, and another $5,000 weekly came in from
Joe Aiello, a Chicago gangster allied with Bugs Moran in the battle
against Al Capone.

The button men saw little of this money. Valachi testified that he
and his companions in murder were getting only about $25 a week,
just enough to live on. He got so cramped for spending money, he
said, that he had to do a little "moonlighting"—pulling off a couple
of burglary jobs to raise some additional revenue. Throughout the
mobs, the Masseria-Maranzano struggle was disrupting life, for a
mobster who had to stay in hiding most of the time for his own skin's
sake couldn't go about business as usual. In this pass, according to
Valachi, Joe the Boss made peace overtures. He was willing to

abdicate as a family chieftain and to become just another soldier in the army if Maranzano would agree to leave him alone. But Maranzano wouldn't deal.

Out in Chicago, Al Capone gave Joe the Boss a helping hand and cut off one source of Maranzano revenue when his gunmen, operating from two apartment machine-gun nests, caught Joe Aiello in a crossfire and riddled him with bullets. Maranzano could afford the loss of this distant confederate and his $5,000 a week, for he now had a conspiratorial trump card up his sleeve.

The continuous blasting, so contrary to the spirit of the Atlantic City agreement that Frank Costello had engineered and so damaging to business, made little sense to two of Joe the Boss's most powerful aides, Lucky Luciano and Vito Genovese. It was obvious to them, in addition, that their boss was losing the war he had touched off with the slaying of Tom Reina. There was only one way to end it, to avert complete disaster, make peace, and get back to business as usual—Joe the Boss would have to go.

Secretly, according to Valachi—and other sources agree—Luciano and Maranzano reached an understanding. Charlie Lucky would arrange for the slaying of his own boss. This would re-establish peace in the brotherhood. It would also, of course, create a vacuum at the top of the Masseria family, and Charlie Lucky, the heir apparent, did not appear distraught at the prospect.

Joe the Boss, not being a mind reader, naturally had no clue to Charlie Lucky's thoughts. He liked Charlie Lucky, relied on him, depended on him. Charlie Lucky in recent years had been handling most of Joe the Boss's detail for him and handling it well. Besides, Charlie Lucky had an old-world flair for living that Joe the Boss liked. Charlie Lucky was almost like a son to him.

So Joe the Boss was agreeable when Charlie Lucky made a date to go out to Scarpato's Restaurant in Coney Island on the afternoon of April 15, 1931. They would have a good dinner, play cards, get away from it all. Joe the Boss liked the prospect.

Others liked it, too—and began to make plans. Judge Samuel S. Leibowitz, of the Kings County Court in Brooklyn, was then a rising young lawyer, laying the foundations for his reputation as one of the outstanding criminal trial attorneys in the nation. He had defended some of the mobsters and was well known and well liked by them. On the morning of April 15, 1931, he was in court trying a case and

his secretary was in his office at 66 Court Street when the door swung
open and in walked Albert Anastasia, the man who in the not too
distant future would be known as the Lord High Executioner of
Murder, Inc.

"What time is it?" Anastasia asked Leibowitz's secretary.

She pointed to a big clock on the wall.

"There it is," she said. "Look for yourself."

"That says twelve o'clock," Albert A. reported, a bit doubtfully.
"Are you sure that's the right time?"

The girl glanced up at the clock, began to get annoyed.

"Sure," she said, "it's twelve o'clock. If you don't believe it, look
out the window at the clock on Borough Hall."

Albert A. looked, pretended to be convinced.

"Is the law man in?" he asked, referring to Leibowitz.

"No, he's in court. He won't be back until one o'clock."

"I'll wait," said Albert A.

He helped himself to a chair and sat there patiently, establishing
for himself an ironclad alibi should anyone ever want to question
him about the events that were soon to take place in Scarpato's
Restaurant in Coney Island.

Charlie Lucky and Joe the Boss were already seated at a table
there. Joe Valachi's version of events departs considerably from all
the official and unofficial reports of the time. Valachi seems to picture a considerable dinner party, attended by Ciro Terranova, Vito
Genovese, Charlie Lucky, "a fellow named Cheech," and Joe Stretch.
According to Valachi, Terranova was so unnerved on the way over,
his hands trembled so he couldn't get the key into the ignition and
he had to be thrown "off the wheel." This cost Terranova such a
loss of face that he was soon afterwards deposed in favor of Trigger
Mike Coppola.

Official and other reports of the time, however, seem to establish,
that there were just two present at Joe the Boss's last dinner—Joe
the Boss himself and Charlie Lucky. They had an excellent meal,
relishing Scarpato's excellent clam sauce, the succulent lobster, and
the Chianti wine. They took their time. When the dishes were cleared
away, Charlie Lucky proposed a game of cards. Joe the Boss was
agreeable.

"Good," he grunted, "just for an hour or so; then I must go."

Lucky called for a deck from the house, and they played and talked for about forty-five minutes. It was now about 3:30 P.M. The restaurant had cleared. Just Joe the Boss and Charlie Lucky, his almost son, sat there at the table in Scarpato's, playing cards. It was at this point that Charlie Lucky politely excused himself and made a trip to the men's room.

He was hardly out of sight, when some crude characters wandered in from the street. They walked right up behind Joe the Boss, bemused by food and wine, and before he could turn his head, they whipped out guns and blasted away. Some twenty shots were sprayed around the premises. Six of them plowed into Joe the Boss's head and body, all from the back. He had no chance to turn and dodge. He pitched forward across the sparkling white tablecloth, his right arm extended as if it had been his play at cards, in his death-frozen grip the ace of diamonds.

Back in the men's room, Charlie Lucky heard the unholy racket.

"As soon as I finished drying my hands, I hurried out and walked back to see what it was about," he told investigating officers.

All he found, of course, was his dear, beloved patron dead. Those who had done the deed had left.

Joe the Boss, who had managed to outrun and outdodge the bullets of his enemies, hadn't been able to elude those of his friends. His failure in this final test wrought profound changes in the underworld. Charlie Lucky, his alter ego, succeeded to his power and perquisites. And Salvatore Maranzano ruled supreme as the boss of bosses. At least for the time being.

Salvatore Maranzano called a big meeting to tell the boys how it was going to be. According to Joe Valachi, Maranzano rented a big hall on Washington Avenue in the Bronx, and some 500 of the faithful attended. Maranzano began by describing the evils for which Masseria had been responsible—the unjustified shootings, the murder of Tom Reina, the war on the Castellemarese.

"Now, it is going to be different," he said. "We are going to have —first we have the boss of all bosses, which is myself."

Maranzano explained the organizational structure that henceforth would govern the affairs of crime. Each family was to have its own boss. Next in rank would be an underboss, and below him a "caporegima," or commander of the troops. "Now, if a soldier wants to talk to a boss," Valachi continued, "he should not take the privilege for him to try to go direct to the boss. He must speak first to the caporegima, and the caporegima, if it is required and it is important enough, the caporegima will make an appointment for the soldier. . . . This is what I called second government."

According to Valachi, it was at this time that the Mafia structure of New York was divided into the five families that have continued to rule it ever since. Maranzano headed his own group, which was soon split into two wings, one under Joe Profaci, the other under Joseph (Joe Bananas) Bonanno. The original Reina family was to be governed by Tom Gagliano, with Thomas (Three-Finger Brown) Lucchese as his underboss. Lucky Luciano sat atop the former Masseria family; under him, Vito Genovese. And in Brooklyn, according to Valachi, Philip and Vincent Mangano were given control, with Albert Anastasia as their underboss. In this, there appears to be some confusion, for the Manganos did not acquire power until much later. At the time, there was just one crime czar in Brooklyn (curiously, a man whom Valachi never mentions), and he was Joe Adonis, as powerful a man as the underworld of his day was to produce and the one to whom Anastasia and his murder goons always owed their primary fealty.

Valachi's account of the early days of the reign of Maranzano continued in vivid detail. The boss of all the bosses, having explained the gangland structure and enlisted his minions in the families of their choice, decided he should have a coronation party. The result, according to Valachi, was a banquet that lasted five days. Every evening the mob gathered and held high revelry until three or four the next morning. This marathon celebration had a double motif: first, to hail Maranzano as the new boss of bosses; secondly, to raise money for the war-depleted treasury. Both purposes were achieved.

Valachi testified he "understood" that the five days netted $115,000. Maranzano, he said, "sent out, for instance, a thousand tickets to Al Capone, and Al Capone sent $6,000. He sent a thousand tickets to Buffalo, and they also sent $6,000. Charlie Lucky himself sent $6,000.

"Them were the big amounts I know. The rest, as they came in, the guests. Frank Scalise would be at the head of a small table. . . . As he would greet the guests as they came in, 'Have a drink'—you know, in Italian. He would go for his pocket, he would throw money on the table. They would follow suit. That was his duty. . . .

"I used to see piles of money on the table every night. Maranzano used to get it at night."

Originally, according to Valachi, the word had been spread that the button men were to share in these "contributions" as a reward for their loyalty in the recent war of the mobs, but Maranzano, with the insatiable greed of a gang chieftain, apparently gobbled all. "I never got a nickel of that, Senator," Valachi told Senator McClellan. "I used to go down, after that I used to go down to the office, I felt that, you know, some day I might be handed something, but I never did."

Valachi was so desperate for money that he talked Buster from Chicago into accompanying him on a burglary, though he knew that it was against Maranzano's rules for any of his troopers to engage in such free enterprise. Valachi reassured Buster by telling him the boss would never know about it, but Maranzano's pipelines of information were better than Valachi knew. The very next day, Bobby Doyle taxed him with having broken the rules by free-lancing in burglary and said the boss of bosses wanted a word with him. Instead of going to see Maranzano, the frightened Valachi took off for Buffalo to pay Steve Maggadino a visit. Bobby Doyle agreed not to let on to Maranzano that they had ever talked.

Maggadino played host to Valachi for about eight days. Then he had to "go to South America somewhere," but, before he left, at Valachi's request, he loaned Valachi $500. Valachi returned to New York; and, figuring that matters had had time to cool, he went directly to Maranzano's office at Park Avenue and 46th Street to make his peace.

"When I got back and I went up to the office, Mr. Maranzano was talking with Charlie Lucky and Vito Genovese," he testified. "As I walked in, they were in the middle of the floor, talking. He dropped them and he walked right over to me and he kissed me. At that time they used to kiss, Senator."

It was, Valachi explained, an entirely friendly kiss.

"You know, I sent the check to Buffalo to Steve," Maranzano told his apprehensive henchman.

"You already know?" Valachi stammered.

"That's all right, don't worry about it," Maranzano told him.

"OK. Thanks," Valachi mumbled.

Relieved, Valachi sat down, and Maranzano went back to his business discussion with Charlie Lucky and Vito Genovese. The $500 that Maranzano paid for him was all he ever got out of the $115,000 kitty that had been collected to reward the soldiers. Valachi said that he never dared broach the matter of any greater reward to Maranzano; one just didn't do that with the boss of bosses. Besides, he figured, Maranzano might have more important matters on his mind and need the money. This conjecture, it developed, was absolutely right.

Not long after his return from Buffalo, Valachi got a summons from Maranzano to report at nine o'clock at night at the boss's home.

"When I got to his house," Valachi testified, "he was bandaging his son's foot, I remember.

"I walked in. He greeted me. I waited until he got through with his son.

"He said to me, 'You know'—now, Senator, I'm telling you. 'You know why I didn't give you any money? You must have been wondering.'

"I said, 'Yes.'

"He was referring to the banquet.

" 'I didn't want to lose you. I didn't want you to get loose. But don't worry about the money.' He said, 'We have to go to the mattress again.'

"The 'mattress' means that we have to go back to war, that is what it means. . . .

"Naturally, I wasn't too happy to hear that. So he told me that we can't get along. He meant he can't get along with Charlie Lucky, Vito. He gave me a list. 'We have to get rid of these people.'

". . . On the list was, I will try to remember as I go along: Al Capone, Frank Costello, Charlie Lucky, Vito Genovese, Vincent Mangano, Joe Adonis, Dutch Schultz. These are all important names at the time."

In this, Valachi was not exaggerating. On that list were the names of men who were to rule the American underworld from that day to the present. The liquidation of any one of them would have made headlines across the nation, and the idea of knocking them all off seemed to indicate that Maranzano was toying with a fatal delusion.

Valachi was worried, but not alone by the eminence of the names on Maranzano's execution list. An order had been passed around only a few days before that Maranzano's boys weren't to go up to his 46th Street office lugging their lethal hardware under their coats because there was a rumor the police might raid the place. Valachi didn't like to be left so naked and helpless. "I'm afraid they are trying to prepare us to be without guns," he had said to his friends at the time. "I just don't like it."

He liked it less when Maranzano told him that he had a meeting scheduled for the next day, a last conference, with Charlie Lucky and Vito Genovese. Valachi protested.

"Can I talk to you?" he said. "Look. After all, if I lose you, I am out in the street. I got all reasons to worry. Must you go to this appointment? Can't you let Angelo Caruso go? If this is your last meeting——"

"No, I got to go," Maranzano said decisively.

The meeting with Charlie Lucky and Vito Genovese was scheduled for two o'clock the following afternoon, September 11, 1931—a red-letter day in the history of the American underworld. Maranzano instructed Valachi to telephone the office at 1:45 P.M. to see if his services were going to be needed.

Not liking matters a bit, Valachi nevertheless telephoned Maranzano's office at the appointed time "and Charlie Buffalo answered the phone. He said everything was all right. He said I need not go down." So Valachi and his friend, "the Gap," decided to forget impending troubles and went to Brooklyn to visit a couple of girls they knew.

They had hardly departed on this pleasurable pursuit before matters ceased being "all right" in Rooms 925 and 926, Maranzano's suite of offices at 230 Park Avenue. Four men, all Jewish, walked through the entrance door. There was quite a crowd in the outer room. Some of Maranzano's boys, including Bobby Doyle, were on hand, and there were a number of other persons waiting to see the boss on business matters. The newcomers identified themselves as detectives. They had come, they explained, to see Maranzano.

The boss of bosses, having been primed to expect such a visit, came out of his inner office, welcomed the strangers and escorted them in. Evidently, from later accounts, the door had hardly closed before Maranzano sensed that something was fatally wrong. He dived for a gun he kept in his desk drawer, but the "detectives," having the drop on him, began blasting away and set upon him with knives. In a few seconds, it was all over. The "boss of bosses" was dead, with four bullet wounds in his body and six stab wounds in his abdomen.

In the outer office, the crowd scattered. The "detectives" came running out and headed for the stairway. As they ran, they encountered face-to-face one of the most ferocious killers-for-hire of the day, Vincent (Mad Dog) Coll. The Mad Dog was on his way in to take care of a commission from Maranzano, but he had arrived just too late. His employer was dead, and the "detectives" who had done the deed, in the fraternity of murder, simply waved to the Mad Dog to get lost—the cops were on the way.

Bit by bit, in after years, Joe Valachi pieced together what had happened. Maranzano's murder was a perfect example of an underworld double double cross. The "boss of bosses" had hired Vincent Coll to attend the scheduled 2 P.M. meeting and liquidate Charlie Lucky and Vito Genovese. But Charlie Lucky was faster with the double cross than anybody. He had contacted his longtime confederates, Buggsy Siegel and Meyer Lansky, and they had put at his disposal Sam (Red) Levine and three other efficiency experts from their Bug and Meyer mob. These were the detectives who had dispatched Maranzano.

The strategic weakness of Maranzano's position was that he had been at a fixed post. He had been waiting in his offices for two guests who had no intention of showing up—and so he was a sitting pigeon for the killers when they arrived a few minutes early, beating Mad Dog Coll to the murder draw. The coup had been plotted with the ruthless efficiency that was the hallmark of one of the best executive brains the American underworld has produced—that of Charles (Lucky) Luciano. Luciano had determined to change the face of the American underworld all in one day, and he did it, not just by the murder of Maranzano, but by a cross-continent carnival of execution that was to make September 11, 1931, memorable in the annals of crime.

On that April day that saw the elimination of Joe the Boss, Gerardo Scarpato, proprietor of the Coney Island restaurant chosen as the execution site, had been stricken with terror. "Take my fingerprints," he pleaded with police when they questioned him. "Take 'em for your books. I may be next."

He was not next, but he was right. On September 11, 1931, Scarpato's body was found in a burlap bag in a parked car in the Prospect Park section of Brooklyn. He had been knocked unconscious by a blow on the head, and then trussed up in such fashion, with his knees drawn up under his chin, that he had strangled himself when he tried to straighten his legs.

This ghoulish touch was only one of many that marked purge day in the Unione. Within a few short hours, the old-line crime bosses who had been born and reared in Sicily and were mostly illiterate— the "Mustache Petes" or "the greasers," as they were sometimes called—were liquidated by the new breed of Americanized, business-oriented gangsters of the Luciano-Costello-Adonis school. Beginning on September 11th and lasting through the next day, some thirty to forty executions were performed across the nation—a purge unprecedented in scope, precise in timing, and as bloody, abrupt, and final as any ever masterminded by a Stalin or a Hitler.

The result left Lucky Luciano enthroned atop the New York underworld, with no formidable rival in sight, and made him, by the same stroke, the dominant voice in Mafia councils across the nation. He was never to lose this stature, not even through a long imprisonment, not even after his subsequent banishment to his native Italy. Some experts have argued that Luciano's take-over in this purge of September 11 marked the death of the Mafia and the succession to power of the Unione Siciliano, but this is largely an exercise in semantics. The basic structure of the Mafia families remained unchanged, and, as events were to show, so did their affiliations with the secret brotherhood in the Sicilian homeland.

The new order brought about inevitable shuffling of family memberships, as well as the kangaroo courts for underworld justice that Frank Costello and his Mafia conferees had charted in Atlantic City in 1929. The purge of September 11th was, in fact, an implementation of those decisions, establishing not only new leadership but new orderliness and business efficiency in the affairs of gangdom.

Joe Valachi was personally involved in some of the details of this reorganization and has explained how it worked. Vito Genovese was Charlie Lucky's emissary in justifying the deed of murder. He painted in darkest terms the misdeeds of Maranzano. Did Valachi know that Maranzano had been hijacking Charlie Lucky's liquor trucks? Valachi protested that he had never heard of such a thing. Did he know that Maranzano had hijacked trucks containing piece goods from Tommy Lucchese? This was news to Valachi, too. Having in this fashion established that Maranzano had been a traitor who deserved what he got, Genovese told Valachi that he was now to consider himself a member of Vito's and Charlie Lucky's family, and then he took Valachi downtown and introduced him to his own trusted lieutenant, Anthony (Tony Bender) Strollo, who was ever after to be Valachi's immediate boss.

On the broader scale, Luciano's system of justice met with Valachi's whole-hearted approval. Luciano created a court of six underworld judges, and before a hireling could be executed, he was to be tried. "For instance," Valachi explained, "a lieutenant wants to have a soldier killed or something like that in that line, he cannot do it no more. If he has anything he wants to do, anything like that, he must come up and talk to these six and state what he has got, what is his reasons before he is able to carry out, which they never did before. That is why the soldiers felt that they have a longer life now than ever, which they did."

Even the blood bath in the Mafia, which Lucky Luciano had engineered on his own, had to be justified to other Mafia chieftains across the nation. According to Valachi, a Mafia grand council meeting was held in Chicago shortly afterwards—in performance and motivation almost identical with the Apalachin conference twenty-five years later —at which Luciano and Vito Genovese defended their indulgence in wholesale bloodletting. A vital part of their defense consisted of Valachi's own report that Maranzano had told him they were about to go to war again and had showed him the list of gang leaders he intended to liquidate. Valachi had told this story to Bobby Doyle after Maranzano's murder; Doyle had relayed it to Genovese and Luciano, and, though the knowledge came to them after the purge, it fitted perfectly into their need for justification. Valachi was reluctant to go to Chicago and testify against his departed boss, Maranzano, but Doyle went. Since Al Capone's name had headed the list of those Maranzano had intended to depose, the grand council's ratification of the purge was almost a foregone conclusion.

With such problems settled, the new underworld began to run smoothly along the lines that Luciano had established for it. Luciano himself and Vito Genovese, then his principal henchman, were not to remain long at the helm. In 1934, Genovese committed the indiscretion of arranging the murder of Ferdinand (The Shadow) Boccia —and of leaving witnesses who might tell about it. The law began to build a case against him, and Don Vitone, as he was sometimes known in the fraternity, departed for the healthier climate of his native Italy, where soon, incredibly enough, he was to attach himself to the court circle of Mussolini, the dictator who had vowed the death of the Mafia. Luciano encountered similar, and for a time even more devastating, misfortunes at the hands of the law. In 1935, New York City went through one of its periodic cycles of reform, and Thomas E. Dewey, then a young and crusading prosecutor, decided to go after Lucky Luciano, the overlord of crime.

Luciano was then living fastidiously as Charles Ross of the Waldorf, but Dewey became convinced that his income derived from sources not fastidious at all. He proclaimed that Luciano was not only the city's king of crime, he was also its overlord of vice, living on the proceeds of a $10 million-a-year prostitution ring, with more than 200 madams and 1,000 working girls paying him tribute. Dewey, with his awesome reputation as the young paladin of the courts, got some of the girls and madams to testify, and in 1936 Luciano was convicted and sentenced to Clinton State Prison at Dannemora for 30 to 50 years.

In the old days, such deactivation of the top command of the New York rackets would have precipitated the kind of crude struggle that so often had wounded or killed innocent bystanders along with the gangsters. But not this time. Luciano's new system functioned so smoothly that the transition in command caused hardly a ripple. Frank Costello, whose role as sage counselor of the mob had been demonstrated by his sponsorship of the Atlantic City conclave in 1929, took over and swiftly established his own reputation as Prime Minister of the underworld. Collaborating with him and running the lucrative rackets of Brooklyn was the equally canny and almost equally powerful Joe Adonis. The Costello-Adonis axis was to dominate the affairs of the American underworld for the next fifteen years; infiltrating and in many instances virtually dominating the machinery of government;

pioneering in the colossal investment of the underworld's blood money in legitimate business enterprises. Under the aegis of Costello and Adonis, the lines of demarcation between the underworld and the legitimate world were to become blurred; crime adopted the camouflage of respectability; and the insidious influences which today threaten to undermine the fiber of American society flowered like lush vegetation in a tropical rain forest.

5

GROWTH OF THE SYSTEM

WHEN the late Senator Estes Kefauver conducted his celebrated investigation of the American underworld in 1951, he found one gangster who more than any other typified the whole range of underworld activity and influence—lord of rackets, proprietor of legitimate businesses, and veritable political boss. In his book, *Crime in America,* Kefauver later wrote that, to him, Joe Adonis "was the evil personification of modern criminality. This man with bloodstained hands [who] for years set himself up as bigger than the law . . . had achieved pre-eminence in all three fields that have become an unholy trinity in areas of the United States—crime, politics and business."

Kefauver did not exaggerate. Joe Adonis had been a topflight power in American gangdom for twenty years. For the past fifteen, in alliance with Costello, he had wielded as much power as any gangster in the nation. He had merged underworld rackets and legitimate business in the manner that has now become so common, so insidious, and so threatening. Not content with paying off politicians, he had actually seized control of the political machinery that nominated and elected them; he had become both the boss of rackets and the boss of politics and government. He was for several years the real political power in Brooklyn; and after he transferred his operations to northern New Jersey, he repeated the pattern and his influence was felt even

103

in the State House. There have been other gangsters, Costello notably, who functioned as czaristic powers in crime, politics, and business; but, in no other criminal career is the pattern so clearly charted, the technique and the dovetailing power so nakedly obvious. If one wants to know how the American underworld functions, how it menaces the legitimate life and government of the nation, one may study with profit the career of Joe Adonis. It is the best and most fully documented case history that we have.

Joe Adonis was known as "the gentleman of the mob." False quiet sat upon him as if he had been to this manner born. When he spoke, his voice was so soft and low that it was sometimes difficult to catch what he said. He ordered in whispers. He had even cultivated the novel habit, not of snarling but of whispering out of the corners of his mouth. But the effect of his whisper was often more electric than that of another's snarl.

When you looked at his eyes, you saw why. They were dark brown —and coldly, inhumanly hard. By the time a man is in his late forties, he usually has had some acquaintance with good humor and his face will wear its traces. There will be little telltale creases about the corners of his eyes, crinkles that are the legacy of past laughter. But Joe A.'s eyes looked out unblinking from skin baby-smooth, without a pucker; they seemed to say that here was a man who, if he had ever smiled, had smiled only with the thick lips set in his heavy, impassive face.

Joe Adonis, as he was known to the mob, was born on November 22, 1903, in a small Italian town about thirty miles south of Naples. His parents were Michele and Maria de Vito Doto, and they christened their son Giuseppe Antonio. In 1909, they emigrated to the United States and settled in the Gowanus section of South Brooklyn, hard by the waterfront.

It was a neighborhood that became known as "the eighth of the eighth," a catch phrase of dark significance in Brooklyn. It signified the Eighth Election District of the Eighth Assembly District—an area that was the cradle of big-league crime. From the "eighth of the eighth," to give just a partial roll call, came such powerful operatives as Frankie Yale, the Mangano brothers, Albert Anastasia, Al Capone —and Joe Adonis.

Joe A. was one of four sons. His father was a small builder and owned some property. Though poor, the Dotos weren't slum poor, and there really was no reason why Joe A. had to go into the rackets, except that he preferred it that way. From boyhood he ran with the tough youth gangs spawned wholesale in this cluttered tenement district. Though sturdily built, Joe A. was short and no match physically for some of the budding musclemen who roamed "the eighth of the eighth." Some who knew Joe A. then insist that he was frequently beaten up by the tougher toughs. If so, this may help to explain two prominent traits of the mature mobster—his reliance on brains and money to dominate brawn, and his absolute conceit in his own cleverness.

Though Joe A. never got beyond the elementary grades in school, he later refined his speech so that he could converse like a gentleman. Only in times of extreme stress would he lapse into the patois of the Brooklyn streets, the idiom of *dese, dose,* and *dem.*

Joe A.'s criminal record begins with his first arrest at the age of twenty-two. The incident is both significant for what happened to the patrolman who arrested him and important because it furnished a barometer by which to measure Joe A.'s meteoric rise in gangdom. At twenty-two, he was just a lowly "soldier" in the mob; at twenty-six, he was a millionaire and one of the bootlegging powers of the Eastern Seaboard.

Patrolman Robert F. Baron was the man who had the temerity to introduce Joe A. to the inside of a police station. Baron's nighttime beat was along the warehouse-cluttered South Brooklyn waterfront. The streets were gloomy and quiet at these hours except for trucks rumbling ashore off the 39th Street ferry. In the area around the ferry landing, there had been a recent wave of hijackings; valuable cargoes of tobacco, rubber, and illicit alcohol had been stolen. And so Patrolman Baron paid special attention to the neighborhood around the ferry slip as he covered his beat on the night of February 26, 1926.

His vigilance was rewarded. He spotted a strange sedan that seemed to be circling aimlessly about the streets, hovering about the ferry landing. Baron hid and waited and watched. When the car stopped and a man got out and raised the hood, pretending to tinker with the motor, Baron pounced. Drawn gun in hand, he lined the car's four occupants against the most convenient wall and frisked them. He came up with two revolvers, a .45 and a .38, and in the car he found a loaded shotgun. Covering his captives with a revolver in one hand, the shotgun in the other, Patrolman Baron forced them to drive themselves to the Fourth Avenue police station.

When the strange group arrived, the precinct captain came out and asked Baron: "What have you got there?"

"I've got a stolen car and a lot of guns," Baron said.

He was right on both counts. It turned out that the sedan in which the four men had been cruising had been "clipped" earlier, a favorite mob technique since such a stolen car, used to commit a more serious crime, can be abandoned without leaving any clue to the identities of those who borrowed it. In this instance, having been nabbed with the car, Baron's four sullen prisoners were questioned and made to identify themselves. One was a short, chunky, not unhandsome youth who gave his name as Joe Arosa. This was the first alias of Joe Adonis.

It would seem that Patrolman Baron had presented the law with an ironclad case. He had seized four hoods in a stolen car, loaded down with an illegal arsenal.

The first test, on the car-theft charge, came in Bay Ridge Magistrate's Court on March 8, 1926. Into court to help Joe A. wrestle with overwhelming evidence swaggered the formidable figure of Frankie Yale, as resplendent as a walking jewelry store, two huge diamonds on his fingers, another glowing from his stickpin, and some seventy-five brilliants studding his belt. Perhaps it was the dazzling radiance of these gems that blinded the law, or perhaps it was the menacing presence of Frankie Yale's glowering bodyguard that caused second thoughts. Whatever it was, the stolen-car case against Joe A. and his fellow thugs was promptly dropped. A month later, the illegal-gun rap was similarly dealt with in the more elevated purlieus of Special Sessions Court, and Joe A. walked away as spotless in the eyes of the law as if the whole dark incident had never happened.

"Frankie Yale went around to the politicians and they were freed," said Patrolman Baron years later, in explaining the mystery to the New York *Post*.

This triumph of the lawless over the law, so typical of those times and of many times since, had one compensating feature. Patrolman Baron was summoned to Police Headquarters, praised and promoted. "You're the type of man I want in the Detective Bureau," Police Commissioner George V. McLaughlin told him, presenting him with his gold detective's shield. It was a proud moment for Baron. It seemed almost as if, after all, virtue might bring its own reward. But

Patrolman Baron hadn't heard the last of Joe Adonis. Nor had the law.

Twice more in 1926, Joe A. suffered the minor inconvenience of arrest, once for robbery, once for grand larceny. Both charges evaporated. In 1927, Joe A. was not so fortunate. He became involved in a street brawl, the details of which have not been preserved; he was charged with disorderly conduct and was actually convicted and fined $25. For years, this was the only blemish on his otherwise spotless record.

These early jousts with authority might indicate that the young Joe Adonis was just another mob punk. He called himself Joe Arosa, James Arosa, and Joe DeMio. None of these aliases stuck to him, however, and the origin of the one that did is misted in underworld legend. One version has it that a Broadway cutie—Joe A. like all rising young gangsters had a pronounced predilection for the species —took one look at his sturdy handsomeness and gurgled, "That guy looks like a real Adonis." Another version is that a pimply-faced Brooklyn hoodlum, having come across the name of the beautiful youth of Greek mythology somewhere in his travels, misapplied it to young Joseph A. Doto, who thenceforth became the Joe Adonis of American gangdom.

Whatever the origin of the name, Joe Adonis soon lifted himself out of the punk class. A young Mafia mobster, he had an infallible instinct for the right connections and a knack for using the profits of one type of crime to enter the next. His first connection at the top was with Frankie Yale, and from Yale he learned, if he had not known before, how easily a corrupted law could be persuaded to protect the lawless. His first racket—and there is some evidence to show that even after he became affluent he never gave it up—was hijacking, and he used the profits of hijacking to set himself up as a speakeasy proprietor. And profits from both hijacking and the speakeasy pyramided to the point where he became a major bootlegger, importing cargoes of good liquor from Nassau and St. Pierre.

The manner in which one racket watered and nourished another rapidly made Joe Adonis a wealthy man and an underworld power. A brief two years was all it took for the transformation. When his first patron, Frankie Yale, was gunned down on that Sunday afternoon of July 1, 1928, young Joe Adonis had already risen so far so fast that he inherited a portion of his fallen chief's rackets. He was not yet top dog in Brooklyn; Anthony (Little Augie Pisano) Carfano was that. But Joe Adonis was next in line behind Little Augie, the No. 1 lieutenant and the man ready to take over.

He was forming, as he was always to form, important alliances. On the upper level, he was striking up a comradeship with Frank Costello and Lucky Luciano; on the lower, he had formed a profitable partnership with the man he was always to dominate—Albert Anastasia, the future Lord High Executioner of Murder, Inc. Anastasia had not yet become the principal enforcer for Mafia chieftains and other crime syndicates across the nation, but he commanded the troops, the sadistic execution squads of Brooklyn that would always be at the command of the Mafioso to whom Anastasia owed his primary fealty—the "gentleman of the mob," whisper-voiced Joe Adonis.

Joe A.'s velvet manner made him an ideal host. He ingratiated himself with his customers in the speakeasy that he established at 260-62 Fourth Avenue, at the corner of Carroll Street, in Brooklyn. The place was known as Joe's Italian Kitchen, and it soon became a rendezvous for the most eminent politicians in Borough Hall. It was not because it was so convenient. On the contrary, the Kitchen was located five long blocks away in the same slum neighborhood in which Joe A. had been reared, a section subsequently described by one of the Kitchen's habitués as "one of the poorest and toughest in the country." Yet it became so fashionable that the Borough Hall crowd went slumming down to the Kitchen like homing pigeons to their dovecotes.

The mystery of this strange allure of the Kitchen for the distinguished was sometimes explained away in later years by saying Joe A. served such excellent Italian food and such pure, undiluted liquor that the combination was simply irresistible. When you went to the Kitchen, said some of the connoisseurs, you could be sure you weren't going to get watered-down joy-juice as you did in most other places around town; you got the real, high-proof article. Few persons were so naïve as to take such rationalization at face value.

Some cynical individuals recalled in after years that a waiter would occasionally sidle up to a VIP and slip a little white envelope half under his plate. The diner never opened the missive in public, just tucked it away carefully in the inside pocket of his jacket—a suspicious maneuver that led the evil-minded to suspect such envelopes contained some of Uncle Sam's favorite folding green. Those prone to such suspicions saw partial confirmation in the fact that the Italian Kitchen ran throughout the Prohibition years undisturbed by the law and, when repeal came, it had no difficulty in getting a liquor license, despite the notorious racket ties of its proprietor.

If little white envelopes were sometimes distributed to important guests by obsequious waiters, other and less obvious maneuvers took place in a secret conference room at the rear of the speakeasy. From the restaurant, a sliding panel and an "icebox door," the kind of heavy, soundproof and almost indestructible door that gamblers favor in their establishments, led to this extremely private caucus chamber. Through this door, rumor had it, passed some of the most powerful politicians in Brooklyn, seeking the money and backing of Joe A.

Such consultations were not the only ones held in Joe A.'s soundproof cubicle. The secret retreat also served as a control room for the rackets. A second passageway led directly to it from the outside of the building. Using this entrance, mobsters came to get their orders from the boss, and through it, too, entered some of the recalcitrant, summoned to "conference." The grapevine had it that, on more than one occasion, such conferees suffered amazing losses of consciousness and were dragged out through this second entrance without disturbing the distinguished diners in the restaurant out front. As a result of such incidents, Joe A.'s well-padded council chamber became known to the mob as "The Slaughterhouse."

Operating from this power base, with ties at the top to Luciano and Costello, with Albert Anastasia handy when muscle was needed, Joe Adonis was in an ideal position to take over the rackets of Brooklyn when misfortune visited Little Augie Pisano. The year 1931 was a hazardous one for bootleggers. The corruption of Prohibition had become such a scandal that the law, to save some kind of face, had to put on a show of enforcement. Even Joe A. got hit with a couple small fines for bootlegging; but he was lucky compared to Little Augie. A suddenly vigorous Coast Guard boarded a tanker and seized a cargo of Little Augie's liquor valued at some $300,000 on the retail market. Even Little Augie's pocketbook felt the pinch of such a loss.

Immediately afterwards, a wave of hijackings broke out along the Atlantic seaboard from Connecticut to the Carolinas. Silk trucks became a special target because their loads could easily be disposed

of and each haul was worth about $10,000. In one of these highway
raids in March, 1931, a Union City police sergeant, James F. Knight,
was shot and killed. New Jersey police set out to avenge their fallen
member; and, after months of investigation, they caught up with a
pint-sized hoodlum, Anthony Curto, who made two confessions: he
had been driving one of the two cars used in the hijacking in which
Knight was killed, and the leader of the raid had been Little Augie
Pisano.

Little Augie was picked up in Brooklyn on the street near his
speakeasy, treated most courteously by deferential cops in the police
station, and held until New Jersey police could bring over their prize
pigeon to make an identification. What happened when this confrontation took place was what almost invariably happens when a
witness faces the awesome power of the Mafia. Anthony Curto blandly
picked the wrong man out of a lineup—and Little Augie Pisano went
free. His brush with the law had been too close for comfort, however,
and Little Augie announced that he was retiring from the rackets and
devoting himself to his string of racehorses and the management of
a hotel in Miami in which he had acquired a major interest. From
that moment in 1933, Joe Adonis became the undisputed rackets boss
of Brooklyn.

His coronation was tacitly celebrated in the wild New Year's Eve
party with which the Kitchen welcomed 1934. The affair lived long
in the memories of those privileged to attend. Joe A. had spent around
$14,000 on interior decorations under the supervision of James Mont,
one of his cronies with artistic pretensions who had done a lot of
work for the mob in beautifying its nightclubs. In the glitter of this
new decor some fifty guests who had paid $10 a plate, far steeper in
those depression days than it would seem now, made merry. Late in
the evening, at the height of festivities, in walked Joey Amberg, the
brutal killer who was the boss of the Brownsville rackets until he
had the misfortune, shortly afterwards, to be shot down. On this
night, Joey was not anticipating any such fate in the new year, and
he bought twenty bottles of champagne at $7 a bottle to add to the
general jollification.

"The last thing I remember of that party," said one of the guests
later, "is somebody filling Jimmy Mont's top hat with champagne."

In subsequent years, various probers focused inquisitive eyes on
the broad range of Joe A.'s political acquaintanceship. Such investiga-

tions established that Francis J. Quayle, then Sheriff and later Brooklyn Postmaster and Fire Commissioner of New York, was a faithful patron of the Kitchen. So was his Undersheriff, Jerome G. Ambro, whom Adonis had backed successfully in a district leadership fight in 1932. So were Magistrate David I. Malbin; James V. Mangano, later Sheriff of Kings County; and Patrick J. Diamond, the district leader in Adonis' own Eighth A. D. (Assembly District).

Ambro, who had had a long public career as a State Assemblyman and a Deputy Attorney General, added some names to this list when he testified before the Kefauver committee in 1951. He said that William O'Dwyer, later the prosecutor of Murder, Inc. and the Mayor of New York, was among those who frequented Adonis' restaurant. Another eminent patron whom Ambro saw "sometimes, many times" in Adonis' place was Irwin Steingut, subsequently Democratic minority leader in the State Assembly.

"You could meet anyone that was anybody in Brooklyn in his restaurant, in his place of business...." Ambro told the Kefauver committee. "Most everybody and anybody...."

Quayle, he testified, "used to be there quite regularly," and was "very friendly, very friendly" with Adonis. He described Francis V. Kelly, leader of the 4th A.D., as another "very good friend" of Adonis. Tom Ryan, leader of the 2nd A.D. and subsequently with the Justice Department, was also in Adonis' tavern on occasion, said Ambro, as was Congressman Cullen "now and then."

Ticking off the names of the Democratic party leaders in all twenty-three Brooklyn districts, Ambro identified about two-thirds of them as among the Kitchen's clientele, and with at least one-third the relationship to Adonis seemed to be especially close. The boss racketeer, who kept his padded "Slaughterhouse" just behind the dining room in which he met these political leaders of Brooklyn, would always circulate most graciously among the tables, using his deceptively soft manner and whispering voice to play the role of simple and genial host.

"He would come to a table and sit down and say 'Hello' and talk," Ambro testified.

The talk would almost always be of politics, and many a public career was furthered by arrangements made right there at Joe Adonis' tables. Ambro testified that it was there, indeed, that he agreed to give the budding career of William O'Dwyer its first major boost.

They were both dining in the Kitchen one day when O'Dwyer approached Ambro. O'Dwyer had been serving under temporary appointment as a city magistrate, and he asked Ambro to say a word on his behalf to Kenneth Sutherland, one of the top Democratic leaders in Brooklyn and a friend of Adonis. Ambro said the word, O'Dwyer became a full-fledged magistrate, and the career that was to lead to City Hall was launched.

How did a racketeer like Joe Adonis get such a clientele of Brooklyn's high and mighty? The answer, it seems, lies in two simple words: men and money. Joe Adonis used both with lavish hand to make himself the deciding factor, the vital difference, in many a close-fought political contest.

Political campaigns, then as now, required a great deal of cash—the kind of heavy cash that can be raised only from selfish interests expecting a *quid pro quo*. So-called legitimate business can and does supply some of this cash, but by no means all of it. From the flush days of Prohibition to today, the one source in America that has this kind of virtually unlimited money to invest in politics—and that has at the same time the greatest need for a return on that investment—is the underworld. Adonis could and did pour thousands of dollars into district leadership fights, a support that it would be extremely difficult to believe entailed no obligation.

Money was, then, the prime, but by no means the only, source of his political strength. Joe A.'s cash was backed by the sheer manpower of his gangster following. In Italian South Brooklyn, his strong arms rounded up thousands of floaters and illegal voters whom they herded to the polls on election day. These voters went from district to district, concentrating on political fiefs where the issue was close, and they carried in their hands printed cards containing the names of the Adonis-approved candidates for whom they were to vote. Opposition election captains, who might have been expected to oppose such procedures, were shoved aside, beaten, or otherwise intimidated. Nothing could stop, at least nothing *did* stop, the illegal flow of Adonis' army of fraudulent voters from one polling place to another. To a desperate politician, they represented an impressive force—the clear difference between victory and defeat.

This difference had been vividly illustrated in Ambro's own personal experience. Originally, he had been supported by Joe A.—and he had won. Later, he broke with Joe A.—and he lost. Ambro told the Kefauver committee that in 1936 a flood of cash, some $30,000 to $40,000, was spent in his 19th A.D. to defeat him as district leader. He testified that "they" put him out of business with "thugs, tough guys and floaters." Asked to identify the "they," he indicated there was no doubt in his mind that Adonis had engineered his defeat, but of course he could never prove it.

Some idea of the kind of muscle that Joe A. threw into such campaigns may be gleaned from a study of a unique organization known as the City Democratic Club, the political clubhouse of Murder, Inc. The City Democratic Club occupied a four-story brownstone building at 367 Clinton Street, near DeGraw Street, in Brooklyn's 3rd A.D. Beginning in 1932, it held annual dinners at which some of the toughest racketeers in Brooklyn, politicians, and businessmen mingled indiscriminately.

Edward P. Flynn, the crack crime reporter of the New York *Post* who submitted Joe A. to his first full-length public exposure in 1940, dug up some of the elaborate souvenir journals of the City Democratic Club's annual affairs. They revealed a most fascinating juxtaposition of names, the close crossties between emperors of the underworld and the rulers of the upper world.

Among the box holders for the 1934 affair, for instance, were Joe Adonis; Louis Capone, a front man for Adonis, a restaurateur and one of the guiding hands of Murder, Inc., destined ultimately to go to the electric chair in Sing Sing with Louis (Lepke) Buchalter for fulfilling a Buchalter murder contract; Albert Anastasia, the Lord High Executioner of Murder, Inc., a man who had already spent eighteen months in the Sing Sing Death House and who had survived when the higher courts reversed his conviction and subsequently the witnesses against him all dropped dead, making a second trial impossible; and Anthony (Tony Spring) Romeo, another of the Murder, Inc., crew, who was to beat two murder raps in the courts before he became a murder victim himself.

This was the unholy crowd of underworld "politicians" whose activities in the City Democratic Club were financed and aided by the distinguished of the legitimate world. The ties showed even more clearly in full-page advertisements, each costing $20, that these upper-crust leaders placed in the souvenir journals of the racketeers' club. Among those expressing their goodwill in such tangible form in this same year of 1934 were a deputy sheriff, an assistant district attorney who helped prepare and present cases to the grand jury, and a man who later became a federal judge. In 1936, when Albert Anastasia was vice-chairman of the ball committee, the late Joseph P. Ryan, head of the International Longshoremen's Association, the union that controlled the docks where Anastasia was such a power, took out a full-page advertisement. So did a former alderman. And in 1938, among the new advertisers, the journal featured the name of an assistant U.S. attorney.

These were visible links; when so much showed so openly, one can only conjecture the real extent of the underworld-upper world alliance perfected by more discreet and far-reaching ties. The combination, in any given test of strength, was almost irresistible. Consider what happened in the September, 1934, primary in the 23rd A.D. in Brownsville.

Hymie Schorenstein had been leader of the district for fifteen years, but he was being challenged by Dr. Maxwell G. Ross. Adonis threw his support to Ross and muscled aside everyone who stood in his path. One of the obstacles whom he summarily removed was a veteran detective who had been attached to the 73rd Squad in Brownsville for nineteen years. He had kept the polls clean by arresting or running out of the district any tough-acting characters who didn't belong there.

"There had never been any gangster trouble at the primaries or general elections in Brownsville until that year," the veteran detective later told Ed Flynn. "In 1934 hundreds of them swarmed in from the South Brooklyn section. . . . It was common gossip in Brownsville that Joe Adonis sent them in to help elect Ross. From my long experience in Brownsville I knew who the strangers were. They came in before the primaries. I started out after them and word got around that I was in their way. A few days before the primary election, I was transferred.

"I was informed later that almost all of the Schorenstein election district captains were either intimidated or slugged at the polls."

The result was inevitable. Ross defeated Schorenstein. It was only one of the victories that Joe Adonis, gangster political boss of Brooklyn, scored in the primaries of 1934. He had set out to capture complete control of the Democratic organization in the so-called Borough of Churches. In this, he did not succeed; but, when the dust had settled, it was estimated that as many as eight of the twenty-three district leaders were his people and that many others, who were not completely in his power, were at least well aware and respectful of his muscle and his wishes.

The long reach of Adonis and the manner in which he could virtually dictate who was or was not to hold key office in Brooklyn is illustrated by the experience of a veteran politician. This man was seeking the Democratic nomination for the office of District Attorney of Kings County, and he was opposed by a party hack rumored to have close ties to the mob. The independent needed all the help he could get, and so he was instantly interested one day when he received a telephone call.

"I have a man here who has seven district leaders in his pocket," the caller said. "He would like to talk to you."

"Who is he?"

"I can't tell you, but can you meet him here at two o'clock?"

The hard-pressed candidate naturally could. At the appointed hour, he arrived at the meeting place and was ushered into a small back room that served as emergency living quarters. There at a table sat Joe Adonis. He wasted no time beating about the bush. He controlled, he said bluntly, seven district leaders; they would do what he said. His support could be had—on certain, very specific conditions. He started to name them.

At this point, the candidate for the office of District Attorney rebelled and interrupted Joe A.

"If I'm elected," he said, "my first order of business will be—*you!*"

With that, he stalked out.

Naturally, he wasn't elected. He was snowed under. The party hack, nominated and elected, went on to preside over one of the blacker administrations of the District Attorney's office in Brooklyn's seamy history.

When even law enforcement at the pinnacle in the District Attorney's office was under the dominance of the mob, it was inevitable that the lot of the lowly detective should be made miserable—and Joe A. had a long and vindictive memory. He had hardly secured his enlarged toehold in Brooklyn politics in the elections of 1934 before Detective Baron, the man who had made the mistake of first arresting "Joe Arosa," found himself broken back to uniform and pounding a beat in Manhattan.

The detective was still boiling with rage at this injustice when,

five years later, New York *Post* reporters found him still unhappily
pounding the pavements. "Why don't you go over to Brooklyn and
get the names of the detectives who were busted for bringing in these
gangsters?" Patrolman Baron asked. It was a good question, and
the *Post* faithfully recorded it; but nobody in official life seemed at
all inclined to try to discover the answer.

As for his own downfall, Baron said this was the way it had been
engineered:

He had been called one night to a house in his district where a
man was beating his wife. Baron had broken up the domestic fisticuffs,
restored peace, and left. He had no sooner got out of sight than the
quarrel was resumed and neighbors called in other police. Then the
wife made a charge that, on the face of it, seemed sheer fantasy—
that Detective Baron had stood by calmly and watched her husband
beat her up without trying to interfere. On such a flimsy pretext,
Baron had found himself suddenly broken and demoted to the beat.

"It was a frame-up to get me out of the way," he said. "The woman
didn't even write the letter of complaint about me herself. I was
bothering the gangsters and I was busted."

The emperor of rackets and politics lived like one; the best of
both worlds belonged to Joe Adonis. With power and affluence, he
began to branch out into respectability. In 1932, he married Jean
Montemorana, and the nuptials supplied their own evidence of Joe
A.'s high standing in the hierarchy of American crime. For one of
the witnesses who signed his marriage certificate was Charles (Lucky)
Luciano.

Status showed in the residence in which the new bridegroom
established his family. Shore Road, as it is called, is one of the most
exclusive residential sections of Brooklyn, and in March, 1933, Joe
A. bought a two-and-a-half-story stucco mansion on the edge of
the district, at 103 81st Street, between Narrows Avenue and Colonial
Road. He later testified in a court action that he spent $50,000
refurbishing the house. Part of this money was spent reinforcing the
walls with concrete to make the structure as bomb proof as possible.

In the privacy of his home, Adonis dropped some of his public
pose of soft-spoken, cultured gentleman and indulged in the gaudy
display of the true gang lord. He had a 30-foot-long barroom built
into the basement. It was overbright with modernistic, glittering

chrome, gleaming mirrors, and an abundance of polished glasses ready to serve every conceivable kind of drink. A full-time bartender reported at regular hours to preside over this tavern in the basement. Upstairs, Joe A. let his taste for show run riot in the appointments of his bathrooms. On one occasion a distinguished party guest, whom Joe A. kept addressing as "Judge," was startled to note that he was washing his hands from a faucet that seemed made of solid gold; but when he remarked about it, Adonis laughed and reassured him. The fixtures, he said, were not solid gold—just gold-plated.

The man whose real character showed in the gaudiness of his home was careful to gild his public image by indulging in all manner of good works. He wangled memberships in the Brooklyn Elks for himself and his brothers, James, Anthony, and Albert, and all became quite active in the affairs of the lodge. As Joe A.'s bootlegging fortune soared, he gave his mother, Mary Doto, a few thousand to spend on good deeds around the family's old tenement neighborhood. Sometimes a family without heat would suddenly get a delivery of coal; another without food would get a stuffed and bulging basket; a third, about to be evicted by the landlord, would find that the rent had been paid; and still others would find life eased by delivery of a huge roast or a turkey. Occasionally, especially around election time, Joe A. would buy up a carload of some 2,500 chickens and, with his mother's help, distribute them all around the neighborhood. Such beneficences gave Joe A.'s mother a certain halo, and Brooklyn newspapermen, tongues in cheek, bestowed upon her the soubriquet of "Mother Elk."

When "Mother Elk" died in July, 1934, her funeral became another Joe A. status symbol. It was one of the largest ever seen in South Brooklyn, surpassing that of many a distinguished civic leader. The passing of "Mother Elk" was an event compounded of all the showy excesses of sorrow so dear to the heart of mobdom and the more decorous, but deferential homage of the respectable. The casket was reported to have cost $7,000. About 175 coaches trailed the hearse to Holy Cross Cemetery. Little Augie Pisano was in attendance. So was a sheriff. So (according to an official check of the license numbers of cars in the funeral procession) were political leaders, office-holders, and men prominent in Brooklyn legal circles. All were paying final tribute to Joe A.'s mother—and homage to Joe A.'s power.

But perhaps the most striking feature of the funeral extravaganza was the flood of floral pieces. The cortege was nearly smothered with them. The whole Borough of Churches seemed to be weeping in flowers.

"Flowers began pouring into the Boyertown Funeral Parlor, 39 Lafayette Avenue, early Sunday morning," the Brooklyn *Eagle* reported. "Soon they had filled the room, then the vestibule. By last night the roses, lilies and carnations were banked along Lafayette Avenue from St. Felix Street to Fort Greene Place. One piece of lilies and roses stood 14 feet high."

In all there were some 400 floral art works, estimated to have cost approximately $35,000 at depression prices. One paper reported it took sixty-five coaches to convey them to the cemetery. Later, an official check of Brooklyn's florist shops indicated that the costliest pieces had all been purchased by one man, a quiet, soft-spoken fellow who paid cash for everything. Joe A. had been expressing his heartbreak at the loss of his mother with the kind of extravagance that the sentimentality of gangland demands.

"There is more of the woman in these top, polished gangster types than there is in most men," says Judge Samuel Leibowitz, who knew gangsters well. "They are at once very soft and sentimental inside— and very hard. They will cry like babies at some tragedy or misfortune in their family—and a few hours later go out and commit murder. I remember one day I was riding out to the Hawthorne racetrack with Al Capone. We were in a Cadillac equipped with a small arsenal, and Capone was telling me how he had stood and wept at his brother's grave that morning. 'It made me feel better,' Al said. 'Now I feel fine.' And he patted the butt of a sawed-off shotgun. Another time, around Christmas, Albert Anastasia stopped by my house with a present—a cake, one of the fanciest concoctions you ever saw. He gave it to my wife, and she thought he was so nice, such a gentleman. She couldn't believe it when I told her the man who had left us the cake was Anastasia. This duality runs through all their lives, all their natures. On the one hand, an almost feminine sentimentality and softness; on the other, hardness, ruthlessness— murder."

Joe A. had wept for his mother with a copious outpouring of money and flowers; now he was to show the flint and steel of his nature, the ruthlessness of the gangster and the petty chiseler. In the spring of 1934 shortly before the death of "Mother Elk," Joe A. decided he wanted a portrait painted of his wife and year-old daughter and commissioned James Mont to find an artist whose talents would do justice to the subjects. Mont settled on Take Styka, a noted Polish portrait painter.

Styka, who had painted the likenesses of Caruso, Marshal Foch, William Randolph Hearst, and many members of European nobility, discussed the project with the well-dressed, obviously affluent "businessman" to whom Mont introduced him. He finally said he would paint the picture, provided agreement could be reached on a suitable fee, and in celebration of this tentative arrangement Joe A. invited him to dinner in his Brooklyn home. Styka later was able to fix the date as March 11, 1934, because that had been a memorable day for him. He had had luncheon with President Roosevelt's mother, and he had dined with "big businessman" Joe Adonis. It was at this dinner, over a drink afterwards in the basement tavern, that the final details had been settled: Styka was to get $4,000 for a portrait of Mrs. A. and child.

Subsequently, Mrs. Adonis and her daughter went to the artist's studio for about a dozen sittings. Styka was puzzled by the fact that they were accompanied on each visit by a burly, hard-featured man who established himself on guard in a chair in the narrow hallway leading to the studio entrance. When Styka inquired about this, he was told that "big businessman" Joe Adonis had become alarmed at the current wave of kidnapings and had supplied his wife and daughter with a bodyguard.

The portrait was finished on April 21, 1934, and Mont paid Styka $500. That was the only money the artist ever got. When his repeated requests for payment went unheeded, he threatened to sue. Mont, he later testified in court, tried to dissuade him from such folly.

"You will never get a cent from Adonis," Styka quoted Mont. "Why don't you get wise to yourself? You are up against the big one, the boss, the big shot. You may get yourself hurt."

An even more pointed threat was made the night before the trial opened, Styka later said. A swarthy, tough-looking man whom he had not seen before called at his studio and told him:

"You know, people who do foolish things sometimes get hurt. Sometimes they get shot. I wouldn't do anything foolish if I were you."

Instead of being intimidated as many were when they received such warnings from Joe A.'s strong arms, Styka was infuriated. He determined to press his suit to the limit. In the end, however, as Mont had warned him, he got nothing but trouble for himself when he bucked the "big shot."

Shortly before the trial, Mont had gone into bankruptcy, listing $46,512.04 in debts and no assets. This became a significant maneuver when Joe A. took the stand and calmly testified that he had paid Mont the rest of the money that was due Styka, and it wasn't his fault if Mont had filched it. Mont, of course, faithfully supported the story.

Despite the neatly meshed defense, the court gave Styka a verdict for $3,500. Instead of paying, however, Joe A. appealed and succeeded in getting the verdict thrown out. Styka tried to reinstitute the action, found himself running into legal roadblocks, and finally gave up in disgust. The incident seemed to show that Joe A., "the gentleman of the mob," was not above a cheap swindle. As Blue Jaw Magoon, one of the Murder, Inc., thugs and informers, was to tell authorities a few years later: "Joe Adonis is supposed to be tight in money matters, which is why the boys don't like him too good." The liking of the boys, of course, didn't matter to Joe A. just so long as they obeyed him—and they did.

All Brooklyn, it seemed, was heeding the power of Joe Adonis. The year of 1933 had been a sunburst year for him; he had succeeded to the underworld barony of Little Augie Pisano—and he had made an eminently right political guess. As a result, the 1934 that had been welcomed in with such hilarity at the Kitchen saw him expanding his power and influence in all directions, merging rackets with legitimate business in a mélange of incredible millions.

The right guess on which so much of this affluence was founded dealt with the New York mayoralty election of 1933. That was the year that Fiorello H. LaGuardia, "the Little Flower," carried the banner of Fusion to the polls against Tammany Hall. Amazingly enough, Joe Adonis, racketeer and Democratic power in Brooklyn, supported Fiorello LaGuardia, fiery reformer.

"The Democrats haven't recognized the Italians," Joe A. told a friend at the time. "There's no reason for the Italians to support anybody but LaGuardia. The Jews have played ball with the Democrats and they haven't got much out of it; they know it now and will vote for LaGuardia. So will the Italians."

Joe A. gave more than lip service to the Little Flower. He contributed a solid $25,000 to the Fusion campaign; and, according to *The New York Times,* he preserved the receipt for his donation for a number of years.

It may have been only coincidence, but it is nevertheless a fact that when LaGuardia swept into City Hall, his new administration brought no drastic changes, no sudden purification of the air, across the East River in the Borough of Churches. City Hall did not disturb Joe A.; indeed, it acted as if it were unaware of his very existence. And so the first four years of the LaGuardia administration were the four years that marked the height of Adonis' power in Brooklyn.

Many sources, legitimate as well as illegitimate, nourished this power. Directly across the street from Joe's Italian Kitchen at Fourth Avenue and Carroll Street, Joe A. established the White Auto Sales Co., an agency for Ford cars. In July, 1934, he also set up in the rear of the auto agency the headquarters for the Kings County Cigarette Service. The cigarette firm achieved an instantaneous success. Joe A.'s strong arms were probably the most persuasive salesmen in all New York, and so, almost overnight, roughly 10,000 of his cigarette-vending machines were installed in bars, hotels, and restaurants all over Brooklyn. Business was so good that one vending-machine company couldn't take care of it all, and in 1936 Joe A. organized the Shamrock Cigarette Service, with headquarters in a building adjoining his White auto agency.

Now it may have been the sheerest coincidence, but it happened that from 1934 to 1937 the very years in which Joe A.'s two cigarette-vending-machine companies were doing such a roaring business, legitimate cigarette distributors were having a tough time on the streets of Brooklyn. There were hijackings of cigarette trucks at gun point all over the place, and police estimated that, in a little less than four years, some $6 million worth of cigarettes were stolen.

Trucks carrying cigarettes to retail outlets in Brooklyn and parts of adjacent Queens County were generally loaded in the Bush Terminal on the South Brooklyn waterfront, in the heart of Adonis' territory. The narrow, clogged streets were ideal for ambush and the average truck driver had no chance. The instant he had to slow down or stop, strange men jumped him, jammed guns against his side, blindfolded, bound, and gagged him, and tossed him into the rear of his truck. A gangster would then take the wheel, and the truck would roll quietly on, as if nothing had happened, to a warehouse used by the mob as a drop. There the truck would be unloaded, its loot stored. And, in a final step, the hijacked vehicle would be driven to some lonely, outlying section of Brooklyn where it would be abandoned, its driver still bound and helpless inside it.

This system worked so well that cigarette firms were forced eventually to resort to extraordinary measures to stop it. Detectives were assigned to ride the cigarette trucks. The cabs of the trucks were made bullet proof, and locks so designed that doors could be opened only from the inside. Sirens were installed to wail instant alarm, and the sides of the trucks were plastered with huge letters so that patroling police could spot them instantly even in the worst traffic jams. These steps finally brought the hijacking wave under control, but in the meantime, for more than three years, Joe A.'s vending-machine companies had enjoyed unrivalled prosperity. As one detective remarked: "Hijacked cigarettes can be sold at 100 per cent profit, and that's a lot better than the legitimate competition can do."

Profits pyramided, and Joe A. expanded. In 1935, he folded the Kitchen and opened a new, swankier restaurant in a better location. He had two other automobile agencies besides White Auto Sales. He had a hidden partnership in two large liquor-distributing companies. And finally he had a controlling-stock interest in the Automotive Conveying Company of Cliffside Park, N.J.—a firm whose trailer trucks had a monopoly on the delivery of new Ford cars assembled at the Edgewater, N.J., plant to agencies throughout New Jersey, New York, Rhode Island, Massachusetts, Connecticut, Pennsylvania, Delaware, the District of Columbia, Virginia, and Vermont. In the eight years from 1932 to 1940, Ford paid this Adonis-controlled company a cool $8 million.

The Adonis tie to Automotive Conveying was first exposed by The *New York Post* in 1940, but eleven years later, when the Kefauver committee probed the rackets, it found the same firm still controlled by Adonis through his fronts—and still enjoying an exclusive contract with Ford to handle all deliveries from the Edgewater plant. Under the circumstances it is interesting to note the manner in which Joe A. came into possession of this million-dollar-a-year plum.

Automotive Conveying had been organized by T. B. Kramer. At first it used chauffeurs to drive cars from the plant to dealers, but Ford eventually insisted on the more economical use of trailer trucks. Kramer had to buy a lot of equipment, and in 1932, in the depths of the nation's worst depression, he found himself badly overextended. Seeking financial help to stave off bankruptcy, he contacted a number of Ford dealers. Eventually, he discussed his problem with the manager of the White Auto Sales in Brooklyn, and the manager put him in touch with Joe Adonis.

Kramer always insisted that he didn't know Joe A., the rackets boss—only Joe A., the businessman. After they were introduced, he said, Adonis took him across the street to the Kitchen for dinner and discussion. There the deal was consummated. Adonis was to put cash into the company and get 49 per cent of the stock; if Kramer still couldn't finance his end of the business, he was to get out and turn the whole thing over to Adonis. No papers were signed. It was "a gentleman's agreement," ratified by a handshake. Joe A. made just one stipulation: he put his own man in as bookkeeper. In four months he invested about $15,000 in the firm; and when Kramer still couldn't meet his obligations, he got out and left all to Joe A. At the time Kramer had been sharing the Edgewater business with another firm. After Joe A. took over, Automotive negotiated its exclusive contract with Ford, and between this and the pickup in business as the depression eased, the cash began to flow in. Kramer, in discussing the deal, always had the highest praise for Joe A. "He went along 100 per cent," he said once. "I didn't see Adonis more than a dozen times while I was doing business with him. He didn't interfere." It was his own fault, Kramer always said gallantly, that he lost out; Adonis hadn't pressured or forced him out.

If so, Kramer's experience was a novel one. For Joe A., in his less genteel dealings, certainly used pressure.

Typical were his tactics in the narcotics racket. The files of the Federal Bureau of Narcotics contain much detail about the powerful secret role played by Joe A. For example, in 1935, according to one of the bureau's informants, Joe A.'s thugs hijacked $20,000 worth of opium that had been smuggled onto a Bay Ridge pier by another mob. From that time on, Brooklyn narcotics importers were compelled to purchase their supplies of drugs from Joe A.'s henchmen "or pay Adonis a percentage of all the narcotics" they brought in themselves. In a later report, dated October, 1939, one of the bureau's crack agents noted that, while Lepke Buchalter's mob had formerly been the big importers of dope in Brooklyn, they had finally been squeezed out by the Italians headed by Joe A.

Direct testimony concerning Joe A.'s role in the nefarious narcotics traffic was brought out during the Federal Court income-tax trial of Johnny Torrio. Jacob (Yasha) Katzenberg described the importance of the trade and Joe A.'s prominence in it. Katzenberg was a man who should have known. For years he had been a foreign agent for Arnold Rothstein, the gambler who originally bankrolled the underworld, and in this capacity he had purchased millions of dollars' worth of liquor abroad in the Prohibition Era. Later he handled Rothstein's enormous investment in narcotics, the last great gamble of his life, and after Rothstein's murder, Katzenberg had served other big-shot racketeers, buying narcotics for the smuggling mobs of Adonis' friend, Lucky Luciano, and the extortion boss, Lepke Buchalter.

In the Torrio trial, Katzenberg testified that, with the death of Prohibition, many of the big bootlegging mobs turned their talents to smuggling in narcotics. Two combines were especially prominent, a Newark group known as the Big Seven, and "another organization by itself—Charlie Lucky——"

> Q: Charlie Lucky?
> A: Yes, sir.
> Q: Is he known as Charlie Luciano?
> A: Yes, sir.
> Q: Who else?
> A: Joe Adonis.
> Q: In Brooklyn?
> A: Yes, sir.
> Q: Who else?
> A: I think that is all.

The remote control that Joe A. exercised over the narcotics traffic in Brooklyn was typical of his operations. He kept himself far removed from the actual crime, but he exacted his tribute. The setup on the docks, where pilfering and loan sharking and extortion were rife, furnished a good example of his methods. Albert Anastasia ruled the world of the docks, but Anastasia, as all informants were to agree in the Murder, Inc., probe, was only the dark, enforcing shadow of Joe Adonis.

No racket was overlooked; all were brought under the dominance of one man. None ran for long outside his sphere; free enterprise was severely frowned upon. The laundry rackets were a good example. In the early thirties these were a disgrace to the underworld. Mobs muscled each other in a disgusting free-for-all; knockoffs and counter-knockoffs threatened the racketeers with mutual annihilation. Then, in late 1934, all rival leaders were called to a meeting in a Brooklyn hotel. According to the word that filtered out, Joe Adonis dominated the parley and laid down the law. The result was a more iron control of all facets of the industry. In this field Lepke Buchalter and his partner, Gurrah Shapiro, were the active bosses; but again, in Brooklyn at least, their power stemmed from the man who had welded the mobs into one vast unit of terror and extortion—Joe A.

The extent to which this evil went is illustrated by the following story. In the midthirties, at the height of Adonis' power, a reputable Brooklyn man bought a new Cadillac. The purchaser was a man who had never been arrested, who had no connection with the rackets, but who in the course of normal business had become well aware of their terrible power in Brooklyn. A few days after he had purchased his expensive new car, he got a telephone call from a man who spoke in a deep, gruff voice, with accents of menace.

"We want eight thousand dollars," the caller said. "We mean business. We know you've got the dough or you wouldn't be buying a new Caddy. You'll be hearing from us again."

With that, the telephone line went dead in the hands of the astonished, and suddenly fearful, owner of the new Cadillac.

A few days later he got a second call. This time he was told the mob wanted to meet him for a personal discussion of his problem. He was warned that if he notified the police, he would be killed.

"We know you got two kids who go to school," the caller added in a threatening sign-off.

Now the owner of the new Cadillac began to quake in earnest, both for himself and his children. Seeking help, he went to a friend and told him the story.

"Go to the police," this friend suggested. "They'll take care of it. Nobody can get away with something like this."

But the man with the Cadillac was either too wise or too fearful, or perhaps it was a combination of both.

"I can't do that," he said. "They told me they'd kill me if I go to the police, and they mean business. If I don't pay, they'll kidnap my kids."

He decided to pay, but to bargain for as good a deal as possible. A meeting was set up with the extortionists on Manhattan's Lower East Side, and for the first time a name crept into the negotiations, that of Lepke Buchalter. After much wrangling, the mob agreed to reduce their shakedown to $5,000. The Cadillac owner protested that this was still too much and tried to arrange a better deal. He even went to Philadelphia and contacted a Philadelphia mobster he was told might have influence with Lepke. Finally, the price was agreed upon—$3,500. The place for the payoff—Joe's Italian Kitchen.

"It all had to be in cash," the victim's friend recalled later. "On the day that had been set to close the deal, the guy came to me and asked me to hold half the money—some seventeen hundred fifty dollars—for him while he went to Manhattan to raise the rest. He didn't want to run the risk of carrying that much money around the streets with him and perhaps being robbed. So I'm left holding the seventeen hundred and fifty, and he goes off to Manhattan, and in a little while he comes back with the rest of it. Then, since Joe A.'s place was in a tough neighborhood, he begged me to go with him and see him to the door at least, to make certain that nothing happened to him or his money."

The friend agreed, and the pair set out for the Kitchen. When they got there, the escort left the extortion victim by the circular entrance on the corner of Fourth Avenue and walked on down Carroll Street. It was a hot day. Some distance down Carroll Street, the door to the side entrance of the restaurant was open. As he passed he glanced through the doorway, and there, sitting at a table in the rear of the restaurant just inside the door was Joe Adonis himself. His heavy face was stolid, impassive; his fathomless brown eyes alert. But what astonished the friend even more than the sight of Joe A. was the sight of Joe A.'s companion. He was a police captain.

"I almost fell through the sidewalk," he related. "I thought to myself, 'My God, here I've been urging him to go to the cops with his story, and there's Joe A. sitting in the rear of the place, with a *captain* no less, right while the payoff's being made up front."

That was the kind of thing that could and did happen in Brooklyn under the reign of Joe Adonis. Sometimes it wasn't even safe for a man to buy a Cadillac.

6

MR. UNTOUCHABLE

O^N THE night of September 16, 1937, Joe Adonis went for a stroll. He was an impressive figure, manicured and groomed until he positively glowed. He was wearing a conservative blue serge suit, white shirt, blue tie. His tan shoes were polished to a high shine, and on his head he wore a dark gray fedora, the brim snapped down.

He had taken no more than a few steps from his big stucco house, with its concrete-fortress walls, when two figures materialized out of the night beside him. They were two of New York's best modern detectives, Ray Maguire, who later became an inspector in charge of the headquarters squads, and Walter Casey, subsequently one of the top racket experts on the Police Commissioner's confidential squad. Casey and Maguire were attached at that time to the Safe and Loft Squad, which had primary responsibility for solving burglaries and hijackings. They had been frustrated for years by the wave of cigarette hijackings in Brooklyn, but at last they had built a case against the all-powerful Mr. A.—and they hoped they could make it stick.

If it didn't stick, the law had another arrow to its bow, a charge called murder. Joe Adonis, for the first time in his life, was in really serious trouble with the law, and he had no one except himself to blame. The all-wise and all-powerful one had made a blunder.

The year 1937 was politically crucial; Fiorello LaGuardia was running for re-election. The undeniable record of the past four years showed that Joe Adonis had lived extremely well under the La-Guardia reform regime. He should never have risked rocking the boat. But Mr. A., usually so canny in such matters, had become blinded perhaps by his own power as the undercover Democratic boss of much of Brooklyn, and he had elected to break with La-Guardia and place all his chips on his party's nominee, Royal S. Copeland.

It was a gamble fraught with incalculable hazards, and almost the instant Joe Adonis made it, some of those hazards became apparent. The Little Flower, who had had a blind spot about Joe A. during his four years in City Hall, suddenly discovered the menace that existed across the East River in the Borough of Churches. In shrill indignation, he lambasted Joe A. as the undercover political boss of all Brooklyn, "a gangster and leader of the underworld," and "a tin-horn gambler." A phrase like "tin-horn" was typical of LaGuardia. It was expressive of his personal contempt, but actually it wasn't very accurate. There was nothing tin-horn about Joe Adonis' millions, his business complexes, his awesome power.

Against this background, the arrest of September 16, 1937, carried with it certain political overtones. It occurred on the very eve of primary day; Joe A. was being quizzed about hijacking and murder at the precise instant when, ordinarily, he would have been manipulating his army of Election Day thugs and floaters.

When Maguire and Casey moved in against Mr. Untouchable of Brooklyn, their case was based on the previous April's hijacking of a truck loaded with 125 bales of crude rubber valued at $7,600. They had a witness who, they hoped, would be able to identify Adonis and place him at the drop used for storing the stolen merchandise. The case looked good, right up to the moment the detectives grabbed Joe A. Then things began to happen to it.

Joe A. insisted on telephoning his lawyer. The lawyer went into instant action and telephoned a Supreme Court Justice in Manhattan. The Justice held a night hearing on a writ of habeas corpus, and Joe A. was freed in the custody of his attorney for appearance next day in Brooklyn Felony Court.

He appeared in court on schedule—and with a most imposing retinue. Just as Frankie Yale had arrived with a small personal army on the day of young "Joe Arosa's" first encounter with the law, so Joe A. now walked into court escorted by six husky, hard-featured, hard-eyed bodyguards. These retainers seated themselves as interested spectators in the first row of courtroom seats, and stared with intense curiosity at the State's principal witness, the trucker who had been trussed up in the hijacking. Perhaps it was only coincidence, but the trucker on the witness stand suffered a complete collapse of memory. He couldn't identify Joe A. He couldn't identify anybody. And so the case bounced right out the courtroom window as if it had the elasticity of those 125 bales of hijacked rubber.

Joe A. started to leave the hall of justice in which he had been so singularly vindicated, but had taken only a few steps when Detective Albert Beron took him by the arm. His immediate presence was requested, Detective Beron said, at the Canarsie police station, where the matter on the agenda was multiple murder.

Police had culled from the underworld grapevine a most intriguing story. In the summer of 1937, three small-timers, possessed of more nerve than brains, had concocted a novel scheme for personal advancement—nothing less than launching themselves on a big-time racket career at Joe A.'s expense.

The three were Andrew Angao, an East Side mobster; Samuel Bianculli, alias Gaspipe Sam; and Vincent Adams. They had been introduced to each other in Elmira Reformatory and had put their combined imaginations to work, figuring out the best road to success that they could take once they got out. The infallible pathway, they decided, lay in setting themselves up in the loan-sharking business in the Brownsville and East New York sections of Brooklyn.

This decision ignored at least one cardinal fact—that both of these territories had been pre-empted by a couple of energetic businessmen who were not likely to permit unsolicited competition. These were Abe (Kid Twist) Reles, field commander of the army of Murder, Inc., and one of the organization's most expert and lethal operatives, Harry (Happy) Maione. Disregarding the trade monopolies of Reles and Maione was a basic mistake, but the ambitious trio compounded this with a strategical error of even graver consequence.

Since they emerged from Elmira in a state of penury, they needed a quick grubstake to finance the initial stages of their loan-sharking enterprise. And with their unique talents for improvisation, they settled on the following plan. Joe Adonis was running a huge floating crap game in South Brooklyn. The game moved from spot to spot to keep out of reach of any misguided zealots of the law, and it was heavily patronized by wealthy suckers and well-heeled out-of-town mobsters. The stakes sometimes ran as high as $25,000. To Angao, Bianculli, and Adams it seemed that this loot was just waiting to be snatched. They would stick up Joe A.'s game, bankroll themselves with the proceeds, and live happily ever after as prosperous loan sharks.

The first stage of the plan worked to perfection. The trio succeeded where the law was constantly failing. They pinpointed the site of Joe A.'s big game, barged in at the height of the play with loaded guns, and swept up the spoils by the bushel. The raid had been everything that they had anticipated, and all that remained was for them to set themselves up in business. But before they could get to that, things began to happen.

On July 9, 1937, Angao was found, riddled with bullets, at Farragut Road and East 78th Street in the Canarsie section of Brooklyn.

Seven days later misfortune overtook Bianculli, alias Gaspipe Sam. His body was found in a blazing automobile on East 89th Street, between Avenues A and B.

And on August 14 the body of Vincent Adams was found at Church Lane and East 89th Street with bullet holes in his head.

To detectives it seemed fairly obvious that the three murders—of two-bit hoodlums who had had the audacity to stick up a Joe Adonis gambling game—might be related. For this reason, they extended the invitation to Joe A. to appear at the Canarsie police station and talk.

With an almost martyred air, Joe A. obliged the cops. He came with his lawyer, sat down, and talked. Why, no, he said in his barely audible voice, he could not imagine who had done those three boys in. He, of course, had no knowledge of them, none at all. He was a reputable businessman, you know, and such bloody incidents were completely foreign to him. He was truly sorry he couldn't help, but then he couldn't understand why the police should have thought he could. He sat there straight-faced, his brown eyes staring into the eyes of detectives, unfathomable pools that gave no clue to the mental machinery behind them. In such fashion the interview dragged along for about 15 minutes, and then Joe A. and his attorney politely left.

It had caused Joe A. practically no effort to brush off the dual suspicions of hijacking and murder; but he was not completely free of the embarrassments, however minor, that stemmed from this arrest. When Maguire and Casey picked him up, they found in his pockets a curious notation. It consisted of two columns of figures marked "In" and "Out." The "In" column totaled $206,283; the "Out" column $188,425. Among the separate entries in the "In" column appeared such names as "Frank C.," "Doc," and "Spic." Among those in the "Out" column, "Doc" and "Spic" again appeared, "Judge" was listed three times, and there was one cryptic notation, "Upstate."

When he appeared in 1951 before the Kefauver committee, Adonis claimed the privilege of the Fifth Amendment against possible self-incrimination when he was asked about his gambling activities. At the end of the hearing, the late Senator Charles W. Tobey, the Bible-quoting New Hampshire Republican, produced the "In" and "Out" memo and asked Joe A. what it meant. Did it perhaps refer to the take of a big gambling game—and the payout and the payoffs? Blandly, Joe A. protested that he had no idea at all. Asked if "Frank C." stood for Frank Costello, he told the committee he really couldn't say; his mind was a blank on the subject; he couldn't even recall that such a memorandum had ever existed—or that it had been taken from his own pockets.

The gambling memo about which Joe A.'s mind went blank when he was questioned by the Kefauver committee was indicative of the new face of the American underworld. Joe Adonis, like all the other major racketeers of his time, had made his initial fortune in the bootlegging and speakeasy racket. With the demise of Prohibition, this source of revenue was cut off; new rackets were needed to bank-roll the empire of crime. And so it is significant that, when Maguire and Casey picked up Joe A. in September, 1937, they found evidence on his person that he was engaged in large-scale professional gambling, for it was as a multimillionaire proprietor of gambling houses that he was soon to establish a second and even more gaudy criminal career.

This shift in Joe A.'s criminal interests was typical of what was happening in the underworld. It was the result of a calculated decision made by the grand council of the Mafia, working in collaboration with other czars of crime, like Longy Zwillman, of Newark, who sat on the board of directors of the Combination.

In December, 1933, with the end of Prohibition at hand, Mafia dons from across the nation rallied in Chicago in a pattern that Apalachin was to publicize a quarter of a century later. Quite a lot of information has leaked out piecemeal to investigators in subsequent years about the decisions taken at this key conclave. The identities of the delegates are not fully known, but there can be no question about the main purpose of the gathering and its major decisions.

There was just one item of crucial concern on the agenda: to find substitute rackets that would be as lush in their multimillion-dollar bounties as Prohibition had been. Some of these alternate sources of revenue lay at hand. The underworld had always had important stakes in the narcotics racket and in gambling; bookmaking and policy had been lucrative sources of revenue for every mob in the nation. Loan-sharking and extortion were also money-makers, the latter especially effective among Italo-Americans with a heritage of knowledge about the menace of the Mafia. In industries where great numbers of these people were employed—such as the garment, trucking, longshore, and food trades—systematized "protection" rackets could be highly remunerative. The rulers of the secret brotherhood determined to cultivate more intensively all of these lines, but the major emphasis would be on gambling—encouraging addiction by every device known to man from slot machines to casinos, from bookmaking and policy to legalized gambling through pari-mutuel machines at the racetracks.

Looking back, it is remarkable how these decisions, taken by the Mafia in secret conclave in Chicago, dovetailed with the birth of the great modern wave of gambling. The year 1933 was the watershed year that marked the end of Prohibition and the beginning of the new era of growth of gambling license. This magnification of an existing, but lesser, racket into an infinite underworld resource was based upon a simple psychological principle: that legalized gambling nourishes the gambling fever and begets illegal gambling. Whether the Mafia dons were astute enough to recognize this basic truth and with devilish ingenuity deliberately fostered the new wave of legalization cannot be said; but it is a fact that the rest of the decade witnessed a tremendous propaganda campaign to sell the public on the idea that the newly perfected pari-mutuels made betting mechanically pure and would eliminate bookmaker and gangster influence at the racetracks. State governments, hard pressed for revenues in those depression days, accepted the argument and jumped at the chance to legalize racing. In state after state, antiracing and antigambling statutes were repealed. The boon to the underworld amounted to billions of dollars annually, for the racing fan who went to the track cultivated the betting habit and plunged ever more heavily in daily wagers with his bookie. The contrast between then and now has perhaps been most strikingly documented in Massachusetts. There, in 1933, two years before pari-mutuels were legalized in the state, a state crime commission found that bookmaking did not even rate notice as a crime problem; by 1960, a successor commission reported that it was the most important racket of the underworld and a major source of official corruption.

The transformation was certainly aided by the secret rulers of the invisible empire. Joe Adonis in Brooklyn began to bankroll big-time, floating crap games like the one that had led the three from Elmira to their doom. In Manhattan, Frank Costello and his partner, Dandy Phil Kastel, pioneered another wing of the Combination's gambling enterprises—slot machines.

As early as 1931, Costello had formed a connection with the Mills Novelty Company of Chicago, the largest manufacturers of slot machines in the nation, and he and Kastel had obtained the New York franchise. They established a whole complex of corporate fronts—the Tru-Mint Company, the Village Candy Company, and the Monroe Candy Company, to name just a few—and they put the "one-armed bandits" into speakeasies, cigar, stationery, and candy stores throughout the city. Most of the machines simply gulped nickels; but some swallowed dimes, quarters, and half dollars—and a few had an exclusive appetite for silver cartwheels. At the height of their operation, Costello and Kastel had 5,186 slot machines on location throughout the city. In some stores, if the slot machines rested on a counter too high for small children to reach, short stepladders would be placed in front so they could climb up and contribute their nickels to Kastel and Costello.

A nickel machine in a good location would take in as much as $20 a day. With more than 5,000 machines working, and the higher-priced ones taking in more than $20 a day, it was estimated that Kastel and Costello were enjoying a *daily gross of some $100,000*.

They had such influence that they even managed to get Justice Selah B. Strong (the same who had issued the gun permit to Joe the Boss Masseria) to issue an injunction forbidding police from interfering with the operation of the machines. When LaGuardia was elected in 1933, he was outraged and instructed his police to ignore the court order, to seize the offending machines wherever they were found, and to smash them to bits. Since each machine cost about $100, such axe-wielding was expensive for Kastel and Costello.

The gambling czars were too canny and too powerful just to sit still and let disaster overtake them. New York police seized and destroyed only some 500 to 600 machines; the remaining 4,500 were spirited away by Kastel and Costello. With their Mafia ties, they did not have to struggle too hard to find another market for their wares. Down in New Orleans, as the Kefauver and McClellan committees both were to document, Carlos Marcello was the local Mafia chieftain, who, having the right contacts in official circles, gladly opened up the whole corrupt Louisiana territory for the Prime Minister of the secret brotherhood. Soon all Louisiana was a virtual fief of the underworld, with the Costello-Kastel-Marcello combine flooding the state with slot machines, horserace wire rooms, and Monte Carlo-type gambling casinos.

Other territories across the nation were being similarly exploited. In 1937, the year marked by Joe Adonis' emerging trouble with the law, the board of directors of the Combination met and decided that the rackets of the West Coast needed the strong hand of an expert organizer. Jack I. Dragna was the powerful Capo Mafioso there, but the directorate voted to send out its own field commander —Benjamin (Buggsy) Siegel, the lethal partner of Meyer Lansky in the Bug and Meyer mob. Though Buggsy was Jewish and so no Capo Mafioso, he went west with all the power of the Mafia hierarchy and the Combination behind him; Dragna became his principal lieutenant; and all the rackets of California were speedily welded into one functioning criminal organization. Individual mob leaders so injudicious as to protest the take-over were shot.

Soon the hot-tempered, insatiable, vicious Buggsy had every racket in California—bookmaking, the offshore gambling fleet, prostitution, and multimillion-dollar movie shakedowns—organized under his command. In the early 1940's, seeking new worlds to conquer, he came upon Las Vegas and began turning the arid desert into a lush, legalized gambling preserve for the mob, an oasis for the lawless.

Such was the system and the manner in which it worked. Generally unperceived by the public and often ridiculed by officials as a pipe dream, the underworld organization of crime, with the Mafia at its core, was stretching out tentacles that threaded the nation from one coast to the other. If local conditions, a suddenly revivified law, made one principality too hot at the moment, the underworld rulers simply pulled up stakes and moved on. Sometimes, as in the case of Costello and Kastel, they found a new paradise for crime in a far-distant state; at other times, as in Youngstown, Ohio, they simply moved across a municipal border.

When LaGuardia trounced Royal Copeland in the mayoralty contest of 1937, storm signals flew for Joe Adonis all over Brooklyn. The Kings County District Attorney's office, in which he had had potent influence, came under a barrage of criticism for its alleged suppression of a murder case, and Gov. Herbert H. Lehman appointed a special investigator, John Harlan Amen, to conduct a probe of Brooklyn rackets. On October 28, 1938, Amen announced that he was looking for Joe A. for questioning about the mysterious disappearance of certain valuable records from the files of Brooklyn's Bergen Street police station. About the same time, William B. Herlands, LaGuardia's Commissioner of Investigations, announced that he was looking into possible financial ties between Joe A. and certain eminent political figures. And Thomas E. Dewey, campaigning for governor, thundered that Joe Adonis was "the public enemy No. 1 of Brooklyn." Nothing much came of all this headline furor, but Joe A. found it advisable to get out of town. He suddenly became a tourist, and the grapevine reported that he traveled first to Canada with his wife and family, then went south to Florida to enjoy the winter sun.

Never again was he to be the Mr. Untouchable of Brooklyn. Soon a new and far more serious threat loomed on his horizon. William O'Dwyer became Kings County District Attorney and began his famous Murder, Inc., probe. Murder, Inc., of course, spelled Albert

Anastasia and Joe Adonis, and any probe that went all the way must eventually land at their doorsteps. But whether O'Dwyer would go all the way remained to be seen.

O'Dwyer started out in an atmosphere of no-holds-barred. He selected for his key assistant a man who was impervious to influence, Burton B. Turkus, a political independent. Turkus, who later told of his adventure against the underworld in the book *Murder, Inc.,* written with Sid Feder, was astonished himself at his selection, but he was promised a free hand by O'Dwyer and he threw himself into the hunt for some of the most sadistic killers the underworld has ever produced.

Going over the records, Turkus found that the celebrated Borough of Churches had become a borough of murder. Some 200 killings, practically blanketing the Brownsville, East New York, and Ocean Hill sections in the northeast part of Brooklyn, had gone unsolved. Such wholesale slaughter obviously was not the result of sporadic, individual passions; it had happened because in Brooklyn violent death had become a business and it had been planned that way. Turkus and O'Dwyer began to apply the heat. They harassed and pressured the stumblebums of the mob. They got little squeals, and these finally led to the big squeal. Abe (Kid Twist) Reles decided to talk.

Reles was a squat, repulsive thug with a photographic mind and thick, powerful fingers ideal for scragging the necks of his victims, a practice that had earned him his nickname of Kid Twist. He had been the commander of the Brownsville troop and the top field agent of Albert Anastasia in the marketing of murder. When he began to talk, he lifted the lid, not just on the murders committed in Brooklyn, but on secrets of underworld organization across the nation. As Turkus later pointed out, he gave authorities the first inside view they had ever obtained into the birth and mechanics of the underworld cooperative known as the Syndicate or the Combination.

Reles told of the Atlantic City meeting of 1929, and he described a later grand conclave in New York in 1934 at which, he said, the earlier decisions were really made effective. According to Reles, Johnny Torrio presided at the 1934 session and helped perfect the actual, working government of crime. Each regional czar was to have his seat on the board of governors. Each was guaranteed protection of his life and loot as long as he did not violate accepted policy or betray the common interest. Mob would deal with mob across the nation. Whatever the deal, wherever its locale, there would be a local mob with the "contacts"; whenever murder became essential to good business, the local boss through this intermob relationship could import specialists for the job at no risk of attracting suspicion to himself. The Combination offered all this—and life insurance, too. None of the rulers could be "hit" without the decision of a kangaroo court, a trial and vote by racket peers.

Under this setup, Reles bragged, the strong arms of Murder, Inc., became the elite enforcers for the entire Syndicate. They practiced their specialty from New York to California and at way stations. They became distinguished in the underworld, said Reles proudly, for their efficiency and dispatch, and even mob bosses who had their own lethal "troops" made special contracts to assure themselves of the services of Murder, Inc. The master extortionist, Lepke Buchalter, who had his own band of efficient artisans, reinforced his hand by paying Murder, Inc., a special annual retainer of $12,000 to handle difficult jobs for him.

All this and more, Reles told. When he began to talk, he wore out stenographers in relays. He had a phenomenal memory that enabled him to recall the minutest details, even the menu he had enjoyed years previously while dining with a prospective victim at his unsuspecting last supper; and in checking such revelations, Turkus always found that Kid Twist had been a model of accuracy. He was so accurate in fact that, in a whole series of subsequent trials, his testimony stood up under the relentless battering of the cleverest cross-examiners available. He could hardly be dismissed as the purveyor of a bad pipe dream when he recited details of some eighty-five Brooklyn murders of which he had personal knowledge, and when he estimated that Murder, Inc., had probably fulfilled approximately 1,000 contracts for the Syndicate across the nation.

The scope of the conspiracy, the grandiose plan of an underworld determined to dominate much of American society by introducing rackets into every field and enforcing its edicts by the terror of organized, cross-continent murder—this was enough to make the head swim. Turkus later recalled that once, in a moment of caprice, he asked Reles what he thought of the international situation. The opening phases of World War II were then dominated by a couple of international gangsters named Hitler and Mussolini. "It's a cinch,"

Reles said, and then drew this comparison: "They're just the same as the Combination. We are out to get America by the pocketbook . . . the whole Syndicate. When we have to, we kill people to do it. Hitler and Mussolini—they're trying to do the same thing. Only, they're trying to get the whole world by the pocketbook. So, they're killing people by the millions to get it."

As evidence of the Syndicate's success in this incredible scheme "to get America by the pocketbook," Reles frequently boasted that Murder, Inc., had "connections." It had connections with other troops of the underworld throughout the nation, and it had other connections that protected it from the inquisitive nose of justice. This protection held good, not just on the lower local levels but even in the higher echelons of the national bureaucracy, Reles hinted. Both he and Lepke Buchalter, in a last desperate bid to escape the electric chair in Sing Sing, murmured mysteriously about the importance of the mob's national connection, but if they ever named names, these have never been revealed.

In his marathon revelations, Reles left little doubt about the internal structure of Murder, Inc. Joe Adonis, he said, outranked Albert Anastasia both in the local pyramid of murder and in the broad structure of national crime. There was no question that he stood high on the national board of the Syndicate; in fact, according to Reles, none stood higher. Reles described Adonis as the Syndicate's coordinator and mediator of intergang disputes. Other songbirds of Murder, Inc., agreed. Blue Jaw Magoon put it this way: "He [Joe A.] is a part of the national Combination. In other words, if he got crossed, the guy who crossed him had the whole Combination on his back." Such testimonials and much other experience led Turkus to conclude: "Some idea of Adonis' eminence can be gleaned from the marked tone of profound reverence that comes into the voice of any hoodlum, anywhere, whenever he mentions 'Mr. A.'"

Even Reles with his detailed knowledge never got close enough to Joe Adonis to build a legal murder case against him. Reles did drop some convincing details, however, and one of these formed a headline springboard for O'Dwyer at one of his numerous Murder, Inc., press conferences. O'Dwyer said Reles had "involved" Joe A. in one murder contract, and he proclaimed he'd send Joe A. right to the electric chair in Sing Sing if he could get the necessary clinching evidence. Ten years or so later, when the Kefauver committee questioned O'Dwyer about this, he couldn't even recall the case. But Turkus fortunately had a better memory.

According to Turkus, Reles had given investigators this account: In the mid-thirties, Dewey was investigating taxicab rackets in Manhattan. A potential witness, who possessed evidence that would have been "very damaging" to Joe A. and some of his racket brethren, was a man named Matty Brown. "Joey Adonis made a personal contract with Albert A." about Matty Brown and Brown's wife, Reles told the Brooklyn investigators. He said he had learned about this when the matter was mentioned during a visit he made with Louis Capone to Adonis' home. Later, he said, Pittsburgh Phil Strauss, another of the Murder, Inc., crew, confirmed the information. "Pep tells me," Reles babbled, "that Albert tells him he got two people to take care of, and it is important because Dewey knows these people are hot. He says Joey A. is interested in this." Reles's information stopped there. He apparently never did learn in detail the mechanics of the plot; but it was a matter of record, according to Turkus, that Matty Brown and his wife mysteriously disappeared, never to be heard of again.

Reles's account made it clear that Joe A. had isolated himself at the summit behind the screen of Anastasia, the Lord High Executioner. If the Murder, Inc., probe was ever to get to the throne-room, it would have to get Anastasia first; and for a short time at least this seemed a distinct possibility. At the moment, however, Joe Adonis was faced with a more imminent threat from an entirely different direction.

John Harlan Amen, Governor Lehman's special rackets prosecutor, had been probing Joe A.'s affairs, and on May 6, 1940, he announced that a nationwide hunt was on to find the mastermind of the Brooklyn rackets. The charges were kidnaping, assault, and extortion.

The case went back to August 1, 1932, and included three lesser characters in the Brooklyn underworld: Isidor Wapinski, fifty, described as a "fringe" figure who was always fast at a swindle; his partner, Isidore Juffe, a man who later blandly admitted that he had bribed and fixed his way through a criminal career of twenty-two years; and Sam Gasberg, at the time a trusted strong arm of Joe A. and also chauffeur and bodyguard for Joe A.'s family.

According to Juffe, Adonis had been a secret partner of Wapinski and himself in several schemes. One had involved the swindling of a trucker and jeweler who had since died. Another had been a decidedly novel "money-making machine," a Rube Goldberg device that was supposed to take a single sample of legitimate currency and print from it scads of bills so perfect that they could not be detected. Wapinski and Juffe actually "sold" a number of them to foolish persons, usually collecting a down payment of several hundred dollars and then forgetting to deliver the machine. One Brooklyn physician, an abortionist, told Amen's investigators that he actually paid the pair $900 for their dandy little money-maker. He had been hoping to work the double double cross. He was being blackmailed by some of the mob, and he figured he could put the dollar-printing device to good use, paying off the blackmailers in the phony currency it would produce.

Brooklyn in those days was a happy world in which one racket was always being topped by the next. For a time Wapinski and Juffe reveled in the endless opportunities almost as much as Joe A., but finally they overreached themselves. The scheme that led to their undoing involved a land speculation in Yonkers. Wapinski and Juffe got a tip that the Yonkers school board intended to buy a certain tract of land for a new school. All they needed in order to make a bundle, they thought, was to purchase the land first, then hold up the municipality for a high price. The idea seemed foolproof, except for the fact that they hadn't the money.

This crass necessity impelled the partners to confide in Joe A. They explained what a cinch they had, how impossible it was to lose; and Joe A., liking the sound of this, invested about $20,000, putting up the money in the name of his brother, Anthony Doto. What happened next is what so often happens to the sure-fire deal: Yonkers didn't buy the tract. This meant that the partners were stuck with a sizable stretch of real estate on which they had to pay taxes, and this was nothing to be stuck with in Depression days. Not even Wapinski and Juffe, who could peddle a money-making machine, could peddle that land. Joe A. was unhappy. His mind began to harbor the dark suspicion that perhaps Yonkers had never intended to use the land for a school, and that Wapinski and Juffe had been playing him for a sucker.

Wapinski and Juffe learned about this trend of Joe A.'s thoughts on the night of August 1, 1932. According to Amen, who made a detailed report on the case to Governor Lehman, Wapinski was walking along the street when a car driven by Sam Gasberg and containing a number of Joe A.'s strong arms pulled alongside. Wapinski was invited to take a ride and under the circumstances, he didn't have much opportunity to refuse. Shortly afterwards, Juffe, who was out on the town with his girl friend, was surprised to receive a similar summons. "Joe wants to see you at the restaurant," Juffe said he was told, as he and his girl were bundled into Gasberg's car.

They were driven to Joe's Italian Kitchen, but Joe A. evidently wasn't there. After a brief stop, Juffe's girl was ejected from the car, and the gang started out again, taking their prisoner to a house on the outskirts of Brooklyn. There Juffe was put into a room adjacent to one in which Wapinski was receiving some ministrations from Albert Anastasia and his helpers. Juffe himself was slapped down in a chair, a tourniquet was placed around his temples, and Gasberg gave this device a few agonizing twists, accusing him of having swindled Joe A. out of $20,000. Juffe denied that he had done any such thing. He later admitted during his trial testimony that he never saw Joe A. during the events of this harrowing evening, but he insisted that he had heard Joe A.'s distinctive, low-pitched voice murmuring instructions in the background.

Finally, according to Juffe, he was allowed to see the beaten and bleeding Wapinski, and then he was told, if he knew what was good for the pair of them, to get on the telephone and start raising some money. Juffe called his girl friend, she contacted Mrs. Wapinski, and between them the women got together $5,000. With this payment, after about two and a half days of imprisonment, Wapinski and Juffe were released. Wapinski was a sight. He had been beaten so savagely that he was bleeding from the mouth and from internal injuries. A protest went back to Joe A. who proved to be magnanimous. He agreed to submit the whole case to decision by an underworld kangaroo court.

The court sat in a midtown New York hotel and heard evidence, according to Amen. It finally decided that Wapinski was innocent, that he had never intended to mulct Joe A. But by the time this favorable verdict was rendered, Wapinski was dead. He had lingered only a month after the savage beating; but unfortunately for Amen, who admitted that he would have liked to develop a murder case, the doctor who had signed Wapinski's death certificate—one who had never treated the man before—had ascribed the cause to angina pectoris, a form of heart disease. Shortly after the death of Wapinski, Sam Gasberg shook the dust of Brooklyn from his feet and went all the way across the continent to Stockton, Calif. There, after depositing some $26,000 in a San Francisco bank, he struck up a friendly acquaintance with a lady in the hotel business and began to live the quiet life.

Such was the story that John Harlan Amen's investigators pieced together. On April 22, 1940, Amen called the first two witnesses before an extraordinary grand jury in Brooklyn, seeking indictments against Gasberg and Adonis. The instant he moved, two strange events occurred—seeming to indicate that Joe Adonis, living in far-off Florida, still had a secure pipeline to keep him apprised even of the secret deliberations of a Brooklyn grand jury. For on the very day this first testimony was given, Adonis disappeared from his favorite hotel in Miami; and across the continent, in Stockton, California, Gasberg also vanished from his regular haunts.

The kidnaping, extortion, and assault indictment against the pair was returned on April 27, 1940, and a nationwide manhunt started. The hullabaloo was terrific. An interstate alarm was sent out for the arrest of Joe Adonis; at least 2,000 photographs and 5,000 circulars describing him and his offense were distributed throughout the nation; and Mayor LaGuardia discussed the possibility of having the New York Board of Estimate place a price on his head.

All this did not help the law locate its elusive quarry. Tipped well in advance, Adonis had made certain preparations which included having two trunks built to his own specifications with saw-proof steel linings and secret panels. When he disappeared from Miami, these trunks disappeared too. Detectives traced them first to Denver, then to New Orleans. Then the trail of Joe A. and the steel-lined, secret-panel trunks vanished.

Gasberg was not so expert in performing the vanishing act. When he left Stockton, he took with him a number of checks, signed by his girl friend and made payable to a variety of aliases. Whenever Gasberg needed funds, he endorsed a check with the proper alias and cashed it. Detectives quickly caught on to his system, however, and established a close watch over the telltale checking account. In early May, when Gasberg, then holed up in Los Angeles, cashed a check endorsed with the name "Sam Glick," detectives spotted the clue as soon as the check showed up at the bank; they followed the trail to Los Angeles and on the night of May 4th arrested Gasberg.

The former chauffeur and strong arm for Joe A. was brought back to Brooklyn for trial, and a few days later, on May 9th, the boss himself calmly walked in and surrendered. He looked not the least like a harried and bedraggled fugitive. He was garbed in his usual dark conservative suit, white shirt and brightly colored tie, gabardine coat and gray fedora with snap-down brim. Not yet quite as subdued as he later became during his second lease on racket life in New Jersey, he displayed a 20-carat star sapphire on the little finger of his left hand. As usual, the thick lips in his full face were clamped tight, and he opened them just once, to say just two words—"Not guilty." In a brief court proceeding, bail was set at $75,000, and Joe Adonis, to whom such an amount was little more than spending money, chose not to raise it. Quietly, all too quietly even for him, he went to jail and sat out the next couple of weeks there.

The timing seems to have been highly significant. Burton Turkus, at the exact moment of Adonis' surrender, was going to trial with the first of his Murder, Inc., cases, based on the testimony of Abe Reles. As he later learned from the underworld grapevine, the Syndicate had formed elaborate plans to counter his legal moves with murder. Buggsy Siegel had left his California racket preserves and come to New York to mastermind the plot to "get" the Murder, Inc., songbirds before they could give their testimony in court. Fortunately, the witnesses were too closely guarded for Siegel and the Syndicate to accomplish their purpose, but this could not have been foretold at the time. One thing could be foretold. If a rash of murders involving key state witnesses in the first sensational Murder, Inc., trial had broken out, the first man officials would have thought of for questioning would have been Joe Adonis, master of the Brooklyn underworld. Accordingly, there was no finer domicile for "Mr. A." than the Brooklyn jail which provided him with the perfect alibi.

Not until May 24, 1940, the day after the first Murder, Inc., trial had ended in a conviction, did Joe A. find it desirable to regain his freedom. Then he did so quite easily. His bail was reduced to $50,000, and most of it was supplied by Pete Savio, also known as Petey O'Brien, a sometime henchman of Albert Anastasia. With this development, Joe A.'s period of personal harassment virtually ended.

Amen went to trial with the kidnap-extortion-assault case in October, 1940. He tried Gasberg separately in the apparent hope that, if the strong arm were convicted, he might become more cooperative and help to bolster the State's case against his master. Under the circumstances it was vital that Gasberg be well defended, and he was. His counsel was Leo Healy, a onetime Brooklyn magistrate and one of the sharpest trial lawyers in the borough.

For any lawyer as astute as Healy, it was obvious that the State's case had one important weakness. This was the character of Juffe. His testimony was the key, but as a witness he was highly vulnerable. He had indulged in a lifelong career of swindle and crime and Healy focused on his past, calling him "a liar and a fixer unworthy of belief." These defense tactics succeeded. The first trial ended with the jury hopelessly split, unable to reach a decision. Amen tried again, and the second trial ended with what Turkus calls an "amazing" verdict. The jurors acquitted Gasberg of kidnaping, but disagreed about the extortion blithely disregarding the fact that, if there had been no kidnaping, there could have been no extortion. It was a courtroom fiasco that made any future move against Adonis practically impossible. Amen himself acknowledged this when he walked into court on February 24, 1941, and moved for the dismissal of charges against Joe A. His action marked the abject collapse of the most serious legal threat that had ever been posed against Brooklyn's premier gangster. At the same time, the air was clearing in other directions.

The Murder, Inc., probe accomplished many things that are seldom accomplished in American law enforcement. It solved a number of gangland murders; it sent a parade of some of the nation's most sadistic killers to the electric chair. Hardly ever does the law solve the murder of a top gangland chieftain. But the Murder, Inc., investigation provided the solution to the slaying of Arthur (Dutch Schultz) Flegenheimer in the Palace Chop House in Newark, New Jersey. Hardly ever does a top czar of the rackets go to the electric chair for having committed murder. But the Murder, Inc., probe was climaxed by an extraordinary triumph—the conviction and execution of Louis (Lepke) Buchalter, a member of the Combination's national board and its specialist in extortion. Then suddenly it all stopped.

The day the sweeping exposé suddenly lost its steam was the day that Abe Reles, "the canary who could sing but couldn't fly," went out the window of his bedroom in the special squealers' suite on the

sixth floor of Coney Island's Half Moon Hotel. He plunged forty-
two feet to his death in the early morning of November 12, 1941;
and in all the years since that day, no completely satisfactory explanation has ever been given of how it came to happen.

Reles's body was found lying out from the wall; various estimates
placed it from a minimum of nine feet to more than fifteen feet away.
Around him fluttered a couple of twisted sheets that could have been
used as an improvised rope to enable him to lower himself to the
window of an unoccupied room directly below his own. A length of
wire had been used to attach this sheet-rope to the radiator in Reles's
room, and the wire had parted. The official assumption was that Reles
had clambered out the window by himself. But why? Captain Frank
Bals, an O'Dwyer favorite in charge of the police detail that had
been supposed to protect Reles's life, insulted the Kefauver committee by advancing the explanation that Reles had just been playing
a little game. What he had intended to do, said Bals, was to re-enter
the hotel through the fifth-floor window, return to the squealers' suite
from the outside, and cry "peek-a-boo" to his shocked guardians.
Listening to this theory, Senator Tobey almost had apoplexy. Even
O'Dwyer, who was steadfast in his admiration of Bals before the committee, said he was convinced that Reles—who had said so often that
he knew he couldn't live for five minutes outside the hotel without
police protection—had died in a fall trying to escape. If these con-
flicting explanations of Reles's motivation for accidentally killing himself made little sense, the physical evidence of the death scene was
even more peculiar. If Reles had gone out the window by himself,
and if he had then been killed in a straight drop as all the official
explanations assumed, shouldn't his body have been found lying
close to the wall? Senator Tobey and a considerable number of fellow
skeptics were inclined to believe that Reles didn't fall but that he
was pitched.

This was also the understanding in mob circles. Joseph Valachi, in
discussing Reles's demise with the McClellan committee, put the
underworld's version of what happened to Reles in succinct terms.
"They threw him out," Valachi said. He could not, of course, identify
the "they."

The belief that Reles's sensational death right under the eyes of
his police guards involved the acme of shenanigans received support
at the time from the haste with which the investigation was closed out.

Here was the prize witness in the greatest murder probe of the century suddenly and mysteriously dead and with him had gone the possible solution to a number of highly important murder cases. In all charity one might have expected William O'Dwyer, whom the Democrats were praising as even a greater rackets buster than Dewey, to have flown into a fury and to have lashed his investigators to ferret out the last suspicious detail.

Instead, the O'Dwyer investigation into Reles's death was finished by noon on the day it happened. Turkus, whose star witness Reles was, didn't even know his No. 1 informer had died until a newspaper reporter told him. He comments cryptically that this "was not, by a considerable margin, the only peculiarity which had developed" in the Murder, Inc., probe. In 1951, after the Kefauver sensation, a Brooklyn grand jury tried to pick up the cold trail and find out what had happened. It concluded that after ten years it was impossible to ascertain many vital facts, but it strongly criticized O'Dwyer's handling of the case. It reported that it was shocked to find no real investigation had been conducted at the time—no real attempt had been made to find out what happened to Abe Reles.

In the murky background of the case was the old specter, the utter corruption of Brooklyn politics by the underworld. John Harlan Amen later disclosed that he had tried many times to talk to Reles; he was aware that Reles knew all the secrets, and he wanted to get him to talk as freely about the protection payments the mob made to Brooklyn politicians as he had about the details of murder. But Amen could never arrange to see Reles alone. He could see him only in William O'Dwyer's office and in William O'Dwyer's presence. "It was something of a farce," Amen said later. "You could see right away that Reles was afraid to talk. I never was able to get him to tell me the names of the officials to whom the mob paid protection money."

Beyond all this there was perhaps an even more vital factor in the case. There have been well-authenticated reports that, as the months of the Murder, Inc., probe dragged past, Reles had been becoming more and more unhappy. He knew that his life would never be worth a nickel unless the murder probe were pressed all the way to the top of the Syndicate. He commented to Turkus that there wasn't any spot in the world he could go where "those bastards" wouldn't get him. In this distinguished company he rated such names as Albert Anastasia, Willie Moretti, Longy Zwillman, Meyer Lansky, Buggsy Siegel, and Joe Adonis. But as the months passed, it had become obvious to Reles that not one of these was being touched.

It was not for lack of opportunity. California authorities had been anxious to get a murder indictment against Siegel—the same Buggsy who had come to New York to mastermind the bumping off of Murder, Inc., witnesses. To indict Siegel, however, California needed Abe Reles and the testimony he could give. When O'Dwyer was asked to loan Reles to California for this purpose, he replied that he couldn't spare him at the time, he was much too valuable testifying in Brooklyn —and then suddenly Reles was dead. Buggsy Siegel could breathe a lot easier. So could Albert Anastasia. One of the first bits of information that Reles had dropped involved Anastasia in what O'Dwyer called, in large newspaper headlines, "the perfect murder case." Reles had happened to visit Anastasia's home one night in 1939 and listened while the Lord High Executioner and some of his thugs discussed arrangements for the murder of Morris (Moish) Diamond, a garment-district figure whom Lepke Buchalter wanted removed because he knew too much. New York State law requires corroboration by witnesses other than those involved in a crime; and in this case, according to O'Dwyer, Reles had not been involved in the slaying and could therefore supply the corroboration needed to convict Anastasia. O'Dwyer announced a great manhunt to find Big Al. The boss killer was sought throughout the nation and in Cuba, Mexico, and Italy. All the time, he was calmly reading the New York newspaper headlines in a hideaway in northern New Jersey; but this fact, unknown at the time, did not detract from the drama of the great manhunt. Curiously, however, in the nineteen months that Reles lived after he began to talk, O'Dwyer never took him before a grand jury to testify against Anastasia; he never obtained an indictment against Anastasia in what he himself had called "the perfect murder case"— and then suddenly Reles was dead.

Dead, too, was the perfect case. And just as startling as the fact of its demise was the nature of it. The Murder, Inc., probe had not yet foundered on the death of Reles when William O'Dwyer, riding the crest of dramatic achievement as prosecutor ran for mayor against Fiorello LaGuardia in November, 1941. Billed as a Democratic Dewey, O'Dwyer made a close race of it, but he lost. On the heels of his defeat came the inexplicable disaster to Abe Reles; and less than a month after that, Pearl Harbor and America's involvement in World War II. Almost immediately O'Dwyer responded to the call of patriotism and took a leave of absence as District Attorney to become an officer in Uncle Sam's Army. But first he cleaned up some tag ends of the Murder, Inc., business.

At his request Burton Turkus prepared a memorandum on the status of the Albert Anastasia investigation. Turkus, who had been the trial attorney, had had nothing to do with the Anastasia case prior to this, and his memorandum was based exclusively on a report to him by O'Dwyer's own Captain Bals summarizing what had happened. Bals's analysis pointed out that when Reles went out the window, the corroboration needed to try Anastasia died with him and there was no case. Turkus, in a confidential memorandum to O'Dwyer dated April 8, 1942, noted this view but refused to accept it. He declared in just about the strongest language possible that "should Anastasia frustrate justice, it would be a calamity to society. Somewhere, somehow, corroborative evidence must be available." He urged "redoubled effort."

There followed one of the most startling developments in the annals of American law enforcement. For just twenty-six days after Turkus had called for "redoubled effort," the slate against Albert Anastasia and his top killers was wiped clean! The "wanted cards" that showed they were being hunted for the offense of murder were removed from police files.

The manner in which this was achieved became a subject for study in the Brooklyn grand jury investigation of 1945 and figured prominently in the Kefauver probe in 1951. What happened seems well established. O'Dwyer throughout his long public career in New York City was served by a hulking individual named James J. Moran— O'Dwyer's Man Friday, as Senator Tobey called him. It was Moran, subsequently sent to prison for running a $500,000-a-year extortion racket in New York's Fire Department, who ordered the wanted cards against Anastasia and two of his ace killers, Dandy Jack Parisi and Tony Romeo, removed from police files and destroyed. Police Sergeant Elwood J. Divers testified: "Moran came in and gave me a list of the cards he wanted taken out of the file, and he told me to destroy them all." O'Dwyer denied to the Kefauver committee that he had ever ordered such an action. Moran denied it too at first, but later admitted that it was just possible he had done it.

Though O'Dwyer insisted that the action was of no importance because Anastasia could always have been indicted for murder any time the State could make a case against him, the removal and destruction of the "wanted cards" as a practical matter meant everything. It meant that the great manhunt for Anastasia was ended. So true was this that "Big Al" even came out of hiding and joined the U.S. Army under his own name. This was a bold act of patriotism that led to the final scene of the farce.

Stationed at Indiantown Gap, Pennsylvania, Anastasia rose to the rank of Master Sergeant, training longshoremen for overseas duty. Then one day an alert Army officer who remembered the old headlines connected Sergeant Anastasia with his past. The Army was quite shocked to realize that the Lord High Executioner of the underworld was a Master Sergeant in its Transportation Corps; and it hastened to notify New York police of the fact. The information aroused little excitement in New York. The police checked their "wanted file"; found no card on Albert Anastasia and told the Army in effect: "We don't want him. You keep him."

Big Al was safe. So was his boss, Joe Adonis, who could probably have been involved in the deeds of Murder, Inc., only through a successful prosecution of Anastasia. So were all the other rulers of the Syndicate. Crime had ridden out the storm in Brooklyn, and just across the Hudson in New Jersey it had found itself a new haven. There, under the guiding genius of Joe A., it was prepared to do business, richer and more powerful than ever.

7

THE LAND WHERE MURDER
WAS BOUGHT

BACK in the thirties, a former state trooper who later had had some contacts with the mob insisted that, in nineteen of New Jersey's twenty-one counties, you could buy your way out of anything, including murder. In the remaining two counties, you could buy your way out of anything *except* murder. Unfortunately, however, his information was not fully accurate, as in one of those two "pure" counties where murder supposedly wasn't for sale, there was at least one case in which it had been bought, and immunity for it purchased, cash on the barrelhead.

When the law in New York began to show signs of conscience, the underworld needed a new nerve center from which to operate. Nature, it would seem, had fashioned New Jersey with special regard to the needs of the Combination. There it lay across the Hudson River, just a short hop from the tall spires and dark canyons of New York; and all one had to do to have the pavements turn from hot to cool was to drive a car across the George Washington Bridge.

When Brooklyn became inhospitable, Joe Adonis, Albert Anastasia, and others of their ilk began to commute across the bridge. They knew precisely what they were doing, for the lotus land of New Jersey—a state from which the underworld could run the world— had been pioneered well in advance of their coming by an emissary who had convincingly demonstrated the completeness of the protection that could be purchased.

The stature of a Mafioso may be judged by his immunity to the law, by the manner in which even the most serious charges take flight before the magic of his money, his power, his influence. When a Mafioso is accused of murder and witnesses falter and lose their memories, he has demonstrated his supremacy over legitimate society, over the law and the courts. Willie Moretti was a Mafioso with just such stature.

Willie Moretti was a self-made man, his American success story as typical in its way as that of any baron in Wall Street. Willie, of course, altered the classic Horatio Alger formula of rags-to-riches and made it read rags-to-roulette—and murder. But it added up to the same quota of millions in the end.

Willie Moretti was introduced to a mobster's world almost from the moment of his birth on June 4, 1894, in an apartment at 329 East 109th Street, New York. This was the heart of the East Harlem section that was to become known in later years as the exclusive preserve of the tough 107th Street mob of narcotics peddlers and killers. Willie, who stood only 5 feet 4 at maturity and in youth was quite slender, got an education fast. He began earning his way as a milkman's helper at the age of five, at twenty-five cents a week; as he grew older, he became progressively a pinboy in a bowling alley and a smalltime club prizefighter. By the time he was nineteen, Willie had his first encounter with the law, an attempted robbery charge brought against him by a neighborhood barber. For a while after that, charges piled up against Willie every time he turned around, but Willie, ever shrewd, finally found the right formula. He found a well-connected lawyer, a gentleman who later became a State Supreme Court Justice; and this eminent representative, who remained a very fine and life-long friend, as Willie assured the Kefauver committee, went down to the District Attorney's office and straightened matters out for him. After this, Willie had no more trouble in New York, and by the time Joe Valachi began to circulate in the hoodlum environment of East Harlem, Willie Moretti was known as a very big man indeed.

Always the picture of innocence, Willie insisted to the Kefauver committee, in a virtuoso performance on the witness stand, that he had always been the most wronged of men. Police, throughout his life, had bothered him with charges for offenses that he never committed. Why, to hear Willie tell it—and he actually used the phrase—he and Al Capone fell in love with each other at a racetrack when they first met because they were both such "well-charactered" men.

This was not the way a Hackensack taxicab-fleet operator named William J. Brady would have told it, but by the time the Kefauver committee got around to questioning Willie Moretti in 1951, Brady had been dead for twenty years.

The story of Brady's misfortune and Willie Moretti's first date with murder goes back to 1931. At the time, Brady had a contract to chauffeur Bergen County detectives on emergency calls. This connection with the law apparently was his undoing. A still that was important to the Waxey Gorden bootleg mob was raided in Wallington, New Jersey, and since such an event was rare, the unhappy proprietors instantly divined that there must have been a squeal. Brady was suspected.

About 6:50 P.M., January 16, 1931, Brady kissed his wife good-bye and walked out the rear door of his home at 95 Summit Avenue, Hackensack, toward his Cadillac parked in the drive. He had hardly stepped out the door when his wife, inside the house, heard a babble of voices suddenly arise. She heard her husband shout: "I didn't do it! I didn't do it!" She heard another voice cry: "Let him have it." Instantly, the house shook as a shotgun roared, and a revolver blasted away. Then came the sound of running feet—and silence.

When his family reached his side a few seconds later, Brady was lying in a heap in the falling snow at the edge of the driveway. His body had been riddled by 23 buckshot. His right arm had been shredded. Three bullets had been pumped into his body at close range. One had nicked his heart, the second had passed through a lung, the third had shattered his left wrist. By rights he should have been dead. But he wasn't. He was alive, fully conscious, able to talk.

Police Captain William Munz, of Hackensack, was among the first officers to arrive at the scene. He and several of his detectives knelt beside the mortally wounded Brady on the snow-speckled edge of the driveway. "What happened?" Munz asked Brady. And Brady told him—told him and others over and over again.

Munz recorded everything in a report drafted the next day, a report that was still in the files of the Bergen County Prosecutor's office twenty years later.

"Detective Dalia asked Mr. Brady who shot him, and he said Willie Moore, Chicago Fat, and Kid Steech," Captain Munz wrote. "The answer was written on paper immediately by Detective Delia [an associate of Detective Dalia].

"We then placed Mr. Brady on a stretcher and put him in the police ambulance and took him to the Hackensack Hospital. On arriving at the hospital we took him to the emergency room. While waiting for a doctor, I asked him who shot him and he answered Willie Moore, Chicago Fat, and Kid Steech. Detectives Dalia and Delia and Patrolman Menke were in the emergency room when Mr. Brady made the statement as to who shot him. Mrs. William J. Brady was also there."

Munz, who in his innocence evidently thought this was good eye-witness evidence, identified the three murder suspects. Willie Moore, he pointed out, was the favorite alias of Willie Moretti, who then lived at 10 Obal Avenue, East Paterson, New Jersey. Chicago Fat was Anthony Sabio, of the Fern Hotel, Market Street, Paterson, and Kid Steech was Joseph Bongiorno, of 10 Obal Avenue, East Paterson.

The case against Willie Moretti would appear to have been quite substantial from the Munz report, but the murder charge did not rest on this report alone. Far from it. Nat Allyn, a detective in the Bergen County Prosecutor's office, was also quickly on the scene, and his account of what Brady said also managed to survive some of the strange developments that were to take place later. According to Allyn, the dying Brady identified his actual executioners as Willie Moore and Chicago Fat. Allyn also noted that a "Mr. Fraser," an assistant in the Prosecutor's office, had taken a detailed deathbed statement from Brady in the hospital.

This makes three separate recitals in which Brady had named his slayers, but even this wasn't all. There was a fourth. Charles Schmidt, then an assistant prosecutor and the man who was placed in direct charge of the murder investigation, also questioned Brady. Schmidt, asked in 1952 about his role in the case, insisted that he "did a good job" from both an investigative and a legal standpoint. The vital angle was the legal one. The courts usually feel free to admit into evidence a statement from a man who is no longer alive to be challenged, or cross-examined, only if such statement has been made in full consciousness of the imminence of death. This was the legal loophole that had to be buttoned up in the deathbed statements, and, according to Schmidt, it was. Brady was fully aware that he was not expected to live because a Catholic priest, who was present when he made his final statement, had already administered to him the last rites of the church.

The sequence of events and repeated statements of the dying Brady would seem to indicate an airtight case. This conclusion rests not upon Schmidt's word alone, but upon the corroborative account of still another important witness at the deathbed scene, Joseph Aloysius Frayne. Then in the mid-stage of a thirty-seven-year career as a Federal agent, Frayne was a special agent for the Department of Justice on the night of the murder. He had never met Brady, but he had talked to him on the telephone earlier that same day and had made an appointment to see him at his house that night.

At the very moment that Brady was being gunned down in his own driveway, Frayne was driving toward Brady's house to keep the appointment. In the snowy night, he had lost his way in the unfamiliar streets of Hackensack, and when he realized that he was going to be late, he stopped and telephoned the Brady house. Someone at the other end of the wire picked up the phone, but all Frayne could hear were background noises, a confused babble and hysterical sobbing. He realized at once what must have happened.

Dashing back to his car, he raced to the Brady home and arrived in time to find the fatally riddled man still lying in the driveway talking to detectives. Frayne heard Brady say that four men had been in the execution squad—Willie and Solly Moretti, Chicago Fat, and Kid Steech. Frayne not only heard this first recital by Brady, but he went along to the Hackensack Hospital and was present at the bedside when Brady made his final and more formal statement.

The veteran Federal agent corroborated Schmidt in the latter's contention that he had done "a good job." The deathbed statement, in Frayne's opinion, had been legally airtight. It included a warning to Brady at the outset that he was dying and that therefore he must be extremely careful to tell nothing but the truth, and near the end of the statement, as Frayne recalled it, there was a paragraph that read approximately like this: "You realize, Mr. Brady, you are about to face your Creator and that you are going to die and we will expect the truth and nothing but the truth." Brady acknowledged that he knew this and insisted that he had correctly identified his slayers.

After Brady died, there was a great manhunt for the alleged killers.

The public, reading the papers, may be excused for naïvely assuming the law was greatly exercised. This was precisely what the public was supposed to believe. But the sequel would seem to indicate that, behind all the headline furor, Willie Moretti and the law understood each other.

The first indication of this came when Willie, who had gone immediately on the lam, walked in docilely and surrendered himself. The second indication followed hard on the first. Though first-degree murder wasn't supposed to be a bailable offense in New Jersey, Willie Moretti accomplished the impossible. A considerate judge set $35,000 bail for him, and Willie, to whom such was a pittance, was promptly sprung.

Then months passed and nothing happened, a clear sign that nothing was ever going to happen. It was nearly two years later, by which time the public had lost almost all interest in the murder of one William J. Brady, that Willie Moretti got a Christmas present. In late December, 1933, the Bergen County prosecutor's office nol-prossed the indictment against Willie Moretti, that is, it dropped the case.

But how could this have happened in view of Brady's repeated statements, especially his witnessed, deathbed declaration?

Charles Schmidt, the assistant prosecutor who had been in charge of the original investigation, was still bitter when questioned by rackets-buster Nelson F. Stamler nearly twenty years later. Schmidt said he had been kept in complete ignorance of the plans of the prosecutor's office to drop the murder charge against Willie Moretti. "I didn't know about it until it happened, until I walked into court," Schmidt insisted. He explained that his superior on the prosecutor's staff, Harry L. Towe, had made the motion to nol-pros the murder indictment. Schmidt made it clear that he had never agreed with the decision, but there had been nothing he could do about it.

Towe, who later served several terms in Washington as a Congressman, was asked for his version of what had happened when he testified before a state legislative committee in 1953. Towe defended his action on the ground of helplessness—there had been nothing else that he could do. Brady's dying statements, he said, the ones available to him at least, could not have been used at a Willie Moretti murder trial because there was no evidence that the victim knew he was dying when he made them.

"These men were out on bail, an indication it was not a very strong case," Towe testified. "I was in charge of the calendar. I conferred with the chief of detectives, and we were in agreement we couldn't proceed."

He added that the County Judge had warned him the State would have either to try the case or to nol-pros it. John Selser, the attorney for Willie Moretti, put pressure on by moving to quash the indictment; but the court refused to permit this and gave the prosecutor's office the honor of admitting the error of its ways. "I made the motion," Towe said.

This action evidently earned Towe the eternal gratitude of Willie Moretti. In discussing the Brady murder with the Kefauver committee, Willie was his usual innocent and protesting self. "Why they implicated me, I don't know," he said plaintively. "He [Brady] was a good friend of mine." A little later, when asked about the politicians he knew, Willie singled out Towe for special tribute. "Well, one I know real well is Congressman Towe, who was the Deputy Attorney General when I was nol-prossed in the murder case; I can't deny knowing him," Willie said.

Towe subsequently made it clear to the State Legislative Committee that he was distinctly unhappy about this accolade. He had never met Willie until he saw him in court the day he was forced by circumstances to nol-pros the murder charge, Towe said, and he had never had anything to do with Willie afterwards. And there the matter rested. Neither the state committee nor the Kefauver committee probed deeper to find out what had really happened. What, for example, had become of that deathbed statement on which Charles Schmidt claimed he had done such "a good job" and which Frayne insisted contained two specific warnings of approaching death?

The answer was that it had simply vanished. Just as the "wanted cards" on Albert Anastasia in the "perfect murder case" were to disappear from the New York Police Department files, so Brady's legally binding deathbed statement disappeared from the files of the Bergen County Prosecutor's office. Police Captain Munz's report had survived; so had Detective Nat Allyn's. But not that deathbed statement. Towe was right about that. It would seem, unless one talked to Schmidt or Frayne, that no such statement had ever existed.

This weird gap at the heart of the mystery intrigued rackets-buster Stamler when he began probing the New Jersey empire of crime in

the early 1950's. He talked to both Schmidt and Frayne and took
statements from them under oath, apparently the only investigator
who ever went to such trouble. So he established that a legally binding, deathbed statement *had* existed. From Frayne, he also got a clue
as to what had happened to it.

Ever since the day that Willie Moretti brushed off that little matter
of murder in Bergen County Court, Agent Frayne had made it a rule
to chat with the cocky, wisecracking hood whenever they chanced to
meet. Frayne, the veteran agent, pumped Willie, the veteran crook,
for information. It was a game they both enjoyed, and usually Frayne
didn't get anything for his trouble. But occasionally Willie, in his
cockiness, would let something drop—as he did one day when he
just couldn't help bragging about that old William J. Brady murder
case.

"You thought you had me where the hair was short," he remarked
to Frayne, practically laughing in the agent's face. "Well, I took care
of that. It cost me twenty-five grand, but I got the deathbed statement
right out of the files."

Frayne, naturally, would have liked to know more; but Willie
Moretti, who couldn't resist tantalizing him with this tidbit, was too
wily ever to part with all the vital details. Who got the money that
Willie Moretti said he paid, and who did the dirty work of filching
the deathbed statement out of the files remain enduring mysteries.

About the outcome, however, there was no mystery. Willie Moretti
had sneered at the most sacred of the commandments and at all the
processes of Jersey justice. He had demonstrated that, as a Mafioso,
he was superior to the law and could fix anything. The high command
of the Combination got the message; and, when it became necessary
to make a strategic withdrawal from New York, it simply transferred
its headquarters over the bridge to the land where even murder could
be bought.

The guile and foresight that run the underworld showed themselves
in the anticipatory speed with which the Combination changed its base
of operations. It did not wait to be chased out of New York. On the
contrary, it correctly assessed the early storm signals and got its most
vital operations out of harm's way before the Murder, Inc., unpleasantness broke about its head.

The timing is fixed by unimpeachable evidence. One hard nubbin of fact was later uncovered in Frank Erickson's expressive bank records. Erickson was the bald, roly-poly, cherubic-faced master of mathematics who had become the Combination's wizard of the layoff. The layoff is a vital process at the heart of the bookmaking operation. It is the underworld's gambling insurance. Say a local book becomes overloaded with bets on a long shot in the third at Aqueduct; if the long shot wins and the book has to pay off all the bettors, he could be ruined. So he bets the long shot with a larger, regional book, "laying off" part of his load; and the regional book, if similarly overloaded, covers itself by passing the burden on to a national clearinghouse. For more than a decade Frank Erickson was the national clearinghouse. He handled the layoff business, for a precisely calculated fee, of course, from bookmakers in every one of the then forty-eight states. The cash flow was tremendous.

Both the magnitude of the business and the date by which Erickson had established his operations in North Jersey were shown by the transactions in an account he opened in the National Bank of West New York on December 31, 1940. This account instantly became the vehicle for the heavy swag that flowed into Erickson's layoff headquarters. Deposits were soon amounting to as much as $100,000 a day, and on a single day, August 10, 1943, they totaled an impressive $152,532.80. This one New Jersey bank account—and there were other accounts handling Erickson cash during the same period—showed total deposits of $2,860,667.98 between December 31, 1940, and June 3, 1943, an average of more than $1 million a year.

The Erickson transactions were not the only indication, however, that the eastern and dominant wing of the great national crime cartel had moved its capital. Far more important was the establishment of a new headquarters in Duke's Restaurant, located at 783 Palisades Avenue, Cliffside, New Jersey, directly across the street from the entrance of the large and popular Palisades Amusement Park. Duke's had a drab-looking front, discouraging to a visitor, but in its appointments it was virtually a replica of Joe's Italian Kitchen. Inside, it had a long bar on the right, booths on the left. Like the Kitchen, it served good food and liquor and had at the rear a separate council room, well padded for sound and well protected against public intrusion. Again, just like the Kitchen, it had a side entrance that gave direct access to this secret privy chamber without the inconvenience of public exposure by passage through the restaurant.

Here was a veritable Capitol of Crime. For more than ten years, it was to be the managerial headquarters of the Combination. Mob power was concentrated here as early as the spring of 1941, a date well established by reports in the files of the Federal Bureau of Narcotics, the only investigative agency that seems to have known what was happening almost as soon as it happened. In one report dated March 31, 1941, the bureau emphasized the importance of Duke's and listed the names of a whole coterie of mobsters whom agents found congregated there on that day. Many of these names were not to come to general public attention or to arouse the curiosity of New Jersey authorities until ten years later when, under the kleig lights of Kefauver, it became imperative to frown upon them. Yet they were the same gangland figures, identified this early by the Federal Bureau of Narcotics, who were to figure prominently in the fantastic gambling operations that made New Jersey the prize fief of the underworld east of the Mississippi.

Some of those named in the 1941 narcotics bureau memorandum are:

John (Johnny Duke) De Noia, the proprietor of the restaurant, then a man about forty, six feet tall and weighing 200 pounds, with black hair and a clean-shaven, pock-marked face. His was the managerial task of running the tavern, handling the staff, and making certain of the security arrangements from bar to kitchen.

Richard Bennet and Peter LaPlaca. These were two of Johnny Duke's top assistants. Bennet, who sometimes spelled his name Dick Bennett, had previously been a narcotics suspect in New York and was known as a Jersey bookmaker; in years to come, he was to exercise increasing authority in Duke's and was to be identified by witnesses as the man who handled many important details for Joe Adonis. Like Bennet, LaPlaca helped to keep affairs running smoothly in Duke's; he also served as a chauffeur and bodyguard for Willie Moretti.

Willie Moretti and his darker, more silent shadow, his brother, Salvatore (Solly) Moretti. The Moretti brothers, Mafiosi of high standing, were to be almost daily habitués of Duke's during the next ten years, the essential fixers and contact men in the manipulations of the Combination.

Anthony (Greenie or Tony Greeno) Guarini, a manager of mob gambling casinos. He was ultimately to be imprisoned in the Kefauver exposé's aftermath for operating some of Joe Adonis' houses of chance.

Arthur Longano, another trusted subaltern of Joe Adonis in the gambling empire.

Thomas (Three-Finger Brown) Lucchese, the boss of one of New York's five reigning Mafia families. Ten years later, after the eclipse of Costello, he was to be widely publicized, not too accurately, as heir to the fallen Prime Minister.

The major name missing from this lineup was, of course, that of Joe Adonis, who became the absolute autocrat of crime in Duke's, functioning as Field Marshal of the Syndicate. There was, however, good reason for Joe A.'s absence at this time. The Murder, Inc., probe was still rushing full-speed ahead in Brooklyn, and no man could yet be certain (since Abe Reles was still alive and singing) where it all might end. But even though Joe A. was making himself scarce, it is perhaps significant that the physical layout of the mob head-quarters in Duke's so closely paralleled that of Joe's Italian Kitchen; significant, too, that prominent Adonis henchmen like Bennet, Guarini, and Longano were already on the scene and extremely active.

As for Adonis himself, the Bergen County countryside, just across the George Washington Bridge from New York, was still too close to the hot seat of investigations and headlines. He needed a racket farther away, out of the glare of the moment's spotlight, and he found exactly what he wanted in the upstate New York racing spa of Saratoga, where, even before the demise of Reles, he became the active director and organizing genius of a large-scale casino gambling.

In one New York State Liquor Authority hearing in 1944, Joe A. was pictured in an omnipresent, proprietorial role at the Piping Rock Casino in Saratoga Springs during the summer racing seasons of 1941 and 1942. Annually, for the month of August, the upstate New York resort becomes the center of the fast racetrack crowd and the gambling millionaires of business and society. Naturally it would be a pity to deprive such fine gentlemen of their sport, and Joe A. and the mob extended themselves to please.

Piping Rock was a high-class, fashionable restaurant that had been operating ever since the thirties. A door led from the restaurant proper into a narrow passageway that connected with a gambling casino equipped with roulette wheels, bird cages, chemin de fer, and high-class dice tables. Two "strong-arm men," former New York policemen, were stationed at the connecting door of the restaurant. Three "spotters" also kept post there and cleared the clientele who, after drinking and dining, thirsted for a little bout with chance. One of the spotters was an expert on the local Saratoga gambling crowd; another knew the Florida and out-of-state playboys; the third certified the credentials of the New York City clique.

The entire operation was supervised by the poker-faced, unwinking Joe A. His favorite station was at a table just inside the door of the gambling casino. There he played gin rummy and kept an eye on the customers filing along the passageway, on the dealers and the croupiers at the tables. His favorite card-playing partner was a comedian who was the star of the nightclub revue. Joe A. and his chosen guests dined nightly in the Piping Rock, always enjoyed the most expensive cuisine, never had to bother about so trivial a detail as a dinner check.

Though *The New York Times* devoted considerable space to these disclosures in 1944, the lush Saratoga gambling operation continued to run unimpeded by the law in the state of which former racketsbuster Thomas E. Dewey was Governor. At Piping Rock, the Arrowhead Inn, and other casinos, the Syndicate operated with perfect impunity. The big play was dominated by the Big Three of eastern gambling and the eastern rackets: Joe Adonis, Meyer Lansky, and Frank Costello. There was no mystery about their interest or their activity; both were widely publicized. Frank Costello, for example, was questioned during a State Supreme Court hearing in 1943 about his interest in Piping Rock, and this was his casual explanation of it:

"There is a Joe Stein which is a good friend of mine," he testified. "I have known him for years, which I consider very honorable. He came to me and gave me this proposition—that he had a lease on a casino in Saratoga called Piping Rock and would I undertake running it?

"I told him I wasn't interested, didn't have no time for it. A few days later he came to me and he says he had some people interested, but they won't take a hundred per cent of it. I say, 'What have you left?' He says thirty.

"I said, 'Well, I will have thirty per cent under one condition. I will finance my thirty per cent, but you will have to look after my interests,

because I will probably never be up there.' Being I trust the man,
I gave him the money, and I have a thirty per cent interest."

In these remarks by trusting Frank Costello, there was no indication that the vague "some people" who had a 70 per cent interest in
Piping Rock were brother moguls of the Syndicate whom Costello
knew perfectly well; there was no hint that the man really running
the affairs of chance and looking out for Costello's interest as well
as his own was Joe Adonis, a peer of the rackets with whom Frank
traded ideas regularly either on the lush greens of the Pomonok
Country Club or in that shadowy back cavern at Duke's. In the same
belittling vein was Costello's estimate of the profits at Piping Rock—
offhand and indefinite. What did his 30 per cent interest net him in
the one month of the Saratoga racing season? "Oh, I would say $9,500
to $10,500; I just don't recollect," Costello said.

Joe A. was more frank in an unusual interview that he gave in
late 1949 (before the disaster of Kefauver's investigation) to Edward
T. Folliard, a topnotch reporter for the *Washington Post*. In this
Adonis said openly that he was a big businessman and his "big business" was gambling. He compared himself to a financial titan in
Wall Street. The Wall Streeter, he said, furnishes capital for legitimate
enterprises; well, he performed the same function for gambling casinos.
He bankrolled them. The motive was exactly the same in both cases,
explained the astute Joe A., attempting to identify himself with the
American profit-revering spirit.

"It's not what we win; it's what we earn," he told Folliard, a bit
self-righteously.

This portrait by Joe A. of Joe A. as the Wall Streeter of the
underworld naturally made no reference to such ungentlemanly practices as hijacking, extortion, and murder that had flourished like
jungle growth during his long reign as czar of the Brooklyn rackets.
In explaining his philosophy of life and business to Folliard, he
made it quite clear that before he sank his money into a costly gambling venture, he had to have the answers to three vital questions.
What was the community like? What were the prospects of action—
that is, patronage or business? What did the law say in respect to
gambling? There were two sides to this last question, the basic one
of the three. Joe A. preferred to make certain, not just that the law
was obliging, but that gambling in the locale in which he intended
to operate was considered a misdemeanor rather than a felony. Thus,

if some blue-nosed crusader came butting into the picture, spoiling a beautiful fix, the worst an underworld Wall Streeter like Joe A. could get would be a relatively mild punishment.

This system of the man whom Thomas E. Dewey, when he was running for governor, had called the Public Enemy No. 1 of Brooklyn worked fine during the regime of Thomas E. Dewey, once he was elected Governor. In fact, one of the most glaring examples that the Kefauver committee uncovered of a gentleman's agreement between the forces of the law and the forces of the lawless resulted from its probe of wide-open gambling in Saratoga Springs, in the heart of Republican upstate New York. The Kefauver committee showed that New York State Police investigated the situation in August, 1947, and found six gambling traps in full career. Joe Adonis and representatives of the Detroit mob, State Police found, were dominating gambling operations at the Arrowhead Inn at the time. When Superintendent of State Police John A. Gaffney received the report, he commented, according to his own testimony, "This looks like a sizable operation." And immediately he put the report in the file and forgot about it.

Badgered for an explanation, the Superintendent explained that State Police weren't supposed to raid over the heads of local authorities, except by special request or on special orders from the Governor. Asked whether he had informed the Governor of the "sizable operation" his detectives had uncovered, Gaffney said he hadn't. He had felt, he testified, that the Governor and the Governor's staff must have known all about it since "it's been going on for twenty-five years to my knowledge." He agreed with Kefauver's statement, "In other words, you just knew you weren't supposed to do anything about it?" Gaffney went even further. Though he tried to soften the statement later, he admitted that he had felt, if he had called attention to Saratoga gambling, he might have found himself "out on the sidewalk."

A similar assumption that the big Saratoga games were untouchable—and supposed to remain that way—pervaded the local police force. One detective testified that he hadn't made a gambling arrest in nineteen years; that he never snooped beyond the public dining rooms of the gambling casinos; and that he felt, if he ever had, he would have been out of a job. The gentleman's agreement with the mob extended even to the point of using the town police car to ferry the mob's cash from bank to gambling casino. Police Chief Patrick F. Rox admitted that he had known of this practice and that he had known about the gambling, but had felt it was to his own best interest to do nothing about it. This obvious desire not to know any more than he had to know probably explained Chief Rox's insistence that, despite the newspaper publicity in 1944 about Joe A. and Piping Rock, he didn't know whether Joe Adonis had ever set foot in his town; he didn't know that Adonis had ever been connected with gambling at the Arrowhead Inn.

In such testimony, the moral of Brooklyn's Detective Baron is expressed in reverse. Baron had tried to interfere with the mob and had been broken back to beat-pounding; here high-ranking police officers—the Police Chief of Saratoga Springs, the Superintendent of New York State Police—had known better than to try. No more convincing example of the dominance of Joe Adonis and the Syndicate could be found than this open acknowledgment that the highest police officers in town and state had felt themselves powerless to act— and had been convinced that they would be cashiered if they did.

Such innocent ignorance on the part of the law was always found wherever Joe Adonis and the Syndicate operated. It made no difference whether the locale was Saratoga Springs or Bergen County. Nobody in official position ever knew what all the world knew. Multi-million-dollar gambling, the profits from which bankrolled as vicious a group of cutthroats as America has ever seen, was dismissed as a little peccadillo, justified by the attitude that boys will be boys and they like to play. Joe A. was just a gentleman—as he said, an underworld Wall Streeter—who accommodated this perhaps illegal, but thoroughly human and understandable desire of the American public for the spice of chance. There really was no harm in it. So ran the rationalization.

It collided, of course, with facts, with truth, with basic moral realities. And nowhere was this collision to erupt in so dramatic and so revealing an explosion as in New Jersey.

8

BONANZA DAYS

THE FACT is not on record, but 1942 should have been welcomed by a New Year's Eve party in Duke's that would have put to shame the famous brawl with which the Kitchen's habitués had greeted 1934. For with the new year, the mob entered upon a long stretch of bonanza days—hardly a murder to ripple the waters and literally billions of dollars cascading down upon their heads, a green waterfall that seemed to mock all ethical and moral pretensions of American society.

The previous year, 1941, had been a horrible time of trials and troubles. Abe Reles had been singing. Hirelings of Murder, Inc., actually had been convicted and started on their march to the chair. Even Lepke Buchalter had been doomed, and such a pall had been cast over the affairs of the underworld that it had seemed for a time even Anastasia and Joe A. might not be immune. But it had all ended in the death plunge of Reles; the dark clouds had blown away and happy days were here again—to rival if not surpass the best of Prohibition.

America was engaged in a desperate world war. This meant that all kinds of persons had all kinds of money. Factories were booming to turn out weapons for the arsenal of democracy; big-league executives, with their cost-plus contracts, had money to burn; and even laborers in the shipyards, airplane plants, and munitions factories, working overtime and weekends, were able to gamble with the best. The world situation might look truly desperate in those first days after Pearl Harbor; men might be fighting and dying by the thousands and the tens of thousands—but there was nothing like a world war to help the cause of the Combination. Fat pigeons cluttered the landscape, and Joe Adonis and his sinister cohorts in the Combination were past masters of the art of plucking them.

So there opened before those unblinking eyes of Joe A. a seemingly endless vista of green. Yes, 1942 and the years immediately following were to be truly glorious. They were years in which Joe A. would wield his field commander's baton as if he were an Eisenhower; years in which he would cavort with Virginia Hill, the Miss Syndicate of the mob; years in which literally billions of dollars would roll in with such a steady surge that the law was corrupted from New Jersey to Florida and, in essence, only the lawless ruled.

How does one tell this story of the incredible fortunes and functions of a day-to-day "invisible government," and the unbelievable corruption affecting even the highest levels of American life? Perhaps the best way is to begin with Duke's, the dingy-looking tavern where it all centered.

Standing before Duke's on a typical day in the war-torn forties, Joe A. looked every inch the millionaire. Always stocky, he had had a certain rugged handsomeness in his youth, before high living had packed 190 pounds on his 5-foot-7½-inch frame. Now he had a tendency to double chins and the dark-brown hair was turning gray. His face, never swarthy but always of surprisingly fair complexion, had been barbered so expertly that it seemed as if the heavy stubble of beard had been shoved back under the skin; his cheeks were so smooth you could have sworn they had never known a whisker. The black, custom-made shoes had been polished until they shone like twin mirrors. Joe A.'s dark, double-breasted suit had that special patina, that silk-like gleam that costs money; and on his head, he wore a wide-brimmed fedora, the brim snapped down over those hard, unblinking eyes.

Swiftly Joe A. strode to the rear of Duke's. He used the side "family entrance," as it was called, that led directly from the parking lot into his well-guarded council chamber. Here he met daily with four members of a functioning Crime Cabinet, the department heads who helped him govern the far-flung, multimillion-dollar rackets of the Syndicate.

Joe A., already as untouchable in Republican New Jersey as he had been in Democratic Brooklyn, sat at the head of the table. At his right hand sat his favorite enforcer, Albert Anastasia, known to the underworld from his gory deeds rather than his physical stature as "Big Al." Next on this board of control came the Morettis, Willie and Solly, past masters of the political fix and the police fix. And finally there was the cadaver-thin, doleful-visaged shadow figure, Anthony (Tony Bender) Strollo, racket czar of the lower Manhattan and New Jersey docks and owner of Greenwich Village nightclubs, a man who as yet had never made the headlines but who had long been known by narcotics agents as "the chief lieutenant" of the exiled Vito Genovese.

This was the power clique that Joe A. joined in his inner sanctum on this typical spring day in Duke's. He had hardly settled himself in the boss's chair before he began to issue orders and the telephone wires began to hum. Call chased call over Duke's phone, Cliffside 6-1799. The legions of the underworld were being summoned. Joe A. had important business to transact.

Though he was not to realize it for some time, his activities on such busy days were often monitored by listening posts across the Hudson. District Attorney Frank S. Hogan, of New York County, was fully aware of Joe A.'s importance in the hierarchy of crime, and he and his aides tried many times to smuggle an undercover agent into Duke's. But they found this impossible. Every bartender and kitchen slavey had been given a loyalty check by mobdom. "You couldn't get near the place," says Vincent A. G. O'Connor, who was at the time Hogan's chief assistant. "Their security arrangements were worthy of the FBI."

Since this was so, Hogan's men had been reduced to checking the periphery of crime's citadel. License numbers were noted, habitués of the gloomy tavern were identified. Criminals from New York who frequented the place were shadowed from their homes to the very doorstep of Duke's, and some telephone lines, under New York State court orders, were legally and patiently wiretapped. Thus, by nightfall, Hogan's detectives had a clear picture of this one day's typical assemblage in Duke's—and of the contretemps that befell one self-judged big shot of the mob who had responded with alacrity to Joe A.'s summons.

The timing had been inopportune from this worthy's standpoint. He had had entrancing plans. The sunshine was bright, the day was warm, the ponies were running at Aqueduct; and he even had a Broadway showgirl lined up to add to the anticipated pleasures of his day.

Then had come the call from Cliffside 6-1799, and all these delightful prospects had to be scrapped. The gangster hopped into his Cadillac and whirled over the George Washington Bridge to Duke's. Obviously, he probably told himself, Joe A. wanted *him* on a matter of supreme importance.

When he walked through the door of the tavern, his ego plummeted into his socks. The place was jammed with strong arms of the mob; the big shot saw at a glance that he had *not* been summoned to an individual meeting of masterminds; he was just one of an army. It was a sudden downgrading of self-esteem not unlike what might happen to a major general who finds himself relegated to the society of sergeants.

Nevertheless, he put on a proud front and announced himself to a flunky with a flourish, his manner saying plainly that, at the mere mention of his name, Joe A. would call him before the dais. He then found a vacant niche and consoled himself with a drink while he waited. The consolation was a protracted process. He had another drink. And another.

Time passed. The door of the inner sanctum opened and shut. Others among the waiting strong arms saw Joe A. and departed. But the big shot was ignored.

That night, Hogan's men heard him moaning over his fractured ego as he bleated the story of his day to a confidante.

"Imagine Joe A. treating *me* like that!" he rumbled in an aggrieved, whisky bass. "I get this call, I give up everything, I dash over there —and then I don't even get in, I don't even get to see him! All I got is a big head."

It was no consolation that most of those who had been ordered to report for duty hadn't been admitted to the presence either. Joe A. had decided suddenly to uproot one of his plush gambling games and find for it a new and safer hideaway; he had called out all the troops, like a good field marshal who wants to make certain that, whatever emergency should arise, he will have on hand the battalions to cope with it. It was a cavalier way to operate, but that was typical of Joe A. He was arrogant. He respected only his own brain and will. He was contemptuous of others.

"There probably never has been a more complete autocrat," said Assistant District Attorney Andrew J. Seidler, who worked closely under O'Connor in Hogan's New Jersey investigation. "He was wholly indifferent to the convenience or sensibilities of his underlings. It was nothing to him to call out two or three times the number of men he could possibly use in one day—as he frequently did—just to make certain that, *if* he did need some special talent, the right man would be handy and *he* wouldn't have to be kept waiting."

Such was the man who dominated the most unusual and probably the most potent crime cabinet in the history of the American underworld. Joe A.'s inner sanctum in Duke's became the focal point for major mobsters throughout the nation. Time and again, in testimony before the Kefauver committee and other crime investigating bodies, top men of the rackets acknowledged that they had "dined" at Duke's. Willie Moretti tried to excuse his constant presence by explaining that the food and atmosphere were so good—"like Lindy's on Broadway." Anthony (Tony Bender) Strollo was more frank and more revealing when he claimed the privilege of the Fifth Amendment against possible self-incrimination in refusing to answer a question whether he had ever been there. When counsel for the Senate Crime Committee asked him in amazement whether it would incriminate him just to acknowledge that he had been in a restaurant, Strollo replied: "I fear it might." No better epitaph could be written for Duke's.

While these tenuous indications of Duke's true importance appear in the records of formal public hearings, the full story has been known for years only to investigators who shadowed the place and watched its day-by-day operations. According to the Federal Bureau of Narcotics, Tuesday was the meeting day for what might be described as the legislature of crime. Regularly each week on this day about twenty criminal overlords and key henchmen would gather for a business luncheon. They would arrive between noon and 1 P.M. "The big men drive their cars into a large garage which is two doors north on the same side of Palisades Avenue," the bureau noted in one confidential memo. "The rest park in the general vicinity."

When the delegates were fully assembled, they would wine and dine as became the rich and successful. Over the drinks and the food, they would discuss their problems, and sometimes these discussions and the decisions to which they led would hold the gathering until 4 P.M. By this hour, sometimes earlier, the guests would disband, and Joe A. and his cabinet would be left to handle the working details until the next regular Tuesday meeting.

The significance of Joe A.'s operation in Duke's is underlined by the stature of the gang rulers who attended some of his Tuesday conclaves. This was a time, in the late 1940's and early 1950's, when the Syndicate was dominated by the Big Six. Two of the Big Six, Jake Guzik and Tony Accardo, were the heirs of Al Capone and represented the Chicago mob; the other four came from the East, then the dominant wing of the combine, and all without exception were identified by investigators as frequenters of Duke's. There was, of course, Joe A. himself. And with him:

Frank Costello, known to the underworld as The Boss or The Prime Minister. Inconvenienced and sometimes embarrassed by Hogan's wiretaps, he made frequent short trips across the George Washington Bridge to the freer land of New Jersey where, in Duke's, there were no wiretaps nor other threats of espionage.

Meyer Lansky, originally the partner with Buggsy Siegel in the infamous Bug and Meyer mob, and one of the nation's top gambling czars, also teamed with both Costello and Adonis in multimillion-dollar gambling rackets at Saratoga and Miami. He is one of the combine whom time and the law seem never to have affected.

Abner (Longy) Zwillman, the ruthless Newark bootleg king who had spread out his millions in infinite legal enterprises, but who still kept a secretive hand in lucrative rackets. Before he committed suicide in 1959, if that indeed is what happened, he had established a reputation for not having guessed wrong on a major New Jersey election in some twenty years.

In addition to these reigning powers, many second-echelon hoods, heirs of the future, were traced in and out of Duke's. Two of the most noteworthy were Vincent (Jimmy Blue Eyes) Alo, a dock and gambling figure sometimes known as Costello's "right bower," and Gerardo (Jerry) Catena, who had close ties to Zwillman, Costello, and Genovese and who recently, since Genovese's imprisonment, reputedly has become one of the two top administrators of the Genovese empire.

This was the setup in the Capitol of Crime. Duke's was the nerve center from which rackets fanned out in expanding rings, and each ring represented untold millions of dollars.

Joe Adonis' special preserve became casino gambling. He was the proprietor of innumerable city and countryside Monte Carlos.

Bergen County, the haven of his principal operations, had had a long history of wide-open gambling and easy official morality, as Willie Moretti had demonstrated. Throughout the thirties, one of the most famous gambling houses in America operated brazenly from a conspicuous perch on the Palisades just north of the New Jersey end of the George Washington Bridge. It was known far and wide as the fabulous Marine Room of Ben Marden's Riviera.

Only a blind man could have missed the Riviera. There it was, thrust out to public view on the very edge of one of nature's most prominent outcroppings. It flaunted an expensive cuisine, lavishly decorated dining rooms, the fame of headline entertainers. These were all legitimate features that impressed the wealthy clientele who came merely to drink and dine. But practically everyone knew that drinking and dining were not the sole functions of the Riviera. For those with the desire, there were the enticing excitements of the Marine Room. This was a feature of the Riviera that the general public never saw. Guards stood at the door, carefully frisking, carefully identifying all who were admitted to this hall of chance; and people soon spoke of the Riviera with the same awed intonation accorded Monte Carlo.

This blatant flouting of the gambling laws and the obviousness of the *quid pro quos* that common sense said must be the only explanation for official blindness eventually made the Riviera a political issue and led to its demotion to the status of a mere legitimate nightclub. The change occurred, perhaps significantly, in the early 1940's, just about the time that Joe Adonis spearheaded the Syndicate's complete takeover of the Jersey rackets. Joe A. was not one to court trouble. Fresh from his Brooklyn experience in which he had paid the penalty for being too obviously politically prominent, he preferred to operate with subtlety and secrecy. Not for him an eye-catching showplace like the Riviera. Instead, he sought inconspicuous sites—

an abandoned factory, an old barn, a Quonset hut in the countryside. He would retain all the lovely, protective drabness like a camouflage and redo the interiors to create a decor and atmosphere that would have done credit to El Morocco. Sometimes he would spend as much at $150,000 on such splendiferous face-liftings. Furnishings were of the costliest materials, paintings by good artists decorated the walls, rugs were ankle deep. The food was always exemplary, the service flawless. Waitresses and cigarette girls were so well proportioned and scantily clad they looked as if they had just stepped out of a Broadway chorus line. Croupiers and stick men in the gambling rooms wore full dress. Glamor, the spice and thrill of secret rendezvous, and the climactic gamble at the tables—all this Joe A. provided to the customers that poured in an unending stream across the bridge from Manhattan.

One of the earliest enterprises of this kind with which a sluggish law was eventually to connect him was a high-stakes dice game in the dilapidated old theater building at 229-31 Walker Street, Cliffside Park. This game was in full swing in November, 1942, and the proprietors were all men whose names were to figure in the wide-open Bergen County gambling of the next decade—Salvatore (Solly) Moretti, Anthony (Tony Greeno) Guarini, James (Piggy) Lynch, and Joe A. himself. Guarini was in direct charge on the premises; but hardly a night passed, according to those who were there, without some of the other bosses appearing on the scene to keep an eye on affairs.

Another of Joe A.'s early enterprises was a Syndicate dice game on Central Avenue in Fort Lee, just two blocks north of the bridge. On the night of July 3, 1943, agents of the Office of Defense Transportation in New York discovered a veritable parade of cars streaming over the bridge to Jersey. These were still the desperate days of World War II, and gasoline was in short supply and supposed to be strictly rationed. Skeptical that the demands of legitimate business could be creating such a traffic jam, Federal transportation agents joined the parade and were swept along to the site of the gambling game. They had no authority to raid the house of chance, but they could and did file charges against the drivers of the limousine fleet—"luggers" they were called—for violating gasoline rationing regulations.

This secondary charge and the more important inferences that might be drawn from the defense agents' discoveries made newspaper headlines. It became incumbent upon the law-enforcement authorities in Bergen County to bestir themselves. They did. Shock, surprise, indignation were all appropriately registered. There was a lot of activity, and a big investigation was ordered to track down the crooks who had treated the law with such lese majesty. It was quite impressive; but, to the surprise of virtually nobody, by the time the detectives reached the scene of illicit enterprise, the Fort Lee gambling den was bare. All that the investigators found were some old, discarded gambling slips and fifteen empty milk bottles. The tensions of an evening of chance make some dice players susceptible to ulcers, and the Syndicate always thoughtfully provided such poor sufferers with the milk and buttermilk needed to relieve their peptic pains.

While detectives stood around, empty milk bottles in hand, the Syndicate blithely shuttled its equipment to adjoining Cliffside, and the next night they were back in business, having lost not a single roll of the dice. Such was the efficiency of Joe A., such the perfection of his arrangements.

Behind such lightning-fast shifts of scene lay intricacies of organization and management that might well have taxed the capabilities of General Motors. Real estate deals had to be negotiated for gambling sites and business offices; contractors and decorators had to be hired; protection arrangements ratified; large staffs, ranging from strong arms and spotters on the doors to cigarette girls and croupiers, chefs and waitresses and kitchen help, had to be organized and paid, their withholding taxes accounted for; friendly truckers must always be on stand-by alert to transfer menaced equipment at a moment's notice; and warehouses must be available so that gambling paraphernalia could be hidden and stored when it was whisked out of sight just a few jumps ahead of a so-called raid. Such were the scope and ramifications of the huge gambling games. The handling of business routine was facilitated by a number of dummy corporations that Joe A. and his partners set up as seemingly legitimate businesses. All had innocuous names that gave no hint of their real purpose—the G & R Trading Company, the B & T Trading Company, the General Trading Company, the PAL Trading Company, and others. Such corporate fronts handled bookkeeping, paid the bills and salaries, accounted for the withholding taxes due the federal government.

The most complete account of the operations of Joe A. and the

Syndicate during this period of the early 1940's is to be found in the files of the Federal Bureau of Narcotics. The bureau keeps a close watch on large-scale mob operations because it has discovered, time and again, that the millions made in gambling to swell the treasury of the underworld are used to bankroll the purchase abroad of huge quantities of narcotics. To the bureau it seemed not mere chance that Joe Adonis had been for years the close friend and collaborator of Lucky Luciano; not mere chance that telephone calls made from the public phones in Duke's had figured repeatedly in major narcotics cases; not mere chance that, of thirty-five criminal figures who had been identified as regularly consorting with Joe A. in Duke's, eleven had past records as narcotics violators or peddlers.

Knowing all this, the bureau devoted a lot of time and energy to the surveillance of Duke's. In September, 1945, one of its ace agents, George White, slipped into Duke's and filed a detailed report in which he described the tavern as the functioning headquarters of the Morettis and Joe Adonis. White's investigation was followed up by another made by Ross B. Ellis. One of the bureau's most resourceful agents, Ellis kept close tabs on the members of the mob and their outside contacts; and eventually, by cajolery and bluff, he cultivated some contacts of his own. From several sources, he began to obtain a private, inside-the-mob dossier on Joe A.'s entire operation. By December, 1945, Commissioner Henry L. Anslinger in Washington and Garland H. Williams, his district supervisor in New York, knew with great precision just how Joe A. was functioning and where his major games were located.

Ellis' informants confided that whenever the law felt forced to act, Joe A. got a prior warning that an "inspection" was about to be made. Then the summonses went out from Duke's, and handymen, truckers, and helpers pitched in with feverish energy. The mob's blueprint called for a flossy gambling house to be dismantled and moved in one hour. This meant that the crap tables, roulette wheels, bird cages, chemin de fer—all the devices for a frenzied evening of risk and loss—had to be carted out and loaded on waiting trucks. The costly paintings and expensive rugs and furnishings had to be transported, too, for the object was to leave nothing but bare boards for the law. When the operation went off smoothly—and Joe A.'s operations always did—the outside help who had been called in to accomplish the magic would report to Duke's the following day to be paid off. They were always happy if they found Willie or Solly Moretti on the premises when they called, for the Morettis were not stingy. They rewarded their loyal help with fat tips. On the other hand, if Guarini or one of the lesser bosses happened to be in charge, all a man got for exerting himself over and beyond the call of duty was his stipulated fee.

This intricate and smoothly functioning organization also facilitated Joe A.'s interstate operations. Roulette wheels and crap tables from Saratoga, for example, were customarily trucked into Jersey at the end of the upstate racing season, and would be stored in a warehouse until Joe A. had decided on a new location for their wintertime use. Such "locations" sprouted up all over the New Jersey countryside and even, in the later stages, stretched into the hills of Bucks County in Pennsylvania.

Bankrolled by fabulous profits, the mob was always open to money-making propositions, even legitimate ones. On one occasion a businessman who had performed some fringe services for the ring found that he needed a loan of several thousand dollars to purchase extra equipment. He telephoned Duke's and made an appointment to meet Solly Moretti there.

"I can go to Duke's, but not inside, and I'm supposed to call first," he explained subsequently to Agent Ellis.

At the appointed hour, the businessman drove to Duke's. Solly Moretti came out of the tavern, and they discussed the proposition in the parking lot. Solly agreed that the deal looked sound to him, but he made it clear that he didn't have the final authority. Just then Joe A. drove up in his Cadillac. Solly went over and explained matters to him.

"He's a right guy," he told Joe A., endorsing the applicant. "I think it's all right for us to let him have the money."

Joe A. listened without saying a word, face blank, eyes blank, not a flicker of expression betraying his thought. But the instant Solly Moretti had finished his explanation, Joe A. was ready with his verdict.

"I'll have to fix it up with Mendel," he said.

He turned to the prospective borrower.

"Come back tomorrow," he ordered.

That was the extent of the conversation. The next day, at the same hour, the applicant went to the parking lot in Duke's. Joe A.

handed him a slip of paper on which was written: "Mendel—Realty Operating Corp., 210 Main Street, Fort Lee."

"Go there. He'll take care of you," Joe A. said.

The amazed borrower had never heard of Mendel or the Realty Operating Corp., but he knew better than to ask questions. Following instructions, he went to the designated address, exhibited the slip Joe A. had given him, and asked for Mendel. A short and extremely stocky man between forty-five and fifty appeared. He had a heavy reddish face, a heavy beard, and nearly three full sets of chins. He carried an envelope with the amount of the requested loan in bills of $100 denomination. The borrower signed a series of notes, one to become due each month. He was to pay off the principal in eighteen months and then to make two extra monthly payments, a total of some 10 per cent for the accommodation. So it was settled, and the businessman departed with his money.

Joe A. was more than the generalissimo and banker of the mob; he was a bit of a playboy, too. The year of 1942 in which he began to tap the gambling gusher in New Jersey was also notable for one other event in his life. It was the year he met Virginia Hill.

Virginia was the leggy, bosomy, chestnut-haired glamor girl of the Syndicate. She had the features of a Hollywood starlet—and the temper and vocabulary of a stevedore. She wore mink like a lady—and she could sock harder than some prizefighters. She was a poor girl from a small town in Georgia, and had worked her way up through the ranks of the mob so successfully that she took hoydenish delight in tossing $7,500 champagne parties. She was a riddle of conflicting complexes, but she wasn't a very hard riddle to read. Most men had to take only one look at Virginia Hill to know the reason for her success in life. As Longy Zwillman told the Kefauver committee with ungallant candor, "She didn't look as if she would be hard to know." She had wide, voluptuous lips and smoky gray-green eyes, seductive behind half-hooded lids. Any way you looked at her, she spelled sex; and had ever since she had begun to acquire and discard husbands at the rather tender age of fifteen.

Her talents were not unique, but her artistry was far from inconsiderable. She had invaded Chicago at the time of its World's Fair in 1934, and before long there wasn't a major mobster who wasn't panting to stuff her handbag with bills. Her philosophy of life seemed to be wrapped up in a favorite saying. "A good girl isn't necessarily a nice girl," she'd tell the boys—and the boys could take it from there.

One of Virginia's first conquests in Chicago seems to have been on a different level than most, though with Virginia it was sometimes hard to tell. He was a mousy, inconspicuous, and worshipful little man named Joe Epstein, a bookie, an accountant, and the income-tax expert for the Capone mob. Joe gave Virginia a leg up and it wasn't long before she was pitching curves at some of the mightiest sluggers in the rackets.

She got to know them all, and they all got to know Virginia. She was the party girl, the star of every big mob blowout. On her calling list were Charlie Fischetti and his younger, handsomer, more suave brother, Joe; Tony Accardo, Murray (The Camel) Humphreys, and Frank Nitti—all of the Capone dynasty; Tony Gizzo from Kansas City; Carlos Marcello from New Orleans; and Frank Costello and Joe Adonis, the top men of the New York mob.

The suspicion has existed for years—the Kefauver committee was positive of it, but couldn't prove it—that Virginia Hill was more than just the sex symbol of gangdom. She was also the cash-and-carry girl, a mink-clad female treasure chest. When fortunes in cash had to be ferried from the Midwest to the East to square the balance sheet of the Syndicate, playful Virginia did the ferrying. It was a service for which she presumably was well paid and it enabled the little girl to widen her circle of acquaintances and to meet charming gentlemen like Joe Adonis.

Virginia got into the cash-and-carry business originally, as she got into so much else, through her connection with Joe Epstein. Joe had devised a system to protect his book against a big hit. If there was a heavy and potentially ruinous play on one longshot horse, he could buy insurance by laying off a big part of the load with Frank Erickson in the East, or, if the race were being run locally, he could handle it more simply by rigging the odds on the pari-mutuel machines at the Chicago track. The rigging was an operation of calculated beauty. Joe would send Virginia out to the track with his credit card; he would total his bets, figure his need, and telephone orders to a confederate just outside the track. The word would be passed along to Virginia, and at the last minute, dolled up like a millionairess, Miss Hill would flounce up to a betting booth, flash the credit card, and

plump down a big bet for Joe—say $5,000—on the nose of the menac-
ing long shot. What this did to the pari-mutuel odds was pitiful to
behold. A 10-1 long shot would be whacked down to 3-1 or even
2-1. If the long shot triumphed, Joe Epstein would collect on his
$5,000 bet, a strike that would help to make the payout from his
book relatively painless. If the long shot lost, Joe had simply spent
$5,000 for insurance, and so many bettors would have dropped so
much more on the gamble that Joe wouldn't even feel the bite. It was
a virtually foolproof system, but it called for one special ingredient
rarely found in mobdom—an absolutely trustworthy agent at the
track. If the holder of Joe Epstein's credit card ever ran amok with
it, the resultant havoc would make strong men shudder. But Virginia,
who had a cash-register mind under chestnut tresses, never ran amok
on someone else's credit; only on her own. She might toss her money
around like confetti, but she handled Joe Epstein's missions with
scrupulous honesty. She passed the qualifying test for a cash-and-carry
girl.

Once having established an enviable reputation for reliability,
Virginia found a glorious future opening up before her. She filled a
need of the Syndicate, namely: When the heavily bet races that
menaced the bookies' bank balances were being run out of town,
the pari-mutuel figures could not be jiggered by last-minute bets
placed by the voluptuous Virginia; then the only protection was the
layoff deal with Frank Erickson in Bergen County. Sometimes Joe
Epstein and his brother bookies in Chicago ended up owing pudgy
Frank as much as $30,000 on the day's play. Naturally, they couldn't
pay off by check; checks and bank balances can be traced, and when
they are, they expose too much about the mechanics and the interstate ties of the mob. The debt, then, had to be satisfied in cash, and
this meant that someone had to convey the cash to New York. Well-
known gangsters always ran the risk of being stopped by some inquisitive detective, and if this happened when they were ferrying such
abundant riches, explanations obviously would be embarrassing. On
the other hand, a beautiful and glamorous girl could go where she
wanted, do what she wanted, see whom she wanted—and no questions asked. Trustworthy Virginia was ideal for the role. Before long
she was practically on a commuter's schedule between Chicago and
New York. She rode the Twentieth Century Limited, an extra-fare

train; she always had a bedroom to herself; and she always seemed to be carrying an extra, especially heavy purse. When she was asked about these trips by Kefauver aides in private questioning, Virginia gave them her hooded, gray-eyed stare, shrugged her shapely, sloping shoulders and quipped: "Maybe I just liked to ride on trains."

Her train-riding brought her into the orbit of Joe Adonis. Both Virginia and Joe A. were always quite reticent about the nature of their relationship. In fact, Joe A. was so reticent he wouldn't even admit to the Kefauver committee that he had ever known the lady. The lady herself wasn't quite *that* bashful. She was a little coy, a trait not ordinarily associated with Virginia Hill, but she was much more frank than Joe A.

In her private revelations to the Kefauver group, Virginia said this was the way it all happened:

She was on one of her regular jaunts into New York sometime in 1942, as she recalled it, and one evening she was perched at the bar in the Madison Hotel, enjoying liquid refreshment like a lady, when a cafe-society playboy who had been playing around brought over a stocky, darkly handsome, extremely well-dressed gentleman of quiet voice and manners.

"Virginia," said Cafe Playboy, "this is Mr. Adams."

Innocent Virginia was quite taken with "Mr. Adams." She sighed and her distinctive gray-green eyes grew soft as she recalled for Kefauver probers years later this momentous introduction. Of course, she explained, she had no idea who "Mr. Adams" was; why, no idea at all. How could she? He was just so nice and so charming that the shy little soul of Virginia was quite captivated by him; in practically no time at all, she discovered that they made a dandy twosome on the town. They had, said Virginia, about half-a-dozen dates before she even realized that the suave and soft-spoken "Mr. Adams" was really Joe Adonis, one of the authentic terrors of American gangdom. This discovery, it seems, didn't trouble Virginia; she valued her men for themselves and never judged them by their reputations. She kept on seeing that kindly gentleman who had told her at first his name was "Mr. Adams," but it was all just in good fun, you know.

The fun lasted, however, for a long time. When Virginia was smitten with the movie craze and went to Hollywood in an effort to break into pictures, Joe Adonis found occasion for frequent "business trips" to the West Coast. He was such a constant visitor, indeed, that Hollywood gossip columnists noted he had been seen strolling hand-in-hand with Virginia on Sunset Strip or dining with her in a quiet, softly lighted corner of the Trocadero. All of this went on despite the fact that Virginia was known in Hollywood as Buggsy Siegel's "girl." She and Buggsy had fallen hard for each other soon after she arrived; but when Joe Adonis appeared, Buggsy was little in evidence, another indication perhaps of the high rating of "Mr. A." Some rumormongers even insinuated that there was a crass financial consideration involved in the blooming romance of Miss and Mr. Syndicate. Virginia squandered money on Hollywood parties, and the underworld opined that not even Buggsy Siegel could keep her in this style—only "Mr. A." The story was that Joe A. used to leave blank checks on her boudoir night table; but Virginia said why, no, she couldn't recall Joe A. ever doing a thing like that. All he ever gave her was charm and a good time; no money, no money at all.

This picture was at least in character as far as Joe A. was concerned. Certainly, he was never in the habit of leaving blank checks around, even for so bounteously packaged a doll as Virginia. But this story of innocent romance doesn't ring quite so true when considered from Virginia's standpoint. The idea that Miss Syndicate would waste her time even on Joe A. without some token of his affection is slightly ridiculous. Virginia Hill simply didn't operate that way.

She made this clear in her dramatic public session before the Kefauver committee. It was a highly explosive performance. Virginia charged into the hearing room wearing a wide-brimmed hat and a platinum mink stole that practically swept the floor. She opened with a volley of curses and closed the same way. Both expressions of her inner disposition were triggered by the annoying persistence of photographers. Virginia, who would have enjoyed preening herself before the Hollywood cameras, didn't relish staging a free show before popping flash bulbs in New York's Federal Courthouse. She swore at the cameramen like a top sergeant, and instructed the committee: "Make them stop doing that. I'll throw something in a minute."

Then she told the rags-to-rackets story of the poor little girl from Georgia. She admitted calmly that she had known, and known well, all the rulers of the mob from coast to coast.

The committee was convinced that Virginia could expose the inner mechanics of the Syndicate if she would, and its members dwelt repeatedly on her most obviously vulnerable point—scads of unexplained cash. Here was a girl who had parlayed her natural assets into continent-wide fame as a spendthrift and lavish party-giver. She had once bought a New York nightclub so she could spend her money in her own spot; she had blown $11,251 in just five weeks at Sun Valley, Idaho; she habitually left bartenders $4.50 tips for 50 cent drinks; she tossed away $7,500 on a one-night affair with champagne in Hollywood. And she had done all this, according to her income-tax returns, on total revenues of $20,000 in 1943, $15,000 in 1944, $16,000 in 1945, and $23,780 in 1946. This conflict with logic was later to turn Miss Virginia into an expatriate, living in Europe to avoid confrontation with an $80,000 income-tax indictment waiting for her at home; but at the time of the Kefauver hearings, such unpleasant-ness was in the future. The committee was just laying the groundwork, and what it wanted Miss Hill to explain was where the money had all come from.

Virginia said it was really quite simple. There were just two pivots to her success formula: first, men; second, horses. The men gave her money, and the horses won. She spoke gratefully of both. Of the horses: "I won it on the horses. I'm just lucky, I guess." Of the men: "Well, fellows would give me things. I would go out with them— like lots of girls did—and they would give me presents. . . . The fellows gave those parties for me. I would not spend my money for those parties. There were always plenty of fellows who wanted to give parties for me."

That was all there was to it. As for crime, Virginia Hill hadn't the faintest idea. She had always gone out of the room when the boys talked business; she had just closed her pretty ears. Federal narcotics agents had been most annoying. They had followed her around all over the country on the theory that, on trips back and forth to Mexico, she might have carried with her some packets of narcotics; but Vir-ginia snapped angrily that she had done no such thing, she didn't know anything about narcotics, she didn't know anything about crime, she didn't know anything.

The strain of the long nonexplanation obviously had frazzled the lady's nerves, and as she stormed out of the hearing room, she let off steam in characteristic fashion. Reporters and photographers trailed her, hoping for final revelations, and they weren't completely dis-appointed. At the elevator bank, Miss Syndicate whirled and planted a gloved right fist squarely on the jaw of slim Marjorie Farnsworth, a reporter for the *New York Journal-American*. Out on the street, heading for a cab, the mob's glamor girl treated reporters to a sample of her invective. After a long series of expressive if not very original epithets, she finished off the photographers with a still-remembered exit line: "You goddamn bastards! I hope an atom bomb falls on all of you."

It was quite a performance, even for Virginia Hill. Yet it was little more than a mild indication of the lady's capabilities. The Senators, in their private session with Miss Syndicate, had been shown even more graphic examples. The first had come when the curious Senator Tobey tried to find out just what special quality had made Virginia Hill the undisputed queen of gangdom.

"Young lady," he asked, "what makes you the favorite of the underworld?"

Virginia took a deep breath and let him have it. It was an answer so earthy that it practically curled the snowy mane of the Bible-quoting Senator from New Hampshire.

While the Senators were still whirling from this one, Miss Hill gave their investigators further insight into the range of her talents. She described the night that she had told off, collectively and individually, some of the most powerful and most dreaded mobsters in America. It had been, by her own account at least, a fantastic scene in which she stood up alone against the rulers of the midwestern ring of the Syndicate. The report, buried in the private Kefauver archives, tells a lot about the Syndicate and the men who rule it.

The event that caused Miss Syndicate to pop her chestnut top is to be found in the murder of Buggsy Siegel. Virginia, evidently, had never forgiven the mob for killing her lover. Three times after Buggsy's demise she became so disconsolate that she overstocked on sleeping pills. Each time—once in Mexico City, again in Miami, and finally in Phoenix, Arizona—stomach pumps saved her life. The Christmas season of 1949 found Virginia back in Chicago, with the glamor of her mob-queen role somewhat worn off. Tight lines of discontent creased her forehead between her eyebrows, and the edges of her wide, curving mouth were harsh, deep-bitten when not adequately camouflaged by makeup. She spent long afternoons in the Clover Bar, gazing across the street at the spot where once had stood the restaurant in which she met Joe Epstein and started on her rise in the rackets. Evenings she would dine at Ciro's or the Chez Paree or the Well of the Sea. She still threw fantastic tips to waiters, but the zip was gone. Miss Syndicate was living in her past, and she knew it.

In this mood she decided to call it quits—but on her own terms. She would throw a last party, a New Year's Eve party that no czar of the Syndicate would ever forget. That she could plan with such certainty seems almost to confirm a persistent report heard by Kefauver investigators. According to this version, Virginia Hill had written some life insurance on herself by setting down in detail her true story—never told on the witness stand. This account contained all the detailed, inside information about gambling, extortion, vice, payoffs—and murders. It named each czar, identified his special field, listed his total take; it was specific about the dates of payoffs to politicians for the protection of the rackets and the fixing of paroles. The most precious secrets of the underworld were contained in this true diary of Virginia Hill, just one step away from revelation; and Virginia had let the mob bosses know that if anything should happen to her it would be just too bad for them, for this masterpiece, packed away in a safe deposit vault, would go directly to the Attorney General of the United States.

Such was the report. It received wide credence, and perhaps accounted for the almost submissive attendance of the redoubtable bosses of the Midwest mob at Virginia Hill's farewell party. Her much-publicized bouts with sleeping pills had made her by this time almost anathema to them, an unenviable headline risk; but she obviously was a lady whom they did not wish to displease. When she summoned them, they came—Charlie Fischetti, Tony Accardo, Murray (The Camel) Humphreys, Joe Aiuppa, even aging Jack (Greasy Thumb) Guzik who was no longer a party boy. These and a lot of others rallied to Virginia's call. The liquor flowed, the atmosphere grew gay almost like old times; but when midnight struck, instead of kissing games, Virginia introduced a new note.

She climbed up on a chair, and she made a speech. Facing her group of guests, as dangerous a bunch as America has ever bred, she screamed and railed and called them every vile name in her extensive vocabulary. She began with gentle designations like murderers, thieves, pikers, chiselers, panderers, lice—and went on from there. She named names and held each mob boss up for a tongue-lashing, and some of the most murderous curs in America sat there and cringed—and took it.

The picture of vituperative Virginia Hill, contemptuously flicking off the emperors of the mob and getting away with it, speaks volumes about Virginia's detailed knowledge and about the characters of the men who had supplied her with it. They wouldn't challenge even a woman unless all the cards were stacked in their favor.

9

THE RACKETS BUST A RACKET-BUSTER

MONEY gives the worst elements of American society domination over the best. The "well-charactered" hoodlums who cringed before the lash of Virginia Hill's unladylike tongue—hands steeped in murder, the double cross emblazoned as their ethic—were some of the most ruthless, unprincipled, despicable villains in America, but they had virtually limitless wealth and all the power that goes with it. As Abe Reles had said, they were out to "get America by the pocketbook," completely cynical in their conviction that with a stranglehold on the purse-strings they could purchase complete immunity for every deed. And seldom were they proved wrong.

Getting America by the pocketbook called for amassing incredible mountains of illicit cash. The volume of money involved staggers the imagination. The very magnitude of the deal, however, carries its own built-in protection; as with the Mafia's whole conception of an "invisible government" of crime, incredulity is one of the strongest deterrents to an aroused public reaction. Yet, to appreciate the insidious influence of the mob, to realize how high and how far this influence extends, one must first understand its virtually boundless financial resources.

Let's take a deeper look at the entire complex of criminal enterprises that Joe Adonis and his Crime Cabinet ran from Duke's. As a primer in this educational process, let's examine the two huge gambling games that were running wide open in December, 1945. Again, Federal Narcotics Agent Ross B. Ellis gathered the information.

The first of these games was being conducted at 1025 McBride Avenue, West Paterson, New Jersey, just over the line in Passaic County. The mob had paid $22,500 in cash for the premises and had spent a small fortune on interior improvements. A staff of fifty well-paid employees was required. The investment was large, but the profits were enormous.

Summarizing Ellis' information, District Supervisor Williams in New York wrote:

"It is conservatively estimated that the average nightly 'play' over the three crap tables, four roulette wheels and three chemin de fer tables is considerably in excess of one million dollars. The house 'take' from this play is unknown. . . ."

The bureau subsequently estimated that Joe A. and Willie Moretti must have been reaping a gross profit of about *$100,000 a week* from the play in this one establishment on McBride Avenue; but even this estimate may have been conservative. On the average straight, "honest" percentages favor the house in this proportion: 1.42 per cent on straight dice bets, with a larger edge on side or "proposition" bets; a 5.26 per cent edge on roulette; 3 per cent at faro and up to 20 per cent on slot machines. If the games are rigged, these percentages, of course, can be raised considerably. Joe A. always protested that he ran an "honest" house and that sometimes he came out the loser on a total night's play. These protestations must be viewed with skepticism. In a lifelong career in crime, Joe A. had always been a devotee of the most ruthless strongarm and extortion methods. The idea that he would operate costly gambling houses and let the clientele escape with just the normal house edge against them appears unlikely.

At the same time that his West Paterson casino was producing a nightly fortune, Joe A. was operating an equally lucrative game miles away in South Plainfield in Middlesex County. This was a "sawdust" crap game with exceptionally high stakes. On December 12, 1945, Ross Ellis, acting on information that he had gathered from inside-the-mob sources, paid a visit to the South Plainfield establishment. It was located some two miles from the main highway down a lonely country road, ideally isolated, with the nearest house about

200 yards to the south. Around the gambling joint was a parking lot capable of accommodating 150 cars. Guards were stationed along the road, and each car as it approached with its payload of players had to blink its lights in a recognition signal. Ellis, having learned of these protective arrangements in advance, made a stealthy reconnaissance on foot. He found that, although cars were constantly coming and going, from seventy to ninety were always in the parking lot between midnight and 3:30 A.M. Since each car brought four or five patrons —a service for which the drivers and cabbies were paid a standard fee of $20 a night apiece—there were always several hundred inside the house making their individual contributions to the bankroll of gangdom. It was not intended that they should escape cheaply or easily. There was only one crap table where one could gamble for as little as $5. Other tables had $10, $20, and $50 minima, and there was one where the figure was $1,000. Ellis, assessing all of this information, concluded conservatively that "several hundred thousand dollars pass over these tables each night."

He found tacit confirmation of his estimate in the edgy wakefulness of the mob itself For the South Plainfield establishment was guarded as if it were Fort Knox. Along the road outside the house, two guards armed with submachine guns were constantly on the prowl. "Both submachine guns carried had the drum type clip so assume they were Thompson submachine guns . . . ," Agent Ellis wrote in his report. "One of the guards so armed passed within 20 feet of your agent on one occasion. . . . From the elaborate guard setup it can be deduced that they have a tremendous investment and are extremely afraid of a holdup."

Ellis' major discoveries during his sleuthing mission to South Plainfield were corroborated by an incident that occurred shortly afterwards. A group of well-heeled Hudson County playboys, who had learned the location of the big South Plainfield game but apparently had not been apprised of its protective arrangements, decided that they would go and see if all the fabulous tales they had heard were true. As they drove along the approach road, the outside guards blinked flashlights at them. The visitors, not aware that their car headlights must be blinked in return, drove serenely on. Suddenly there was a shout from the underbrush, followed by a fusillade. Submachine-gun bullets, aimed low, kicked up dirt all around the tires of the approaching car. White and shaken, the visiting players braked to an abrupt halt.

"Where do you think you're going?" an angry guard, weapon at the ready, demanded of the driver.

The visitors breathlessly explained their mission, with stress on the innocence of their intentions. The guards eventually were convinced.

"All right," one of them said. "You can go on, but if you come again, don't forget to blink your lights."

Recovering from his fright, one of the players asked curiously whether the guards weren't afraid of waking up the police with all this loud gunplay.

"Oh, we don't have to worry about the police," the guard replied. "It's a holdup we're afraid of."

This fear was certainly well justified, the players concluded, once they were inside the gambling hall. So many bills of large denominations were lying around on the tables that the newcomers were flabbergasted. After they had recovered enough to count, their tally showed that, on any given roll of the dice, at least $100,000 was at stake. And the rolls were fast and furious all night along.

Inevitably, with gunplay in the night and motorcades rolling along the highways at the most unlikely early-morning hours, even Joe A. and the Syndicate could not keep word of such Golcondas as the West Paterson and South Plainfield halls of chance from seeping out into the press. The *Newark News,* New Jersey's largest newspaper, focused a critical spotlight on the colorful West Paterson operation and correctly described it as a Joe Adonis gambling game. In the face of such exposure, it became necessary for authorities to go through some investigative paces. Attorney General Walter D. Van Riper asked Prosecutor Manfield M. G. Amlicke, of Passaic County, to look into the truth of such allegations and report. On January 6, 1946, the Prosecutor informed the Attorney General that his staff had made "several investigations" of the McBride Avenue premises, some even before the *Newark News* article had appeared, and had failed to discover any traces of gambling. His agents had been told, Amlicke said, that the place was just "a businessman's club and restaurant, catering to members, their wives and friends exclusively." Van Riper added that he had asked the Federal Bureau of Investigation whether it had any information about the law's being broken in nightly gambling at McBride Avenue, and the FBI assured him that it had not. The implication was that, once more, the press had indulged in gross exaggeration.

Dealing with the South Plainfield embarrassment was not quite so simple. The Hudson County players, returning from their safari, told of their adventure and described the heavy wagering and the gunplay in the night. Sometime later the *Newark News* sent to the scene two reporters who proved better sleuths than the detectives: they actually found the gambling establishment. Once more publicity produced a brief official flurry. On February 1, 1947, Prosecutor Matthew F. Melko announced in New Brunswick that his agents had raided the South Plainfield game which he called "the biggest dice game in the East." Just how the Prosecutor could know this was not quite clear, for his raiders had found the place deserted. One man tinkering with his car some distance up the road was arrested. But in the gambling hall itself all that the detectives garnered for their initiative was a bunch of $1,000 money wrappers that had been discarded and were littering the floor. Prosecutor Melko confided sadly that he suspected there had been "a tipoff."

Such were the rewards of the mob for flouting the gambling laws in New Jersey; what the rewards of the law were for permitting all this have never been estimated. A rule-of-thumb, vouched for by Milton Wessel and other racket experts, holds that in such operations the lawless and the law usually split the profits fifty-fifty. This may help to explain why, during the decade the Jersey rackets ran wide open, newspaper reporters could always find abundant evidence of what was going on—and the law could never find anything.

It would be a mistake, however, to suppose that even a play of $1 million a night at a couple of flourishing gambling traps represented the major resource of the mob. On the contrary, the McBride Avenue and South Plainfield establishments, remunerative as they were, actually counted as no more than a couple of tributaries flowing into the great mainstream of the Combination's wealth.

Consider District Attorney Hogan's discovery, when he managed to seize the records of Frank Erickson, that the king of the bookies had been in partnership with Meyer and Jake Lansky, Joe Adonis, and others in gambling at the Colonial Inn just outside of Miami. Erickson's records showed $685,538.76 in net profits in just one twelve-month period. This, remember, was Erickson's own official accounting, and the Colonial Inn was just one casino; other gambling traps in Florida, Saratoga, and Las Vegas were pouring in additional cascades of treasure.

Consider, too, the take from bookmaking—with wide-open horse rooms and a fantastically elaborate telephone network—which probably surpassed the take from gambling. Frank Erickson's own income-tax returns, not likely to be inflated indicators of his rewards as layoff king of the nation, showed net income of: $184,354.71 in 1946; $194,841.35 in 1947; $169,819.58 in 1948; and a mere $113,460.25 in 1949. Such figures probably only hinted at Erickson's total take. He himself casually admitted that he paid one man $20,000 a year just to bank his money for him; he made a practice, so investigators said, of keeping $500,000 in cash lying around, in case of an emergency. Three "dummy" Erickson bank accounts uncovered by New York investigators in a New Jersey bank in 1945 showed deposits totaling $6,683,362.20 in a little more than four years. And all this was just Erickson's share of receipts at the top of the bookmaking racket, his reward for handling the potentially dangerous layoff play. The sucker play that didn't have to be laid off was inevitably much heavier than this. Throughout Bergen County, at the peak of the operation, bookies rented some 2,600 individual home phones to handle the heavy daily play from New York. One official estimate insisted that *four billion dollars a year* was wagered over this network.

As a result, one New Jersey State Senator charged on the floor of the legislature that the Syndicate of Crime was making a gross profit of *one million dollars a day* out of the Jersey rackets. The sum was so grandiose that it was jeered as a wild exaggeration; but, considering the enormity of established figures, it was perhaps closer to the truth than most persons were willing to concede.

The corruptive power of such staggering sums of money virtually defies description, as hearings before a state legislative committee later were to demonstrate.

It infected the humble householder who was delighted to rent out his phone for $50 a week to a bookie using it to take bets a few hours each day.

It infected the police departments and the local governments in at least ten Bergen County towns, spread out along the west bank of the Hudson. To a man, they saw no evil and heard no evil, and when evil reared its ugly head, they insisted it was a mirage that, if you just blinked, would go away.

It infected the county, whose law-enforcement officials were as blind as the local cops and whose Prosecutor once expressed doubt that Erickson and Costello even knew where Bergen County was.

It infected the state; in Trenton, the highest officials in New Jersey turned their heads aside for years, and neither saw nor heard—not even when New York officials publicly announced that the underworld had set up shop in Bergen.

And, in the end, it affected even the prosecution of murder. For when Willie Moretti was finally bumped off at high noon in a public restaurant, the investigation of his violent departure was pressed at such a gingerly pace that a state legislative committee later concluded it was marked more by fear to learn than an eagerness to solve.

Doubtless the most corrosive single influence was the bookie telephone network. The mob's offer of $50 a week just to let one of its agents have exclusive use of a householder's phone between noon and 6 P.M. proved irresistible to thousands of persons. On nights when there were fights or college basketball games, the visiting bookie might require use of the phone until 9:30 P.M., but he was always quiet and unobtrusive. And for accommodating him, there was that windfall of $50 a week! When rackets-buster Nelson Stamler tried to clean up Bergen, he encountered an almost universally corrupted public opinion. Again and again he heard the same refrains: "Everybody's doing the same thing. What's wrong with it?" And: "What about the cop on the street? He makes fifty bucks a week, and he has a big home and a flashy convertible that must have cost a year's salary. Where do you think he got that kind of dough?"

Stamler found that corruption began at the top, with the politicians and officials sworn to uphold the law, and that cynicism for all law soon seeped down to the average individual. A graphic example of this occurred before a Bergen County grand jury long before Stamler was sent into the county. An assistant prosecutor, one of the few who tried to do something about the situation, had developed a flawless case against a bookie. He wanted an indictment. But the jury balked and refused to indict. "What do you want us to do?" one of the jurors asked. "Indict ourselves?"

In a county where even a lowly bookie had an almost completely perverted public sentiment on his side, Joe A. and his fellow mob bosses didn't have to worry. For them the protection was even more ironclad, and more active. Investigators who tried to cross the river to spy on them were harassed out of town by local cops.

District Attorney Hogan's men learned the hard way that, when they tried to get evidence against Joe Adonis, they had to contend not just with the mob, but with brother officers of the law on the west bank of the Hudson. As long as Joe A. stayed in his tight little empire across the river, Hogan couldn't touch him. But if he came over to New York, if he engaged in illegal activity there, Hogan would be free to pounce. The only way to catch Adonis in the act of crime was to set a plant over his New Jersey home and tail him when he came out on the longshot chance that he might commit an indiscretion justifying his arrest.

Consequently, two of Hogan's detectives drove to New Jersey and parked diagonally down the street from Joe A.'s home at 1020 Dearborn Road, Palisades Park. The house was a square, block-like structure, large, of solid brick, with six white pillars supporting the curved portico above its front entrance. Its windows were elongated loopholes, high, narrow, and arched at the top. It was a fort-like, gloomily protective house that squatted on a well-groomed plot 75 by 100 feet; and, interestingly enough, it was located only three-and-a-half blocks from the more imposing, Spanish-type mansion of Joe A.'s confederate in crime, Albert Anastasia.

Hogan's detectives had been parked down the street from Joe A.'s residence only a short time when a local police car came cruising along, drew up, and stopped.

"What are you fellows doing here?" the local cop wanted to know.

"We're detectives from New York," Hogan's sleuths explained.

"Doesn't make any difference who you are," the cop insisted. "Nobody parks here. Come on, get moving."

Dumbfounded, Hogan's detectives drove off, feeling more like the hunted than the hunters. But they were persistent men. Time and again they returned to Jersey and tried to set up watch near that solid brick house at 1020 Dearborn Road; and time after time they would be chased away.

Years afterwards, O'Connor and Seidler, the assistants who handled the New Jersey investigation for Hogan, would shake their heads in disbelief as they recalled the manner in which the forces of Jersey law cooperated with the mob in fighting off investigations by the law.

"Our fellows would hardly get over there when they would see the local cops coming," Seidler said. "Trying to stall for time, they'd jump out and raise the hood, pretending they had engine trouble. But this didn't fool the local cops for a minute. 'Come on,' they'd say in bored tones. 'We know you guys. Get moving.'"

Hogan's detectives weren't the only ones who found the ever-watchful law casting a protective mantle over Joe A.'s castle at 1020 Dearborn Road. Newspaper reporters and even U.S. Treasury agents were rushed as well.

Irving Lieberman of the New York *Post* had an experience almost identical to that of Hogan's agents. He had been sent out to interview Joe A. Turned away at the door, he went back to his car to wait and watch, hoping to catch the overlord of gangdom leaving his home. In a few minutes, a local cop came cruising along and snapped: "Move along, move along. Nobody is allowed to park around here." Irv, a short, wiry, and tenacious reporter, pretended to obey the order. He drove around several blocks, then returned to his original observation post. His car motor had not cooled before another police car drove alongside, and a man in a police lieutenant's uniform called to him: "Follow me to the police station." Having no choice, Irv obeyed. Once inside the station house, the lieutenant whirled on him. "You're going to get out of town and get right away," he declared. When Irv started to protest, the lieutenant cut him off abruptly. "You got no business here," he said. "You get right back where you came from. Get out of here—and stay out." And that was that.

Agents of the Intelligence Unit of the U.S. Internal Revenue Bureau didn't fare any better. Fully aware of the tremendous flow of cash into the hands of the mob in Bergen County, Treasury agents tried to shadow some of the racketeers in the hope of developing income-tax cases against them; but, just like Hogan's detectives and reporter Irving Lieberman, the revenuers were shadowed, badgered, hounded by local cops.

"They were always on the lookout for us," one Treasury agent said later. "It got so bad that the police chief in one North Jersey town would be on our tails almost the minute we crossed the bridge. We had to take two or three cars and split up and go off in all directions at once, and some of us would get rid of him—for a little while any-how."

When the protection was so ironclad that even U.S. Treasury agents could be run out of town, the dominance of the lawless over the law had achieved its fullest expression. The underworld, indeed, was running the world—and nobody seemed to care.

For the underworld, the impossible was only an obstacle to be overcome. Sometimes, it became the possible in one gigantic leap, as happened on February 2, 1946, when Charles (Lucky) Luciano, living up to his nickname, was sprung from a virtual life sentence in prison.

Gov. Thomas E. Dewey, who as a young rackets-buster had put Luciano behind bars, was the man who, in later years and from the more mellow vantage point of the governor's chair, commuted Luciano's sentence and released one of the most dangerous criminal minds of our times. It was a startling about-face; and behind it lay an equally startling rationale—that Charlie Lucky deserved his freedom because he had been such a great wartime patriot that, in other circumstances, he might have received the Congressional Medal of Honor. Though this explanation was ridiculed at the time, there was at least one hard nugget of disgusting truth in it: the American military during the war, intent only on victory, actually had entered into a working partnership with the Mafia.

Norman Lewis in *The Honored Society* has recounted in great detail how American invasion forces, almost the moment they landed on the shores of Sicily, got into direct contact with Mafia chieftains whom Mussolini had not succeeded in exterminating. On July 14, 1943, Lewis recounts, an American fighter plane flew low over the town of Villalba and dropped a packet that fell near the church. A yellow flag, displaying the letter "L" in black, had been stretched over one side of the plane. The packet dropped near the church contained a smaller replica of this flag, and it was passed along promptly to Don Calogero Vizzini, the ruler of the Sicilian Mafia. Shortly afterwards, when American tanks appeared upon the scene, one of them flew the distinctive "L" flag. Don Calo at once appeared, identified himself by displaying the flag that had been dropped, and helped, to some degree at least, to smooth the path for the Sicilian conquest. The upshot, according to Lewis, was that the American military were so impressed by the knowledge, efficiency, and goodwill of these anti-Mussolini "patriots" whom they had discovered in the Sicilian countryside that they armed their wonderful collaborators

and turned the machinery of local government over to Don Calo—
and the Mafia.

There can be little question that the yellow-and-black "L" flag was
a symbol that stood for "Luciano." Lewis writes:

> The exchange of silk handkerchiefs, in fact, had become the
> equivalent of a Mafia password when an identity had to be
> established. In 1922, for instance, a certain Lollo, an associate
> member of the Mafia in Villalba, committed a murder so out-
> rageously ill-planned, and carried out with such an arrogant dis-
> regard for concealment, that his arrest and conviction were in-
> evitable. Don Calo, by a certain flexing of his powers, arranged
> to have Lollo supplied with false identity documents and smug-
> gled to the United States. On his arrival in New York, Lollo was
> met by a group of friends who had been alerted to expect him,
> and to these he identified himself by a yellow silk handkerchief
> given him by Don Calo, which in this instance carried the initial
> "C." The bold black "L" on the flags at Villalba on those fateful
> days in July stood for "Luciano." Lucky Luciano, originally
> Salvatore Lucania, had been born in Lercara Friddi, the next
> town of any size up the main road from Villalba to Palermo,
> and, as head of the Mafia in the United States—which he had
> almost certainly become—Luciano would have been in regular
> contact with his opposite number in Sicily. There has, of course,
> been considerable speculation what, if any, *quid pro quo* was
> offered Luciano for his services, but there is no doubt that in
> 1946 he was freed from prison . . . and deported to Italy. No
> unassailable evidence of any overt connection between Don Calo
> and Luciano emerged until later that year, when they occupied
> adjoining suites in a Palermo hotel.

Lewis' account spells out the murky background of deeds that
respectable society is not too principled to commit, just too fastidious
to acknowledge. Though Dewey justified his release of Luciano on
the grounds of patriotic wartime services and the custom of releasing
prisoners, even murderers, if they were deportable, no one in authority would ever acknowledge that Charlie Lucky had distinguished
himself by contributions of inestimable value. What appears from the
sketchy and embarrassed official record, as it was dragged out in
the Kefauver committee inquiry, is essentially this:

In 1942, Naval Intelligence was greatly concerned about the danger of sabotage and espionage along the sprawling New York water-

front. The great French liner *Normandie,* converted to a troopship capable of carrying an entire division, had burned and sunk at her Manhattan pier in a mysterious disaster; German submarines seemed to be supplied with uncannily accurate information about sailing dates and cargoes of convoys bound for England. Navy Intelligence was anxious to establish a counterforce on the waterfront, and it was suggested that perhaps the underworld mobs could help. Some of the more scrupulous officers at Navy Headquarters at 90 Church Street reacted with horror, but urgency overrode ethical sensibilities.

The late Lt. Cmdr. Charles Haffenden (USNR) was placed in charge of Operation Underworld Counterespionage. Haffenden contacted District Attorney Hogan, and Hogan assigned Murray Gurfein, then his assistant in charge of the rackets bureau, to work with the Navy. With Gurfein's help, an approach was made to Joseph (Socks) Lanza, czar of extortion in the huge Fulton Fish Market and the neighboring Lower East Side docks. Lanza was then under indictment and about to go to trial, and Gurfein made it clear to him he could expect no deal. "Socks" decided to be a patriot and help anyway, but shortly afterwards he told Haffenden there were "certain elements" along the waterfront who wouldn't cooperate unless they got the word from Charlie Lucky.

Again Haffenden contacted Gurfein. The assistant DA telephoned Moses Polakoff, Luciano's lawyer, and Polakoff reported back that he had discussed the situation with Meyer Lansky, who in turn had broached the matter to Charlie Lucky. The ex-whoremaster of Manhattan was confined at the time in Dannemora, a prison in the farthest reaches of upstate New York. He let it be known that he felt he couldn't cooperate very effectively from this remote distance, and so arrangements were quietly made for his transfer to Great Meadow Prison, just north of Albany, the "country club" of New York State penal institutions.

With Luciano ensconced in more comfortable surroundings, there now began a fantastic series of pilgrimages from New York to Albany. Polakoff and "Socks" Lanza made the first trip and explained the proposition to Charlie Lucky. Polakoff said later that Luciano appeared surprised, but agreed to do whatever he could to help. So, during the next three years, Polakoff made some two dozen such trips to Great Meadow, ten with Meyer Lansky, three or four with Lanza before "Socks" himself was sent to prison, nine with Mike

Lescari, one with Costello, one with Willie Moretti, and one with Mike Miranda. Polakoff always insisted that he had no idea what was discussed during these prison conferences held under the aegis of Naval Intelligence; he always sat off to one side, and besides everybody was jabbering away in Italian.

Just what Charlie Lucky told such emissaries, whether in sheer patriotism they always discussed only the affairs of war and nothing else, are mysteries that probably never will be resolved. According to some versions, Charlie Lucky sent out word to the boys—to Joe Adonis heading the Crime Cabinet in Duke's, to Albert Anastasia whose brother, Tough Tony, ruled an impressive stretch of Brooklyn docks, and to Vincent Mangano, general overlord of the Brooklyn piers. That these orders were effective is suggested by the fact there was virtually no sabotage in the vital port of New York during the remainder of the war.

Even if one grants that Charlie Lucky made notable contributions to the war effort, some thorny problems remain in considering the generosity with which he was rewarded. Did his actions justify release from prison after serving only nine and a half years of his thirty-to-fifty-year sentence? There were many who didn't think so. One of these was Supreme Court Justice Philip J. McCook, who had originally imposed sentence on Luciano. In 1943, George Wolf, who represented both Costello and Luciano, argued before Justice McCook that Luciano's patriotic endeavors entitled him to a reduced sentence of ten years, an action that would automatically have made him eligible for parole. But Justice McCook ruled that it would be wrong to liberate the boss of crime when many of his henchmen were serving longer stretches for far more trivial offenses.

Rebuffs such as this never discourage the underworld. The Mafiosi are always convinced there is a way, if one can but find it; and when one tactic fails, they try another—and another and another. With their money and contacts, many tactics are open to them. In Luciano's case, they decided upon an end run around the obstruction of Justice McCook; on V-E day, Luciano's astute mouthpieces, Polakoff and Wolf, applied to the New York State Parole Board for clemency, again citing Luciano's high patriotism and noteworthy, but unspecified, contributions to the Allies' triumphant cause.

Now some strange things began to happen. New York gossip columns of the time noted rumors in underworld circles that large sums were being amassed to finance Charlie Lucky's expensive tussle with the law. One columnist reported that $100,000 had been raised to meet "legal expenses." Across the nation minions of the mob were moaning in pain. The word evidently had gone out from Joe A.'s Crime Cabinet in Duke's, and heavy assessments had been imposed on the bankrolls of mobsters throughout the country. Out in St. Louis, Paul Meskil, a reporter with a flair for knowing what goes on in the underworld, found all of his mob acquaintances wearing faces hounddog sad.

"They're breakin' our backs to kick in to get this big sonofabitch out of jail in the East," victims of the special assessment complained.

Underworld scuttlebutt has long insisted that, by such cross-continent effort, some $250,000 was raised to defray Charlie Lucky's "legal expenses." Whether this sizable fund had anything to do with the outcome, no man can say; but it should perhaps be noted that Socks Lanza, whose patriotism by all accounts had equaled Charlie Lucky's, did not receive equal consideration from the law. He served out his seven-and-a-half-to-fifteen-year term.

Only for Charlie Lucky was liberation to come prematurely. The New York State Parole Board recommended that his sentence be commuted; and, since Charlie Lucky in his less patriotic days had never bothered to become a naturalized citizen, it also suggested he be shipped directly back to his native Italy. Governor Dewey went along with the parole board and signed the order for Charlie Lucky's release and deportation.

Almost instantly there occurred a scene that should have given the Governor second thoughts, for it was another of those brazen incidents that seemed to say the underworld does indeed rule the world of law and order. On February 9, 1946, just a week after Dewey had acted, Luciano was taken from Ellis Island and escorted by immigration officials to Pier 7 at the Bush Terminal in Brooklyn. There he was to be placed aboard the frowzy little Liberty ship *Laura Keene* for the voyage back to his homeland.

Immigration officials had invited reporters to a shipboard press conference with Luciano, and quite a crowd gathered for the anticipated face-to-face meeting with the overlord of the New York rackets. The newsmen and photographers had proper passes and, in addition, were accompanied by Harry Ratzke, the Immigration Bureau's assistant superintendent of security. But, as the group approached the pier entrance, they found their way barred by a line of fifty tough-looking Anastasia dock wallopers. All carried ugly, sharp-pointed bailing hooks.

When Luciano drove up at 2:30 P.M., he was greeted with an outburst of cheering, but when reporters tried to follow for the shipboard interview, they found their way blocked.

"Nobody goes on the pier because somebody might get hoited," one of Anastasia's stooges told them. "We gotta watch out for lawsuits. Somebody might trip over something."

Ratzke, informed of this decision, snapped: "That's nonsense. Follow me."

But it quickly became apparent that the authority of an Immigration Bureau assistant superintendent didn't count for much.

"Where d'ya think you're goin', chum?" challenged the tough, runty-looking boss of the dock wallopers.

"I'm from the Bureau of Immigration, and I'm taking these boys to see Luciano," Ratzke told him.

"I don't give a damn where you're from," came the answer. "You ain't got no right to take nobody on this pier."

The stevedores closed in around Ratzke, swinging their bailing hooks, toying with them, idly. Ratzke got the idea. Meekly he asked —well, would it be all right if *he* went aboard ship and saw Mr. Luciano? Permission was granted, but the reporters and photographers were forced to back off under the threat of being thrown bodily into the river. Ratzke was gone only a few minutes, then he returned to announce the obvious: Luciano had said to hell with the goddamned press; he wasn't seeing anybody.

"I want you fellows to know it wasn't the Bureau of Immigration that kept you off the boat," Ratzke told the reporters lamely.

The same restrictions did not apply to others. Before the *Laura Keene* sailed that evening, there was a send-off party that should have kept Lucky suspended in air halfway across the Atlantic. All the emperors of the mob came to wish the chief hail and farewell. They brought hampers crammed with wines and liquors, lobster and caviar, and all were passed like royalty through the stevedore line guarding the pier. Frank Costello came, and Joe Adonis, and Albert Anastasia. Mike Lescari, an associate of Longy Zwillman, an old boyhood friend of Lucky's and one of the favorite consultants at Great Meadow, was also on hand. So were Meyer Lansky and a half-dozen politicians, including an ex-judge. When at last the revelry ended and the *Laura Keene* pulled away from the pier, the stevedore honor guard sent Lucky on his way with a rousing cheer, and one bull voice bellowed over all the rest: "Keep the old chin up, Boss. You'll be back in the driver's seat soon."

It was a prophetic remark.

From the moment of his release, Lucky Luciano became an international menace to law and order—and an acute embarrassment to Governor Dewey, the man who had let him go. To deal first with the second aspect of this development, whenever reporters or investigators tried to find out why Luciano had been released, the ground underfoot shifted like quicksand. First, it was said he had been of inestimable help in the Sicilian invasion. But Gen. William J. (Wild Bill) Donovan, commander of the wartime spy service, the Office of Strategic Services, declared emphatically Luciano hadn't been of any help at all. High Navy officials denied Charlie Lucky had ever assisted them. The Army declared he hadn't aided it. Just one man recalled and acknowledged his contributions. Commander Haffenden, who had gone back to civilian life and was New York's Commissioner of Marine and Aviation at the time of the *Laura Keene* farce, testified before the Kefauver committee that, in 1945, he received a letter from Charles Breitel, law secretary to Governor Dewey, asking whether Luciano had contributed to the war effort. "I answered that letter," Commander Haffenden testified, "and I said he had been of value . . . I used the word 'great,' which was probably overvaluing it, to be frank." Haffenden could not recall any specific services Luciano had performed which might have misled him into using the word "great." He was recovering from war wounds at the time, he explained, and he just felt "great" toward the whole world.

Governor Dewey himself did not emphasize the patriotism factor in explaining his actions. Luciano's war service from prison had been one reason, but not the "compelling" one, he said. He argued that it had been customary to release felons who could be deported, and he said his three predecessors had commuted the sentences of fifty-seven such aliens, including eighteen murderers. Of course, none of these had been a Luciano, but this, it seemed, did not matter. Taking their cue from the Governor, Republican press agents tried to convince the public that Dewey had acted wisely and thriftily by shipping

Luciano back to Italy, thus sparing us the cost of housing, feeding, and guarding him.

Such flimsy rationalizations discounted, of course, the structure of the Mafia and Luciano's high standing in it. Once freed from prison, the onetime king of New York City vice became an even greater menace than he had been previously. From exile in Italy, he began to run the international narcotics racket, and the results were soon apparent. Heroin, smuggled into our ports from countries around the Mediterranean basin, became a menace such as America had never seen before. Addiction began to sweep the nation; in New York pushers even invaded the school yards and began turning teen-age boys into addicts and thieves—and girls into addicts and prostitutes. The Federal Bureau of Narcotics, trying to combat this wave of evil, traced narcotics deal after narcotics deal back to Luciano and quickly became convinced that Charlie Lucky was the brains and real over-lord of the international narcotics racket.

Before the end of 1946, Luciano made a daring move that showed just what kind of a criminal menace Dewey had unleashed. Though Italian police supposedly were keeping close tabs on his movements, he slipped out of Italy and over to Cuba. There he rented a lavish penthouse atop one of Havana's fanciest hotels and began to deal with Cuban politicians. He was also within easy communication of New York, a circumstance that quickly led to unusual developments.

One famous Broadway and Hollywood star, the idol of teen-age fans, learned that his old friend Charlie Lucky was in Havana and flew down to see him. In honor of their reunion, Charlie Lucky threw a classic party that roared full tilt into the early morning hours. As ill fortune would have it, the great star's arrival in Havana had been duly noted in the press, and next day, a group of Girl Scouts appeared at the hotel to see their idol. The eager girls, with a nun as chaperone, were herded into an elevator and delivered to the penthouse. The door stood ajar. The visitors timidly ventured in. What met their innocent young eyes was a scene of chaos. Bottles littered the floor; lingerie was draped from the wall brackets; and bodies in various degrees of nudity were scattered wherever they had fallen. A white-faced nun marched her charges back into the elevator and reported to her mother superior. The mother superior forwarded the incredible report to her bishop, and for a moment it seemed that all kinds of scandal might erupt in the press. This prospect caused the Federal

Bureau of Narcotics no end of consternation, for the bureau did not want Charlie Lucky to know that it had him under close surveillance and was aware of his presence in Havana. Wires were pulled, the news suppressed—and Charlie Lucky remained for a time in ignorance of the watch that was being kept upon him.

So he continued to function as elder statesman and the man with the determinative voice whenever ticklish issues divided the secret rulers of gangdom. Just such an issue was up for decision at this time, and all the reigning powers of the Combination were traveling to Havana to consult with Charlie Lucky about it. The Crime Cabinet in Duke's was represented by its most prominent members, Joe Adonis, Albert Anastasia, and Willie Moretti. The names of the other delegates read like a blue book of the underworld: Frank Costello, Charlie Fischetti, Vito Genovese, Tony Accardo, Joe Profaci, Phil Kastel, Meyer Lansky, Vince Mangano, Lil Augie Pisano, Mike Miranda, Joe Bonanno, Joe Magliocco, Tommy Lucchese, Carlos Marcello.

The problem that had brought these emperors of the Combination to a crime conclave with Charlie Lucky in Havana was Buggsy Siegel.

This handsome, psychopathic hood and onetime partner of Meyer Lansky had become carried away with his own power and was threatening to fracture all the rules of the combine. Sent out to California as the emissary of the Syndicate, he had put crime there on a professional basis—and then he had discovered Las Vegas. When Buggsy had his great vision, Las Vegas was just squatting there in the desert, doing nothing much except fleecing the few two-bit suckers who came along. But what enchanted Buggsy was that gambling had been made a legitimate profession in Nevada, and he saw in this simple fact enormous possibilities. He would build on the desert a fabulous hotel; he would dress it up fancy, with all kinds of class, the sexiest showgirls, the best revues, headline entertainers; attracted by such irresistible allure, the wealthiest sheep in the nation would flock to their own shearing.

So was born the idea for the "fabulous Flamingo Hotel." Buggsy got so carried away by his vision that the Flamingo devoured money the way a boa constrictor does lambs. Originally expected to cost $1.5 million, the Flamingo cost $6 million before it was finished. Even Buggsy Siegel didn't have this kind of money, and when cash ran short he would depart for the East and return carrying satchels bulging with the product of the federal mint. On one occasion, he plunked down two such heavy valises on the desk in front of one of his startled legitimate advisers and grunted: "Let me know if it's not enough." The bags contained some $400,000 in cash.

By the time the Flamingo was finished, the mob moguls who had entrusted Buggsy with their racket millions were getting restive. They wanted some sign they were going to get their money back. The Flamingo, however, was at first just an expensive flop. It seemed to devour as much money in the operation as it had in the building, and Buggsy became desperate. One of his chores in the West had been to open up the territory for the racing wire run by the Capone mob out of Chicago. Buggsy, in his usual ruthless way, had knocked off all competition; but now, needing cash to keep the Flamingo afloat, he decided to keep the racing wire and all its rich rewards for himself. So he violated a cardinal rule of the Combination—and the national board met with Charlie Lucky in Havana to decide what should be done.

The result of their deliberations was made explosively clear on the night of June 20, 1947. Buggsy Siegel had been staying alone in the pink Moorish mansion in Beverly Hills that he maintained for Virginia Hill. Virginia, after one of their famous lovers' spats, had just taken off for Europe. Afterwards, there was much speculation that Joe Adonis, as a reward for past favors, might have tipped the lady it was a good time to disappear; but Virginia herself always insisted she had had no intimation that her beloved Buggsy was in deep trouble. On this night, however, Buggsy had returned home after dining out and had just settled himself with the *Los Angeles Times* on a chintz-covered love-seat in front of a picture window. Outside, a sharpshooter drew a deadly bead with a carbine and opened up on Buggsy with a full clip. The steel-jacketed slugs literally tore the handsome mobster apart.

He had hardly collapsed on the floor, police in fact didn't yet know that he was dead, when out in Las Vegas a delegation composed of Little Moey Sedway, Morris Rosen, and Gus Greenbaum calmly walked into the Flamingo and assumed control. And from the East, at almost the same instant, a new figure appeared upon the Las Vegas scene—Joseph (Doc) Stracher, a Newark gangster with a long record and a close associate of such gambling moguls of the Combination as Meyer Lansky, Joe Adonis, Longy Zwillman, and Willie Moretti.

Word filtering out from the underworld was that the boys had held "a meet" in some unnamed Newark hotel (Duke's was never mentioned in such reports of the period, only some vague "hotel") and that they had designated Doc Stracher to look out for their investments in Las Vegas. Stracher, in close association with Meyer Lansky, has ever since been one of the reigning powers behind some of the fanciest hotels and gambling casinos along the Strip.

So had the underworld made its decisions—and power shifted from the stiffened hands of Buggsy Siegel. His murder marked a turning point in the story of modern gangdom. For the first time since Frank Costello and Lucky Luciano had imposed a rule of order on the mobs following the Masseria and Maranzano slayings in 1931, the national board of the Combination had met, tried, and condemned one of its own. So Buggsy had become the first of the ruling powers to go—and go violently. He was not to be the last.

With the underworld ruling in such highhanded fashion, springing a Lucky Luciano from a virtual life sentence, holding kangaroo courts and carrying out death sentences, the question inevitably arises: What happens to the honest investigator who tries to uphold the law and buck the power of the mob?

The fiasco of the official raid on the South Plainfield gambling game that Ross Ellis had so thoroughly scouted and Prosecutor Melko had billed "the largest dice game in the East" nettled an upright jurist, Supreme Court Justice Frederic R. Colie, who was then sitting in Middlesex County. Taking seriously his judicial obligation to see that the law was enforced, Justice Colie formally requested Attorney General Walter D. Van Riper to appoint a special deputy to investigate gambling and all its ramifications. Van Riper himself was a controversial figure. Even while holding office as the state's highest law-enforcement officer, he had twice been indicted by Federal grand juries, one charge involving black-market operations, the other the kiting of some $400,000 worth of checks; and though ultimately he had been cleared on both counts, he had hardly been a crusading attorney general. Nevertheless, a Supreme Court Justice's official request could not be ignored, and so on April 16, 1947, John J. Winberry was sworn into office to conduct a rackets probe.

Winberry, who lived in Bergen County, was a stockily built man with a square, solid, determined face. He had been a captain in the

U.S. Marines and later a Federal investigator, working for the Treasury Department on fraud cases. As a lawyer, his technique mirrored this background. He lacked the flamboyance often associated with the term "rackets-buster," relying more on the plodding thoroughness of a Treasury expert accustomed to depend on the hard facts of balance sheets and figures. Critics were later to concentrate upon him with a vicious intensity, belittling his ability and picturing him as wildly irresponsible. The clear and well-established record shows, however, that he was honest, tenacious, and possessed of an unquenchable crusading fervor.

Aided by undercover men, Winberry soon developed a clear picture of the underworld conspiracy that fanned out across the state from its hub in Bergen County. He traced phone calls, cultivated informants, developed detail on the telephone network that had turned Bergen County into such a bookie pest-spot. By mid-December, 1947, Winberry felt he was ready to make his first big move. Later he recalled in detail exactly what happened.

"On December 18, 1947, I went to Trenton and requested seventeen State Troopers to raid eight horserooms my agents had uncovered in Perth Amboy," he said. "The State Police referred my request to Gov. Alfred E. Driscoll at ten minutes to twelve.

"Gov. Driscoll notified Van Riper that the troopers were being assigned to raid gambling in Perth Amboy. At ten minutes after one, one of my undercover men in Perth Amboy telephoned me that he had heard the word being passed: 'Lay off all bets for a few days. The heat's on.'

"Someone had leaked the news to the mob and the word had gone out within an hour and twenty minutes. The raids could not be pulled."

If the mob's pipeline was so reliable—and this on the very highest levels in the state—that it could grant such protection for current operations, it stood to reason that it would be even more difficult to get evidence against the South Plainfield gambling game that had gone out of existence some seventy-five days before Winberry was appointed. The game had run without interference from the law for eighteen months; but its operators were now dispersed, its activity had ceased, and there was no chance of obtaining the kind of vital evidence that could have been furnished by a successful raid. Doggedly, Winberry turned to the records. He traced details of local property ownership; he went to State Banking Departments in New York and New Jersey and examined check cashers' accounts, studied incorporation papers, probed through business- and income-tax returns, pieced together a pattern of contact by cataloguing the number of telephone calls that had linked the racket center in Bergen County to South Plainfield. Bit by bit, he compiled a remarkably detailed picture of the gambling operation and the manner in which it had been run.

The casino itself had been a concrete-block structure that, Winberry found, had been designed and built for the very purpose for which it had been used. It had been constructed without a building permit; and though it had been a gold mine for its operators, it had never even been assessed by South Plainfield for tax purposes. It had been located on property belonging to a retired policeman of the town, and the local public pretense had been that it was a "gymnasium" where boxers trained for ring encounters.

Intriguing as these details were, they were not half so significant as the facts that Winberry uncovered by probing through financial records. He discovered a partnership tax return that had been filed, most appropriately, under the name "Four Clovers." This listed the six men who had been the directors of the "Four Clovers" enterprise, and it showed that, in the years 1945 and 1946, the six had divided among themselves an income of $293,450. The lion's share in both years had gone to three major partners—Angelo DeCarlo, William Rega, and Eugene Catena, a brother of Gerardo (Jerry) Catena, the principal lieutenant of Longy Zwillman and one of the coterie in constant attendance at Duke's. The lesser partners—Anthony Santoli, Dominick Rega, and Joseph Panigrosso—had received small amounts ranging from $5,000 to $12,000. The largest single take had been that of Eugene Catena, who had pocketed more than $100,-000 for his eighteen months' activity in South Plainfield—$57,600 in 1945 and $45,250 in 1946. In the latter year, DeCarlo and William Rega, who had each drawn $30,000 in 1945, had shared equally with Catena. Here again was documentary evidence of the tremendous spoils that feed the underworld. All six operators of the South Plainfield game were relatively inconspicuous figures; none was within several leagues of a Moretti or an Adonis. All had "notorious records," as Winberry later informed the Kefauver committee, yet each had been compensated at a rate even a well-placed business executive might have envied.

The evil of the situation, in Winberry's view at least, did not end there. He became convinced, as Federal narcotics agents and many honest investigators at every level are convinced, that a mob battening on such a tremendous flow of cash, and protected in its illicit activity, obtains carte-blanche authority to commit every crime from narcotics peddling to murder. Tracking telephone calls, Winberry had become intrigued by a phone located in a house in the vicinity of the South Plainfield game which quite obviously had been used as a channel of mob communication. Winberry traced a heavy load of calls that linked this number with racketeers large and small all over the state. Calls had been made repeatedly to several of the top six operators of the South Plainfield game; someone had been in contact with Longy Zwillman. Furthermore, the pattern seemed to Winberry to bear a direct relation to four New Jersey gang murders. These murders in Middlesex, Union, Passaic, and Somerset Counties had never been solved, but the telephone links that he had uncovered led Winberry to declare in his subsequent Supreme Court deposition: "It is my firm belief that these murders are part and parcel of the operations of the gambling syndicate which has its headquarters in New Jersey and of which the South Plainfield operators are members."

By the time he had developed this picture, Winberry knew that he was on the trail of a Syndicate operation of mammoth proportions. He felt confident, too, that he could prove gambling charges against the principal operators and the employees of the South Plainfield "Four Clovers" game. Winberry worked hard at a novel method for identifying victims who could give direct testimony against the gamblers. The link between the two was the check casher. Heavy plungers always go to a game fortified with huge rolls of cash; but once they have lost all, with the fervor of play still hot upon them, they begin to write checks against their bank accounts. Mob credit experts were always on hand to determine just how far a plunger should be allowed to plunge, and the checks that settled the evening's accounts were handled by check cashers who turned the paper into currency.

Winberry, by plowing through records, identified the credit man who handled the paper from the South Plainfield game and the check casher in New York with whom he did business. The check casher's records supplied names of persons who had played and lost and who, in consequence, were witnesses capable of giving direct testimony against the operators of the South Plainfield dice hall. With this chain established, Winberry was ready to act. In October, 1948, he filed a memorandum with the assignment judge in Middlesex County. He named the six principals of "Four Clovers" and eighteen hired hands, against all of whom, he said, he was prepared to seek indictments.

Under the circumstances, such success must be considered excellent progress, but Winberry wanted more. He felt he could successfully prosecute the personnel of the "Four Clovers" enterprise, but he knew that the Syndicate operation, whose trails he saw everywhere, was much larger than that. What he needed as the final justification of his appointment and long months of work was the one vital element that he still didn't have—the link connecting the lower-echelon workers at the South Plainfield game with the masterminds who directed the whole vast conspiracy.

Throughout his investigation, Winberry had kept in close touch with the office of District Attorney Hogan in New York. He had found it, as the Kefauver committee was to find it later, one of the best-informed spots in the nation on the ties and maneuvers of the big-time underworld. Hogan's office had helped Winberry when it could, and he had helped it. For just at this time, while Winberry was probing the South Plainfield game, Hogan's aides had launched an investigation into the mammoth Bergen County operation and the ties of Bergen County mobsters to New York. By mid-August, 1948, Hogan had developed such specific information that word went out in Bergen County—and newspapers publicly proclaimed it—that "the heat's on." Joe Adonis shut down his gambling games, Frank Erickson suspended his bookie operation, and New Jersey officialdom rushed into action. Eminent law-enforcement authorities crossed the river in a parade and thundered at Hogan's door, begging to be informed. Among the information seekers was Attorney General Van Riper. On August 19, 1948, New York's Assistant District Attorney O'Connor, as he was later to testify before the New Jersey State Legislative Committee, gave Van Riper specific details about the Bergen rackets. "We told Van Riper the New Jersey mob operation was headed by Joe Adonis," O'Connor declared flatly.

Against this background of a definitive warning by New York officials, the final act of the Winberry drama came to a surprise conclusion.

O'Connor and his principal aide in the New Jersey investigation, Andy Seidler, had both come to like the earnest but often frustrated Winberry. They recognized his almost insurmountable problems in trying to accomplish law enforcement in the face of official lethargy in New Jersey, and they felt that, while Winberry had gathered considerable evidence, he had not succeeded in developing the airtight case that would be expected of him after the fanfare surrounding his appointment and the length of his probe. It is almost axiomatic that a much-ballyhooed investigation must produce dramatic results, or the investigator is highly vulnerable.

O'Connor decided to speak his mind during one of Winberry's visits in early November, 1948.

"I agree with what you're doing, John," he said, "but I'm afraid you're going to have to come up with more than you have. If you don't turn up something pretty big, if you don't really put up, the first thing you know you may find yourself on the spot."

Winberry listened and sat for a few moments in deep thought. Then he heaved a big sigh.

"I guess you're right," he said. "I guess I'll have to take the bull by the horns."

Scanning his list of lowly laborers in the South Plainfield enterprise, Winberry picked the ones about whom he had the most information and who would be the best prospects for his great gamble. What he planned was to barge straight in on some of the hired hands, and to try by bluff and brashness to startle or scare them into talking. To O'Connor this seemed like the most desperate of longshot chances, but Winberry was convinced he could make it work—and, anyway, it was his only hope.

Taking with him a New Jersey State Police Sergeant and a detective from the New York Headquarters Squad, Winberry went to Brooklyn on Friday afternoon, November 12, 1948. He called first upon Jack A. Natiello and confronted him with the positive facts he had unearthed about the South Plainfield game and his role in it. Winberry was impressive and effective. Natiello was convinced that he was trapped, and talked. He admitted that he had been employed with several others in the South Plainfield gambling game. For Winberry this was a major break.

Elated, the New Jersey investigator pressed his luck. On the morn-

ing of November 13, 1948, he paid a sudden visit to another Brook-
lynite, Joseph Carlino. Carlino at first refused to talk, but Winberry
kept after him.

"What's the matter with you?" he demanded. "What are you being
so close-mouthed for? You want me to tell you? You're scared I'm
going to get something on you in that murder case. Well, you're right.
It's the murder case I'm interested in; I don't care about the gambling, I know all about that. But I'm going to get to the bottom of
that murder case if it's the last thing I do, and if you know what's
good for you, you better talk up."

Winberry was roaring in fine impassioned style by now, and Carlino, with the prospect rising before his eyes of being dragged feet
first into a murder case, decided he had better do just what Winberry
advised him to do. He talked. When he did, he provided the very
link that Winberry had gambled so desperately to get. Carlino admitted that he had worked with about twenty others in the South
Plainfield game. It had been, he conceded, a house run by "the Syndicate." He identified Joe Adonis as the boss of "the Syndicate" and
said he had worked for Joe A. in several other gambling dens besides
the one in South Plainfield—specifically in Fort Lee and West Paterson, New Jersey, and in Miami, Florida.

This, as Winberry said in his later memorandum to the Kefauver
committee, was "vital information." It was the first direct evidence
tying Joe Adonis to the South Plainfield game; it was direct testimony
that could lead to the prosecution of the top mob ruler in New Jersey.
It filled in that fatal gap between the lower-level field hands and the
man who directed their activities. And it came, it must be remembered, as striking corroboration of the information Hogan's office
had given to Van Riper almost exactly three months earlier when
it had told the New Jersey Attorney General that Joe Adonis was the
brains of the mob in New Jersey. Under the circumstances, what happened next is one of the most amazing reversals of logical expectation
in the history of law enforcement. For instead of the rewards of
triumph, Winberry was suddenly confronted with disaster.

After his talk with Carlino on November 13th, a Sunday inter-
vened before the next act, but on Monday morning, November 15th,
things started to happen. Attorney General Van Riper announced he
was holding up Winberry's payroll. The Attorney General's mood

was reflected in headlines that read: "Van Riper Holds Up Winberry Bills—Angry at Deputy's Failure to Wind Up Middlesex Gaming Probe."

Since an investigation could not be continued without funds, Winberry took his case to the press and the public. He could not, of course, reveal all the details of his investigation, but he described it in general terms and accused Van Riper of attempted "sabotage." He declared that he expected to seek the indictment of about twenty-five persons in the South Plainfield gambling case "in approximately two weeks" if he was not "interfered with further by the Attorney General." Van Riper's reaction was prompt. He fired Winberry and in an angry blast, he said he should have dismissed the special investigator earlier and implied plainly that Winberry was a bungler who had been getting nowhere.

These developments astounded Hogan's aides, O'Connor and Seidler, who had advised Winberry and had been applauding his successful gamble.

"Can you beat it?" O'Connor asked years later, recalling the event. "I suppose in a way you would have to say I was responsible for getting Winberry fired. Here I was urging him on for fear that if he didn't come up with really hot evidence he would get fired, and he takes my advice, barges in, gets the most fantastic break and gets the evidence—and we knew he got it, no question about that because we had one of our own detectives right there—and almost the minute he accomplishes all this, he's fired!"

With Winberry officially decapitated, the great investigation of gambling that Justice Colie had spurred moved swiftly to its denouement. A new Deputy Attorney General, completely unfamiliar with the case, was named to succeed Winberry, and in two months he closed out the probe. Winberry was examined before the Middlesex County grand jury in what he described as a hostile atmosphere; he was subjected, he later told the Supreme Court, to a virtual cross-examination in which "even the sneer and the snarl were employed" and only about half of his information was elicited. Three indictments were voted. Dominick Rega, one of the three lesser lights among the six partners of "Four Clovers," was accused of maintaining and operating a gambling establishment. And Jack A. Natiello and Joseph Carlino—the two men who would have been Winberry's major witnesses—were indicted for aiding and abetting! They were the only two employees in the list of eighteen whom Winberry had previously named to the court who were molested by the law.

Though Justice Colie had called months earlier for the imposition of stiff prison terms on convicted gamblers to curb widespread lawlessness, Rega was given a suspended sentence, released on probation and slapped on the wrist with a $3,500 fine; Natiello and Carlino likewise drew suspended sentences and were fined $1,500 each. This was not quite all. The Middlesex grand jury, in closing out the probe, passed a resolution formally censuring Winberry for making irresponsible charges that widespread gambling was flourishing in the fair state of New Jersey. As for Joe Adonis, nobody even mentioned him. As far as the law was concerned, Joe A. didn't even exist—which, of course, was just the way Joe A. wanted it.

Even this was not quite the whole picture. In February, 1948, the seven-year term of Justice Colie on the Supreme Court had been due to expire. There had been rumors that the antigambling, antirackets Justice might not be reappointed by Governor Driscoll. Many newspapers of the state had rallied to Justice Colie's support in editorials pointing to his excellent record and urging his retention. Governor Driscoll had evidently agreed, for he reappointed the Justice. But in September, 1948, after a new State Constitution had gone into effect, the Supreme Court was reduced from nine to seven members. Then it suddenly developed that there was just no room on the high bench for Justice Colie. He was dropped and downgraded to the post of Judge in the Appellate Division of Superior Court.

It was all just a coincidence, of course; but when such coincidences repeat themselves in a pattern that comes to seem like a rule of life, one can hardly wonder that some persons with acutely developed instincts for self-preservation get the feeling that it hardly pays to buck the underworld.

10

POWER AT THE TOP

WHEN one talks about mob muscle, one inevitably talks politics. The simple truth is that the American underworld could not have achieved its power and immunity had the political climate of the nation not been almost totally corrupt. The operations of the underworld are so mammoth they cannot be conducted in secrecy; they must flourish in an atmosphere of official permissive blindness. It is impossible to run a 2,600-telephone bookie network or to spangle an entire countryside with gambling casinos to which players are ferried in Cadillac fleets without causing even the most stupid minions of the law to suspect that illegal enterprise is being conducted under their noses. To operate as Joe Adonis operated in Duke's, as the Syndicate whose forces he directed operated across the breadth of New Jersey, there must be sweeping and ironclad protection, the kind that can be guaranteed only through politics and the purchase of official complaisance.

The public usually assumes that such arrangements are consummated only with the corrupt politicians who dominate America's big-city machines. The reality is more subtle and much more damning. So tremendous is the underworld gold mine that it infects not only the innately corrupt; it infects the innately incorruptible. It purchases influence not only from the dishonest political boss, but from

214

the reformer who would oust him in the cause of the public good. If a politician does not want to be left for dead on the battlefield, he needs campaign money in vast amounts—and such heavy financing can be obtained only for a *quid pro quo*. This is an axiom of American politics. It explains the all-pervasive influence of the underworld, the manner in which it is able to sway even men who are not purchasable.

Joe Adonis' $25,000 contribution to the LaGuardia campaign and his immunity in Brooklyn during the first LaGuardia administration strikingly illustrated this fundamental and paradoxical fact of political life. It was no isolated example, something that happened once and was not likely to happen again. On the contrary, it was inevitable that it would happen again; and, in his New Jersey operation during the Forties, Joe Adonis was again to demonstrate that the underworld purchases its immunity from all manner of surprising sources. For his wholesale New Jersey operations were conducted, not under the aegis of a corrupt, old-line political machine, but under the rule of perhaps as effective and efficient a reform administration as New Jersey had ever known.

New Jersey, like many states, had been torn by eternal political strife pitting the so-called reformers against the bosses; but in New Jersey, the battle lines had been more fiercely drawn and the contest given an unreal, black-and-white coloration because of the continued dominance of one man, the late Mayor Frank Hague of Jersey City. So powerful was Hague that he once brashly bragged, "I am the law," a statement, incautiously thundered in public, that was to haunt him throughout the closing years of his long reign. His rule over Jersey City and populous Hudson County was so complete that it was commonplace for his floaters to vote the names of the departed members of the electorate found on tombstones in the graveyards; no statewide election could be considered decided until Hudson's floodtide of votes had rolled in and it could be determined whether Hague's machine had managed to enlist enough dead voters to control the result.

To counteract Hague, the Republicans needed an equally powerful, well-oiled machine. They found it in Bergen County. Bergen became such a stronghold of the G.O.P. that it was sometimes called "America's foremost Republican county." It was expected to return majorities of 75,000 to 100,000 votes for Republican candidates, and sometimes it did even better. In 1952, for instance, it gave President Eisenhower a margin of 119,000 votes. Such one-sided balloting made Bergen the dramatic and effective counterweight to Hudson, and the county became the hearthstone and breadbasket of state-wide Republicanism. If some of the important contributions to the bread-basket were made by the mob, nobody worried too much. For though it is still not politic publicly to acknowledge so distasteful a fact, mob contributions to political campaigns play an extremely important, sometimes pivotal role in American politics. In Bergen County a neat system—the $100-a-plate political dinner—was devised to give such donations the appearance of legitimacy. Mobsters or mob fronts often bought at least 100 tickets for such affairs, a lump sum con-tribution of $10,000 every time a dinner was held. And there were many dinners.

The double moral standard of American politics is implicit in such arrangements. In one of his franker moments before the Kefauver committee, Mayor William O'Dwyer of New York said bluntly: "It doesn't matter whether it is a banker, a businessman, or a gangster —his pocketbook is always attractive." Such a pragmatic philosophy on the operating front of politics is cloaked by the sedulously cultivated myth that there is somehow a vital difference between the act of an official or candidate in personally taking racket money and "the party's" taking it for "campaign purposes." The fiction is that the candidate doesn't have to know what is going on and is not bound by it. However the facts, which over the long course of years spell out an unvarying pattern of potent mob influence, argue otherwise.

In Bergen County, the political machine which Joe A. and Willie Moretti helped to bankroll was largely instrumental in turning New Jersey, for a whole decade, into a totally Republican state. In the twenties and thirties, Hague had been able to elect governors, al-though the Republicans, with their grip on the rural counties, almost invariably controlled the legislature. The resulting duality of bossism had corrupted, to a great degree, both law enforcement and the courts. Hague, with his puppet in the governor's chair, had the power of appointment to vital positions; the Republican bosses, with their majority in the Senate, held a veto through their power of confirma-tion. It followed all too frequently that prosecutors and judges, to obtain their positions, had to demonstrate that they were men of such pliable backbone they could serve not one boss but two. Blank resignations were sometimes signed and deposited, one with Hague, one with the rural Republican boss; and anytime a judge or prosecutor offended, he could be removed simply by typing in a date on the blank resignation and mailing the document to the governor. Only the rare man of exceptional stature and integrity could rise above the evils of such a system.

Though the Republicans took part in every smelly appointment deal, Hague's Democratic governor usually shouldered the onus of making the initial error, a personalization of responsibility that gave weight in the public's eyes to sanctimonious Republican breast-beatings about how horrible things had become. The manifold benefits to the G.O.P. were obvious. Republican bosses reveled in the benefits of the dual-boss system but suffered few of its penalties. Whenever a public scandal erupted, they could blame all on the monstrous evil of Hague. And all the time they maintained their own counterpoise to Hague in the racket warrens of Bergen County. In the end, the combined pressure of all these forces became too much even for Hague. The 1940's and early 1950's saw Republican control solidified at both the executive and legislative levels.

Out of this political stew, compounded of many diverse and paradoxical ingredients, there emerged one highly unusual man. He was Alfred Eastlack Driscoll, often called the best executive New Jersey had had since the days of Woodrow Wilson. Driscoll certainly bore no resemblance to the usual political hack. Anyone familiar with the convolutions of Jersey politics in those days knew this, if only because it was so patent in the way ordinary political hacks regarded him. The county Republican bosses, who liked to pose in public hand-in-hand with righteousness, privately viewed him with the deep resentment only a professional can feel toward an amateur who flouts the rules. The bosses gagged on the fact that Driscoll, as governor, seemed to take seriously the need of public and private virtue to which a sensible politician gives only appropriate lip service. A governor so dedicated was a constant living reproach; he was also a potential menace, likely to kick over the traces at what the bosses considered an entirely normal deal. Human nature being what it is, many leaders of his own party chafed under the Driscoll halo and privately regarded it as composed of no better tinsel than their own. But in the meantime, Driscoll was the governor, he was also a Republican, and the Republican bosses had to live with him and put their best smiles forward, little as some of them liked it.

The man who could arouse such contradictory emotions was obviously no ordinary personality. Son of a well-to-do paint manufacturer and descendant of forebears who had marched with Ethan Allen and the Green Mountain Boys in the Revolution, Driscoll was a lean six-footer, with a curly, unruly shock of hair that seemed in perpetual need of combing. He didn't care much for dancing or the social whirl, but much preferred the rugged outdoor life. In 1926 he and four friends traveled by canoe from Edmondton, Canada, down the Mackenzie River to the Arctic Circle. Then they made their way along the unexplored Rat River into Alaska and followed a series of streams that were only vague, dotted lines on the map until they reached the Yukon. This and similar rigorous trips into the Far North won Driscoll membership in the Explorers Club, one of the relatively few organizations to which he belonged.

On the professional side, Driscoll, having studied at Harvard Law School, established a law office in Camden. He continued to live in Haddonfield, where he had been brought up, and he organized a town professional football team on which he played. He also taught Sunday School in the First Presbyterian Church and, for a time, lectured on constitutional law at Rutgers University. He got into politics during a local campaign to straighten out Haddonfield's tangled school problems, and he did such a good job he was rewarded by election to the Borough Commission. This in turn proved a stepping-stone to his election as State Senator in 1938.

From the start Driscoll was against bosses. In 1938, a Clean Government movement was sweeping large parts of Jersey, and Driscoll affiliated himself with it and was elected as an antimachine candidate. In the Legislature he quickly earned a reputation for independence, a quality not greatly admired by political bosses. But surprisingly enough, when the post of Alcoholic Beverage Commissioner became vacant in 1941, Driscoll rather than a party favorite received the plum. Several factors apparently contributed to his selection: the bosses were at loggerheads, Driscoll had strong backing among the more independent party elements, and his appointment to the liquor-control post got him out of the hair of the "regulars" in the Senate. What the "regulars" hadn't figured on, since it had never happened before, was that Driscoll would use his new position as the spring-board to the governor's chair.

As ABC Commissioner, Driscoll was astute enough to attract reams of favorable publicity. When liquor firms delivered cases of free refreshment at his door, he sent back the gifts. His decisions on liquor licenses and revocations were delivered with a seemingly judicial impartiality, a freedom from influence, that endeared him to the press of the state. The image of an independent and incorruptible public executive was created, and in 1946, Driscoll received the backing of the still-powerful remnants of New Jersey's Clean Government forces for the Republican nomination for governor. In a heated primary campaign, he defeated former Governor Harold G. Hoffman, long a popular performer on the hustings, and went on to trounce the Democratic candidate in November by a margin of 221,000 votes.

An important factor in Driscoll's initial success was the backing of the powerful Bergen County Republican machine. A key figure in obtaining support for him in Bergen was John J. Dickerson, the strongest and most influential Republican leader in the county. A real estate man with an ideal politician's hail-fellow-well-met personality, Dickerson had been the mayor of his home community of Palisades Park and director of the Bergen County Board of Freeholders, the county governing body that keeps a grip on the purse strings. In the political wars of 1946, he became Driscoll's campaign manager.

Success in the November election was followed by a series of achievements that enhanced Driscoll's stature in the public eye and overshadowed periodic, ugly rumblings about wide-open racketeering in Bergen. For years New Jersey had creaked along with an archaic state constitution. The most capable of the State's governors had recommended repeatedly that the ancient document be scrapped in favor of a more modern governmental structure. Wilson, Walter E. Edge, and Charles Edison had all advocated such a course, but all had failed to get action. Driscoll, however, succeeded. He was instru-mental in calling a State Constitutional Convention in the summer of 1947 and in securing a new charter that was widely praised as one of the best in the nation.

Under the new constitution, the Governor's power to run the machinery of state government was increased greatly. Even more important, the State's judicial system, long the target of welling and caustic complaint, was reorganized and streamlined, with almost dictatorial watchdog powers concentrated in the hands of the Chief Justice of its new Supreme Court. This was a key post, the governor's most important single appointment, and Driscoll, to the eternal shock of many of the bosses of his own party, named to it a man so eminent it was impossible publicly to quarrel with his choice. His selection was Arthur T. Vanderbilt, a powerful Clean Government leader in Essex County, long recognized as one of the top legal minds in the nation, and a former president of the American Bar Association. Though Vanderbilt and Driscoll had quarreled politically, the Governor did not hesitate to name his onetime critic to the office of Chief Justice. And Vanderbilt proceeded to run it with such tough independence and rectitude that political hirelings, who love only the amenable man, were to moan for years about the tragedy of the choice.

This typical expression of Driscoll independence was accompanied by notable administrative achievements. He pushed through plans for the $225 million New Jersey Turnpike, an essential link between Philadelphia and New York, despite vigorous opposition in his own party to the creation of a toll road. He spent additional millions improving the state's highways, accomplishing more than any other Governor before him. Yet he also achieved some notable economies in government. He reorganized the administrative machinery, consolidating seventy independent state agencies into fourteen major departments, eliminating jobs and saving some $2 million a year. A $50 million emergency veterans' housing program was carried out without Federal aid, state employees' salaries were raised 33 per cent, teachers' minimum salaries were doubled—yet New Jersey, which had no sales or income tax, kept its budget under control with fewer and lower imposts than are levied by most states.

All this added up to a remarkable record of achievement on many diverse levels, and the man who accomplished it had about him an air of sincerity and informality that impressed both the public and astute political observers. He was careless and indifferent in dress and lacked completely the pompousness that often overtakes a politician who has acquired distinguished title. Joe Alex Morris, in an admiring

Saturday Evening Post profile that implied Driscoll was perhaps the greatest governor New Jersey had ever had, wrote of him:

> His appointment schedule seldom runs on time. He is likely to leave his wallet lying on a table somewhere. He lets correspondence pile up maddeningly as he patiently listens to the complaint of a citizen he had never heard of before and will never see again. He dashes out into the corridor to investigate a loud pounding on the steam pipes and stays to find out exactly why the plumbers are at work and how much it will cost the state. He refused for months to turn in an expense account for official telephone calls at his home—the bill ran over $200 most months —and the budget director finally had to have the company transfer the charges directly to his own office for payment.

This was no press-agent-inspired portrait. It was all in keeping with Driscoll's character. One summer, while the Governor and his wife were weekending at the Jersey shore, the small congregation of a little resort church was startled to see the door open quietly and the Governor and his lady tiptoe down the aisle to take seats inconspicuously in their midst. When the service was over, Governor and Mrs. Driscoll departed just as unostentatiously. Their car was a battered old jalopy, and the Governor himself did the driving. There was no limousine, no chauffeur, no State Police guards, no fanfare.

On another occasion Driscoll had stopped at a roadside diner one night with his characteristic genius for inconspicuousness, and he was amused to find himself the subject of a heated discussion among the clientele. The counterman, who was arguing with several customers, finally closed off the discussion with the belligerent statement: "O.K., O.K., maybe Driscoll is dumb, but at least he's honest!"

Not many persons in New Jersey would have so characterized Driscoll's mental abilities, but the vast majority certainly would have agreed with the verdict about his honesty. Yet this was the man under whose administration Joe Adonis and his councilors ran with absolute impunity the multimillion-dollar affairs of the underworld.

Never did public image and public fact so contradict each other. In fact, it is doubtful whether one could find a more startling example of the insidious evils of a system that virtually requires "the party," for success, to deal for underworld cash. Implicit in such arrangements for financial and political support is the necessity for the man

at the top, even a man as exceptional as Driscoll, to remain as blind
as possible to ugly realities.

The chain of command is the ideal protective device to isolate
the commander-in-chief from unpleasant truths. When asked what
happened, he can always point to the subordinate in whose probity
and ability he has placed implicit trust—and the subordinate can
always point to *his* subordinate, and so on down the chain until final
responsibility is fixed on the last and lowliest member on the team.

In Bergen County, the chain of command in matters of law enforcement ran through the office of the county prosecutor, filled in this
critical period of the latter 1940's by a large, bumbling, politico
named Walter Winne. Winne belonged to the Republican clique in
the county headed by State Chairman John J. Dickerson, and so he
had the inside track when he was first given the appointive plum in
1944. In the next four years, as the State Legislative Committee later
noted, his office was rocked by repeated disclosures of wide-open
bookmaking and casino gambling and by the angry cries of New
York mayors that the underworld had made Bergen its bucket shop.
Winne always had some cover up, logical or otherwise, and so, like
a man living in a vacuum, he presided for four years over as do-
nothing an administration as even Joe Adonis could desire.

A unique inside view of how it all looked from the prosecutor's
office was given at a later date to both the Bergen County grand jury
and the probing State Legislative Committee by John E. Selser, who
had been named by Winne as his First Assistant Prosecutor.

Selser had been the attorney for Willie Moretti in the Brady murder
case, and within a few years, he was to represent both the Morettis
and Joe Adonis. But he was emphatic in stating that when Winne
named him First Assistant Prosecutor, he fully intended to do as good
a job for the law as he had ever done for his private clients. He was
tested at once. Almost as soon as his appointment was announced,
before he had even taken office, Selser received a surprise visit from
Solly Moretti.

"From now on you get one thousand dollars a month," he said
Solly told him.

"What for?" the astonished Selser asked.

"Well, we are making money, so you are entitled to make money,"
Solly explained, putting the proposition in instant focus.

"What for, Solly?" Selser asked again.

"Just because you know we are making it, so you get it."

Selser lost his temper and warned Solly to get out of his sight and never come back. Then he went promptly to Winne and reported the bribe offer. The Prosecutor, he testified, patted him on the back and said he was proud to have such an assistant. Nothing, Winne said, could have convinced him more that he had picked the right top aide. According to Selser, he and Winne discussed the possibility of bringing an action against Solly Moretti, but they decided that, since they hadn't taken office at the time, there was no legal basis for a charge.

Subsequently, during his tenure in office, Selser was disturbed repeatedly by reports of gambling and corruption that were too detailed and seemingly authentic to be ignored. He always insisted that he thought Winne personally was a fine man, but that he put too much trust in some of his office help, especially in his Chief of Detectives, Michael Orecchio. The reports of wide-open gambling games became more prevalent than ever during the busy summer of 1948, and Selser described his efforts to uphold the law—and how they were frustrated.

On one occasion, he said, he was told about a big game going on in Costa's Barn in Lodi. This was in either June or July, 1948, a full month or two before Hogan's detectives discovered the same game in operation. Selser told Winne, and the Prosecutor ordered his detectives to investigate. Though Winne was later to insist that he couldn't find Costa's and wasn't even sure there was such a place, no such uncertainty appears to have been in his mind at this time; for, according to Selser, Winnie reported back to him that an investigation had showed there was some furniture in the place because "someone was going to open a restaurant" there. Selser checked back with his private informant, who snorted and told him: "Well, I lost six hundred dollars in that 'restaurant.' "

The First Assistant Prosecutor decided to play detective and see for himself. With his young son, Bob, he drove along Route 6 to Lodi. He had no great difficulty in locating the gambling "barn" that Bergen detectives and Winne later were to insist they couldn't find. Stopping near Costa's, Selser pretended that his car had broken down. He got out, raised the hood, and went through an elaborate pretense of tinkering with the motor. All the time, he made careful note of the

Cadillacs rolling in and out, carrying customers to Joe A.'s big game. The next day he drafted a memorandum concluding that the place was "a gambling casino," and handed it to Winne personally. The Prosecutor appeared shocked and said he would have the charge "immediately investigated"; but once more nothing happened, nothing was done.

Selser testified that the wide-open telephone bookie network in the county led to complaints that were in themselves a clear indication of what was going on. Home owners who had the misfortune to have telephone numbers closely corresponding to some of those being used for betting purposes reported that they were constantly annoyed by misdirected gambling calls. When the telephone company was informed of these complaints, Selser said, it changed the phone numbers of the disturbed householders—not the numbers of those more important phones being used by the bookies.

As if all this wasn't serious enough, Selser received another report in the summer of 1948—a second huge gambling game was being run in the Aristocrat Baby Carriage Factory in Fort Lee. Once again the tip came from a personal friend whom he trusted; he reported to Winne; the Prosecutor told him he had already had the factory investigated and found the reports false—there was no gambling there. Selser, not completely satisfied, decided himself to investigate.

Taking Orecchio and Detective James Stewart with him, but giving them no hint of the nature of their mission, Selser drove to Fort Lee police headquarters. There he picked up a local police captain and hurried on to the baby carriage factory. The raiding party went to the third floor, which had been identified to Selser as the gambling den, and found that this was partitioned off from the rest of the building.

"There was a door in the rear of the partitioned area," Selser testified. "The door was locked. I asked the man in charge of the building for the key. He said there was none. I asked how to get in. He said he didn't know."

Selser said that Orecchio volunteered to climb the fire escape and look in. He did, and reported there was nothing in the room. The watchman kept insisting that the blocked-off room was "just an old drying room" that hadn't been used for years. Selser, suspecting that he was being given a run-around, was furious.

"I told the Captain to go to the Fire Department and get some axes," he testified.

The night watchman protested, arguing that the Prosecutor had no right to damage the property.

"I'm going in," Selser told him determinedly, "if I have to chop the door down myself."

Seeing there was no way to hoodwink an official with his mind so firmly made up, the watchman finally took the investigators down to the second floor where he removed some crates and rubbish that had been piled against a wall, revealing a concealed door. There was a sliding panel in the wall, and a metal door behind it. The door opened on a stairway that led to the "unused drying room" on the third floor. Selser and his party mounted the stairs and came out in an empty room.

"The light fixtures were not the kind you would expect to find in a grim hole," Selser testified. "I rubbed my hands on the floor. There was no dust. I called the man in charge a liar, with adjectives, over the nonuse of the room for years. I asked him what the room was used for. He said he didn't know."

Selser said that he returned to Hackensack and filed a report with Winne, charging that the baby-carriage factory had been used for gambling purposes.

"Was anything done?" Selser was asked by the legislative committee.

"You'll have to ask Mr. Winne," he replied.

Selser's activities as volunteer detective brought swift repercussions. He testified that "a couple of days" after his adventure in the baby-carriage factory he got a telephone call from a man he didn't know "that if I didn't mind my own goddamn business there was going to be a funeral in my home."

Coupled with the threat was another surprise visit, this time from Willie Moretti.

"He asked me why I was being foolish," Selser testified. "I said, 'Willie, I'm not being foolish. I'm trying to be sensible.'

"He said: 'How would you like to be U.S. Attorney?'

"I said: 'Willie, please. I'm grown up. I'm a Republican. Republicans couldn't get jobs as U.S. Attorneys. You couldn't get it for me anyway. Of course, I would like to be a U.S. Attorney, but you couldn't get it for me.'

"He said he could get it for me. He had associations in Washington."

But that, said Selser, was the last he heard of *that*.

It wasn't, however, the last he heard of corruption in Bergen County. He recalled that on one occasion he entered a popular bar and grill in Hackensack late at night. A mob hanger-on who happened to be in the place had imbibed more than was good for him; and, seeing Selser, he became obnoxious. Selser tried to brush him off, but this only made the fellow more offensive and finally he wisecracked that, since his boss was paying Selser off, Selser at least could afford to be polite.

The public insult brought Selser storming to his feet, and he had to be restrained from slugging the offender on the spot. The next morning, when he entered the Prosecutor's office, he was still fuming. Deliberately, in the full hearing of all the staff, he blew his stack. He described what had happened the previous night, and concluded with a threat.

"I said if anybody was taking money in my name, I'd shoot the S.O.B. with my service revolver even if I had to go to the chair for it," Selser recalled.

The office staff was rocked. So were the boys at the bar and grill. Stopping in there a few days later, Selser heard that the mob had been talking about his peculiar reaction and had come to the conclusion that he had really flipped his lid. Selser was such an exception to the general rule of take and let live that nobody could understand what possessed him. One of his gangland clients later described the moral standards of Selser's fellow officeholders in the county in these words: "Clear your mind about us trying to corrupt public officials. We are fighting them off all the time to prevent them asking for more."

Even without this kind of direct confirmation, the situation was so obvious to Selser at the time that he urged Winne, whom he still liked and respected, to appoint a secret investigator to probe the conduct of his own staff. "You are going to get the shock of your life," he predicted to Winne. "You can't know what is going on." But Winne, in Selser's view, was such a fine man that he couldn't credit the things Selser tried to tell him. He refused to take Selser's advice, and once more nothing happened. That is, nothing happened to anyone except Selser.

When Winne was appointed to a second term, he decided to drop his troublesome First Assistant Prosecutor of whom originally he had been so proud. Once more, the one man who had tried to live up to his oath of office was the one man to get the axe. Of course Winne appeared genuinely unhappy about the axe-wielding, but he said "the party leaders" had decided Selser shouldn't be retained because he wasn't "active enough" in politics.

Evidently no such charge of political inactivity could be brought against Winne himself. The "party leaders" were solidly behind him, and in the spring of 1949, Governor Driscoll yielded to the party powers in Bergen and renamed the Prosecutor whose administration already had caused some acute embarrassment. Even more significant than the mere reappointment, however, was the fact that Driscoll, a governor of more than ordinary stature, took the step in spite of a direct challenge flaunted in his face by John J. Winberry, the ousted rackets-buster who simply refused to keep quiet.

On February 14, 1949, Winberry wrote Driscoll a personal letter crammed with specific detail on the racket situation in Bergen. It said in part:

> I have read your statement to the effect that you intend to "crack down" on gambling in New Jersey. While I applaud your statement, I must accept it with reservations in view of the fact that the newspapers of New Jersey have been pounding at the notorious conditions which have existed ever since you became Governor, without a single public move on your part until this date.
>
> The attempt made by former Attorney General Van Riper to place full responsibility for gambling upon local officials was a farce, in the opinion of everyone familiar with law enforcement. All officials know that gambling cannot exist in any municipality unless the Prosecutor of the county is lax. And no lax Prosecutor can stay in office unless the Attorney General, who, under the law, is in charge of law enforcement, ignores his duties and responsibilities. . . .
>
> The public press has stated that you may reappoint Van Riper's close friend, Prosecutor Walter Winne. If you do so you are obviously not interested in suppressing gambling in this County, for apparently everyone but Mr. Van Riper and Mr. Winne knows that Bergen is one of the largest gambling centers in the East.
>
> The bookmaking kings of the nation, Frank Erickson, Frank Costello and Joe Adonis, have been publicly reported as operating in our midst, after having been forcibly denied the hospitality

of New York City. These men are known to be "big time operators."

Winberry stressed that New York officials had issued lists of hundreds of telephone numbers being used by the bookie network in Bergen. He pointed out that Assemblyman T. James Tumulty, from Democratic Hudson, had named 200 Bergen gambling places in a speech on the floor of the legislature. But nothing had been done.

> . . . The contemptuous flouting of the law in Bergen has greatly decreased the respect for our model court system [Winberry wrote]. Efficiency in our court system becomes a mockery if the breakdown in law enforcement in Bergen is whitewashed by the Governor, through the reappointment of a Prosecutor who has proved himself incapable of coping with the situation.

This last thrust was one that could be guaranteed to hurt. Driscoll prided himself on the new state constitution and the model court system he had been instrumental in establishing, and so Winberry's accusing letter put him to a kind of special test. Under the circumstances, with the heavy preponderance of facts on Winberry's side, it is fascinating to discover the manner in which these explicit charges were brushed away. As the State Legislative Committee later revealed, the deed was done by a triple play, with an error at every base.

Driscoll, who faced a campaign for re-election in 1949, had rid himself of Walter Van Riper and appointed a new Attorney General of far different personality. The new man was Theodore D. Parsons of Red Bank, New Jersey, a lawyer with a sound professional reputation in the state. Parsons was a slender, thin-faced man, an inveterate pipe-smoker. He dressed in a dark, conservative suit and looked much more like a church deacon than a fighting prosecutor. The impression was not entirely fanciful, for Parsons often filled in as a lay preacher in country churches.

This was the man to whom Driscoll referred Winberry's waspish letter. And Parsons "investigated" by funneling the charges directly to Prosecutor Winne himself! Since an accused man can hardly be expected to conduct a rigid and impartial investigation of himself, Winne's findings on the subject of Winne's efficiency could hardly have surprised the Attorney General or the Governor. Nevertheless, Winne went to such extremes in his self-exculpation that his letter merits quotation.

His reply, addressed to Parsons and dated February 28, 1949, said:

> I have your letter of the 25th enclosing a letter addressed to
> Governor Driscoll from John J. Winberry, dated February 14,
> 1949, which is as you state undoubtedly prepared for release to
> the press. I suppose I ought to comment on his letter although
> I do not believe that any good newspaper or many of our citizens
> pay much attention to Mr. Winberry. I have never seen him in
> my life. He has no law practice that I know about and certainly
> does not belong to our Bar Association and does not have any
> standing as a lawyer in Bergen County. You probably know his
> recent history as Deputy Attorney General.
>
> As I stated heretofore, when Harry Moore was Governor and
> we had a Democratic Prosecutor, there were open gambling
> establishments in this County. The same thing is true in Hudson,
> Monmouth and other counties. Certainly in my County there
> has been nothing of the sort since I have been Prosecutor. . . . I
> do not know whether I ought to ask a Grand Jury to indict
> Winberry or whether I ought to sue him or ignore him.
>
> As far as Frank Erickson and Frank Costello being in this
> County, *I doubt very much if they know where Bergen County
> is.* It is true that Adonis lives in Bergen County and has a very
> substantial business in Cliffside Park [hauling cars for Ford] but
> I have never had any evidence of his activity in New Jersey in
> any illegal matters.
>
> . . . I conferred many times with Hogan's office and they
> absolutely refused to furnish me with any information regarding
> the alleged gambling place in Lodi. *I am of the opinion that no
> such place existed.* [Italics added.]

The shell game now went into its final shuffle. Parsons reported to
Driscoll that Winberry's charges could be disregarded. And Driscoll
reappointed Winne. Even the Republican majority on the State Legislative Committee that later investigated the Bergen mess gagged at
the whitewash. It wrote:

> Under date of March 30, 1949, and after Winne had been
> reappointed, Parsons wrote to Winberry saying that when he was
> appointed by the Governor he had been directed to enforce the
> laws of this State impartially and honestly. He wrote further that
> his department, which was charged with the enforcement of the
> law, had not and did not intend to exhibit indifference toward
> any County of the State. His letter stated that since he had been
> in office an investigation had been made of existing conditions in

Bergen County. This investigation, he wrote, resulted in the disclosure of no evidence warranting his office to take any current action.

Regardless of the source of this complaint and regardless of the fact that Parsons had been in office since February 4, 1949, nevertheless, Parsons is to be censured for having referred this complaint about Winne to Winne himself, instead of having a thorough and independent investigation made. Such an investigation would have disclosed that the charges made by Winberry in his letter to the Governor were based upon fact.

The Winne-Parsons-Driscoll whitewash in the spring of 1949 brought its anticipated rewards in November of that year when Governor Driscoll rode triumphantly back into office, defeating his Democratic opponent, Elmer Wene, a South Jersey chicken farmer and former Congressman. Even this final victory was not achieved without producing one more sensational episode. Jim Bishop, who has since become the author of several best-selling books, was serving at the time as Wene's press agent. He later testified before the Kefauver committee that during the campaign, a Democratic functionary in Essex County, obviously a go-between for racket boss Longy Zwillman, came to him with a proposition.

"He said Zwillman would go as high as $300,000 for Wene," Bishop testified. "I asked him what was expected in return. He said, 'Zwillman does not want to be hurt by the Wene administration if Wene is elected.' I asked what else, and he said Zwillman wanted a friend in the State Attorney General's office. Apparently, he [Zwillman] wanted to name the Attorney General."

Bishop testified he reported the offer to Wene, who promptly snapped: "I don't want to have anything to do with it."

So the mob, which evidently did not feel entirely secure with Parsons, had to be content with the security arrangements it already had. Bergen turned in its usual thumping Republican majority; Driscoll was re-elected; and it seemed at the time as if Joe Adonis and his crime coterie in Duke's might reign forever.

A man's best plans often founder not on the major threat that he foresees and for which he can prepare, but on the unlucky chance, the minor incident. It was not the big game for which Joe Adonis could arrange the big fix that was to be his undoing and cause all his protective arrangements to come unglued; it was a trifling, chance affair with which he personally had not the slightest connection. This mischance, which seemed at first to raise a cloud no larger than a midget's hand, was a so-called charity gambling party in the plush Park Avenue duplex-penthouse apartment of Mrs. Vivienne Woolley-Hart, a flashy female of the international set.

She went by the name of the British coal baron who had been the fourth of her six husbands. Of all her marriages, this was the one that had given her the greatest notoriety as a result of the colorful didoes that seemed almost invariably to accompany her lavish party-giving. On one occasion, two eminent guests had resorted to fisticuffs. On another, an elephant and the Maharajah of Cooch-Behar had collaborated in an unrehearsed comedy act that had most of London in stitches. Vivienne had been throwing one of her more extravagant parties in the Maharajah's honor, and it had occurred to her that the presence of an elephant would give the affair the proper exotic touch. So an elephant by the name of Rosie had been rented from a circus. The Maharajah was so pleased at Mrs. Woolley-Hart's thoughtfulness that he climbed upon Rosie's back to drink a toast to his hostess. What no one had taken into consideration, however, was that Rosie was a dancing elephant. Finding the Maharajah on her back, she was inspired to go into her routine; but the Maharajah, unprepared for the exhibition, lost his balance and was dumped unceremoniously into a huge champagne-punch bowl.

Rosie the performing elephant, the Maharajah of Cooch-Behar, and even the wealthy Woolley-Hart himself were all in Vivienne's past by July of 1948. Her major interest at the time was operating the Gallery Vivienne, devoted to sponsoring young artists. In these circumstances, she was receptive to the suggestion that she rent her Park Avenue penthouse for $750 for an elaborate party that would further the cause of charity.

Ostensibly—and, as far as Mrs. Woolley-Hart knew, legitimately— the affair was designed to raise funds for the Medical-Surgical Relief Committee, then buying surgical equipment for hospitals throughout the world. Arrangements for the party were made with Mrs. Woolley-Hart by Charles (Chick) Farmer, a press agent, and William (Bill) Buckner, a society playboy. No suspicions about the purposes of the party were aroused until a couple of days before it was to be held. Then the reputable medical-surgical group evidently sniffed a

professional hand in the extended glove of charity, for it canceled its
sponsorship of the affair. But too late. Elaborate arrangements had
been made for a gala night; and the party, practically on the verge
of its first cocktail, wasn't to be halted without a sip.

It was held on Wednesday night, July 28, 1948. Chauncey Gray's
orchestra from El Morocco played on the terrace. A sumptuous supper was served to guests whose names registered in italics with New
York gossip columnists. Maxie Rosenbloom, the former prizefighter
and darling of the nightclubs, was there. So was Puk Paris, one of
the most curvaceous charmers of café society. So were a number of
Texas oilmen with flashily gowned companions. There were also
some nineteen dealers manning tables devoted to roulette, chemin de
fer, bird cages, and dice.

Inevitably, the party made quite a splash. By July 31, a Saturday,
gossip columnists goggled in print over the more glamorous among
the 100 guests and described some of the fancy play that had gone
on. One of the guests, it was reported, had stormed out shouting that
the games were crooked and he'd been robbed.

These lurid details caught the eye of District Attorney Hogan. To
him it was apparent that this kind of gambling was a far cry from the
innocent play at a church bazaar. And so, as soon as he reached his
office on Monday morning, August 2, 1948, he called for O'Connor,
his chief assistant.

"Have you seen the stories about this Woolley-Hart charity gambling party on Park Avenue?" Hogan wanted to know.

O'Connor said he had. He and his chief agreed that the affair bore
all the earmarks of a skilled, professional gambling ring in action;
and Hogan at once ordered a full-scale investigation. All the resources
of the District Attorney's office and the Police Department were
thrown into the hunt. Aiding O'Connor were two assistant district
attorneys, James J. Fitzpatrick and Seidler, and police cooperation
was insured by two of New York's best modern police executives,
Conrad Rothengast, then in charge of all detectives on Manhattan's
fashionable East Side, and James R. Kennedy, then the Inspector in
direct charge of the division. So began an intensive six-week investigation during which detectives sometimes worked day into night.

They began by calling in for questioning a number of café society
figures whom the newspapers had identified as attending the party.
Some, it developed, had been quickly undeceived and disgusted at

the shoddiness behind the Park Avenue facade. "They were just a bunch of bums running the affair," Maxie Rosenbloom told investigators. "I never shoulda worn a Tux."

Others agreed. Several of the players, investigators learned, had become suspicious about the charitable aspects of the affair and had stopped payment, or tried to stop payment, on checks they had issued to cover their losses after they ran out of cash. A number of witnesses identified Farmer and Buckner as the men in charge of arrangements for the party, but said that they hadn't had charge of the gambling. The work of the nineteen professionals manning the tables had been under the supervision of a third man, but none of the players seemed to know who this man was. Detectives tried to locate Buckner, but he had left the city. Farmer, when questioned, insisted that he didn't know the identity of the mystery man.

O'Connor and his assistants kept pressing the hunt, widening the circle of their investigation. Under steady questioning, the trails began to fan out in all directions. Some of the guests at the party had known others; as each new name was revealed, the witness was called in, questioned, persuaded to give the names of acquaintances he had seen at the game. Bit by bit the whole story began to emerge. A constantly expanding investigative process finally brought detectives to the one man who could help them most.

He was Dr. H. L. Hsieh, a fabulously wealthy Chinese merchant. One colorful legend was that when Dr. Hsieh left China, he brought with him to America a mysterious large wooden chest. This securely padlocked, constantly watched chest contained some $4 million in gold, rumor said. Whether this was true or just a fanciful story, one thing was indisputable: Dr. Hsieh certainly had money at his disposal. He was a slim man with polished manners, a fine and expensive taste in clothes, impassive of face, courteous of manner. He was a favorite of professional gamblers everywhere. He had tried his luck at Monte Carlo and in the gambling halls of Jersey; and everywhere he had tried it, his luck had been bad. He sometimes dropped $30,000 to $50,000 in a single night without the twitch of an eyelid. As may be gathered, gamblers were passionately fond of Dr. Hsieh. They loved both his money and the insatiable eagerness that, each time he lost, drew him back to their tables for another bout with chance.

As O'Connor and Seidler developed the picture by questioning their widening circle of witnesses, it became obvious to them that the professional gamblers who had manipulated the Woolley-Hart party had envisioned Dr. Hsieh as their *pièce de résistance* for the night. Before the party was held, they had extended themselves to make sure of his presence. And they had made certain that he would have society he liked.

It was an open secret among the café set at the time that Dr. Hsieh was greatly charmed by a striking product of the nightclubs named Marion Saunders. A flaxen blonde, she wore her long hair pulled to one side, and her eyes and features were made up to give her an exotic, almost Oriental look. When she walked into the District Attorney's office, she had a costly sable stole draped around her shoulders, and a huge diamond bracelet glittered on one arm, above a plainer bracelet composed of pearls.

Appreciating the effect Miss Saunders had on Dr. Hsieh, the gamblers had included her in their guest list. They had arranged that she and Dr. Hsieh should have an exclusive, specially placed table on the terrace, where the strains of Chauncey Gray's orchestra would be conducive to the proper atmosphere; and they provided the only brand of liquor that Miss Saunders would touch, Napoleon brandy. In this perfect setting, Dr. Hsieh stuck his money right into the plot, and when he did, the incredible happened. He began to win.

In all his ill-starred career at the gambling tables, Dr. Hsieh had been permitted only to dream of a night like this. Luck was with him. No matter how wildly and foolishly he bet, he kept winning. Watching this performance, observing how their most logical expectations were being shattered, the professional gamblers began to turn green around the gills.

"You should have seen them," a guest later told O'Connor and Seidler, chuckling at the recollection. "When Dr. Hsieh kept right on winning, they liked to have fell through the floor."

The gamblers were not alone in their shock. Dr. Hsieh was equally embarrassed. Long had he dreamed of a night like this, and when it came, it was on the one night he didn't want it. Still under the delusion that the Woolley-Hart game was being run for charity, he felt positively guilty about winning; and when he found he couldn't lose, the joy went out of the evening for him and he abandoned the play.

Dr. Hsieh had been taken so many times by so many gamblers that he had acquired an eye as professional as the gamblers themselves. He described for Hogan's assistants every detail of the play. He knew exactly what devices had been used; he diagramed the apartment and showed the exact spot each bit of equipment had occupied. He remembered the odds and the action, and he confirmed that he had seen some of the dealers in professional gambling houses in New Jersey where he had lost in the past.

But not even Dr. Hsieh could give investigators the one clue they most wanted, the name of the man who had supervised the gambling action. Baffled, O'Connor and his assistants turned to bank records for a lead. They had learned that $19,260 worth of checks had been made out by the victimized guests. Payment had been stopped on about $9,600 of these when rumors of a professional gambling tie-in began to circulate; but the rest of the checks, nearly $10,000 worth, had cleared through the banks. The endorsements on these canceled checks led Hogan's investigators to a sensational discovery. Once they began studying these endorsements, they found unraveling in their hands the skein of a mammoth conspiracy they had never envisioned when they started out. Suddenly, instead of probing a small Park Avenue charity party, they found themselves on the trail of Joe Adonis and the Syndicate.

It happened this way:

Each check that had been cashed at the Woolley-Hart party had two endorsements. One read: "Finance Company of America." The other was just a numeral—the mysterious figure "88."

"We knew this numeral was important, but we couldn't figure out what it meant, it baffled us," O'Connor explained. "If we had only known what it represented, we could have saved ourselves a lot of time and trouble. Eventually, we found out it was a check-casher's code, the number by which he could identify the man who had cleared the checks with him."

This key unlocked the mystery that had stymied investigators. The figure "88" was the code mark of Stephen Tolk, known to gamblers throughout the nation as a chemin de fer expert and onetime proprietor of New Jersey gambling houses. He was the elusive "third man" who had directed the gambling operations at the Woolley-Hart party. Up to this point the probe had been concerned chiefly with tracking him down; but hardly had investigators learned that Stephen Tolk was Mr. 88 when they began to make other discoveries that dwarfed this one. The new and all-absorbing interest stemmed directly from that second endorsement on the cashed checks—the Finance Company of America. For this was the check-cashing firm of Max Stark, otherwise known as Joe Adonis' man Mendel.

The instant Hogan's men established this tie-up they struck pay dirt. They uncovered the colossal financial affairs of a man who handled so many millions that he disrupted the operations of an entire bank.

Max Stark, whose importance as the financial custodian of Joe Adonis' enterprises had been spelled out three years before in the reports of Narcotics Agent Ross Ellis, was a one-man walking treasury, part-owner of a bank, and a banker's nightmare.

"We found that the New York State Banking Department in early 1948 had monitored the account of Max Stark, making note of every item over a period of several days," O'Connor explained. "From the banking department report, we got the names of a few people whose checks cleared in that period. We interviewed these people, and we found in every case that they were customers who had suffered heavy losses in the New Jersey gambling houses."

By questioning officials of the Merchants Bank of New York, Hogan's aides developed a startling picture. Daily, accompanied by a couple of burly guards, Max Stark would appear at the Canal Street branch of the bank, lugging satchels filled with bills of all denominations. It was a poor day when they contained as little as $30,000. Other days Stark would bring in $50,000, and sometimes he would even dump as much as $90,000 in front of a bewildered teller. This hoard of greenbacks had to be sorted, counted, and then exchanged for an equal amount in crisp, new currency, as gamblers always pay off the lucky winners in shiny new bills—a psychological trick of the trade that greatly enhances the thrill of winning. "Often," says O'Connor, "Max Stark would need $50,000 in new bills of $100 denomination."

The Merchants Bank of New York was kept busy. As one of its officials acknowledged before the Kefauver committee, the Canal Street branch found that the mere processing of Max Stark's daily tidal wave of currency was tying up the services of a teller and a bookkeeper all day long. It snafued the normal operations of the bank and left other customers snarled up in long queues waiting for service.

Bank officials finally appealed to Stark to take his business to the central office of the bank where there was more help. They promised that special arrangements would be made to give him the very best of service. For Max Stark was not only a wealthy customer, he was also an important part-owner of the bank. There were just 20,000 shares of Merchants Bank stock outstanding, and Stark had fortified himself with 2,000 shares—a 10 per cent interest that practically guaranteed him proper courtesy.

When Stark obligingly transferred his daily cash shuffle to the main office, officials extended themselves to please him and the head teller was assigned to count and recount the flood of gambling cash which sometimes took as long as five hours a day.

"We estimated—and we believed the estimate was most conservative—that Max Stark's cash totaled $200,000 a week," O'Connor says. "Remember, $30,000 was a poor day for him, and often he brought in as much as $90,000—nearly half as much in a single day as we allowed for the whole week. For this reason, we felt that our estimate of a $40,000-a-day average was ultraconservative. But when we sat down and figured out what this meant, we were truly shocked. Multiply it out and you will be shocked yourself. A cash flow of $200,000 a week, multiplied by 52 weeks in the year, comes to better than $10 million. When we hit that figure, we knew we were up against an operation so huge that it could only be a major project of the Syndicate."

Yet the flow of $10 million in cash through the pudgy hands of Max Stark in a single year did not tell the whole story, nor anywhere near it. Examining the records of his account in the Merchants Bank of New York, Hogan's accountants found that, in 25 months from July 1, 1946 to July 25, 1948, Stark had banked $6,810,847 worth of checks. Adding checks to cash produced a figure of $13,500,000 as representing the annual play in Joe Adonis' gambling casinos in New Jersey. "Actually, that figure was ultraconservative," O'Connor explains. "We felt certain that this was probably closer to a $15 million to $20 million-a-year operation."

And it may well have been a lot more than that, for Hogan's estimates were based on just one bank account—the transactions of Max Stark in the Merchants Bank of New York, where the records were within New York's jurisdiction. But this was not Max Stark's only bank account, nor was it by any means the full record of his business.

The complete records were in New Jersey, and these have never been revealed to this day.

The $15 million to $20 million-a-year figure projected by Hogan's investigators, it must be remembered, represented the total gambling play, not the total profit. Just what percentage of those crisp new greenbacks that Max Stark collected every day was paid out each night to winning bettors, no one knows. Hogan's experts felt that, on the basis of the one Max Stark bank account details of which they knew, they were safe in estimating a $10 million annual gross profit for the Joe Adonis casinos. The Kefauver committee, which later studied the Hogan evidence, felt that it was being conservative in placing the profit figure at one million dollars a month, or $12 million a year.

Once they had glimpsed the magnitude of this operation, Hogan and his aides found that the one-night Woolley-Hart charity gambling stand, the offense that had started them on the chase, was relatively insignificant. They secured indictments against Farmer, Buckner, and Tolk, all of whom pleaded guilty to gambling charges. This disposed of the lesser offense that had been committed in New York, but it did not of course affect the fantastic operation that was taking place just across the Hudson. This lay in the preserve of another state. What could Hogan do about it?

The New York District Attorney sat down with his aides and discussed the problem. Under New York law it is a misdemeanor to conspire to commit a crime, and therefore it would be possible to find an indictment for conspiracy in the operation of a gambling enterprise. But could New York indict for conspiracy to commit a crime when the crime itself was taking place in another state? That was the ticklish point.

Hogan himself made the eventual decision.

"He felt we should endeavor to set a precedent in view of the booming rackets," O'Connor said afterwards. "He felt that by digging into the Stark case we could get closer to racketeers who headed the New Jersey operation and its offshoots in New York."

With this decision, the New York probe steamed full speed ahead on its newly charted course. O'Connor and Seidler, with their detective aides, followed the same strategy they had adopted in the Woolley-Hart case. They obtained the names of prospective witnesses from the signatures on checks that had cleared through Max Stark's bank account; then they called in these heavy losers, discussed the situation with them and appealed for their help in breaking up the New Jersey gambling racket. Sometimes the victims were amazed to discover how badly they had been victimized.

"These were men of real means," Seidler recalled. "They had the money, and they could afford to lose. They didn't feel it the way you or I would. But, even so, sometimes they had no idea how much they were going for. I remember one man especially. He didn't know what he had lost until we totaled up his checks and showed him. The checks, of course, represented just what he had lost after he had run out of cash, for all of these players carried a fat roll to the game. But just the checks alone came to $36,000 in a few months' time. When we showed the man this, he was surprised and shocked. 'You've opened my eyes,' he said. 'I'm glad this happened. I worked too hard to lose money like that, but I didn't have any idea it was that much, I was having such a good time.' "

From such players, suddenly faced with the magnitude of their folly, Hogan's agents developed an explicit, vivid picture of the nightly carnival with chance in the New Jersey countryside. Joe Adonis, when he had had to terminate his multimillion-dollar games in West Paterson and South Plainfield, had opened up a new gambling gusher in Bergen County, in the rural atmosphere of the small town of Lodi. Here on Route 6, behind a gas station, was a Quonset hut that became known as Costa's Barn. The Barn was a drab-looking structure on the outside, but money had been spent with a prodigal hand to make its interior decor out-dazzle Broadway. The waitresses and cigarette girls were alluring creatures; the dining room was presided over by a maître d'hôtel who was later to establish his own famous New York restaurant; and the menu included wines and dishes to tempt epicurean palates. Food and drinks were all on the house; all that was required of the sated guest was that he play and lose his money.

Such was the original Costa's Barn, one of the most splendid of the Syndicate's "carpet" joints. From swank hotel or Park Avenue apartment, a wealthy player needed only to dial a Passaic number in New Jersey and fix the hour of his departure. At the appointed time, a gleaming Cadillac with liveried chauffeur would draw up before his residence and whirl him off across the George Washington Bridge for a night of excitement in the New Jersey countryside.

In May, 1948, this system changed. Joe A. demoted Costa's from a "carpet" to a "sawdust" joint. Instead of the lavish dining room, there was a snack and sandwich bar. It became primarily a dice game, with only one table for chemin de fer. The individual chauffeur service was also abandoned; but, even so, between 250 and 400 players a night continued to make the trip to Costa's. They departed from a midtown New York parking lot between Sixth and Seventh Avenues. There two dispatchers kept a fleet of twenty Cadillacs rolling all night long. As soon as a payload of four or five players had collected, a driver who was getting the usual $20 a night for his services would gather up his passengers and head for the game. The Cadillac fleet followed Route 6 to Little Ferry, where a transfer point was established at a bar and grill known as Charlie's. Here the customers would alight and wait for other cars to pick them up and transport them to Costa's. Car lights would be dimmed when approaching the Barn, and the players, as they got out and passed through the door, found themselves in a vestibule guarded by sentinels armed with rifles. Here each arrival would be identified and each politely but thoroughly frisked before being passed through an inner door.

Hogan's assistants, after they had identified some of the employees in Costa's, asked one of the dealers whether these elaborate precautions had been adopted from fear that authorities might try to sneak detectives into the Barn and stage a raid. The dealer's reply was the same as the machine-gun-toting guards at the South Plainfield game had given.

"No," he said. "This was just to prevent a holdup."

Having pieced together the mechanics of the Costa's Barn operation, Hogan's staff sought the kind of incontrovertible, eyewitness evidence that would enable them ultimately to bring action against the bosses.

"Any number of those who played and lost at Costa's described for us just how Joe A. supervised the operation every night," O'Connor said. "He didn't actually run any of the tables himself, but he was always there, the boss, the lord of the manor. Some of the witnesses also placed Solly Moretti at the game, another director of the enterprise."

The New York investigation of misdeeds in New Jersey had reached this point when, in mid-August, word filtered back to Joe A. and the Crime Cabinet that sat in Duke's. Inevitably, with Hogan's men questioning so many witnesses, there would be at least one loyal enough to mobdom to funnel back a tip that trouble was brewing. Adonis reacted swiftly. On August 17, 1948, he closed down the Lodi game. On the following day Frank Erickson suspended operations at his huge layoff headquarters, and the 2,600 telephones in the Bergen County bookie circuit went dead. Throughout the underworld rumbled that dire phrase, "The heat's on."

By this time, however, Hogan's agents had worked so long and so hard that they had their own pipelines into the Jersey rackets. Just as the underworld had been tipped to what they were doing, so they were now tipped to what the underworld was doing. This game of intelligence and counterintelligence led directly to one of the most priceless Gilbert-and-Sullivan sequences of the entire Jersey drama.

About ten o'clock on the night of August 18, 1948, a group of weary investigators were sitting around Vince O'Connor's office. "We had been going night and day, and we were completely pooped," Andy Seidler recalls. "We just didn't have energy enough to get up and go home, and we sat around chewing the fat about the case." In the group were Conrad Rothengast and Jim Kennedy and Captain William Grafnecker, then in charge of Hogan's detectives. Grafnecker remarked that he had been getting rumbles from some of his Jersey contacts.

"What kind of rumbles?" Seidler asked.

"I hear Joe A. has shut down the game, and now they're closing up the Jersey wire rooms until they see which way the wind blows," Grafnecker said. "By God, we must be getting too hot for them!"

Everybody was too exhausted at the moment to do more than grunt; but the next morning Seidler, who had been a newspaperman before he became a lawyer and an Assistant District Attorney, took a fresh view of the matter. Since the mob was already well informed about the extent and aim of Hogan's investigation, he reasoned, no harm could come from some publicity, and it might lead to a lot of interesting good. Seidler decided to stir things up and see what might develop.

As soon as he reached his office in the Criminal Courts Building, he called an Associated Press reporter whom he had known well for years. He suggested that, if the reporter asked O'Connor the right questions, he might get some interesting and newsworthy answers. Having dropped the hint, Seidler strolled into O'Connor's office and was just sitting down when the phone rang. His reporter friend began asking O'Connor questions. O'Connor, asking not to be quoted directly, gave the Associated Press as much as it was possible to give out at the time about the extent of the investigation and the resulting sudden shutdown of mob operations in New Jersey. The AP wires moved the story to all member papers, and across the Hudson, the New Jersey press once more headlined the news that the heat was on and that the flourishing underworld was going underground in Bergen.

One of the Jersey papers did even better than that. The Newark *Star-Ledger* was not quite so ignorant as Jersey officialdom about the location of Costa's Barn in Lodi, and it dispatched a photographer to the scene. The cameraman found the Quonset hut and started to shoot pictures. The instant that he did, things began to happen. Two guardians of the premises rushed the photographer and started to beat him up. They punched and kicked him and smashed his camera. But fortunately they didn't succeed in getting his plates, and the photographer, once safely back in Newark, developed a picture of Costa's Barn which the *Ledger* promptly used and which New York officials later exhibited in court as visual proof that such a place actually did exist.

This assault on a photographer made headlines in New Jersey and fanned the wave of newspaper publicity. The normally quiescent world of New Jersey officialdom, rudely jolted, came to life like a disturbed ant hill. On August 19 harried officeholders from across the Hudson began to beat on Hogan's door. One Jersey prosecutor, face contorted in a frown of perturbation, came, questioned, and departed —wreathed in smiles of relief because the mess wasn't in his county.

Hard on his heels came a second and even more distinguished caller. This was Attorney General Van Riper, the man who was responsible for law enforcement in all of New Jersey. Exuding personal charm, Van Riper explained his thirst for details and went directly into a long conference with O'Connor and Seidler. O'Connor was later emphatic in statements to the press, in his testimony before the State Legislative Committee, and in his testimony at New Jersey trials, about the extent and thoroughness with which he had briefed the New Jersey Attorney General.

"We told Van Riper the New Jersey mob operation was headed by Joe Adonis," O'Connor said. "We gave Van Riper the description and location of the Lodi game. We described the premises, told him how it was operated and gave him the names of several dealers and credit men at the game.

"We described for him the system of transportation to and from the game and told him that, in the sawdust operation, passengers were transferred at a grill named Charlie's and then taken to the game in other cars.

"We emphasized the importance of Max Stark. We gave Van Riper the name and address of Max Stark and told him that Stark's records were the source of literally hundreds of witnesses who could testify about the New Jersey gambling. We stressed that these records should furnish much more information than we had been able to obtain from one bank account, and we explained to him what that account showed. Van Riper appeared shocked. At one point he exclaimed: 'Why, he [Stark] is as guilty as if he was a teller in a cage at the game!' He left, thanking us for our information and promising a thorough investigation."

Van Riper had hardly disappeared when a third delegation arrived. This was headed by Michael Orecchio, the former plumber who had been elevated to Chief of Bergen County Detectives under Prosecutor Winne. Orecchio was accompanied by two detectives, and his party was soon closeted with New York investigators.

"We understand from news stories that you have some information about New Jersey gambling operations," Orecchio said. "Mr. Winne sent me to check on the news stories."

Again, patiently, O'Connor recited all the details. He took Orecchio step by step through the Woolley-Hart charity game investigation, showing him just how the evidence was developed; he described how the trail had led to Max Stark, the check casher, and explained how the questioning of witnesses whose names had turned up in Stark's bank records had led to information about the Lodi game.

"Where's the place supposed to be?" Orecchio wanted to know.

Captain Grafnecker gave him explicit directions on how to get there. Then once more O'Connor took up the story.

"I told them—Orecchio and his two aides—that this game, from our investigation, was a mob operation and that it was Adonis' game —Joe Adonis' game," O'Connor later recalled. "I said, 'Now, chief, you understand as to witnesses——' and at that point Chief Orecchio put up his hand and he said, 'Now, we don't want the names of any witnesses.' He said, 'If there is a leak we don't want it ascribed to our office.' I said: 'That's fine. It is not our policy to give out names in a pending investigation.' "

Once more, for Orecchio's benefit, O'Connor stressed the importance of Max Stark as the vital financial cog in Joe Adonis' far-flung, multimillion-dollar organization.

"I said," O'Connor recalled, " 'But the key to this whole picture is Stark. Stark is in New Jersey. His records are in New Jersey. If you get his records, you will have hundreds of witnesses, because his records will show the names of people who drew the checks that they gave at this house; so we have a handful compared to what his records can give you.' "

Orecchio, like Van Riper, departed breathing fire and brimstone. But the fire burned to ashes before the echoes of the protestations had died away along the Palisades. On August 21, 1948, just two days after Orecchio had visited Hogan's office, Prosecutor Winne said the New York District Attorney hadn't given him a list of any gambling places in Bergen at all. "All they gave me was rumors," he said. The next day, August 22, Winne was asked specifically about the gambling in Costa's Barn in Lodi, and he answered: "Until I get some names, some witnesses I can question, I will not believe that there is any such place." He added that he would like to talk to Adonis, but "I don't know whether he will come."

It was a plaintive remark that seemed to indicate the freedom of choice lay with Joe Adonis, not with the law of New Jersey which most citizens would have presumed to be superior.

Van Riper did a little better, but not much. He carried through on his promise to pick up Stark's records. These were obtained on August 26, 1948, but testimony some years later at the trial of Orecchio showed that nothing effective was ever done with them. Van Riper simply turned the records over to Winne, and the Bergen County Prosecutor acknowledged in trial testimony that he never ordered any of the persons whose names appeared on the records brought in for questioning. He also testified that he and two detectives had spent two hours hunting for Costa's Barn and couldn't find the place. The lack of follow-through on the Stark records especially annoyed Hogan's aides. Their information showed that Stark kept the most meticulous accounts, listing every check that cleared with him by name, date, bank, and endorser. They were convinced that Stark's full records, as

O'Connor had told Orecchio, would yield hundreds of names of potential witnesses compared to the handful that they had, and they were extremely anxious for the chance to examine the records themselves. But this opportunity was one they never got. Winne announced that examination by his accountants had showed that the checks clearing with Stark were those of reputable businessmen, not those of racketeers. "Of course!" O'Connor snorted in disgust. "These were the checks of the players at the games!" Ignoring this obvious point, Bergen County simply turned the precious records back to Max Stark; it took no action against him.

In New York, even though the essence of the crime that was being committed lay beyond the pale of his jurisdiction, District Attorney Hogan showed what can be accomplished by a prosecutor who really wants to prosecute. He and his aides prepared their conspiracy case against Max Stark and one of Stark's assistants. On September 13, 1948, a New York County grand jury handed up a criminal information against Bergen County's triple-chinned check casher and one of his employees. "Two Indicted Here for Acts in Jersey," *The New York Times* proclaimed.

Across the Hudson the silence was as the silence of the grave.

11

THE $228,000 BRIBE

I N September, 1948, with the Woolley-Hart exposure looming, Joe
Adonis was overheard by Hogan's detectives thinking out loud to
a confrere. "This Woolley-Hart party has caused me more trouble
than anything I've ever had in my life, and I don't know where this is
going to lead to," Joe A. confided.

The shrewdness of this remark impressed Hogan's aides. "Look
at that," O'Connor afterwards said, with something of the admiration
one accords an especially astute and capable adversary. "Even that
early in the case, Adonis had the foresight to see just how serious this
might be for him. It shows just how clever he really was."

And the aftermath showed how powerful the Combination really
was. For despite Hogan's investigation, despite prosecution, despite
exposure, despite headline publicity, the underworld remained immune, sacrosanct, virtually untouched for two more years in Bergen
County.

In New York, Hogan brought Stark to trial. He spread upon the
court record the incredible financial details about the activities of
the multiple-chinned check casher and the fantastic millions in gambling money that rolled into Joe Adonis' coffers from Costa's Barn.
The evidence was so overwhelming that Stark was convicted; but he

fought the conviction and ultimately got the case thrown out on a technicality—the contention that, though Hogan had indeed proved a colossal conspiracy, he hadn't been able to show that the actual deed of conspiring had taken place *in* New York.

The widely publicized conviction of the treasurer of Joe Adonis Enterprises made it incumbent upon Bergen County to exhibit some pretense of vigor. A sacrificial offering was needed, and Anthony (Tony Greeno) Guarini was chosen by acclamation. Guarini, the stalwart Joe A. henchman whose activities in Duke's had been spotted by the Federal Bureau of Narcotics a full ten years earlier, later testified in the Bergen County trial of Detective Chief Michael Orecchio about the manner in which he happened to be arrested on March 1, 1950, as a result of the Max Stark disclosures in New York.

Guarini insisted he had never met Orecchio until the former plumber called on him and asked him to be a good fellow and submit to an arrest for running that terrible gambling game in Costa's Barn.

"He said he was sick and tired of hearing about gambling and wanted to get the case cleaned up," Guarini testified. "He told me that, if I helped him out, he would appreciate it—and for that appreciation, I got one to three years in State Prison."

The departure of Guarini for State Prison left Joe A. and the Crime Cabinet in Duke's at liberty to operate in their usual freewheeling fashion. With Bergen in the spotlight, they simply moved their big games farther away, and about June, 1950, they set up shop in Mt. Freedom in Morris County, at the extreme northern end of the state.

This farcical sequence later drew the scorching criticism of the state legislative probers.

"To properly appraise conditions as existed in certain municipalities in Bergen County from 1945 to 1950 would be to paint a picture of uncontrolled gambling, of blindfolded public officials and of an indifferent or frustrated public," the Republican majority on the committee conceded. The committee remarked caustically on "the anomalous situation" that arose when New York convicted Stark for crimes committed in New Jersey, and it concluded: "It is apparent . . . that the situation in Bergen County should have been known to many law enforcement officers and particularly those connected with the office of the Bergen County Prosecutor and in the municipalities in which gambling was rampant. The failure to take action between 1948-1950 was inexcusable."

Events now conspired to build remorseless pressure against Bergen County and the racket warren it harbored. In Washington the Senate was becoming restive, and an investigating subcommittee began to pry into underworld scandals. The first sensational, headline-making revelations came on April 28, 1950, when the committee, then under the chairmanship of Senator Ernest W. McFarland (Democrat from Arizona) called to the witness stand the balding, pink-cheeked Frank Erickson, king of the bookies.

Erickson had been assured by the committee that he could testify freely, that nothing untoward could happen to him as the result of any testimony he might give—and he believed it. Calmly, therefore, he rattled off details about his business. He acknowledged that he operated in every state in the union; that he netted better than $100,-000 a year; that he had his layoff headquarters in Cliffside Park, New Jersey, and a business office to coordinate his affairs at 487 Park Avenue, New York.

This last admission was all that District Attorney Hogan needed. His detectives had been keeping the Park Avenue office under surveillance for some time, hoping to get evidence to justify a search warrant. When Erickson obligingly furnished them with the details they needed, they pounced. On May 3, 1950, while Erickson was talking shop with his brother Leonard, Hogan's raiders came barging through the door. They seized all of Erickson's records, almost a truckload, and found that they had stumbled on a gold mine of information.

Two of the more interesting exhibits were meticulous balance sheets prepared by I. George Goldstein, a Newark accountant, detailing the gambling take at the Colonial Inn in Hallandale, Florida. These showed clearly the interstate ties of top-level mobdom, for the interests of the New York mob and the Detroit mob had merged in the Colonial Inn gambling. Goldstein's account revealed that from November 1, 1945, to October 31, 1946, the gross profit from the Colonial Inn was $685,538.76. After a deduction of $40,760.50 for "charities," the net profit of $644,778.26 was split among the partners. Joe Adonis, who had only a 5 per cent interest in the business at the time, netted $34,276.94. Mert Wertheimer and his associates in the Detroit mob held 32½ per cent of the stock, and took out a handsome $222,600.10 share of the profits. Another Goldstein account for the Colonial Inn, dated March 15, 1948, showed that the New York mob had taken over control of the operation. Joe A. and Meyer Lansky each had a 15 per cent interest, Jake Lansky had 16 per cent, Vincent (Jimmy Blue Eyes) Alo 8 per cent, and Frank Erickson 5 per cent. The cash distribution this year was $215,891.33, of which Joe A. collected for his private purse a neat $32,785.70.

With this kind of evidence in his hands, Hogan moved swiftly. Following the same tactics he had adopted in the Max Stark case, he called in the businessmen who had bet and lost to develop his case against Erickson. One wealthy bettor confided to the DA's men that he had dropped $1 million since 1936 betting on the ponies; another, who said he began as a $2 bettor, admitted that the gambling virus infected him so badly that he ended up losing $20,000 in a single day. Erickson, Hogan's investigation showed, had condescended to provide direct, personal services to the extremely wealthy who lost well and at Christmas time had expressed his appreciation of their patronage by touching little gifts. In 1948, for example, Erickson had purchased from Tiffany's 1,000 gold, monogrammed tie clasps at a cost of $29,000 just to let the well-heeled boys know he hadn't forgotten them, and the following Yuletide he had distributed gift certificates for 124 hats worth $20 to $25 each at a total cost of $2,157.60. The result of these discoveries was that Hogan obtained the indictment of Erickson on sixty counts charging conspiracy and bookmaking; Erickson pleaded guilty, and on June 22, 1950, he was sentenced to a two-year term in New York City's Rikers Island Penitentiary.

Over in New Jersey, there was only silence—and inaction.

Still the scandal refused to die. In Washington, Estes Kefauver got the Senate to approve his bill creating the Special Senate Committee to Investigate Organized Crime in Interstate Commerce, and Kefauver took over the work that had been started by McFarland. With John Winberry prodding him on, the new Senate crime buster quickly focused a glaring spotlight on racket operations in New Jersey.

Lt. Walter Casey, the New York Police Department's racket expert, testified about the far-flung operations of Joe Adonis and the manner in which New York detectives had trailed big-league mobsters from Manhattan to the door of Duke's. Henry Silver, an employee in Joe

A.'s gambling houses, testified that he had worked as a clerk at the gaming tables and drew his pay through the mob's dummy corporations. Withholding statements were introduced into evidence showing that Silver was paid $3,350 in 1947 by the L & C Amusement Company, Joe Adonis proprietor, and that in 1948 he was paid $1,500 by the PAL Trading Company, Joe Adonis proprietor. Silver agreed that he had seen Joe A. in several of the gambling halls in which he worked and that Joe A. ate in them and walked around surveying the operations.

Explicit testimony—but it wasn't the only testimony. As the summer dragged by, Kefauver repeatedly needled New Jersey officials with additional evidence. He put Goldstein, the accountant, on the stand and publicized the size of Joe A.'s personal take. In 1946, the same year Joe A. was getting $34,276 from the Colonial Inn in Florida, he was paid an additional $76,581.14 by the G & R Trading Company and $12,328.60 from the B & T Trading Company. In 1949, Joe A. drew $7,240.20 from the PAL Trading Company and $43,093.80 from the General Trading Company. These, it was emphasized, were just isolated items in Joe A.'s total income; they represented amounts of which Goldstein had knowledge because he had prepared the business accounts of the dummy firms. But even Goldstein had no idea of the grand total of Joe A.'s resources because, he said, he did not work on the master's private ledgers.

The slow buildup of disclosures reached a climax on September 12, 1950, when Kefauver picked up Hogan's revelations about the fantastic banking operations of Max Stark and gave them a headline whirl. He followed this with the unkindest cut of all, calling to the stand two distinguished representatives of law enforcement in New Jersey—Michael Orecchio, the Bergen County detective chief, and Frank Nicholas Borell, the police chief in Cliffside Park, a man who for years had seen nothing particularly wrong about hanging out with the mobsters who congregated in Duke's.

Rudolph Halley, the committee counsel, asked how much Orecchio was worth financially. The detective chief, who explained that he also ran a private real estate and insurance business, estimated his net at "say around twenty-five or thirty thousand dollars."

"Do you have any other cash in the form of bills or currency?" Halley demanded.

"I have a safe-deposit box," said Orecchio.

> Q: Do you keep currency in that box?
> A: Surely.
> Q: How much do you have in that box?
> A: I have $10,000 in that box.

Orecchio explained that he kept this cash sum on hand because a man never knew when a profitable deal for a piece of property or some other investment might crop up and fast action would be required. Of course, he acknowledged, no such handsome opportunity had reared its head as yet, but a man never knew when it might. Senator Tobey, exasperated, asked sharply:

"Could you draw that cash quicker than you could draw a check?"

"Not necessarily, sir," Orecchio replied politely. "It is merely my way of doing business, that is all."

Borell, the Cliffside Park police chief, was even more casual about his financial affairs. Asked how much money he had in banks, he replied: "Approximately $50,000, $60,000, $70,000. It could be $80,000 or so." This nonchalant attitude toward money in chunks of tens of thousands of dollars led to some sharp questioning. Well, Borell explained, he had some six or seven bankbooks, and it was really hard for a man to keep count. Also, he had a safe-deposit box with some $15,000 in it, and he had, say, $15,000-$17,000 worth of government bonds. He acknowledged that he made only $4,500 a year as police chief, but he pointed out that he ran some concessions in Palisades Amusement Park. It was this private business interest, Borell insisted, that gave him a total income of about $25,000 a year. He conceded that he had frequented Duke's and had seen Joe A. there a lot, but, he said, he hadn't gone to Duke's "so much in the last three years, due to the fact that I can't stand the food. The food is very good, but it is not good for me."

This constant prodding by Kefauver had no effect in New Jersey. In its 1951 report, the Kefauver committee noted that Hogan's exposure and conviction of Max Stark had resulted in only a single, inadequate prosecution across the Hudson. "Following this conviction, Guarini was indicted and pleaded guilty in New Jersey," the committee reported. "No others were indicted in New Jersey, despite the fact that the name of James Lynch appeared on the back of almost every check as endorser. After Guarini 'took the rap' for the entire group, the houses continued to operate in New Jersey until the early part [actually, the summer] of 1950 when they closed down. There were no further prosecutions in New Jersey until after this committee publicly aired the situation."

The extent of the force-play that moved New Jersey to act has to be described in some detail to be believed. In addition to the pressure being exerted by Kefauver from Washington, District Attorney Hogan in New York was preparing his master case—a conspiracy indictment against Joe Adonis himself, based on the meticulously assembled eyewitness evidence that placed him constantly on the scene as the director of the great gambling game in Costa's Barn in Lodi. New Jersey officials were as aware of Hogan's activity as they were of Kefauver's disclosures, for Nelson F. Stamler, at this point the favorite rackets-buster of the Attorney General's office and the Driscoll administration, had been in constant touch with Hogan's office. As early as January, 1950, according to Hogan's own assistants, he had been informed in considerable detail of the major case they were preparing against Adonis.

During these same critical months of 1950, Stamler was also in frequent contact with Kefauver in Washington and the Senator made no secret of his determination to get the Jersey mess cleaned up, one way or another. Kefauver made it clear that, if Jersey didn't act, his committee would come in and practically blow the lid off the State House. He finally told Stamler that he intended to question Governor Driscoll himself, especially with regard to a $25,000 loan made to his 1946 campaign by Joseph Bozzo, a political figure in Paterson and an admitted acquaintance of Joe Adonis, Longy Zwillman and Willie Moretti. Stamler later testified before the State Legislative Committee that he returned to Trenton and reported all this to his boss, Attorney General Parsons.

"That man is not kidding," he said he told Parsons. "We had better do something about it. If we don't, there's going to be a lot of trouble."

Parsons, Stamler said, appeared very upset. The Attorney General indicated that he wanted to go into Bergen County, and in this Stamler felt that Parsons was sincere. But evidently there were restraints upon Parsons. Nothing happened. Indeed, on September 29, 1950, the New Jersey press quoted Parsons as denying he had any intention of sending a special rackets-buster into Bergen. "How can

I when I have not yet had a report on any New Jersey tie-up with New York gamblers?" the Attorney General wondered mildly.

Stamler later testified before the State Legislative Committee that Senator Kefauver was shocked by this bland statement. Wrathfully, according to Stamler, Kefauver told him that the Senate committee was going to subpoena Governor Driscoll to appear before it on October 12, 1950. "He said the Governor would have to appear," Stamler testified.

Only after Stamler had relayed this news to Trenton did New Jersey finally act. On October 20, 1950, a full two years and two months after the Woolley-Hart disclosures, Stamler was finally named to supersede Prosecutor Winne and conduct a probe of gambling and official corruption in Bergen County.

Stamler, with his working knowledge of Hogan's New York evidence for background, lost no time. On October 30, 1950, he swore out warrants for the arrest of Joe Adonis, Solly Moretti, James (Piggy) Lynch, Arthur Longano, and Anthony (Tony Greeno) Guarini. Guarini was still in State Prison serving out his previous sentence, but the others were at liberty and the following day, October 31, they all walked docilely into the Bergen County Courthouse in Hackensack and surrendered to the law.

The scene in Stamler's office was unforgettable. Joe A., the underworld mastermind who had given new dimensions to the word immunity, hadn't felt the nip of handcuffs in ten years; and, though he doubtless believed at this point that he could wangle his way out with relatively little difficulty, he didn't like what was happening. Lips grim and compressed, hard eyes staring murder—"the coldest goddamned eyes I've ever seen in a human face," Stamler comments —Joe A. nevertheless seemed determined to act the part of the gentleman of the mob if it killed him. His conduct was in stark contrast to his expression. His manner remained soft as silk, his voice so low Stamler could hardly hear him.

"Mr. Stamler, you have your job to do. You do it the best way you can," he told the dumbfounded rackets-buster.

Stamler wanted to question Joe A., on the chance that he might be able to obtain a few choice tidbits of information. He knew that, naturally, Joe A. wouldn't talk in front of a stenographer, and so he ensconced him in a room well wired for sound by State Police detectives.

"It wasn't any use," Stamler recalls. "He spoke so low and soft we couldn't get a thing on tape. The State Troopers thought he did it on purpose for fear he was being bugged, which he was, but I think it was just the manner he had cultivated. He always spoke in whispers."

In Stamler's outer office, Willie Moretti starred in the impromptu mob scene. Willie hadn't been indicted, simply because he had been astute enough to have his brother, Solly, front for him and had never shown his face in a gambling establishment; but when Joe A. and his three fellow unfortunates, with lawyers and bondsmen, trooped into Stamler's office, Willie trailed along. His purpose seemed to Stamler quite obvious. Willie wanted to see how things would go, how tough Stamler was inclined to be; and while he was watching for little clues that might tell him what he wanted to know, he kept bouncing around Stamler's office, his usual wisecracking, ebullient self. He joshed with the State Troopers, patted acquaintances on the back, and attempted, with broad jocularity, to make light of it all.

"Come on, come on," he said at one point to the troopers. "Why don't you boys forget it? We'll all go to Florida and have a good time."

He waved his arms expansively, including the whole room in his invitation. Then suddenly he whirled on Stamler.

"And that means you, too," he said.

Everybody laughed. Everybody, that is, except Joe A. He watched Willie's antics, but they didn't amuse him. His was a deadpan face to which the grimly bitten-in lips and the hard eyes gave a look of restrained menace. Lt. Eugene A. Haussling, of the State Police, nudged Stamler and nodded at Joe A.

"Look at him," he whispered. "He's really boiling inside."

So was the pot of crime and corruption in New Jersey.

The arrest of Joe Adonis had an almost immediate repercussion—the unfolding of a mysterious story about a $228,000 State House bribe.

With the arrest, Attorney General Parsons asked Hogan in New York to help the Jersey prosecution by turning over the evidence he had gathered. Hogan was then just finishing his two-year investigation. On November 9, he obtained criminal informations against Joe A., Solly Moretti, and the same three helpers whom Stamler had arrested, and he disclosed that he was turning over his voluminous and iron-clad grand-jury testimony to Stamler. This action intensified the pressure on the mob, and the mob's reaction to it was swift and startling.

On the night of November 12, 1950, a gangland delegation descended without warning on the home of State Republican Chairman John J. Dickerson, the powerful Bergen County boss who had been for so long the campaign strategist and political sponsor of Governor Driscoll.

Only one full version of this bizarre meeting has ever been told. That version belongs to Dickerson. He gave it more than two years later in testimony before the state investigating committee. A tall, beamingly expansive man who seemed to be practically shaking hands with everyone in the packed galleries when he testified, Dickerson pictured for the committee the shock that he had felt when he opened his door on this quiet Sunday night and confronted the sinister visitors from the nether world. He had been clad in pajamas and lounging about his home in Palisades Park when the doorbell rang. And when he opened the door, there were three of the five members of the Crime Cabinet that sat regularly in Duke's.

Closest to Dickerson—a stocky, balding figure with quick-darting eyes and the saucy grimace of the perpetual wiseacre—stood Willie Moretti. Slightly behind Willie was his thinner, more somber image, his brother Solly Moretti. And bringing up the rear, stolid-faced and almost ominously silent, was the Field Marshal of Crime, the masterful Joe Adonis himself.

Dickerson, who said he thought he had met the two Morettis just casually once before but had never met Adonis, testified that he was startled by the sudden appearance of these visitors and that, not knowing quite what to do with them, he led the way downstairs to his basement playroom. There, he declared, with Willie Moretti acting as the spokesman for the delegation, this conversation took place:

"He [Willie Moretti] said he was tired of being pushed around up there in Bergen County; that he had paid out a lot of money and that he didn't intend to take this laying down, and I believe he used a term 'unless something is done about it, he is going to blow the lid off' and language along that type. . . .

"So I said to him, 'Well, what do you come to me about this situation for?'

"And he said: 'Well, you are . . . state boss, you are state top man of the Republican party and we want this stopped.'

" 'Well,' I said, 'I know nothing about this. Who have you been paying it to?'

" 'Well,' he said, 'I have been paying it to Harold Adonis.'

"I said, 'Harold Adonis?'

"And he said, 'Yes.' "

Harold John Adonis, it must be explained, was no relation to gangdom's Joe A. He was a tall and flamboyant man of Greek extraction —dapper-mustached and flashily dressed. A publicity man, he had done campaign-promotion work for Governor Driscoll in 1946 and subsequently had been rewarded with appointment as a clerk in the Governor's office in Trenton. He was variously described, depending on who told the story, as a very special and confidential clerk or a very inconspicuous and unimportant clerk whose desk was tucked away in a cubbyhole far out of normal range of the Governor's eyes. In any event, in the spring of 1949, a time that coincided by chance with the heavy rumblings about wide-open rackets in Bergen and Passaic Counties, Harold John Adonis was dismissed from his State House job. It had been discovered that he was an inefficient clerk. But he was not so inefficient, nor so much out of favor, as to be in complete official disgrace, for some months later, in the gubernatorial campaign of 1949, he handled some of the radio publicity urging the re-election of Governor Driscoll.

Such was the man to whom Willie Moretti told Dickerson he had been paying a bribe. The State Republican Chairman testified that his instantaneous reaction was one of incredulity.

"It seems fantastic to me that they would pay any man like Harold Adonis with the little or no authority that he had," Dickerson told the legislative committee.

> Q: Did you tell him that?
> A: I did tell him that, yes.
> Q: What did you say?
> A: Virtually what I have just told you. I just couldn't understand it. I said, "How long has this been going on?"
> And he said, "I think we have been paying $12,000 a month for nineteen months."
> Q: To Adonis?
> A: To Adonis.

Q: Did you ask him how he was paying it?

A: Well, he said he had paid twelve thousand dollars a month for nineteen months, and I said, "When did all this take place?"

And he said, "We started paying him the early part of 1947."

And I said, "Well, when?"

And he said, "I think it is maybe February or March," and I said, "What could a fellow like Adonis do for you?"—Harold Adonis I am referring to—and he said, "He was in the Governor's Office." And he said, "Of this $12,000, $10,000 was going to Governor Driscoll and $2,000 was being given to Harold Adonis for handling it."

Q: Did he say—

A: And I said, "Well, I think it is hard to believe of Harold Adonis, but no one can ever sell me on the idea that the Governor ever got a dime." And he said, "Well—"

And I said, "I think you have just been sold down the river," or something along those lines.

Q: Did he say they were nineteen consecutive months?

A: Well, I inferred it, yes. When you say that, I didn't ask him specifically. . . . And then he continued with the story and he said, "He was not going to stand for Stamler pushing him around."

He said that he had paid—I am not, I don't know his exact phraseology—he said he had paid someone fourteen thousand dollars in Passaic County for Stamler to close up the Passaic probe. [This was an earlier and abortive probe of bookmaking.]

Q: Did he say who the person was to whom he paid it?

A: He did not say.

Q: Did you ask him?

A: I did not ask him. And he said that they wanted an answer on this and they wanted me to call the Attorney General and they wanted me to tell the Governor and to tell them as quickly as I could, and they were coming back the next night for their answer.

In this manner Dickerson eventually put on the record the details of the gangland ultimatum that posed the threat of a state-wide, state-rocking scandal. Just as significant as the Moretti disclosures, however, was the way in which New Jersey officials conducted the investigation of the fantastic allegation which they all insisted they did not believe.

The first play was Dickerson's. He testified that he telephoned Parsons and told the Attorney General it was imperative they meet as soon as possible the next morning. Parsons informed the disturbed

State Republican Chairman that he was driving to Hackensack in the morning and had planned to pick up Stamler at Stamler's home in Elizabeth on the way. Dickerson's reaction to this information is to be evaluated, in the light of subsequent events, as highly significant. Stamler was the administration's trusted rackets-buster, but Dickerson obviously, even at this early date, did not want to include him in discussing this matter. Of course Stamler himself had been involved, by indirection at least, in Willie Moretti's allegations. On the other hand, Dickerson didn't put a particle of faith in Willie Moretti's truthfulness, and in addition, since Stamler was in charge of the Bergen County probe, logic dictated that he should be informed as promptly as possible of the vital disclosure that had just been made by one of the most important gangsters whom he would have to question. This, however, was not Dickerson's view at the moment. He told Parsons bluntly that he did not want Stamler present, and so it was arranged for the Attorney General and Dickerson to meet alone.

The meeting took place at 7:45 A.M. Monday, November 13, 1950, just outside the Pennsylvania Railroad Station in Newark. The two men walked around the streets bounding a parking lot in the vicinity, and while they walked, Dickerson told Parsons of the surprise visit made by Adonis and the Morettis to his home the previous night. Dickerson insisted to the State Legislative Committee that he told Parsons the full story, including the alleged division of the money between Harold John Adonis and Governor Driscoll. "Unquestionably," Dickerson said, he told the Attorney General that Willie Moretti was returning that very night for his answer.

This "unquestionably" became eventually one of the most questioned adverbs in the entire legislative probe. The state committee, reacting to a suggestion by the press, wanted to know why State Police detectives had not been on hand, why Dickerson's home had not been wired for sound, why no independent record had been made of every word Willie Moretti uttered on his second visit when it was known a full twenty-four hours in advance that he was coming. No such procedure had been followed, Parsons told the committee, because he had *not* been informed by Dickerson of Willie Moretti's scheduled second call. He first learned of this, Parsons maintained, by reading of it in newspapers a couple of years later.

The same tender question about this initial oversight in the state investigation was raised with Governor Driscoll when he appeared as a witness before the state committee. Dickerson had testified that, after his morning consultation with Parsons on November 13, he drove to Trenton and waited until late afternoon when the Governor returned from an appointment. He told the Governor all, Dickerson said, just as he had told Parsons all. This was not, however, the way Governor Driscoll remembered it. The Governor testified in June, 1953:

"I have no present recollection of being informed that these men were going or had any intention of returning to Mr. Dickerson's home.

"My first state of shock, followed by a state of anger, occurred the moment someone suggested—Mr. Dickerson suggested that there had been anything wrong in this State House. That was enough for me. And it was that first statement that spurred me into immediate action. But as to whether or not I knew or didn't know about a return, a possible return meeting, I must report to the committee that I have searched my memory and I have no recollection of being told of any such repeat engagement."

This, then, according to both the Attorney General and the Governor, was the reason the State missed its first chance to get positive evidence about the alleged $228,000 bribe. They, said both Parsons and Driscoll, simply didn't know. And so there were no detectives in the shrubbery when Willie Moretti returned as he had said he would to the home of John Dickerson on the night of November 13. Dickerson's word was the only word on what followed, and it was given to the state committee in this question-and-answer sequence:

Q: Did he [Willie Moretti] come alone?
A: Well, there was a car in front and I don't know whether anyone was or was not in the car, because I opened the door and, of course, you don't know my house, but there is one step, a one-step outside platform, and I opened the door—
Q: Did he phone in advance of his coming?
A: He did not.
Q: He just rang the bell?
A: That is right.
Q: And you were waiting his visit?
A: He said he would be back and I knew he would be back sometime, at least I expected him to be back sometime.
Q: What did he say?

A: And I opened the door and he didn't actually say anything. I said, "I talked to the Governor and I talked to the Attorney General. They know nothing about this and as far as they are concerned the investigation will proceed." And he never answered me and turned on his heels and went away, and I closed the door and that was the end of it. . . .

Q: Did you report to Mr. Parsons about that return visit of Moretti, of Willie Moretti?

A: I don't recall talking to Parsons again about it.

Q: At any time?

A: At any time.

The investigation that was touched off by Dickerson's reports to Parsons and Driscoll now proceeded like some kind of game. As the account of the alleged $228,000 State House bribe passed down the investigative chain, vital details filtered out at every step of the way until the detective lieutenant who was ultimately in charge of the investigation didn't even know he was investigating a purported State House bribe.

Parsons, despite Dickerson's reticence where Stamler was concerned, drove to Hackensack from the Newark parking lot and told Stamler the details. Only, he said, he didn't mention one key item: the supposed split of the state bribe money, $2,000 to Harold John Adonis, and $10,000 to Governor Driscoll.

The next day, November 14, 1950, Parsons conferred with Colonel Charles H. Schoeffel, then Superintendent of State Police. Schoeffel kept detailed notes on what he was told, and he later testified: "I never heard the story about Moretti coming back to the house. And I never heard about the split-up of the money. I learned that first in this Chamber."

After his talk with Parsons, Schoeffel set the investigative wheels in motion by briefing his deputy, Major Arthur T. Keaten. Only, Keaten testified, all *he* was told was that Schoeffel had some information that Harold John Adonis might have been getting $12,000 a month from gamblers, and the object was to get a check on Adonis' income.

Keaten now called in the man who was to do the investigative chore, Lieutenant Hugo Stockburger—and all Stockburger was told was that there was to be a confidential check on Harold John Adonis' income. He didn't know anything about the gangland delegation's visit to

Dickerson, and it was three or four weeks before he heard somewhere that there was supposed to have been a payment of $12,000 a month. All he knew when he started his investigation, Stockburger testified, was that "Adonis may have had some connection with Bergen County gambling."

This, it seems, was achieving the nadir of the inconsequential with a minimum of executive effort. In view of the lack of zeal for fullest truth on the highest levels of the state, it is little wonder that not very much happened—not immediately, at any rate—to Harold John Adonis.

The flamboyant Adonis, then in his early forties, had been a fringe figure in New Jersey politics for years. A publicity woman who knew him well described him as a typical "pusher," eager to meet all the bigwigs in the state and generally successful in ingratiating himself with them. The personable Adonis began his climb with the aid of a fine tenor voice. He sang in the choir of the Second Presbyterian Church in Newark and became friendly with the pastor, Dr. Lester H. Clee, a politically ambitious leader in the New Jersey reform movement of the late thirties. When Dr. Clee ran for governor on an independent ticket, however, Adonis evidently saw the handwriting on the wall and switched his allegiance to Harold Hoffman. After Hoffman, he moved on to the Driscoll camp and went to Trenton with a winner.

Until scandal struck, Adonis had been known to newspapermen in Trenton as the executive clerk of Governor Driscoll; after scandal struck, administration spokesmen insisted vociferously that he had never been anything more than a mail clerk who hardly ever came to the Governor's notice. This description did not quite square with certain hard realities. For even after it had been discovered in the spring of 1949 that Adonis was so inefficient he must be dismissed he was obviously not in such complete disrepute that he had to be shunned. Months later, during Driscoll's campaign for re-election, he was still a constant and evidently welcome sight around campaign headquarters; and though he didn't have authority to sign tabs, he was notoriously well-heeled, entertained lavishly on the Governor's behalf, and handled some radio campaign publicity.

When Lt. Stockburger, considerably in the dark about the purpose of it all, started his investigation into the affairs of Harold John Adonis, he naturally began with the publicity man's home and neighborhood. Right away he discovered evidence of the kind of affluence one does not usually associate with a $4,100-a-year governor's clerk. For Harold John Adonis, his wife, and three children lived in a new and spacious two-story brick home located on a beautifully landscaped two-and-a-half-acre plot in Roseland, a suburb of Newark. It was a home, Lt. Stockburger quickly discovered, that had been built and paid for on the spot—in cash.

The detective, in trying to carry out the task he had been assigned, developed an intriguing picture of the wide swath cut by the former governor's clerk. He discovered, for example, that on March 11, 1949, just eleven days after he had been dismissed from state service, Adonis breezed into the Livingston National Bank and opened an account with a deposit of $2,000 in cash. The Livingston bankers told the detective that Adonis had advised them to let all the politicians in the neighborhood know he had honored their institution with his business; it would be good public relations for the bank, he said—do it a lot of good. The bankers were not impressed. Adonis, they told Lt. Stockburger, was "quite windy." Perhaps their judgment was colored by the fact that Adonis' account, opened with such a flourish soon after he had been dismissed from the governor's office, did not continue to prosper. It was built up to $2,600 in a short time, but then a steady series of withdrawals depleted it to about $50.

As Lt. Stockburger pressed his investigation into the fortunes of the bombastic former clerk, it became obvious to him that Harold John Adonis had not prospered nearly so well after leaving his $4,100-a-year job in Trenton as he had while he held it. For in the year before the axe fell in Trenton, Adonis appeared to have been loaded with cash. He had indulged in a spending spree of awesome proportions, beginning on April 23, 1948, when he paid $5,000, half in cash and half by check, for his two-and-a-half-acre plot at 170 Passaic Avenue, Roseland. On this land Adonis promptly began constructing a handsome home. Each Saturday night while the house was being built, Adonis would appear upon the scene, unroll a fat wad of bills and pay off all the workmen—carpenters, electricians, and masons—in cash. Lt. Stockburger testified that Adonis paid out these eye-opening amounts: electricians, $700; plumbers, $900; carpenters, between $3,300 and $3,400; masons from $7,000 to $8,000. He also paid $2,700 in cash for rugs and linoleum, $6,236.06 in cash for lumber, and $2,601 in cash for a Buick. In all, in this one twelve-month period from the spring of 1948 to the spring of 1949, Lt. Stockburger found, at least $43,892.51 had passed through Adonis' hands.

The State Police detective had no idea where all the money had come from, he told the state legislative committee in 1953; after all, he had not been instructed to find *that* out, though if he had happened to come across any outside sources of income for Adonis "of course I would have followed them up." No such discovery having come his way, Lt. Stockburger simply reported to his superiors that Harold John Adonis had indeed spent a lot of money. The detective's first report was dated November 17, 1950, two days after he had been assigned to investigate, and it was followed up by other reports dated November 20, 25, and 30. By the end of the month Lt. Stock-burger had a full picture of the scale of expenditures indulged in by the $4,100-a-year former clerk, but no move was made by him or anyone else in state authority to ask Harold John Adonis the simple question: How come?

Lieutenant Stockburger testified he looked at the Roseland home from the outside, but he never went up the steps, never rang the door-bell, never asked whether Adonis was present. One reason that he didn't, he said, was that the local postmaster had told him Adonis was away in South America. Adonis had indeed been in Venezuela in the fall of 1950, but he had returned and at the time the State began looking into his affairs he was living calmly with his wife and family in the house he had built with cash. Lieutenant Stockburger himself subsequently discovered this by the simple expedient of checking on Adonis' telephone calls. The telephone company record disclosed a surprising fact—that Adonis, for a mere clerk, had had consider-able conversation with one of the most powerful men in the state, Republican State Chairman John J. Dickerson.

The telephone company listed seven calls made by Adonis to Dickerson. The first had been made on November 1, 1949, in the final days of the Driscoll re-election campaign, and the last two on November 29, 1950, seventeen days after Adonis had been named to Dickerson by Moretti as the go-between in the $228,000 State House bribery plot. The first call on this last day had been made at 6:02 P.M., the second at 7:04 P.M. Adonis himself later said that the

primary purpose of these calls was to try to collect $800 he claimed
was still owed him for his services in the Driscoll campaign of 1949.
But this, he said, wasn't all that he and Dickerson discussed. "We
talked briefly of my experiences in Venezuela," Adonis said, "and
of my plans to return to Caracas within a few days." Adonis insisted
that he had also talked to other New Jersey politicians and officials
about his plans, making no secret of his intention soon to leave the
country.

It seems a pity that this vital point should have been one of the
details to escape the attention of Lt. Stockburger and other New Jersey investigators. Naturally, had the State known, the State would
have been eager to ask the key man in the alleged $228,000 bribery
conspiracy some pertinent questions before he left the country, perhaps forever. But, alas, the State did not know, and in December,
1950, Adonis went off quietly to Venezuela, attending to his own
private business concerns.

Not until some time after he had departed did the public of New
Jersey first hear of the smothered scandal. This came on January 4,
1951, when Governor Driscoll, in a press conference in Trenton, told
reporters that Adonis was being sought for questioning in connection
with the Bergen County gambling investigation. The vague reference
didn't attract too much attention at the time. The following day the
Newark News called Adonis in Venezuela, but he said simply that it
was "fantastic" to imply he knew anything about Bergen County
gambling. He positively didn't. However, he said, he was too busy
with his own private interests in South America to come back home
to testify. And there the matter rested for the time being.

It was still resting when, some months later, Adonis flew back to
the United States on June 27, 1951, and went directly to his home in
Roseland. His conduct suggests that he was unperturbed by the slightest apprehension. After all, why should he be fearful? When he first
went to South America, he carried with him letters of recommendation from some of the highest officials in the State—from Colonel
Charles H. Schoeffel, Superintendent of State Police, subsequently
charged with investigating him; and from New Jersey's two U.S. Senators of the moment, H. Alexander Smith and Robert C. Hendrickson.
Everyone concerned later explained that the letters given Adonis were
just courtesy "form" letters, but they had at least enabled the onetime

governor's clerk to appear in South America under distinguished aegis, and evidently, as far as anyone knew, the blessing still endured at home. For without revealing the slightest tremor indicative of a man who knows he is much wanted for questioning, he calmly took his family on a long automobile trip, first to Canada and then to Florida, with a long stopover in New Jersey between.

His presence in Roseland was no secret, but State authorities who wanted so badly to question him, as Governor Driscoll had revealed in January, had taken no precautions to make this possible in June. No watch had been established over Adonis' home, no arrangements had been made with local authorities to pass along a tip when this sought after man appeared. Many people in Roseland knew that Harold John Adonis had returned home; but—and here again one encounters incredible official timidity, a disinclination to act in any affair even remotely connected with the sinister and all-powerful Syndicate—the local police weren't going to ask for trouble themselves.

Chief Russel O. Williams of the Roseland police force, in talks to reporters Earl Mazo and Carol Taylor, expressed himself succinctly on the subject many months later.

"He was here all right," the chief said, referring to Adonis. "We used to see him walking along the street. But nobody asked me to do any investigating, and I'm not going to be any Schuster, sticking my neck out and getting myself shot on a corner for talking."

His reference was to Arnold Schuster, a handsome young former Coast Guardsman and detective buff, who had happened to spot and recognize one of the most notorious bank robbers of the age, Willie (The Actor) Sutton. He had notified Brooklyn police, and Sutton had been arrested. Schuster's feat was widely publicized.

According to Joseph Valachi, Albert Anastasia became so incensed at the glorification of Schuster that he flew into a maniacal rage and ordered Schuster shot as an object lesson to any and all who might be inclined to inform on the underworld. The death sentence was carried out on a dark evening in early March, 1952; and, like virtually all gangland-ordered executions, the Schuster murder was never solved. The impunity with which the underworld could commit such a deed pointed a lesson that even the most retarded citizen could understand: inform against the underworld at your peril; the law cannot protect you.

Chief Williams evidently understood the official ethics of his time. The lame-and-halt state investigation had not inspired him with any zeal to go out and stir up trouble when it was obvious that the most powerful officials in the state weren't anxious to have trouble stirred up. So 1951 passed into history, and nobody on any investigative level in New Jersey expressed any further curiosity about Harold John Adonis.

12

ROADS TO MURDER

AT 2 A.M. on October 31, 1950, the telephone rang in the home of John E. Selser, the former chief assistant to Prosecutor Winne and the man who had been let out of office because he was too active hunting gamblers and "not active enough" in politics. When the sleepy Selser answered it, he found Willie Moretti on the other end of the wire. Willie was badly upset. He had learned the Nelson Stamler had sworn out warrants for the arrest of Joe Adonis and his brother, Solly, among others, and he wanted to know: Would Selser represent them and see what could be done? Selser agreed.

This was the opening incident in a long chain that was to lead to the dissolution of the invisible government that had functioned for so long in Duke's—and to a whole succession of murders that would change the face of the American underworld.

The first scene in this many-act drama centered around the efforts of the mob to get the law to impose only farcical punishment. Selser was convinced from the first that the evidence against Adonis and the others was so tight that they had no alternative except to make the best deal they could in return for guilty pleas. Selser later revised this judgment and concluded that he had given his gangster clients bad advice. Testifying in the state inquiry in 1953, he said he had become convinced that, had Joe A. and the rest stood trial, they would have been acquitted, no matter what the evidence against them. So low, he felt, have modern morals fallen.

"The world is made up of hypocritical people who pretend to lead decent lives and know in their souls that they don't," Selser testified. ". . . These men [Joe A. & Co.] were opportunists who provided a nice place where people who went to church could gamble. I would describe the situation in Bergen County as idiotic. The public did not want the law enforced. I know the law was flouted by the church-going public who now talk of righteousness."

These bitter afterthoughts may have been prompted by the fact that the plans of the mob finally went awry. In appearances before a Bergen County grand jury and before the State Legislative Commit-tee, Selser testified in detail about the intricate maneuvers he had undertaken on his clients' behalf. Many a deal underlies the sup-posedly stern and solemn rites that are enacted in a courtroom when some mogul of the mob is haled before the bar of justice for sen-tencing. But it is rare indeed that the whole behind-the-scenes frame-work is exposed to public view. The Jersey drama was different. Sel-ser told all, describing both the deal he had made and the double cross that had come out of it.

It began in the office of the Bergen County Freeholders. Shortly after the Bergen County grand jury had indicted his clients, Selser testified, he walked into the office one day and found John Dickerson on the telephone talking to Attorney General Parsons in Trenton. "Tell Parsons I would like to talk to him," Selser told Dickerson.

Dickerson relayed the message and reported that Parsons said: "Call me in a couple of days."

Selser did just that, and an appointment was made for him to see the Attorney General in the latter's law office in Red Bank. There Selser told Parsons that he wanted to enter a plea to one count of the indictment, the conspiracy count, the one that carried the lightest penalty.

"You can't take a plea," Parsons told him.

"What do you mean I can't? Of course I can," Selser argued.

"I don't want you to."

"That's different. Why not, though?"

"I don't want a plea. I don't want to have my investigation stopped."

At this point the Attorney General was being very tough indeed. But Selser was persistent. He and Parsons met again and again, perhaps as many as a dozen times, he said, and finally a mutually satisfactory agreement was reached.

"There was very definitely a deal made," he testified.

The terms were these: Parsons agreed to accept a no-defense plea from Joe A., Solly Moretti, and their three cohorts. They were to get light, eighteen-month-to-two-year sentences, and with time off for good behavior they would be out of jail in about one year.

Secondly, there were to be heavy fines. Parsons, according to Selser, attached considerable importance to this. He wanted to collect enough to defray the costs of the state's special probe in Bergen. The amount agreed upon was $50,000.

And lastly, the most sensitive item of all, there was to be absolutely no probation. Joe A. was insistent on this. Two major points were involved. A man at liberty on probation must not consort with disreputable characters. If Joe A. should be seen in conversation with another hood in a nightclub, for instance, this would constitute a violation of probation for which he could be sent back to prison. This strict provision of the probation laws led to the second consideration. A gangster like Joe A. under probation would be virtually at the mercy of unscrupulous and rapacious law-enforcement officers. Anyone in uniform could hold a club over his head by threatening to report him unless he paid off, and Joe A. knew from long experience just how insatiable such demands could be. On this point, Selser had his instructions and could not yield. He quoted Parsons as finally assuring him: "There will be no probation." Selser added: "He [Parsons] told me there would be a one-and-a-half-to-two-year term, and he told me that would be it. It was distinctly understood there would be no probation."

Having achieved this meeting of minds, Selser demanded one more assurance—that the Bergen County Court would go along. Parsons, he said, told him: "I'll call you back in a couple of days and let you know." Subsequently, reassured by the Attorney General, Selser agreed to bring his clients into court and have them enter pleas.

One significant aspect of these negotiations is that they were conducted behind the back of Attorney General Parsons' own special rackets-buster, Nelson Stamler. Parsons, in his subtle way, let it be known that only he and Selser were to talk; Stamler was to be kept in the dark. At their first conversation, Selser testified, Parsons said any additional negotiations had to be with him and not with Stamler. "I didn't want to tell him [Stamler] that Parsons said I couldn't talk to him," Selser testified. "After all, I wasn't looking for a sock in the nose."

Against this secret background, Joe A., Solly Moretti, and their three less-distinguished associates appeared in court on May 21, 1951, calmly admitted they had been bad boys, and threw themselves on the mercy of the judicial system. This willingness to abandon the battle without so much as a skirmish astonished the press at the time, but the scene in the courtroom was so blatant that it presented little challenge to the cynical imagination. Selser, in fact, put the essential element on the record when he remarked for all to hear that the pleas had been preceded by "hard bargaining." Attorney General Parsons, who had appeared personally in court to supersede Stamler and handle all arrangements, bristled at the imputation and denied emphatically that any deal had been made. But it was obvious that there was at least one highly shocked and surprised man in the courtroom—Nelson Stamler. *The New York Times* reported that the pleas "appeared to surprise Mr. Stamler," who "conferred briefly with Attorney General Parsons and then asked Mr. Selser for an explanation."

The press was quick to point out that, technically, Joe A. and his fellow mobsters could be packed away for eighteen years if they were treated wtih maximum severity; but few, noting the gangsters' willingness to take this chance, had any doubt of the law's intention to treat them with gentlemanly consideration.

A week later, on May 28, 1951, in the courtroom of Judge J. Wallace Leyden, Joe A. and Solly Moretti and the others appeared on schedule. The Field Marshal of Crime was his usual handsome and well-groomed self. His carefully barbered hair was slicked straight back; his conservative suit had that certain indefinable, rich patina; his shoes were highly polished mirrors. Before the curtain went up, Joe A. chatted with representatives of the press. For so poker-faced and close-mouthed a man, he seemed especially amiable. He held no grudge against anyone, he murmured softly; the prosecuting officials were simply doing their duty; and as for him—well, that was the way the cards had fallen and he'd take like a man whatever the court decided was fair.

This turned out to be a highly evanescent mood. When the courtroom proceedings got under way, the sunny atmosphere suddenly congealed into forbidding ice. No Aleutian williwaw ever wrought a more drastic change. The cause was hidden and the changed atmosphere mystifying at the time, but the simple drama of events went like this:

Attorney General Parsons, again on hand to assume control of the State's case, recommended the one-and-a-half-to-two-year term agreed upon in his private consultations with Selser. Then Judge Leyden began to speak. Seldom does a judge choose to be more severe than the prosecuting official, but it quickly became obvious that Judge Leyden was kicking the Attorney General's lenient recommendations out the window. Later there would be rumors that stern Chief Justice Arthur Vanderbilt had expressed himself in no uncertain terms about the pending sentences in Bergen County. Whether this influenced Judge Leyden or whether he acted from other motives, this was what he did: He imposed a two-to-three-year term on each of the defendants. He levied fines totaling $75,000. And, worst of all, he doomed each of the prisoners to five solid years of probation after their release from jail.

The mob was furious at what they considered a double cross. The press noted at the time that Selser was visibly upset and angry. Joe A., who had come so jauntily to court, turned dour almost beyond recognition. Suddenly his scowling visage really looked the part of the overlord of Murder, Inc. This abrupt switch to murderous fury baffled newsmen at the time, for though the two-to-three-year sentence was more severe than had been anticipated, it didn't seem that it was *that much* more severe. Not understood at the time was the extreme importance the gangsters attached to the final item in their pact with Parsons—no probation.

Long afterward, Stamler was to regard that scene as a turning point in the Jersey drama. Joe A.'s sudden transformation from smiling good sport to human thundercloud struck him as a signal of storms to come.

"He was grim and you could see that he was boiling inside," Stamler later said. "But he kept it all under control. As he passed me, he said something out of the corner of his mouth, but he whispered as always. He spoke so low that I couldn't hear what it was he said."

Willie Moretti was cast in another mold. In the corridor outside the courtroom, he was literally wild with fury.

"Willie was harsh and noisy, a real pig," Stamler recalls. "His approach was: 'What the hell you doing to my brother? Who the hell you think you are?' On the day of sentencing, Willie was in the hallway screaming, 'You can't do that to my brother.' "

As Judge Leibowitz had noted, there is a strange thread of softness and sentimentality existing side by side with murder-hardness in the veins of the mob. To Willie Moretti, his brother Solly was sacred—it was a fraternal devotion that was to spur further acts of the Jersey drama.

With the jailing of Joe Adonis and Solly Moretti, the Crime Cabinet that had sat in Duke's and handled the affairs of the invisible government for nearly a decade began to dissolve. But it was not yet impotent. Three of the Big Five were still free to operate—Anthony (Tony Bender) Strollo, Willie Moretti, and Albert Anastasia, the grim Enforcer. And their power was still such that they were able to pull off the fix of the century.

In Brooklyn's not so placid Borough of Churches, another nation-racking scandal was brewing. A squat, beefy, completely amoral and unlovely individual named Harry Gross had become the bookie czar of Brooklyn. Some years earlier, hit by a succession of long shot winners, Gross had gone broke operating his Brooklyn bookmaking business, but he had managed to stage a comeback with the aid of kindly cops who had actually raised the necessary bankroll to get him back in action. On the second round, with this eminent official backing, Gross got really rolling in high gear. Soon he had a $20-million-a-year business, and his payoffs for protection amounted to a minimum of $1 million a year.

Unfortunately for Gross, at this time Miles F. McDonald became Kings County District Attorney and began to probe reports of the multimillion-dollar Brooklyn bookmaking operation. William O'Dwyer, who by now had just begun his second term as Mayor of New York, publicly denounced McDonald for conducting a "witch hunt," but as the heat of the "witch hunt" intensified, O'Dwyer suddenly felt the call to higher statesmanship and, with the blessing of President Harry Truman, went off to Mexico as U.S. Ambassador. There he was to stay for years.

With O'Dwyer south of the border, McDonald lined up a sensational bribery-conspiracy case against eighteen New York cops whom

Gross testified he had paid off. The reverberations shook all New York. The Police Commissioner and a flock of his principal aides quit under fire, and there was wide speculation that the first cop-bribery trial prepared by McDonald in Brooklyn would be only the first step in tracking a long spoor that led up and up, how high no one knew. This first trial, then, became the crucial test. If it was not stopped, it could produce all kinds of horrors. Stopping it, therefore, became the top-priority project of Joe A.'s still-functioning government of crime in New Jersey.

Perhaps not fully recognized at the time were the long-existing ties between Harry Gross in Brooklyn and Joe A.'s Syndicate operations on the west bank of the Hudson. Gross had once run a horse-room in Bergen County, where every horse-room, down to the hiring of its lowliest personnel, had been under the iron control of Joe A. and his strategy board in Duke's. Even after Harry Gross's Brooklyn operations became so vast and so profitable that he gave up the Bergen County enterprise, a community of mob interest and mob ties continued to exist. These were apparent in the identical procedures followed by Harry Gross in Brooklyn and Joe A. in Jersey.

Joe A.'s Jersey mob and Gross's Brooklyn ring used the same retail outlets to procure little gratuities for their official friends. As McDonald's detectives discovered, one retail television store on Manhattan's West 25th Street handled business for both mobs and also became the New York hangout for some of the rulers from Duke's. Harry Gross patronized the store when he bought expensive TV sets as Christmas gifts for the policemen on his pad; similarly, the Jersey mob used it, both for gifts to friends in high places and for their own personal business. The firm installed and serviced the set in Duke's and those in the homes of Tony Guarini and Albert Anastasia, among others, and Anastasia held regular court in its West 25th Street offices, gathering about him not only mob hirelings of note but several prominent prizefighters and their managers, with whom the mob had cordial relations.

In like fashion the books of a certain fashionable gentleman's tailor on Manhattan's West 52nd Street revealed the all-important link between the Brooklyn and the Jersey mobs. Gross testified before the Brooklyn grand jury that on one occasion he sent all the plainclothesmen in an entire Brooklyn division to this particular haberdasher to be fashionably outfitted; and the clothier's books, when they were examined by McDonald, showed that Joe A.'s coterie in Duke's had introduced some of their policemen friends to this same skilled tailor. Thousands of dollars' worth of apparel, more than one man could possibly wear, had been paid for as well by Sammy Bender, brother of Tony, the most inconspicuous of Joe A.'s four top councilors.

These well-established ties became important in early September, 1951, when Miles McDonald and his assistant, Julius A. Helfand, went to trial with the first menacing cop-and-bookie corruption case in Brooklyn. They had, of course, one essential witness—Harry Gross. And on the evening of September 11, 1951, Gross gave his two police guards the slip, jumped into his freshly serviced Cadillac, and vanished from his home in Atlantic Beach, Long Island. After a brief but frantic hunt, he was found late the following day placing a bet at the $100 window of the Atlantic City race track. Brought back to Brooklyn, questioned by McDonald and his staff, Gross insisted that his mysterious disappearance had been inspired only by his desire for a last fling before he was cooped up under rigid guard during the trial. But it quickly became obvious that Gross had been moved by far stronger compulsions.

When McDonald and Helfand put Gross on the witness stand, he went along with them and testified—up to a point. That was the damning part of it. He told his story right up to the brink of the first direct accusation; but when he was asked to identify the first cop whom he had paid, he balked. He refused to say another word, and in a gesture of supreme contempt for the law, he actually rose and stalked away from the witness stand. It was probably the most brazen fix ever engineered in an American courtroom. Had Gross not testified at all, McDonald and Helfand could have put off the trial and tried to revamp their case; but once he had begun to testify, and then balked, a directed verdict of acquittal—the complete exoneration of all the accused bribe-taking cops—became mandatory under the law. It was a complete jobbing of justice made possible only because Gross's conduct had been directed to this precise point by an astute and unscrupulous legal brain, reinforced by the authoritative dictation of the implacable arm of the Syndicate.

Miles McDonald's post-mortem investigation established beyond doubt that the deed had been performed by Joe A.'s well-drilled brain trust. Both McDonald's investigation and word filtering out through the underworld grapevine show, essentially, what happened.

Brooklyn cops and politicians, who had harbored Joe A. and Albert Anastasia even when they were running Murder, Inc., realized that the critical threat posed by Miles McDonald's probe necessitated a desperate remedy; and so they contacted their old friends who had moved to New Jersey but were still conveniently handy. Now a cardinal rule of the Syndicate is that it must protect its protectors even if it has to kill its own to insure silence. For only then can it offer the guarantees of safety that will enable it to do business with these same policemen and politicians, or others just like them, once the furor of the moment has died away and affairs have returned to crooked normalcy. This was the motivation that impelled the rulers of the Jersey mob to slip word to Harry Gross, virtually on the threshold of a Brooklyn courtroom, that he must come to parley. He was to be given a simple choice—death if he talked, a fortune if he didn't. The mob of course could have knocked him off the moment he slipped away from his police guards; but such crudity might have whipped up a greater scandal and caused no end of trouble. The deft payoff and the complete sabotaging of the State's case in court by legal process was the more sensible and satisfactory way of handling the affair.

And so on that night of September 11, when Gross performed his famous vanishing act, he did not drive directly to Atlantic City as he had told McDonald and Helfand. Brooklyn investigators at the time were mystified because Gross's car, serviced just that morning, seemed to have more mileage on it than could be accounted for had Gross taken the direct route across lower Manhattan and through the tunnel to New Jersey. The mystery of this extra mileage was later explained when Brooklyn authorities learned that Gross had taken a detour to get his orders and his payoff from the Syndicate.

There are two versions about the site of this conference. The underworld grapevine suggested a vague "house in Newark," the kind of designation it always used during the decade in which Joe A. was running the affairs of crime from Duke's. The second version, which seems more compatible with the extra mileage on Gross's car, is that the escaped bookie made a long trek to the north over the George Washington Bridge to a secret rendezvous in Bergen County.

Accounts of the parley agree that four representatives of the mob were present. Some versions insist that Meyer Lansky was one, but nearly all informants seem positive on the identities of two—Albert Anastasia and Willie Moretti. The other conferees are reported to have been representatives of the corrupt police and political powers in Brooklyn.

The inducement offered Gross to cooperate in sabotaging the State's case is said to have been a princely $125,000. The voluble Willie Moretti, all sources agree, did the talking for the mob, backed up by the glowering and terrifying presence of Anastasia. The conferees wanted Gross to perform his witness-stand balk for a 25 per cent down payment; but Gross, who had been a crook long enough not to trust other crooks, held out for 50 per cent on the spot. Finally, after much haggling, he agreed to be content with $60,000 and a promise for the rest—a pledge that, naturally, was to prove worthless. Just how this $60,000 was paid and what Gross did with it are mysteries that McDonald's investigators never could solve.

This is the seemingly credible account, vouched for in its essentials by investigators who deem their underworld sources reliable, of the last colossal fix arranged by the surviving moguls of the Crime Cabinet that had ruled for so long under the aegis of Joe A. in Duke's. It is perhaps not without significance that this night parley with Harry Gross, in which Willie Moretti played a stellar role, preceded by only three weeks another sensational event in which Willie again was the principal actor.

The fall of 1951 was a time rife with plots and conspiracies. Both the official world and the underworld were being shaken, the first with threats of multiple and disastrous disclosures, the second by the thrust to power of the most ruthless and vengeful figure in modern gangdom —Vito Genovese.

Genovese as the right-hand man of Lucky Luciano had climbed to high power in the Mafia by the mid-1930's. He ruled the Italian lottery in New York and New Jersey, from which, according to his estranged wife, Anna, he picked up more than a million dollars a year. With Anthony Strollo as his principal lieutenant, he dominated gambling, loan-sharking, and other rackets along the sprawling Manhattan and New Jersey waterfronts. His power was such that, when Lucky Luciano fell before the zeal of the crusading Dewey, he almost automatically would have taken Luciano's place as ruler of the New York underworld—except for one thing. Unfortunately for Genovese, there was pending against him the little matter of murder.

In 1934 a small-time Brooklyn hoodlum, Ferdinand (The Shadow)

Boccia, had steered a wealthy sucker to a crooked card game run by Genovese and his associates. The fleecing took place in the restaurant operated by Boccia's uncle at 533 Metropolitan Avenue in the Williamsburg section of Brooklyn; and when it was over, the wealthy businessman had contributed $116,000 to the mob. Boccia naturally expected a fat reward for engineering the affair, and he let Genovese know that he assessed his services at $35,000. Genovese put him off, saying he had a big deal winging and he needed all the cash he could get his hands on at the moment, but if Boccia would just be patient, he would be well taken care of.

Patience was not Boccia's long suit. He became irritated at the stall and committed the fatal indiscretion of deciding to take at gunpoint some of the money he felt was rightfully his. With a pal, Willie Gallo, he invaded a garage used by Tony Strollo as a drop for bootlegged whisky, and held up Strollo himself for $5,800. Treating Strollo with such incivility was like spitting in the face of Vito Genovese—and Genovese promptly decreed the death penalty.

Ernest (The Hawk) Rupolo, who was later to tell all, bungled the job of killing Willie Gallo, but the executioners assigned to Boccia were more efficient. They caught up with him at another card game in his uncle's restaurant. The suspicion of authorities quickly fastened on Genovese, and Don Vitone, as he had become known in the Mafia, decided that the climate of his native Italy would be healthier for the time being.

He had reason to believe that he would be well received in his homeland, for he had been back before. In 1933 he and his wife, Anna, had made a well-heeled pilgrimage to the land of Il Duce. According to Dom Frasca, a New York newspaperman who later chronicled Genovese's career, Don Vitone on that occasion had carried a letter of introduction to Achille Pisani, secretary of the Fascist party. Though Mussolini was making headlines with Cesare Mori's crusade against the Mafia in Sicily, Pisani and Genovese had little difficulty in understanding each other. Don Vitone wined and dined and wenched the Fascist bigwig, a successful wooing that seemed to prove, as Bill O'Dwyer was later to tell the Kefauver committee, that it doesn't matter who a man is, businessman or racketeer—his pocketbook is always attractive.

When the Boccia murder unpleasantness made it necessary for Don Vitone to make a second trip to Italy, he took with him his bulging wallet; and from time to time, during most of the eight years he stayed abroad, his wife replenished his resources with trips across the Atlantic. Though Mussolini hated the Mafia, it soon became clear that he bore no ill will for the New York Mafia chieftain who had so much to recommend him. Genovese quickly became a favorite in high Fascist society. His money bought him women, power, and recognition. On the one hand, he became the head of Italy's Camorra Society, blood kin of the Mafia; and on the other, he went into legitimate enterprises. He bought a power plant in Nola. He contributed $250,000 to the construction of a Nola municipal building. And Benito Mussolini, in gratitude for such a sterling contribution to the Fascist cause, rewarded Don Vitone with the title of *commendatore,* the highest civilian award in all Italy.

Vito Genovese was useful to Il Duce in other ways. Back in New York, there was a fiery anti-Fascist editor, Carlo Tresca, who was putting out an Italian-language newspaper called *Il Martello,* "The Hammer." Tresca attacked the Duce in the most savage terms, and as part of his documentation of the case against the Italian dictator, he derided the close association of the Mafia-hating Duce with Vito Genovese, the Mafioso wanted on a murder charge in New York. The vitriol in Tresca's pen scarred the sensitive hides of Il Duce and Don Vitone, and the inevitable happened. Carlo Tresca was standing on the corner of Fifteenth Street and Fifth Avenue about 9 P.M. January 11, 1943, when a gunman walked up behind him and calmly blew his brains out. Officially the case was never solved, but agents of the Federal Bureau of Narcotics have put on record, in sworn testimony before investigating committees, their subsequently acquired knowledge of the affair. According to informants, Genovese passed the word across the Atlantic, and Carmine Galante, who was to become a terror of the modern underworld, did the deed.

World War II and the invasion of Italy by the American army disrupted this paradoxical relationship between the Mafia chieftain and the dictator who hated the Mafia. For Il Duce, the war spelled disaster and death; for Don Vitone, only new opportunity and power. Like a big cat, Don Vitone leaped agilely from one side of the fence to the other, and when American forces came up the Italian boot, they found Don Vitone waiting to receive them with open arms.

Once again, as in Sicily, the Mafia worked closely with the military. Vito Genovese became virtually indispensable to the American brass, and so high did they rate him as man and patriot that they had no hesitation in signing for him the most glowing of testimonials, which were found later among Genovese's personal effects:

June 9, 1944

This is to certify that Vito Genovese has been employed by me as my personal interpreter since the 28th of January, 1944. He has been invaluable to me—is absolutely honest, and as a matter of fact, exposed several cases of bribery and black-market operations among so-called civilian personnel. He has a keen mind, knows Italians as do few people, and is devoted to his adopted home, the U.S.A.

CAPT. CHARLES L. DUNN
Provincial Officer, Nola.

November 8, 1943

TO WHOM IT MAY CONCERN:

The bearer, Vito Genovese, is an American citizen. When the undersigned arrived at Nola District, Mr. Genovese met me and acted as my interpreter for over a month. He would accept no pay; paid his own expenses; worked day and night and rendered most valuable assistance to the Allied Military Government.

This statement is freely made in an effort to express my appreciation for the unselfish services of this man.

MAJOR E. N. HOLMGREEN, U.S.A.
Civil Affairs Officer
Allied Military Government, Nola

December, 1943

TO WHOM IT MAY CONCERN:

During my service as Civil Affairs Officer in authority March 26, Nola Commune, Vito Genovese was my interpreter and acted as my assistant in many matters. He served without any compensation whatever. I regarded him as trustworthy, loyal and dependable, and attest to the fact that he has been most helpful and has been of service to the United States.

MAJOR STEPHEN YOUNG, U.S.A.

Orange C. Dickey, an agent for the Army's Criminal Intelligence Division, discovered the patriotic Don Vitone's darker side. In the spring of 1944, Dickey began an investigation of widespread black-market operations in the Foggia-Naples area. Wheat, sugar, and olive oil were being stolen from Army depots by the ton and funneled

into the Italian black market. Army trucks were used to transport the
supplies outside the military encampments; rendezvous would be made
with private trucks and cars to which the cargoes would be transferred—and the trucks would then be burned. On June 4, 1944,
Dickey obtained statements from two Canadian soldiers involved in
the black-market ring. They admitted that they had driven a number
of the stolen and heavily laden trucks to their rendezvous points and
then on to the vineyard near Nola where Dickey had discovered a
sizable truck graveyard. According to the Canadians, the password
for the operation had always been, "Genovese sent us."

Dickey pursued his investigation for two more months until he felt
he had an ironclad case against Genovese as the head of a huge black-
market ring. During his investigation, he also learned that counterintelligence suspected Genovese of being a spy. It appeared to Dickey
that Don Vitone was a man who should be arrested, and he made
the pinch. When he did, strange things started to happen. It quickly
developed that the Army brass had positively no enthusiasm for
pressing charges against their indispensable interpreter. Genovese had
ingratiated himself so well at the top—and perhaps knew so many
secrets—that no one in the Army hierarchy would move against him.

Frustrated Agent Dickey had notified the FBI as a matter of routine of the prisoner he had on his hands, and he finally got word back
that Genovese was wanted in Brooklyn for that old Ferdinand Boccia
murder. The Army evidently breathed a great, gusty sigh of relief at
this prior claim on Don Vitone, and Dickey was assigned the task of
escorting the man nobody wanted back to the States.

Genovese, despite his great patriotism and affection for America,
did not seem especially anxious to return. In later years, Dickey testified before the McClellan committee about his trials in the Genovese
case, and in response to a question by Robert Kennedy, then McClellan's chief counsel, he described some of the inducements that were
dangled before his own eyes.

"At various times," he testified, "I was offered many things. At
one point, I was offered a quarter of a million dollars to let this fellow
out of jail. On one occasion, when I was offered another sum of
money, I had with me an officer by the name of Lieutenant Dillon."

Dickey refused all such bribes and turned Genovese over to the
Kings County District Attorney's office. Even before he did so, the
State's case had suffered a fatal blow. Rupolo was scheduled to tes-

tify against Genovese about the arrangements for Boccia's murder, but under New York law, the testimony of an accomplice is not enough; there must be corroboration from some independent, outside source. In the Boccia case, Assistant District Attorney Julius Helfand thought he had the corroboration that he needed. Rupolo recalled that Peter LaTempa, a cigar store salesman with unsavory associations, but not himself involved in the plot, had happened to be around and to overhear some of the details of Boccia's execution. LaTempa was held as a material witness and was placed, at his own request, in the Brooklyn City Jail for safekeeping.

There, on January 15, 1945, the fate that had overtaken Abe Reles overtook LaTempa. LaTempa, who suffered from gallstones, had obtained a prescription for some pain-killing tablets. On this January morning, he asked for some of his medicine. A glass of water, with the tablets dissolved in it, was given him. LaTempa drank the potion —and, in minutes, he was dead. The city toxicologist later reported he had died "of an overdose of a sedative." The glass of water he had been handed had contained enough tablets "to kill eight horses," the toxicologist found.

With the key witness thus eliminated and with no replacement available, Vito Genovese on June 11, 1946, walked out of Kings County Court a free man—and fully able to take up where he had left off some ten years earlier as a ruler in the top echelon of American crime. Just thirteen days after his release, on June 24, 1946, chieftains of the clans gathered to welcome him home, to signalize his victory over the law and to do him homage. The party was held in a small private banquet room in the Hotel Diplomat in midtown Manhattan; and, though the mobsters themselves weren't aware of it, their privately uttered thoughts were recorded for posterity by the FBI which had had an advance tip and had wired the premises for sound.

Genovese was welcomed back into the world of the American Mafia, as protocol required, by the eldest Mafia chieftain present. This happened to be Santo Volpe, the Pittston, Pennsylvania, Mafioso who went by the soubriquet, King of the Night. Volpe embraced Genovese and led him to the leather-upholstered chair, the seat of honor, at the head of the long, rectangular banquet table. One by one, the other assembled Mafia chiefs paid their homage to the man who had hobnobbed with one of the world's most powerful dictators and who had just added to his prestige by doing a classic, Mafia-style jobbing of American law.

Despite the conviviality of this gathering, Vito Genovese was not completely happy. He had been away a long time, and though Anthony (Tony Bender) Strollo had minded the store for him and even sat on the Crime Cabinet that met in Duke's, this was not the same thing as holding the real power. Others had acquired that in his long absence. Frank Costello was known as "The Boss" or "The Prime Minister"; Joe Adonis actively commanded the legions of crime from his field headquarters in Duke's; Albert Anastasia was the Enforcer for this ruling dynasty; and the Morettis were the fixers and influence men. Vito Genovese, who should have been heir to the mantle of Luciano, found himself blocked off.

Joseph Valachi was later to describe to the McClellan committee the extent of Don Vitone's unhappiness.

"Well, when he came back," Valachi testified, "he was mumbling and grumbling and he was giving hell to Tony Bender, as 'You allow these people to sew up everything and tie up everything,' but Tony told him, well, he told him to make the worst of things, so that is what I have been doing. Well, he said, 'I didn't tell you to get chased out of Duke's.' . . . Yes, he felt that Moretti, Albert and Frank—and I don't remember whether Joe Adonis was included in this, but he felt that they had everything sewed up."

Genovese kept grousing, but there could be no doubt that, almost from the moment he was released from prison, he had become again an awesome power in the Mafia. Tony Bender Strollo, who ruled Greenwich Village and the Lower West Side of Manhattan, had always owed him fealty; and, as Valachi testified, "you see us boys in the Village actually belonged with Vito Genovese. In other words . . . if Vito Genovese had any trouble, he depended on Tony Bender and his crew, which is us. Second, Mike Miranda, and third, Richy Nowak. That was his stronghold."

In 1949, the mob threw a big bash at the Copacabana, Frank Costello's favorite stamping ground, and when Vito Genovese appeared, he was treated with such marked and servile respect that New York detectives concluded he was, as of that moment, the single most powerful figure in the American underworld. It became the fashion in the press of the time to call him "the kingmaker" of the underworld, a kind of Mafia elder statesman; and, though this designation was not completely accurate, it did reflect both the degree of his power and the anomaly of his position. He was such a menacing figure that even the ruling Costello-Adonis dynasty treated him warily and with respect, but as long as Joe Adonis ruled in Duke's and kept his iron hand on the preponderance of the troops of the underworld, Genovese's was more a potential than an actual and dominating power.

All of this changed when Joe Adonis, Solly Moretti, and the rest were packed off to prison in the Costa's Barn gambling disaster. With their departure from the scene, the delicate balance of power was drastically altered. A vacuum began to develop, a situation made to order for the ruthless power grab of Vito Genovese. For some time he had been laying the groundwork, nibbling away at the prestige of the ruling coterie in Duke's, his special target, Willie Moretti.

The personality of the brash, wisecracking Willie was wide open to the kind of undermining assault that Vito Genovese launched. For some two years before the climactic events of 1951, Don Vitone kept insinuating that Willie Moretti, afflicted by syphilis, was suffering from a weakening of the brain cells and was babbling in a manner that threatened to disclose the most precious secrets of the criminal conspiracy.

"Rumors started getting around between us," Valachi testified, "that Vito is sore, and there is no money, and the agitating about Willie losing his mind. . . . That is about two years before the talk like that was getting around, only in our regime, our group."

Vito Genovese talked this way, Valachi explained, "only to Tony Bender, and his close ones. In other words, it was between us. One time he was known to say, 'What are we, men or mouse?' "

One thing was certain—Vito Genovese was no mouse.

Willie Moretti was at the boil. Much credible evidence indicates that he burned at the "double cross" he felt had been pulled on him in the sentence meted out to his brother, Solly. As Al Capone had wept at the grave of his brother, Willie Moretti grieved at the unjust fate that had sent Solly to prison—despite all the money he had paid out during the years to purchase influence in the right places.

Willie was also deeply worried. Solly's introduction to prison life had been rough. The story comes from John Winberry, the dogged investigator who had recruited a task force of private informants in Bergen County. Winberry had been able to do this despite his dismissal from the Attorney General's office, because he had never compromised and even the members of the mob respected this quality in him and knew he was a man to be trusted. The result had been a flock of inside-the-mob contacts, one of them a flunky of Willie Moretti's. Shortly after Solly went away, this character confided to Winberry that all was not well in the State Prison in Trenton. One of the first persons Solly had encountered there had been Anthony (Tony Greeno) Guarini. Guarini, who had been chosen to take the rap for the entire mob in the first place, had then been subjected to double indignity—a second indictment and a second sentence in the Costa's Barn case. If Willie Moretti felt he had been double-crossed, Tony Guarini was convinced he had been double double-crossed; and when Solly Moretti arrived in prison, Guarini upbraided him as a lousy fixer and a dirty double-crosser, and proceeded to give him what was described as "a helluva beating."

All of this added yeast to the ferment in Willie Moretti. Stamler had him before the Bergen County grand jury for a brief and routine appearance in the spring of 1951. Willie blandly denied all. He had never made any payoffs to anybody. He had never engaged in the rackets in his life. He wouldn't, he said, know John Dickerson "if I fell over him." This last statement was going a bit too far in view of Dickerson's own positive account of the manner in which Willie had made that startling Sunday night visit to his home and disclosed the story of the $228,000 State House bribe. Willie evidently became aware that this head-on conflict of testimony laid him open to a perjury indictment, for early in June, 1951, he reappeared in Stamler's office, told Stamler he had not "understood" the questions that had been put to him and would like a chance to correct his testimony. Here was a chance, it would seem, to get some direct and invaluable evidence about the State House bribe mystery, but Stamler did not seize the opportunity; he did not call Willie Moretti back before the grand jury. It was an omission on his part for which he later was to be severely criticized in the state inquiry.

Stamler's justification has always been that he could see Willie was seething inside. Willie indicated to him very clearly, he says, that he might be willing to testify much more fully in the fall than he would if called back at once in June. Willie said that he just wanted to get away from it all, just wanted to go off to his spacious seashore home in Deal, New Jersey, just wanted to think things over for the summer. It was clear to Stamler that Willie, who had become accustomed to wielding all kinds of influence and fixing everything, still couldn't quite believe it was beyond his power to ameliorate Solly's fate. He still expected to be able to work some miracle that would spring Solly from prison before his time. Stamler himself was convinced that the age of such miracles had passed, in Willie Moretti's case, at least, and so he was content to let frustration have its effect, anticipating that he would have a much more talkative witness in the fall.

Independent corroboration for Stamler's version comes from a potential witness who never was called in the state inquiry. This was a Bergen County businessman who had been backed right through the wall by a combine of the mob and the politicians. According to his story, the collaborators had desired his well-situated place of business to set up a gambling game even larger than the one that had run in Costa's Barn. They offered to buy him out; and, when the businessman wouldn't sell, they began a series of official harassments that finally drove him into bankruptcy. Still hoping to right the wrong through litigation, the businessman had gone to the Jersey shore in the summer of 1951 to seek the aid of Willie Moretti, who had knowledge of the entire affair and could help by testimony if he would.

"I went down to Monmouth County and spent a whole week around Monmouth Park [the beautiful flat-racing track at Oceanport, just outside Long Branch], waiting to see Moretti," this man later related. "Finally, on August 7, 1951 [he exhibited ticket stubs to prove he had been at the park that day], I caught up with him in the paddock. I told him the whole story. . . . He said: 'Them crooks. I pay . . . and this is what I get. A double cross.' "

According to this source, Willie spoke freely about the payoffs he had made and of the manner in which the protection he had bought had failed him when he most needed it. He meant to blow the whistle, he intended to get revenge, he said. As an indication of this determination, he agreed to testify for the harassed businessman when his case came up in court.

This vengeful Willie Moretti, according to Nelson Stamler, was the same man whom he encountered in the corridors of the Bergen County Courthouse in Hackensack just sixteen days after the Harry Gross fix that was still cloaked in underworld mystery. Stamler bumped into Willie by accident and found, he later testified, that

Willie was practically flipping his lid. He remarked, Stamler said, that he had always operated "just like the president of a racetrack, strictly pari-mutuel"—his way of saying he had always paid off. Willie said he was ready now to go before the grand jury, and he wanted "to testify against plenty of people."

"What people?" Stamler asked.

"Some of the county leaders," Willie replied.

Stamler later told the State Legislative Committee that he whipped out a subpoena and served it on Willie on the spot. He admitted to the committee that he didn't keep any record of the subpoena; it was, he said, just a blank, a spare, that he carried with him for such emergencies. Stamler admitted, too, that he had not followed what would have seemed like normal investigative procedure—to take instant advantage of Willie's eagerness and get his story on a record before he could change his mind. Stamler wanted to do this, he says, but Willie was spouting so loudly and intemperately, resorting to unprintable abuse, that he feared any statement obtained under these circumstances would be useless.

"He was cursing almost every other word," Stamler later recalled, "and we decided to let him calm down, get his thoughts in order, and then try to get the truth from him before the grand jury."

So Stamler scheduled the appearance of Willie Moretti before the Bergen County grand jury for October 10, 1951, a fateful delay.

On the morning of October 4, Willie drove from his home in Deal to Cliffside Park. Since Duke's had closed its doors, he and Albert Anastasia had fallen into the habit of meeting in another rendezvous in the same block, across the street from the Palisades Amusement Park. Their new hangout was Joe's Elbow Room at 793 Palisades Avenue. The Elbow Room was not mob controlled as Duke's had been; it was simply a convenient place for two elder statesmen of the rackets to meet, sit at a table, and discuss matters of the moment. On this particular morning, Willie Moretti's chauffeur parked his master's shiny, new, cream-colored Packard convertible just down the street from the Elbow Room a few minutes before 11:30 A.M.

Willie got out of the car, leaving his well-marked racing sheet, fruit of his communion with the morning line, on the seat behind him. As he started toward the door of the restaurant, a man who had come out on the sidewalk, apparently looking for him, rushed up to him, shook hands effusively and followed closely at his heels as stocky Willie

Moretti, not a premonition on his mind, walked through his last door.

Subsequently, Mrs. Dorothy Novack, thirty-three, a waitress in the restaurant, gave authorities a picture of the reception committee that had assembled to meet Willie. It was shortly after 11 A.M., she said, when two men entered the deserted restaurant and seated themselves at the counter. They ordered coffee and cake and had just about finished when two more men appeared. These later arrivals selected a table in the middle of the restaurant, directly in front of the door, but they did not appear to be particularly hungry. One ordered a glass of orange juice; the other had no appetite at all. The first two men who had been sitting at the counter now moved over and joined the newcomers at the table. The waitress described all four as stocky Latin types, men in their fifties. Shortly before 11:30 A.M., one of the men left the party at the table and went out to the street, looking up and down. When Willie appeared, the lookout rushed up to him and almost smothered Willie with his demonstrative greeting.

As Willie and his escort entered the restaurant, the three men at the table all stood up. They shook hands with Willie warmly, and they talked away in a tongue the waitress felt certain was Italian. This flow of cordial discourse was interrupted momentarily when one of the men asked Mrs. Novack to bring them all menus. The waitress turned and went through the swinging door into the kitchen to get silverware for the table. Hardly had she disappeared when, in the restaurant behind her, the most infernal racket broke out.

When the startled waitress and the kitchen help peered out through the swinging door, the restaurant was deserted except for Willie Moretti. The four gentlemen who had welcomed him so effusively were gone, and they had left behind them a recumbent form.

The fifty-seven-year-old Willie lay on his back, his feet stretched toward the door, legs apart, the toes of his polished shoes pointed up. His red tie had been half-twisted around his neck as if somebody had tried to throttle him. One hand was clutched at his chest like that of a man trying to rid himself of some smothering pressure; his other arm was outstretched, flung wide across the floor. Two pools of blood were spreading around his shattered head. And almost directly above him was a gaudy sign reading: "Chicken in the Rough—$1.50."

13

HOW NOT TO SOLVE A MURDER

AMERICANS for years have been beguiled by a comfortable cliché—
"crime doesn't pay." But as the Mafia had demonstrated time
without end, it does pay and it pays in such astronomical figures that
the average man has difficulty comprehending the facts. At the core
of their vast conspiracy lie two techniques—the fix and murder. The
fix has purchased influence all up and down the chain of American
politics and government; but when, despite the fix, circumstances get
out of hand, there is just one final resort—murder. It is on murder
and the threat of murder that the underworld counts for its success.

It is murder that makes the Mafia able to defy all the processes of
American justice; murder that guarantees its emperors their immunity. It is murder and the threat of murder that silence the lips of vital
witnesses, that cause a man caught in gangland's toils to blank out
his mind and know nothing about events that happened right before
his eyes. The menacing power of the underworld is far more immediate and more real to him than the vague and often ineffective
guarantees of protection by the law. A vastly corrupted American
law-enforcement system has long excused its own derelictions by
rationalizations such as those that for so long deluded Youngstown's
citizens: "Who cares if the rats bump each other off?" An indifferent
citizenry has accepted this exculpation of official failure and has

largely adopted the attitude that gang murders don't matter. On the contrary, they are the murders that matter most, for as long as gangland can enforce its edicts with such finality, it can and will maintain a system superior in its power to all the judicial machinery of the nation.

In October, 1963, the McClellan committee was shocked by testimony that showed the incredible immunity of the underworld when it commits the cardinal offense of murder. Police Superintendent O. W. Wilson of Chicago told the committee that across the nation 62 per cent of "run-of-the-mill murders" are solved. But, he said, Chicago had had 976 gangland killings since 1919, an average of twenty-three a year, *and only two had been solved.* The odds in any given case, Wilson pointed out, were roughly 500 to 1 that a gang member could slay with impunity.

"The most nefarious action of those engaged in organized crime is their resort to murder to maintain discipline within their organization," Wilson told the committee. ". . . These killings were executions —executions of competitors—executions of those who would muscle in on profitable illicit operations—executions of those who welshed on money due—executions of those who informed to law enforcement agencies or competitors—executions of those who stood in the way of ambitious labor racketeers."

The rule of murder is graphically expressed in the Chicago statistics, for the Windy City's experience is not unique—it is typical. Gang murders are almost never solved. And one of the reasons they are not is that there is all too often no great desire, no passionate commitment, to solve them. As a case history in official lethargy, as a vivid illustration of how *not* to solve a murder, the Willie Moretti investigation was a classic.

The telephone call came into the Cliffside Park Police Department at exactly 11:28 A.M., October 4, 1951. Officer Frank Neffgen, who was on desk duty, deduced only that there had been a shooting of some kind in Joe's Elbow Room. He telephoned Dr. Sol H. Sklor, who answered emergency calls for the department, and asked Dr. Sklor to go and see how bad it was. When Dr. Sklor arrived, he found a patrolman standing by Willie Moretti's outstretched body, and he saw at a glance that things were not just bad, they were fatal. Chief Frank Borell—he who had been so casual with the Kefauver committee about his tens of thousands of dollars, he who said he hadn't made a gambling arrest in thirty years because he hadn't known about any gambling—arrived almost immediately, took one look at the body lying on the restaurant's tile floor and identified the victim, applying to him his old racket name.

"Why," he said, "it's Willie Moore."

Dr. Sklor, who had pulled an envelope out of the dead man's pocket and read the name on it, looked up and said: "I'm sorry. It's Willie Moretti."

Chief Borell didn't say anything.

Dr. Sklor, having no patient whom he could help, looked around to see what he could see. The partly full glass of orange juice that one of the killers had been sipping still sat on the table. Two bullets, quite flattened, were on the floor by the body. The doctor picked them up and gave them to Chief Borell. Another bullet was imbedded in the table top; still a fourth in the woodwork near the door. It was obvious that Willie Moretti had been the target of a fusillade.

Something else became obvious very quickly: that this was a murder investigation that wasn't going to get anywhere.

Never did an emperor of crime pick a more unpropitious time to get himself killed. For October 4, 1951, was the opening day of the World Series at Yankee Stadium. The New York Giants of Lippy Leo Durocher, the team that had just pulled off the Little Miracle of Coogan's Bluff by beating the Brooklyn Dodgers on the wings of Bobby Thomson's thunderous home run, were on their way to humbling the Yankees by a 5-1 score; and all during those first hours, while Willie Moretti still lay outstretched on the restaurant floor, police and detectives kept going out to take a look at the game on a nearby television screen.

"Willie was almost ignored," said reporter Bill Longgood, who was there. "What I remember most about that afternoon is the police rushing back and forth telling each other the score of the ball game. There was poor Willie stretched out dead, murdered, on the restaurant floor, but hardly anybody paid any attention to him."

State Police witnesses later conceded unhappily to the probing State Legislative Committee that the initial stages of the investigation had been so incredibly bungled that newspapermen, spectators, almost anybody who had any desire, had handled the physical effects like the orange juice glass that might have had fingerprints and been valuable as evidence. The committee wanted to know whether any potential evidence had actually been spirited away in the confusion; but police witnesses reacted with horror to this suggestion and were positive no clues had been so completely lost. Under the circumstances, it would seem that such certainty could have expressed little more than a pious wish.

Only one high prosecuting official arrived quickly on the scene— Nelson Stamler. Photographers got a picture of the tall, husky rackets-buster, dressed in a light summer suit, staring down at the restaurant floor where his most important witness had been forever silenced. Stamler was soon to boil over at the conduct of the Willie Moretti murder probe, but he gave no indication of it then. Indeed, his first reaction was strangely ambivalent for a man whose star witness had just been killed. Walter Arm, a star reporter for the *New York Herald Tribune,* quoted Stamler's off-the-cuff impression that the murder was "gangster-inspired." Stamler added: "I don't know why, but it was a good thing. Poetic justice, I'd call it."

The justice ceased to be poetic to Stamler once he discovered, as he swiftly did, that he wasn't to be permitted to have anything to do with the murder probe. The prosecutor who was to handle that chore was Harry L. Towe—the same Harry L. Towe whom Willie Moretti had recalled with such gratitude for having nol-prossed his murder indictment in the William Brady affair. Towe's injection into the case stemmed from a decision made by Parsons almost a year earlier when he first sent Stamler into Bergen. The Attorney General had decided then to split the duties of the prosecutor's office into two parts. Stamler was to concentrate on the gambling-and-official-corruption probe while the regular work of the office would be handled by another appointee.

A former judge, Francis V. D. Lloyd, had originally handled this normal office routine. Lloyd and Stamler seem to have gotten along well; but in the fall of 1951, Lloyd, who was not in good health, expressed his desire to give up his post in Bergen and a successor was named. The choice fell on Towe, who had the strong backing of John Dickerson and other leaders of the Bergen Republican machine—the very machine that stood in potential danger of being blighted by the possible exposés of Stamler.

Towe, who was serving as a Congressman in Washington (he had been there nine years and was in the middle of his fifth term), suddenly abandoned the nation's capital and returned to Bergen to take up what would appear to be a not particularly inviting task, that of being one-half of a county prosecutor in the midst of bursting scandals. The transfer had been made on October 1, 1951, just three days before Willie Moretti was murdered.

Political gossip at the time offered a couple of rational explanations for this strange move. It was suggested that the Bergen post was to be only a stepping-stone for Towe. One report was that he would eventually succeed Parsons as attorney general; another, that he was being groomed as the organization's candidate for governor. Towe himself denied that he had been motivated by any such alluring prospects. When he testified in the later state inquiry, he said he had become tired of the burden of maintaining two homes, one in Bergen and one in Washington; he had become tired of commuting between the two; and since he would get the same pay, he had decided he would be better off as a Deputy Attorney General handling the Bergen Prosecutor's office. He could "recall no discussions with anybody" about the shift; he couldn't "remember anyone suggesting it"; it had been all his own idea.

At the time of Moretti's murder, Towe said, he was on his way to the Yankee Stadium in the company of John Dickerson, Sheriff Martin Ferber—a stalwart Dickerson supporter—and Richard Drukker, a Passaic County publisher. Towe said he was paged at the ball park, left at once, and got back to Cliffside Park about 2:30 P.M.

He clashed almost immediately with Stamler. Stamler afterwards testified that Towe, almost as soon as he took office, "told me he wanted me the hell out of there [Bergen County]" and that, on the afternoon of the murder, Towe told him peremptorily to keep his nose out of the murder investigation. Towe at first denied before the state committee that he had ever talked to Stamler on the day of the murder, but later admitted he might have; he at first said he had no recollection of having told Stamler to keep out, "although I may have."

The quarrel between the two prosecutors became so acrimonious that Parsons called both men to his Red Bank office and laid down the ground rules: Stamler was to handle the probe of crime and corruption, Towe, the Moretti murder case. Ironically, no one except Stamler was connecting Moretti's murder with its background. Towe was asked by the state committee if he thought at the time that the

Moretti murder had anything to do with gambling, and he replied: "I don't know if I had the actual thought." The state committee noted that "Parsons failed to attach any significance to a possible relation between the charges of the receipt of protection money by Harold Adonis and the murder of the man who said he had paid protection money to Harold Adonis." The committee stated it thought Stamler's conviction that he should have handled the murder probe "may have had merit" and that "the assignment of Towe may have been injudicious."

This original snafu was indicative of the more complete one to come. Though the murder had taken place in a business section in midday, no effort was made to canvass the area for potential witnesses for at least two months, as Major Keaten of the State Police later acknowledged before the state committee. Willie's pockets were searched for possible clues, but there was so much confusion, Major Keaten conceded, that no one could ever be absolutely certain that the list of effects as finally compiled was definitive.

Among the clutter in Willie's pockets, detectives found some $1,850 in cash; a lot of keys, including one to a safe-deposit box; and a number of business cards, on many of which were jotted telephone numbers, initials, and cryptic notations that undoubtedly meant something to Willie but not much to anyone else. There was also a newspaper clipping, dated October 14, 1950. The story quoted Governor Driscoll as expressing the hope that no gambling witnesses would get shot in the Bergen probe, and it quoted Willie as scoffing, "He don't have to worry—this ain't Chicago." Another clipping dealt with Willie's appearance on a radio program just a month before his murder. Then he had quipped: "Old gamblers never die. They just fade, fade and fade, and then retire peacefully."

All of this was grist for the journalistic mill, but it didn't help solve the murder. There were, however, a couple of elements in the case that, it would seem, should have been helpful to authorities. There was Mrs. Novack, the waitress who had served all four of Willie's slayers and had had a good look at all of them, undistracted by any other chores since they were the only persons in Joe's Elbow Room at the time. In the hours immediately after the murder, the information that newspapermen got from police sources seemed quite optimistic. It was said that all four men were familiar to Mrs. Novack, since they all had been in the restaurant previously. It was said even that there was a positive identification of one of them. But as time passed Mrs. Novack's recollections began to "fade, fade and fade," and officials finally said that she really couldn't identify or describe anybody except in vague, general terms.

Even without the waitress' recollection, there were a couple of items of evidence that might have been important. The killers, in the haste of their departure, had left two hats behind them on the hatrack. Their mute evidence suggested that the gunmen who had done Willie Moretti in had come from New York. The band of one bore a label: "Howard's of Brooklyn." One of the hats bore a tag from a cleaning establishment in the Greenwich Village area of lower New York; but, as the McClellan committee was later told, "this unfortunately was prematurely released to the press and by the time the investigators got to this hat-cleaning place, the slip or bill was missing."

The law, as can be seen, was having a terrible time wrestling with evidence. It was having a comparably hard struggle with motive. Before long authorities bought the story that Vito Genovese had been spreading for two years—that Willie had been bumped off because his softening brain and gabbing tongue had made him a danger to the mob. This thesis was supported by references to Willie's supposedly dangerous admissions before the Kefauver committee; and vast sections of the public, never having read Willie's testimony, never having had occasion to wonder why Frank Erickson's far more frank and damaging admissions had never led to murder, accepted this widely purveyed version as probably true. Anyone, however, who has read Willie's words in the Kefauver transcript quickly discovers that all the evidence there points, not to a softening brain, but to a quick and agile one.

Willie had been called before the committee on December 13, 1950, just a month to the day after John Dickerson had turned down his demand for protection for his brother and Joe A. There was, of course, no reference to this in his testimony; no suggestion that he had ever had anything to do with the rackets; no intimation that all the eminent gangsters he admitted knowing were anything but "well-charactered" men. When Rudolph Halley picked up this phrase and wanted to know if Costello and Luciano and Capone weren't really ruthless racketeers, the exchange went like this:

Moretti: Well, I don't know if you would call it rackets.

Halley: How would you put it?

Moretti: Jeez, everything is a racket today. (Laughter in the hearing room.)

Halley: Well, what do you mean by that?

Moretti: Everybody has a racket of their own.

Halley: Are these people you are thinking of when you are talking about the mob?

Moretti: Well, the newspapers call them the mob. I don't know whether they are right or wrong. If they would be right, everybody would be in jail; is that right?

Halley: Is that what you mean when you say the mob, these fellows that you meet at the racetracks and the gambling places?

Moretti: People are mobs that makes six per cent more on the dollar than anybody else does.

Again titters of mirth swept the hearing room, and Halley, obviously hitting nothing but foul balls, switched the questioning to Willie's political contacts. Willie said blandly that he was a man with a lot of friends and that naturally, as a man with a lot of friends, he knew a lot of politicians. Asked to name a few, he insisted, "I don't care to reveal their names right at present." The committee, in one of its most considerate moods, deferred to Willie's delicate sensibilities on this point. It pressed him only mildly, and Willie produced just one name of a politician he couldn't deny knowing and feeling grateful to —Harry Towe. Halley let the point go, as if his question had been satisfactorily answered, and asked Willie about his political contributions. And Willie declared: "I never made no contributions—only my voice."

This was the kind of testimony that was a motive for murder? John Selser, who probably knew Willie Moretti as well as anybody, told the State Legislative Committee he had been almost ready to accept the official theory about Willie's murder until he read Willie's Kefauver testimony. He knew, he said, that Willie was "a strange lad" who "would tell you almost anything at any time," but after he studied Willie's performance before the Kefauver group he became convinced that Willie was "mentally capable—more so than the examiners."

The complete ineptitude of the noninvestigating murder investigation, which seemed all too eager to embrace Vito Genovese's propaganda about Willie's softening brain, did not become apparent until two years later when Major Keaten of the State Police took the stand before the state investigating committee. Keaten, whose nickname on the force was Buster, was a stockily built man, bland-faced, with a high forehead, and glasses. He had been sent into Bergen to help Towe with the Moretti murder investigation, but this action hadn't been taken until a week after the murder. When he arrived, Keaten found everything in great confusion. He conferred with Towe, and he evidently learned that virtually nothing had been done for he quoted himself as telling Towe: "There is no use crying over spilt milk. We'll have to start from scratch."

Keaten actually was starting from much farther back than he knew. He had supposed, he said, that the neighborhood around the murder scene would have been canvassed immediately after the crime, and it was not until two months later that he learned even this elementary step had not been taken. Trying belatedly to rectify matters, Keaten sent his detectives out on a house-to-house canvass, and one of them, N. Thomas DeGaetano, came up with a most peculiar discovery.

On December 13, 1951, DeGaetano called at the home of Mrs. Caroline Hilbert at 14 Marion Avenue, Cliffside Park, adjacent to Joe's Elbow Room. Mrs. Hilbert recalled that on the day of the Moretti murder she had been listening to the Arthur Godfrey program and Godfrey had been just about to sign off, a couple of minutes before 11:30 A.M., when she heard the fusillade of gunfire in the nearby Elbow Room. Five shots had been fired in rapid succession, she said; then there had been a momentary pause—and a sixth. Mrs. Hilbert ran to her window, from which she had a clear view of the entrance of the Elbow Room, and as she looked out, she called to her next-door neighbor, who also had heard the shots. While the two women stood staring, they saw the killers leave the restaurant. Two of them, Mrs. Hilbert said, got into a green car parked across the street; and three others (not two as police had been told, a discrepancy that might possibly be accounted for if a lookout had been established on the street) walked almost casually, with no trace of hurry, down the street to Marion Avenue, where they got into a blue car. Both cars bore New York license plates, and both roared away, vanishing quickly.

Mrs. Hilbert had obtained only a momentary glimpse of the departing killers, and she did not feel that she could ever identify any of them. Nevertheless, it had seemed to her that she ought to tell someone what she had seen. What she did next was explained in the official report DeGaetano filed and that was read to the legislative committee:

"It was established that she [Mrs. Hilbert] was friendly with John Dickerson, with whom she discussed this information, and he advised her not to get involved, to take care of her health and not to worry."

Mrs. Hilbert, DeGaetano noted, had been under a doctor's care for high blood pressure.

It was this report by DeGaetano, Major Keaten explained, that sent him to see John Dickerson on December 19, 1951. Dickerson, he said, assured him positively that "at no time did she [Mrs. Hilbert] give him such information. If she had, he would have given the information to Mr. Towe."

This conflict induced Keaten to send DeGaetano back to see Mrs. Hilbert. With the detective on this second trip, Keaten sent Lt. Louis Borneman and a woman sleuth. After questioning Mrs. Hilbert again and getting essentially the same story from her, DeGaetano then asked her this question: "I understand you did not discuss this with John Dickerson?"

And Mrs. Hilbert replied: "I did not *see* John Dickerson. I don't think I have *seen* him in a year." (Italics added.)

The form of this question which practically begged for a negative answer, asked by the same detective of the very woman who had originally told him exactly the opposite, obviously surprised the State Legislative Committee. Keaten was subjected to some close questioning about why this key question had been put in negative form. DeGaetano never said, Keaten testified, how he came to understand that Mrs. Hilbert hadn't seen John Dickerson, and *he* never asked DeGaetano about it.

"Does DeGaetano's statement say that she [Mrs. Hilbert] didn't *talk* to John Dickerson?" Augustus C. Studer, counsel for the committee, demanded.

"All she says is that she hadn't seen him," Keaten replied.

"Nothing is said about whether she phoned him?"

"No, sir."

Keaten capped these disclosures with another almost equally amazing. He testified that Mrs. Hilbert and her neighbor never had been called before the Bergen County grand jury probing the Moretti murder, but that both women *had* testified before a federal grand jury. Though murder isn't a federal offense, the federal panel had dug into the Moretti case because the abandoned hats and the license plates suggested that the killers had been imported from New York and so had crossed state lines. The fact that a federal jury, wedging into the case on this strictly secondary legal premise, had been interested enough to locate and hear eyewitnesses who were never before the Bergen County panel obviously nettled the state committee. The effect of Keaten's testimony had been to lift the lid on a murder probe as limp and ineffectual as the state's inquiry into the celebrated $228,000 bribe plot.

In such manner was this murder case, potentially the most explosive in modern New Jersey history, investigated. If, looking back, the vigor of the probe does not appear to have been excessive, there was at least one other aspect of the case that seemed at the time to be of some significance. This, like so much else in the Moretti case, involved the delicate balance of timing—the timing of murder. For Willie Moretti collected the brutal wages for his misspent life at the precise moment that Nelson Stamler's probe of gambling and official corruption was roaring along in high gear. In fact, on October 3, 1951, the day before Willie was gunned down, a Bergen County grand jury, acting under Stamler's direction, handed up nonfeasance- and misfeasance-in-office indictments against the Mayor, the Police Chief, and the Police Commissioner of one of Bergen's racket-ridden towns, and against Michael Orecchio, the Bergen County detective chief. After Moretti's murder, the Stamler corruption probe began to encounter snags and much of the steam went out of it.

Two Bergen County grand juries which worked with Stamler later were openly critical of the state administration and passed resolutions supporting Stamler for his activities in trying to break up the Bergen rackets and purify the official atmosphere. One member of the first jury that sat from January, 1951, to June, 1952—a responsible Bergen County businessman and a lifelong Republican—subsequently described the sudden chill that cooled off the probe in these words:

"At first we were clicking one-two-three. Everything was going right. Then we started reaching out to go higher. But all of a sudden something went wrong. We ran into a blank wall. I don't know what happened or what the connection was, but somehow it was tied up with the Moretti murder. After that, we couldn't get anywhere."

There remained to be performed just one familiar rite—that drama known as busting the rackets-buster.

When Nelson Stamler was first sent into Bergen County, bookies began taking odds on how long he would last. Bergen was famous as "the graveyard of rackets-busters"; and once in 1943, during the heyday of the Adonis regime, a Bergen County grand jury had actually censured a special prober who had been sent into the county to clean up—and, inferentially at least, had blessed some of the most ruthless hoods in America. Under the circumstances and especially since Stamler had been sent into the county by the very administration that would have to be exposed by a thorough cleanup, there were inevitably widespread doubts about how far he would go, and what would happen to him if he really tried to go all the way.

Anyone who studies Stamler's performance finds about it the quality of ambivalence. During the early period when he was flinging gangsters to the wolves, he seems to have been operating with consideration for the restrictions imposed by the Driscoll administration through Parsons. Gamblers at this point were fair game, but not their official and political protectors. Somewhere along the line, however, something happened to Stamler. He became determined to go a lot farther than anyone in power in the state wanted him to go.

The Driscoll administration later was to contend that he kicked over the traces and began a personal vendetta against it out of pique because he had not obtained the promised appointment as Prosecutor of his native Union County. Perhaps this had something to do with it, but looking at the record, it seems more logical that Bergen County itself wrought a great deal of the change in Stamler. It was a shocking eye-opener to him. When he came into the county, he had a reputation as a rackets-buster, built on some peripheral campaigns he had conducted in the outlying regions of central and southern Jersey. He considered himself a competent and knowledgeable prosecutor; but Bergen County quickly convinced him that, until then, he had been nothing but a rube from the sticks.

The evils that result from the complete perversion of the law when the forces of the law owe fealty to racketeers began to get to Nelson Stamler. In a *Saturday Evening Post* article that he later wrote with

Stanley Frank, he recalled one especially horrible incident. He described it this way:

> Laws meant to protect the rights of citizens were flouted so
> callously that the most flagrant offenses went unpunished. Two
> sisters, ten and twelve years old, were criminally attacked by a
> caretaker of an estate in Englewood. The mother of the girls
> immediately tried to make a complaint to the police, but was
> told to return later in the day. Within the hour, the caretaker's
> brother, a well-known bookie in town, offered the mother several
> hundred dollars to forget the rape of her daughters. When the
> mother indignantly refused the money, the bookie hinted broadly
> that very unfortunate accidents would befall the family if she
> did not keep her mouth shut. The mother, who had told no one
> but the police of the attack, recognized the futility of pressing the
> charge. The caretaker was never prosecuted.

The law had fallen too low for Nelson Stamler and too low for
two grand juries, composed of some decent Bergen citizens, whose
activities he directed. Both Stamler and the grand jurors began to
throw off all restraints, their indignation aroused by two especially
glaring cases of official ineptitude—the limp performances of the law
in following the Harold John Adonis bribe case and the Moretti murder mystery.

The bribery case, with its explosive potential, had been simmering
all this time beneath the surface of public knowledge. The State Police
investigation had been completed by January, 1951, and on February
12, Colonel Schoeffel, Parsons, and Stamler conferred in Parsons'
office in Trenton. But no action was taken. Stamler always contended
that Parsons ordered him not to move; Parsons emphatically denied
it. But the record makes clear that the Attorney General had assumed
personal command of this inquiry from the start, and so in all logic
the responsibility for inaction would seem to be inescapably his.

Not until September, 1951, according to Stamler, was he permitted
to take up the Harold John Adonis matter. And it was not until
December 12, 1951, with Willie Moretti already two months dead,
that Dickerson was called before the jury to give his version of the
Moretti-Adonis visit to his home exactly thirteen months earlier. On
January 9, 1952, Major Keaten testified. He acknowledged he had
never questioned Willie. Solly was still in prison but wouldn't talk,
he said. And Joe Adonis, whom Keaten had finally got around to

questioning on January 2, had disclaimed all knowledge of any payoffs. Keaten appeared at his bland best as he simply related Joe A.'s convenient denial, never questioning Joe A.'s word that multimillion-dollar rackets could run wide open for a decade without a fix of any kind. As for Harold John Adonis, Keaten said, he certainly had had the cash, but there was nothing in the state investigation to show how he got it or "whether this was payoff money." And so the first Bergen grand jury went out of office without finding indictments.

Both this jury and its successor, however, had been shocked by what they learned about their own county in the secrecy of the grand-jury room; and, in the fall of 1952, the second grand jury began to rake over the almost dead ashes of the $228,000 bribe story. Its activities were not exactly welcomed. In October, Attorney General Parsons appeared before the panel and delivered a legal opinion that, had it been accepted, almost certainly would have nullified the whole investigation. The Attorney General told the jurors there was "a very grave question" whether they had "jurisdiction over the Adonis case." Stamler pointed out that the jury felt, since the gambling had taken place in Fort Lee and Lodi, the alleged bribery that had permitted the games to run was within its jurisdiction. "You may be correct," Parsons said. But again he expressed his grave doubts.

Despite this unfavorable opinion from the highest law-enforcement officer in the state, Stamler and the jury went ahead. They encountered all kinds of roadblocks. In a subsequent showdown between the jurors and Parsons, one juror told the Attorney General that the first time Major Keaten had appeared, he had "refused point blank" to divulge the Harold John Adonis file and "it wasn't until we had brought pressure to bear that the man answered the questions we asked. . . ." Another juror told Parsons bluntly that "it was only through our own efforts that we got whatever evidence we did accumulate." The result was that, on November 7, 1952, only five days before the statute of limitations would have expired, barring all action, this second Bergen County grand jury indicted Harold John Adonis and the dead Willie Moretti for conspiring to obstruct justice. Eleven days later, on November 18, the jury voted a second indictment against Adonis for common-law bribery—an action that Stamler himself felt was illegal but that he insisted was undertaken at the request of Parsons to give the state a charge sufficiently serious to procure the extradition of Adonis from foreign parts.

Disclosure of the first indictment exploded the long-hidden scandal into prominence. It was a turning point in the Jersey story. Stamler's relations with his superiors, strained severely by altercations over the Willie Moretti murder probe, were ruptured beyond repair. The Driscoll administration publicly put its best face forward. It claimed pride in the achievement. The Governor and Attorney General Parsons praised each other and lauded the State Police in public statements. Governor Driscoll added a glowing commendation of Dickerson for having come forward so promptly and reported the gangsters' visit to his home. In this chorus of mutual congratulation and praise, there was one conspicuous omission: no state official on any level administered a pat on the back to Nelson Stamler, the rackets-buster who, after all, had produced the result which so pleased everyone.

Behind the camouflage of press statements, there was white-hot fury. A memorandum prepared a few months later by one of the most capable newsmen covering the State House in Trenton gives a vivid, inside view of the birth and development of what became known in political circles as the "Get Stamler" project. This comprehensive memorandum states:

> The indictment [of Harold Adonis] set off in the Trenton State House the "Get Stamler" project. . . . Both [Governor Driscoll and Attorney General Parsons] pointedly omitted any mention of Stamler in public statements, and privately cursed him and accused him of bringing a "thin" indictment that could never stand up. . . . At least a dozen underlings in the State House in Trenton took up the party line, calling Stamler every manner of name in hopes of taking the heat off what was really happening now that someone close to the Governor was indicted.
>
> (Incidentally, an amusing sidelight: Dickerson, as a witness, was to appear before the grand jury in Hackensack in mid-October to be questioned about the visit of the three gangsters to his home. He asked to be excused temporarily, and permission was granted. He couldn't appear as a witness, he said, because he had to introduce General Eisenhower in Hackensack that day. As a matter of fact, Mr. Dickerson did introduce Gen. Eisenhower, and the general, speaking from a platform not 200 feet from the grand jury room, did a violent job of lambasting crime and corruption in Washington.)
>
> To get back to the Stamler project . . .
>
> It appeared from observers in the State House that it centered around Leon Milmed, Gov. Driscoll's personal counsel and a

deputy attorney general. Milmed started issuing statements to the press (not for attribution but as "background," of course).

There were visits by representatives of the Governor and Attorney General to various newspaper offices, where publishers and editors were told all sorts of horrible things about Stamler— that he was "sore" because he hadn't been appointed Prosecutor of Union County, in accordance with Gov. Driscoll's promise; that he was tired and sick and therefore not to be completely trusted; that there had been a report the mob had given him $14,000. . . .

The project, of course, has been continued and been accelerated by the Legislative hearings. The Attorney General has 37 deputies, two assistants and a State Police force of 500. At least seven of the deputy attorney generals and a dozen of the top State Police officials have been doing *nothing else* for several weeks other than working up the case against Stamler.

One attaché in the Attorney General's office, a civil service career man with about 35 years service, said he had never before seen such activity, such feverish work and so much excitement. It even dwarfs what went on there during the Lindbergh Kidnapping investigation and trial.

The aim of the project is a simple one: it is to so blacken and smear Stamler that everyone else looks good by comparison. Those in the thick of it admit it is a tough job because the public is so well aware that Stamler is the only state investigator who has achieved *any* results in six years.

The background pressures pictured here, although they were unknown to the public at the time, must have been obvious to Stamler, and there is little doubt that they led to the final eruption. With his entire career and prestige at stake, Stamler began to fight back, and in angry frustration, he developed an unfortunate tendency to make extreme statements that, as he afterwards admitted to the legislative committee, sometimes simply were not warranted by the facts. He became involved in continual public sniping in the press with his boss, Attorney General Parsons. When Parsons sent State Police to the Netherlands to bring back Harold John Adonis, Stamler charged a plot to "get Adonis before I have a chance to question him." He boiled incessantly over the inept handling of the Willie Moretti murder investigation, and he suggested in one statement that "maybe" things had been handled the way they had because he and his staff "could have found out who did it." Finally, he embraced the theory that "politicians" had ordered the murder of Willie Moretti.

This politico-murder theory had first been spelled out by Clendenin Ryan, a wealthy Samaritan who had hired private detectives at his own expense to investigate the Jersey rackets. In testimony before the Bergen County grand jury on December 20, 1951, Ryan had declared:

"Just the slightest investigation shows that the mob itself not only had nothing to do with it [the murder] but did not even know who ordered the execution. Solly Moretti, who is now in the penitentiary, says that he knows positively the mob did not do it. Willie's execution was ordered by someone who was afraid Willie would talk and explain the situation as it really existed in Bergen County. . . . This is a clear-cut case of murder to prevent testimony concerning gambling and corruption."

Stamler in time came to the same conclusion, and he didn't make much secret of the way he felt. In the article he later wrote for the March 21, 1953, issue of the *Saturday Evening Post,* he said:

> Willie was a big wheel in the underworld hierarchy, all right, but the mob did not knock him off. I am convinced that gunmen hired by politicians murdered Willie.
>
> The underworld itself had nothing to fear from Willie. Although he freely admitted he was a professional gambler and a very dear friend of the top racketeers in the country, he always suffered profound lapses of memory when grand juries and the Kefauver Committee asked him questions that implicated his buddies. But the politicians had good reason to fear Willie. He was enraged at them for failing to reduce his brother Solly's jail sentence as they had promised. Two days before he was shot down in a tavern in Cliffside Park [actually the lapse of time was a week, according to Stamler's later version] Willie told me he would blow the whistle to the grand jury on the politicians who had double-crossed him after taking his bribes, and orders, for years.

By the time Stamler broke into print with this charge, he had already joined John Winberry in the fraternity of ousted racketsbusters. His angry statements to the press had needled Parsons to the point where on January 27, 1953, he went to Hackensack and publicly fired Stamler. The act precipitated a stormy session with

Stamler's second Bergen County grand jury. The jury was then at a critical stage of its work. It felt, as did Stamler, that there was a connection between the Harold John Adonis and Moretti cases. And it had been trying to pinpoint the sources of the mysterious influence that had protected the mob in Bergen so long and so well. In a direct confrontation with Parsons, protesting the dismissal of Stamler, one juror bluntly told the Attorney General: "We feel—it is my opinion, and I think the rest of the grand jury is of the same mind—that we are getting awfully close to home and people are going to squirm. Now I will put it right on the table. . . . The fact is that we don't think our effectiveness is being utilized to its full extent, because of the fact that we are changing horses at this point."

Parsons insisted his firing of Stamler must stand, and with this decision, the curtain came down on the Bergen inquiry. The jury never got any closer to home, and the people, whoever they were, stopped squirming. The state investigating committee later concluded that, though Stamler had given Parsons ample provocation for firing him, the Attorney General had exercised "poor judgment" in acting as he had just at the critical stage of the Bergen inquiry.

Politically, also, the timing and the judgment were poor. The firing of Stamler, the only man who had ever sent Joe Adonis to jail, the only man who had ever really tried to clean up the mess in Bergen, provoked state-wide repercussions, and no fewer than nine resolutions for investigations were introduced in the state legislature. Finally, a joint committee, safely dominated by Republicans, was appointed to serve under the chairmanship of Senator Harold W. Hannold, of Gloucester County. The committee took some 7,000 pages of testimony; and, partisan though it was, it nevertheless presented a report severely condemning the lack of law enforcement in Bergen and the evident reluctance and sluggishness with which the Adonis and Moretti cases had been investigated.

Willie Moretti's murder changed the face of the Eastern underworld. It removed from the scene the third member of the "Big Five" Crime Cabinet that had sat in Duke's, and it shifted power from the long-dominant Costello-Adonis wing of the Syndicate into the ruthless hands of the man who had been waiting for the opportunity—Vito Genovese.

The timing of the Moretti murder had an impeccable artistic touch,

coming as it did at an opportune moment for quite a number of
people, and the manner in which the Moretti murder probe was conducted said clearly that Jersey officialdom was possessed of no passionate fervor to discover just who did Willie in. Yet Clendenin Ryan
and Stamler were wrong in believing that "the mob" had nothing to
do with the murder; on the contrary, this was a mob murder all the
way. It marvelously served a dual purpose: it protected the mob's
longtime protectors in Bergen County, guaranteeing them precious
anonymity forevermore; and it placed the real underworld power in
the hands of the man who had been thirsting through several frustrated years to grab it.

The Moretti murder was the first in a long skein of underworld
violence traceable directly to Vito Genovese. The rule of order that
Costello had drafted at Atlantic City in 1929 and that Luciano had
imposed after the purge of the "greasers" was now about to be
scrapped. The guns of Genovese's troop would do the talking, and
when they were through, Don Vitone would not have a serious chal-
lenger for power in the Eastern underworld.

In this chain of violent ascension to the throne, the Moretti murder
was the first link. And the key man in engineering it was almost certainly the thin, doleful-featured Anthony (Tony Bender) Strollo, the
fifth of the high councilors who had sat with Joe A. on the crime
board in Duke's. All his life Bender had been Vito Genovese's man,
his dependable right bower, and the threads of the Moretti murder
trace directly back to him.

The connecting link was a Brooklyn and Greenwich Village gangster, John (Johnny Roberts) Robilotto, also known as the Mortician.
Robilotto was the customer in Joe's Elbow Room whom the waitress,
Mrs. Novack, had been so certain at first that she could identify.
Though she later became less positive, she was right all the time. We
now have Joseph Valachi's word for that. Valachi had been a partner
of Johnny Roberts in a loan-sharking operation, and Johnny knew
Valachi had never liked Willie Moretti from their youthful days together in hoodlum's kingdom on the East Side. With this much for
background, here is Valachi's account of the Moretti murder:

"I was in my place in the Lido at the time . . . and I got this news
from the radio. . . . And I quickly went downstairs and called up Tony
[Strollo], my lieutenant, and he told me, 'Go about your business.'
In other words, I wanted to find out if there was any trouble.

"So now, that night I wasn't in my restaurant, and when I got to my restaurant that particular night, I was told that Johnny Roberts was there and he waited a couple of hours for me, and then he was there to celebrate. I understood what that meant, and he left word with the waiter.

"Well, the next time I saw Johnny would be maybe a few months later, and by this time Johnny was arrested. There was a couple of hats left in the restaurant, and naturally I ain't going to talk to Johnny in plain English, or in plain talk, and I got to curb a little. I didn't want to put him on the spot and he ain't supposed to tell me nothing. So I asked him how did he stand with the hats . . . and he said, 'Don't worry about it, it ain't my hat, and it belonged to the other guys.' "

Johnny Roberts, demonstrably, on the record, was a Strollo man. In 1949, the year after the Woolley-Hart party had focused District Attorney Hogan's attention on the mob operation in New Jersey, Hogan's detectives discovered that the Jersey crime cartel was running a huge policy game based on the total daily transactions reported by the Treasury's Cincinnati Clearing House. Not only was this particular numbers racket a flourishing one; it was rigged. The mob had its inside man in a key position in the clearinghouse; and, after determining from its play which numbers would do it the least damage if they hit, it had its agent falsify the reported totals. Here again one encounters the insatiable greed of the mob. It was taking an estimated $1 million a month out of Joe A.'s gambling casinos, another estimated $140 million a year out of the Bergen bookie network—and yet it couldn't be satisfied to run an on-the-level policy racket in which the normal odds were 1,000 to 1 in its favor. It had to make certain the suckers didn't have even their 1,000 to 1 chance. The result, according to Hogan, was that the rigged policy game put another $50 million a year gross profit into the mob's pockets.

When Hogan's detectives, with the cooperation of Attorney General Parsons and the New Jersey State Police, smashed the operation in a raid in late July, 1949, they caught some important fish. On the raided Newark premises, they found Danny Zwillman, a cousin of racket czar Longy, and in his possession were all the books and records of the ring. These established that the ring's cash had been handled through the West 35th Street Trading Company, a check-cashing concern located at 218 West 35th Street, New York. Proprietors of the firm were Emilio (Sammy) Strollo, the brother of Tony, and John Robilotto. There were other, on-the-record ties. Hogan's detectives discovered that Robilotto was listed as the president of a cigarette-vending-machine business in which Tony Strollo was a heavy investor. He also shared with Tony financial interests in a number of Greenwich Village nightclubs. "The plain fact is," said Vincent O'Connor at the time, "that Robilotto is and always has been a Strollo man."

These Strollo ties became significant when Jersey police, acting on Mrs. Novack's tentative identification, began following the trail of John Robilotto. They discovered that he had vanished from his home at 755 Anderson Avenue, Cliffside Park, on the very day that Moretti was gunned down, and he hadn't been seen in New Jersey since. He hadn't returned even to pack his belongings, but had had the furniture trucked to a three-and-a-half-room apartment at 10 Downing Street, Manhattan. Detectives eventually caught up with Robilotto on July 2, 1952, at Eastern Parkway and Bedford Avenue, where the Mortician was known as a prosperous bookie.

Taken to the Grand Avenue police station in Brooklyn, Robilotto was questioned by Bergen County sleuths and New York detectives led by Lt. Joseph Leary. Eventually, a bit of what was supposed to have transpired in this closed-door session leaked out to the press. Robilotto admitted, detectives said, that he might have had breakfast in Joe's Elbow Room shortly before Willie Moretti was murdered, but he insisted he wasn't on the premises at the time of the gunplay. Though Robilotto was positive about this, he wasn't positive about much else; he just couldn't remember what he had done that day. An indication of the extreme terror that mere mention of the Moretti murder never failed to arouse in the underworld showed through Robilotto's almost frantic protestation to the cops that he would "talk about anything but that."

Robilotto was held without bail in Brooklyn as a fugitive from Jersey justice. In Hackensack, authorities described the Mortician as a former close associate of Willie Moretti and Albert Anastasia. Curiously enough, no mention was made of Robilotto's far closer ties to Tony Bender Strollo, the man who now, as deputy for Genovese, was filling Joe Adonis' shoes as the Field Marshal of Crime.

This incomprehension of basic realities—New Jersey officials never were to let on they were aware of the function of Duke's or the lines of power so clearly delineated in the Crime Cabinet that sat there—certainly did not help to speed the prosecution of John Robilotto. Having located him, New Jersey had him indicted for the Moretti murder and announced it would bring him swiftly to trial. Robilotto bucked like a steer against extradition and appeared on July 31, 1952, for a hearing before Justice J. Vincent Keogh in Brooklyn Supreme Court.

Changing the story he had originally told detectives, Robilotto now argued that he had never been in New Jersey on the day of the Moretti murder; he had been in New York all the time. This contention was bolstered by the testimony of an attorney, Michael P. Direnzo. Direnzo gave his address as 10 Downing Street, the building Robilotto claimed as home, and also—a circumstance that went completely unnoticed at the time—he happened to be the attorney for Tony Bender Strollo. So Strollo's attorney testified that he knew Johnny Robilotto, Strollo's man, had been in New York on murder day because he had met the Mortician in Gambler's Court at almost the very moment Moretti was being gunned down in New Jersey. On cross-examination, Direnzo had trouble with his powers of recall. He couldn't remember whom he had talked to on October 3 or October 5, 1951, the days before and after the murder, nor could he recollect what had happened on a specific day just two weeks previously. Under the circumstances, Justice Keogh was not impressed, and Johnny Robilotto was sent off to face the charge of murder in New Jersey.

Now events came full circle, working their devious way with a certain poetic justice. The swift trial that New Jersey had trumpeted in July had failed to materialize by September. Instead, on September 11, 1952, Robilotto was released in $25,000 bail, a bond even less onerous than the one that had been imposed on Willie Moretti twenty years earlier in the William Brady murder case. Now history began to repeat itself, and the law's beneficence to Willie Moretti in the Brady case was to be extended in equal degree to Willie's slayer. Before setting bail for Robilotto, Judge J. Wallace Leyden was briefed in private session on the details of the State's case. The briefing was handled by an assistant prosecutor who was later to be roundly criticized by Stamler's last Bergen County grand jury for his open association with representatives of the very Bergen political organization he was supposed to be investigating. The result was that

Judge Leyden announced, "I have come to the conclusion at the present time the information or proof of the prosecution is not great" —and so he freed Robilotto.

The Moretti murder case now matched the old Brady affair. Like the murder indictment against Willie Moretti in that long-forgotten crime, the charge against John Robilotto hung fire for three years, gathering dust in the closet with other New Jersey political skeletons —and then it was quietly dismissed for lack of evidence.

14

CHANGING OF THE GUARD

THE changing of the guard now became all but official. The "Big Five" who had sat for so long in Duke's had been reduced in effect to the "Big One"—Anthony (Tony Bender) Strollo, the most mysterious and inconspicuous of the truly powerful mob rulers. Standing always in the shadows, he had a positive genius for letting others capture the headlines and the appearance of importance. Behind Strollo lurked, of course, the dominant Mafia chieftain to whom he had always given fealty, Vito Genovese, but those who knew the underworld at the time did not underestimate the pivotal importance of Tony Strollo.

"The only man left with all the threads of the organization in his hands, and the only one in the clear able to do business for the Combination, is Strollo," Chief Assistant District Attorney Vincent O'Connor said in the spring of 1953. "Speculation as to his recent rise is sound. His rise coincides with the fall of Adonis and Moretti's death."

About the same time an authoritative FBI source gave a similar assessment and traced the development of the underworld hierarchy. "Genovese was the old kingpin," he said. "Strollo was one of his young henchmen. Frank Costello took over from Genovese, and now

311

Strollo has inherited Frank's toga. You'll remember that, when Costello became involved with the law, there was a lot of publicity about
Thomas (Three-Finger Brown) Lucchese taking over and becoming
the top man in the underworld. Well, our informants tell us: 'Three-
Finger Brown? Uh-uh, that's the malarkey. Not Brown—Strollo.' "

Strollo never actually achieved quite so dominant a position. He
was never to be the no. 1 man, but rather the no. 2 man wielding the
power of Vito Genovese. Yet he had his own following, and on the
operative front he was to be the key cog in virtually every maneuver
of the Eastern underworld during the next decade. In him were
merged two forces, the old-line Mafia authority of Vito Genovese and
his own personal command of the "Young Turks" inside the Mafia.
Though Strollo himself was a contemporary of Adonis and Costello
and though his hound-dog-sad face sometimes made him look even
older than they, he was really the leader and spokesman of the young,
brash hoods on the rise. He was constantly surrounded by them, and
his authority over them apparently was complete.

Some hint of the self-effacing Tony Strollo's personal power could
be seen when he went out on the town for a night. He usually cavorted
in his personal fief, Greenwich Village, and he would select some
inconspicuous nightclub for the evening's celebration. Before he set
foot inside the door, however, his Young Turks would invade the
place like scouts scenting out a possible ambush. They would case
the bar, the diners, the kitchen, the entire premises; and only when
they had satisfied themselves that no hostiles were in evidence would
Strollo enter with his immediate bodyguard and retinue. Then a couple
of thugs would be placed on the door, all other customers would be
turned away with the curt notice that the joint was full up for the
night, and Tony and his Young Turks would take over.

The autocrat who could pre-empt an entire nightclub for his personal pleasure sometimes demonstrated his absolute authority over
the rambunctious Young Turks in the very presence of the law. Inspector John J. Shanley, then head of New York's Central Investigation Bureau which compiles dossiers on the mob, told the McClellan
committee of one striking instance when Strollo and some of his
young toughs were picked up for questioning. One of the troop especially "was supposed to be a very tough man."

"The arrest was of a minor nature and this fellow was showing his disregard of the arrest activity," Inspector Shanley testified. "He was clowning around in the station house. While he was doing this, the detective told him to keep quiet. Still he clowned.

"Bender said one sentence to him, 'Why don't you sit down, Frank?' Frank sat down and never opened his mouth for the rest of the night."

The man whose mere suggestion was more effective than an official order was born in New York City on June 14, 1899. He had lived a lifetime in the rackets, but the law had hardly brushed him. In 1926 he had been arrested for carrying a gun, but the charge had been dismissed. Until 1949 this had been the only spot on his record. Yet Federal Narcotics agents, who knew him by his original gangland nickname of Tony Benda, had identified him early in his career as the chief lieutenant of Vito Genovese.

In maintaining his nearly spotless police record, Tony Bender Strollo had developed a number of baffling techniques. Even early in his career, a gang leader on the rise, he was infinitely circumspect. New York detectives who tailed him in those days became accustomed to finding him holding almost nightly court on a certain East Side street corner. There Strollo would loiter nonchalantly and meet his henchmen as they came along. Sometimes he would get into a car with one and cruise quietly around a few city blocks as he discussed the "our thing" of the moment. It was a most frustrating technique. No business was transacted over a vulnerable telephone wire nor in a closed room that might be bugged; whatever was done took place in the privacy of a slowly moving car, and though detectives might observe the suspicious association between Strollo and a lot of unsavory individuals, they could gleam not a particle of evidence on which to hang a prosecutor's hat.

With the passage of time, Strollo, like all wise gangsters, gave himself a legitimate business front. In 1938 he obtained a real estate broker's license from the New York State Division of Licenses and set himself up in business at 270 Broadway. When the mob shifted its operations to New Jersey, Strollo shifted too. He still maintained his New York business office, first at 270 Broadway and later at 166 Bleecker Street in Greenwich Village; but he established his residence in Palisades, New Jersey, as early as 1943, and during the latter years of the decade he lived with his wife, Edna, at 1015 Palisades Avenue.

It was during this period that Hogan's investigators spotted Strollo as one of Joe A.'s four major associates on the Crime Cabinet in Duke's.

The Strollo-Genovese control of the eastern underworld necessitated at the outset the cleaning up of unfinished business. Of the Crime Cabinet that had sat in Duke's, Joe Adonis had been pretty effectively eliminated by the law, for, in addition to his gambling sentence, the federal government had come up with a number of actions, including a deportation case. Robilotto and his fellow executioners had taken care of Willie Moretti. But Willie's brother, Solly, still lived—and so did Albert Anastasia.

Solly was the first of this pair to go. On the morning of May 6, 1952, he was discovered in a coma on the floor of his cell in Trenton State Prison. He was taken to the prison hospital and there he lingered, unconscious, until he died on June 8.

The underworld grapevine has always insisted that Solly Moretti was helped on his last journey, that his coma was induced by a blow on the head. But there is nothing in the official record to substantiate this. According to prison records, Solly died of a cerebral hemorrhage. He had been given, the records say, a skull X-ray which showed no external injuries. No autopsy was performed, however.

Solly's departure left only one member of the original Crime Cabinet in Duke's as a possible competitor of Tony Bender Strollo—Albert Anastasia, the veteran Lord High Executioner of Murder, Inc. But Anastasia also was having his troubles, and these began with Willie Moretti's murder.

On that day, Big Al had demonstrated that he was still sufficiently well connected to have been entrusted with knowledge of coming events. And just as he had done years before on the afternoon of Joe the Boss Masseria's last dinner, he had thoughtfully provided himself with an airtight alibi. This time, Big Al had developed the most excruciating pain in one knee. He was afraid he might have cracked the knee joint, or something, and so he had packed himself off to St. Mary's Hospital in Passaic where, by coincidence, an X-ray machine was taking a picture of Anastasia's leg at virtually the instant guns began to chatter in Joe's Elbow Room.

"He had the perfect alibi," Nelson Stamler later said. "The time the X-ray was taken was stamped right on the plate, and it corresponded within a few minutes with the time of the murder. It was incontrovertible evidence that Anastasia was in the hospital at the time Willie was killed."

There were signs at the time, however, that all was not serene in the underworld. The Lord High Executioner went almost directly from the hospital to his cliffside palace at 75 Bluff Road, Fort Lee, New Jersey, just north of the Palisades Amusement Park. And there he stayed. He was surrounded by bodyguards. Floodlights turned the lawn around his Spanish-style castle into day on the darkest night, and a squad of fierce Doberman pinscher watchdogs roamed cease-lessly behind a ten-foot-high fence, tipped with barbed wire. The in-dications certainly were that Big Al felt his own life might be in danger, but he stayed secure in his fortress and rode out the storm.

Other troubles now came his way. On March 10, 1954, the Internal Revenue Department moved against him, charging that he owed the federal government $250,000 in income taxes. The case stemmed from a colossal wartime swindle in which Big Al and his gangster associates had played the government of the United States for a sucker.

During World War II, while Master Sergeant Anastasia was patri-otically devoting his services to the nation at Indiantown Gap, his brother, Tough Tony, was still the czar of a vast section of the Brooklyn waterfront. Thus Big Al had plenty of longshoremen for muscle. Using this resource, he began to form stevedore companies to which the Army issued exclusive contracts for loading government vessels at Brooklyn docks.

The contracts were all drafted on the customary cost-plus formula that was an open invitation to legal larceny. Under this system, an unscrupulous contractor simply loaded on "costs," since he was guar-anteed his own percentage of profit above the "cost" figure—and, naturally, the higher the "costs" the higher his profit. In Brooklyn, Tough Tony organized a stevedore company which promptly loaded so many longshoremen on its payroll it was a wonder the piers didn't sink. In a matter of months, this firm cleaned up more than $100,000; and when the federal government became suspicious of the size of this bite, Big Al met the emergency by setting up a new and fancier front. He called this the Sancor Corporation, and it professed to be composed of experts in the art of repairing ships.

The most cursory examination of Sancor would have shown that its expertise derived more from mayhem than from maritime matters; but, by one of those coincidences that seem always to favor the heavily bankrolled moguls of the mob, no such elementary study was made. Even the qualifications of Sancor's front men—C. Don Modica, of Hasbrouck Heights, New Jersey, president, and Benedicto Macri, secretary-treasurer and active boss—were clearly open to suspicion. Modica was a bizarre character known in the underworld as "The Professor," a title accorded him for tutoring the children of Joe Adonis, Albert Anastasia, and Willie Moretti. He had acquired a master's degree in social science from St. John's College in Brooklyn and had taught the philosophy of education for five years at New York University; but also he was a jailbird, having done time for a $3,500 swindle in Queens County, Long Island, and for practicing medicine without a license in Delaware. In all his background, there was nothing to show that he knew one end of a ship from the other. Macri was a little more knowledgeable, but not much. He had, at the time, no police record, an indication of clean living that was deceptive, but the only training he had had for his new role as a ship-repair expert had been gained as a longshoreman on the docks and during a short period as a welder. In 1949, Macri was indicted for a New York garment district murder but even before this, it shouldn't have been hard to discover the truth—that he was really nothing but a strong arm and stooge for Albert Anastasia, the Enforcer of the mob.

Of all this, however, Uncle Sam was unaware, and Sancor, which established a shipyard in North Bergen, New Jersey, was promptly showered with federal beneficences, jobs that eventually totaled more than $5 million. But Sancor couldn't rest content with its legitimate swindle. It had to have more.

One of its most outrageous illegitimate swindles was perpetrated after Master Sergeant Albert Anastasia came marching home from war to take personal charge of his company. Sancor's employees later told federal investigators that Albert A. showed up around the yard constantly. And soon Sancor developed a curious interest in home building. Anastasia had acquired a piece of property on the Palisades, and to this site, in 1947, Sancor began to send men and supplies. Both were charged off to Sancor's ship-repair operations, for which the government was paying, but both were devoted to the construction of a cliffside palace for the Lord High Executioner of the underworld.

The home-building caper was brought into clear focus by the Kefauver committee in its private session with Anastasia.

"Who was the contractor for the building of your house?" Rudolph Halley asked the Enforcer.

"I decline to answer on the ground it may tend to incriminate me," Anastasia said.

Halley warned that only one conclusion could be drawn from his answer, that the committee would feel its suspicions about his mansion-building chisel were confirmed. But Anastasia doggedly refused any further explanation. Officials of Sancor similarly sought refuge in the Fifth Amendment when the committee tried to question them about the doings of the firm. They had good reason for reticence, for former Sancor employees, by this time, had let federal investigators in on a number of secrets. The workers had described how they had labored for weeks on "the big house," as they called Anastasia's palace, and they had described the incessant theft of tools and materials from the yard, a calculated campaign of looting conducted in an obvious design to bleed the firm to death.

This objective—Sancor having served its purpose and reaped the cream of war profits—was achieved on June 6, 1947, just about the time that Anastasia's mansion was finished. On that day Sancor filed a bankruptcy petition in Federal Court, Brooklyn, listing liabilities of $717,626 and assets of only $232,955. Everybody had been cheated. Hundreds of small business concerns were victimized for materials or services they had furnished Sancor. The corporation's 390 employees lost their last week's pay. And Uncle Sam was left holding the bag for some $600,000, the amount the federal government claimed was due it in taxes and as compensation for the damage Sancor had done to its ships while pretending to repair them.

"It was one hell of a strange yard," a U.S. Maritime Commission official commented in 1950. "They did as much damage to our ships as they repaired. There seemed to be evidence of culpable negligence."

Albert Anastasia and Joe Adonis rode high, and they had good reason to be well satisfied with themselves. Big Al had acquired, at comparatively little expense, a stately mansion that could be used as an ideal haven for supersecret, top-level conclaves if circumstances made it inadvisable to meet in Duke's. Nelson Stamler in his probe of the Bergen rackets became convinced that Anastasia's home provided an alternative council chamber for the top powers of mobdom and that much of the strategic planning of the Syndicate took place there.

"The site was perfect," Stamler points out. "The house was right on the Palisades, with a sheer drop in front. Nobody could approach it from that direction or observe what was going on there. All the mob had to worry about was the rear, and that was well protected by the high fence, the floodlights and as evil a set of watchdogs as you'd ever find anywhere. Our State Troopers always felt certain that they could tell when something special was stirring at Anastasia's house because then the lights would all be turned on and the dogs would be let loose to roam the yard."

But, alas, there came a time in the aftermath of the Kefauver exposures, when Internal Revenue agents began to assess the cost of building Anastasia's cliffside castle and of his extravagant way of life; and they concluded that, at a minimum, the Lord High Executioner had spent three times the money he had reported as total income. Hence the uncharitable tax-dodging charges—and another case of history repeating itself.

In the past, whenever the law camped hard on the trail of Albert Anastasia, key witnesses for the prosecution had always wound up dead. There was no reason to suppose that matters would be different now.

One of the witnesses whom the federal government had called before a grand jury had been Benedicto Macri—the same Macri who had been secretary-treasurer and front man for Sancor and who had been acquitted in October, 1951, of the New York garment district murder of William Lurye. This verdict had been achieved, as the State later showed, only because Anastasia had paid and threatened the key State witness into committing perjury. Now, summoned before the federal grand jury, confronted with Sancor records and the testimony of its former employees, Macri apparently found it impossible to back up the play of his boss. He testified, and though the exact nature of his testimony has never been revealed, Anastasia apparently considered that it placed him in personal jeopardy.

On April 25, 1954, just a month and fifteen days after the indictment of Anastasia, Vincent Macri, brother of Benedicto, was found dead, two bullets in his head, his body stuffed into the trunk of his own parked car in the Bronx. Five days later, twenty-five miles away, perched by a river bank in Harrison, New Jersey, police found a blood-smeared car in which Benedicto Macri evidently had been taken for his last ride. Benedicto himself had vanished without a trace.

With the elimination of the Macris, the federal government ran into trouble and watered down its charges; but, nevertheless, in October 1954, it put the Lord High Executioner on trial, accused now of defrauding the federal government out of a mere $11,742 in income taxes during 1947 and 1948. One of the key government witnesses still left alive and unterrified was Charles Ferri, a Fort Lee plumbing contractor, who testified he had installed $8,700 worth of pipes in Anastasia's cliffside mansion. Ferri's testimony was vital to what was left of the Anastasia income-tax case; but, despite it, the trial ended in a hung jury. The government had to begin all over again, and a second trial was scheduled for May 10, 1955.

Before this could be held, Ferri, who was sixty-eight, left the plumbing business and went with his wife, Marie, sixty-one, to North Miami, Florida, to enjoy their final years in placid retirement. On April 28, 1955, Ferri received a federal subpoena to appear as a witness in Anastasia's approaching second trial in Camden, New Jersey. That evening Ferri and his wife visited their daughter and son-in-law, Mr. and Mrs. Michael Lopiano, who lived nearby. They left the Lopianos late in the evening to return to their home—and that was the last ever seen of them.

The next morning, Michael Lopiano, Ferri's son-in-law, was driving past the Ferri home and sensed that something was wrong. The porch light was still lighted, the morning paper lay on the lawn, and the front door was wide open. Entering the house, Lopiano found just one living thing—a cheerful parakeet.

A shattered vase lay on the floor of the living room. Draperies had been ripped from the windows. Blood smeared the carpet, the curtains, and the furniture in several rooms. A trail of blood led from the living room to the carport where Ferri's Cadillac was parked. Some twenty feet from the car, police later found Ferri's bloodstained shoes. In the days that followed, State Police combed Florida, but of Marie and Charles Ferri, no trace has been found to this day.

Back in New Jersey, Albert Anastasia was now ready to admit that he might have chiseled a little on his income taxes. On May 23rd he walked into Federal Court in Camden and most obligingly pleaded guilty before Judge Thomas M. Madden. He could have drawn ten years in prison and a $20,000 fine, not too stiff a punishment, it would seem, for the master of murder; but his attorney, Anthony Calandra, reacted with righteous horror and argued that for the law to be unkind to Big Al would really be gross injustice.

"Since 1935," the lawyer assured Judge Madden solemnly, "there has not been a blemish on his record. He has rehabilitated himself."

And so Anastasia got what has come to seem almost customary treatment for moguls of the mob, a slap on the wrist—the maximum fine of $20,000, which meant absolutely nothing to him as punishment, and a year in prison, which with time off for good behavior meant a mere ten months.

Back in Manhattan there was the law-crippled figure of the man who had been known as The Boss and The Prime Minister. The Kefauver hearings had focused a blinding spotlight on Frank Costello, and in their aftermath The Boss had been pelted with federal legal actions like a man plastered with snowflakes in a blizzard. He had been sent to prison for contempt in refusing to answer some of the Senators' questions; he had been convicted of income-tax dodging and sentenced to another five years; and he was trying to fight off a denaturalization and deportation case, based on the government's contention that he had concealed his criminal record when he became a citizen. All of these actions crimped Costello's style as a czar of the rackets, but he was reluctant to step aside.

In March, 1957, Costello was freed from prison on a legal technicality after serving eleven months of his five-year income-tax evasion sentence. He returned at once to his old haunts in Manhattan and apparently tried to take up right where he had left off. But he quickly discovered that circumstances had changed. According to one report, the boys threw a party for The Boss in one of the city's fancier bistros. All of the ranking thugs of the day were there to do him honor; but, if Costello had envisioned the affair as a kind of second coronation party, he was soon undeceived. His fellow Mafiosi quickly let him know that they weren't there to welcome him back to power; they were bidding him a polite farewell—that carried with it an implicit warning. From all the evidence, Costello did not heed the warning.

On the night of May 2, 1957, Costello and his wife went out on the town. They had dinner with some friends, then went nightclubbing. About 11 P.M. Costello recalled that he had to get back to his apartment to receive an expected telephone call from one of his lawyers, Edward Bennett Williams. With a partying companion, Philip Kennedy, he hailed a cab and was driven to the Majestic Apartments at 115 Central Park West at the corner of 71st Street. As the cab pulled up in front of the door, a large black Cadillac stopped behind it, and a fat, flabby-looking man in a dark suit, with a hat pulled down over his forehead, got out and shuffled to the main entrance of the apartment building.

Costello got out of his cab and hurried to the door that a doorman held open for him. As he passed through the door, he entered a foyer which was separated from the lobby of the apartment house by a glass wall. Crossing the foyer in rapid strides, Costello passed the pudgy man in dark coat and hat without giving him a glance. In that instant, the pudgy one moved. His hand whipped out of his coat pocket. It held a gun.

"This is for you, Frank," he cried.

And with the words, he fired a shot point-blank at Costello's head.

Costello started to turn as he heard the voice behind him, and this slight movement saved his life. A .38 caliber slug slashed along the right side of his head, ripping his scalp just behind the ear. The fat gunman, evidently thinking he had accomplished his murder mission, whirled around the instant he had fired the shot, and waddled out to the waiting Cadillac.

Costello was taken to a hospital to have his dented skull patched up, and while this was being done, New York detectives thoughtfully examined the contents of his jacket pocket. They found some $800 in cash and a cryptic note showing that the Prime Minister was still being bankrolled by large gambling revenues. "Gross Casino Win as of 4-26-57—$651,284," the note read. The total was broken down this way: "Casino win less markers [that is I.O.U.'s]—$434,695. Slot wins—$62,844. Markers—$153,745."

Investigation by the Nevada Gaming Control Board subsequently showed that these figures matched item for item the officially reported gambling revenue for the first twenty-four days' operation of the plush Tropicana Hotel that had just been opened in Las Vegas. Dandy Phil Kastel, the lifelong gambling partner of Costello, had been one of the original backers of the Tropicana, and the note in Costello's pocket, though Costello blandly protested that he had no idea what the thing meant or how it got there, would seem to indicate that the gang boss had a major financial stake in the welfare of the new Tropicana.

The bungled assassination attempt signaled the dawn of a new and more violent era. It clearly said that new forces were taking over from the old regime that had run affairs for more than twenty years without this kind of unseemly violence at the top. Though no one at the time had a very clear idea who these new forces were or what they represented, no doubt existed as to their intentions, for they adopted a novel technique of publicly calling their shots and warning their enemies.

I was the medium that they chose to convey the message. Why this should be so, I have no idea. In 1953, as a crime expert for the New York *World-Telegram and Sun,* I had written a series of articles on the North Jersey racket situation, and these had played a major role in broadening the probe of the State Legislative Committee into the fields of political corruption and protection of the rackets. Perhaps this was remembered; perhaps someone figured my crime articles would be read by those for whom the message was intended. In any event, only two hours after the firing of the bullet that creased Costello's skull, a tough-talking caller tried to reach me by telephone at the office, and not getting me at that hour, left a message. Its burden: the Costello shooting was only a sample of what was to come; its propaganda justification: Costello had been shot because the old regime had been too ruthless in dealing with its followers.

"They stepped on some good guys' toes," the caller said. "All I can say is that, if Albert or Freddie steps in, they'll get it too."

The reference to "Freddie" puzzled authorities, but no one had any doubt who was meant by "Albert." That could mean only Albert Anastasia.

In the months that followed, some of the tracks in the jungle began to become clear. New York detectives, tracing the overconfident marksman who had thought to do Costello in with one pistol shot, found the trail leading them to Vincent (The Chin) Gigante, a hulking Greenwich Village character, sometime chauffeur and full-time hanger-on of Tony Bender Strollo. Gigante was on the lam for several weeks, during which, according to much physical evidence, he went on a drastic reducing diet in the hope of eliminating his fatman's waddle and confusing witnesses. Eventually he returned, went to trial—and was acquitted. The acquittal resulted largely from the inability of Frank Costello to recall a single detail about the man who had tried to blow his brains out at such close range. The Mafia code of omertà having been thus preserved once more at the expense of the law, "Uncle Frank" retired into the shadows as an elder statesman of some stature but with decidedly diminished power.

No such graceful withdrawal was to be permitted Anastasia. It took some months, but on the morning of October 25, 1957, it became evident that the telephone caller who had tried to contact me after the Costello shooting had been no crackpot, but a well-informed individual who knew precisely what he was talking about.

Around 10:15 A.M. on this quiet October Friday, Big Al walked into the barbershop of the Hotel Sheraton at Seventh Avenue and 55th Street. He seated himself in chair No. 4 and told the barber, Joseph Bocchino, that he wanted "the works." He wasn't long in getting them.

Bocchino had hardly covered the Lord High Executioner's face with lather when two men, one stout and sallow, the other thin and dark, strode purposefully in from the lobby, scarves wrapped around the lower portions of their faces. They walked right up behind chair No. 4 and drew two guns, one a .38, the other a .32. At point-blank range, they opened fire on the back of Albert Anastasia's unsuspecting head.

The first shots struck with such impact that Anastasia was literally blown out of the chair. His legs kicked out in front of him and broke off the foot-rest. Propelled erect by the bullets, he slammed into a counter laden with shaving and hair lotions, spun as another shot hit him and crashed face down on the barbershop floor. His killers stood over him, pumping bullets at his back; then, their morning's work finished, they turned, strode swiftly out and made for the nearest subway.

"The old order changeth," an assistant in District Attorney Hogan's office commented succinctly.

The nature of the change was again underlined by a telephone call I received only some two hours after Anastasia had been so violently deposed. The message was tough, fast, and to the point.

"You remember I called you last spring right after Costello was shot, and you printed a warning we issued to Anastasia not to butt in?" he asked.

"Yes," I said.

"Well, we're giving another warning now. This time we're telling Frankie—and I don't mean Costello—not to interfere. And we're not fooling."

"Who do you mean by Frankie?" I asked.

"Frankie C., but it's not Costello," the caller said. And before I could ask another question, he slammed down the phone.

The riddle of this second warning proved baffling to authorities. Who was Frankie C.? A couple of possibilities suggested themselves. Frank Carbo had long been known as the underworld's commissioner of boxing, the rigger of crooked fights. It could be he. Or it could be —and the underworld grapevine later insisted it was meant to be— Frank Casino, a Long Island gambling power with ties to Costello and the old top leadership.

Joseph Valachi was later to give an inside-the-mob view of the pressures that had led to the Anastasia killing. Big Al, he said, was considered "the mad hatter" of the underworld because he "killed left and right for nothing," as he had in the Arnold Schuster case. He was intractable, unpredictable—and besides he had had a head-on clash with Vito Genovese. Anastasia reportedly had been outraged by the Strollo-Genovese attempt to assassinate Costello, and he was infuriated, as Genovese had been after his return from Italy, to find himself blocked out of participation in the most lucrative rackets. An especially sore point with him was the fact that he had been frozen out of any share in the lush Havana gambling casinos then being pioneered for the mob by Meyer Lansky with the collaboration of Fulgencio Batista, Cuba's dictator. Anastasia, according to some reports, had tried to go over the heads of the now established Strollo-Genovese hierarchy and set himself up in the Havana gambling business independent of the Syndicate. He had been blocked, but the effort had not sweetened Vito Genovese's disposition. The result was that a face-to-face confrontation ended in a shouting match and the grim Genovese threat: "Mind your own business or you'll be next."

This ultimatum having been delivered, Genovese decided to take no chances. He feared Big Al, with reason, and determined to get Anastasia before the Lord High Executioner could get him. He knew that Anastasia's underboss was the extremely ambitious ex-boot-legger, Carlo Gambino, and through Tony Bender Strollo, he began to proposition Gambino. The deal was elementary in its simplicity and potential reward: eliminate "Big Al," Gambino was told, and you can become the boss of his family with the blessing of Don Vitone.

Gambino liked the sound of this and quietly made arrangements with Joseph Profaci for the loan of some expert killers to do the deed. Profaci turned the chore over to his then-loyal Gallo wing, heirs to the title of Murder, Inc. Joseph (Joe Jelly) Gioelli, the top Gallo "enforcer," and Ralph Mafrici, a thin and sadistic man who liked to use the knife, were given the contract to execute the Lord High Executioner.

This account of the machinations leading up to the Anastasia murder has been corroborated in its essentials by another informer besides Valachi. He is Sidney Slater, a member of the Gallo clan who has spent the past several years singing to District Attorney Hogan. According to Slater, he was in a nightclub a couple of nights after the Anastasia killing when Joey Gallo came in with Mafrici, Joe Jelly, and two other mob members. They had some drinks and the talk naturally got around to the violent fate that had overtaken Big Al in the Sheraton barbershop. Joey Gallo laughed ghoulishly and said:

"From now on, Sidney, you can just call the five of us the Barbershop Quintet."

That told Slater all he needed to know.

The elimination of a longtime underworld power like Albert Anastasia created a void. The new rule of murder rampant created a problem. Both were compelling reasons for the historic rally of the Mafia at Apalachin on November 14, 1957, only three weeks after Big Al's death.

According to Joseph Valachi, Vito Genovese called the Apalachin parley. He had planned originally to have "the meet" in Chicago, but Steve Magaddino, the powerful Mafia chieftain of the Buffalo-Toronto area, talked him out of it and was instrumental in getting the Mafiosi to assemble at Joseph Barbara's hilltop mansion. If the Federal Bureau of Narcotics' information is good, Magaddino had at least one seemingly good argument on his side. Mafia rulers had met the previous year at Apalachin—and nothing had happened; the law hadn't been aware. This time, thanks to Sergeant Croswell, it was to be different; and, according to Valachi, "Vito never stopped beefing about that. . . .

He said if it was not for him [Magaddino] we would have gone to Chicago."

Many vital underworld issues were up for decision at Apalachin, but there can be little doubt that the first item on the agenda dealt with Genovese's justification for the assassination of Anastasia. Hinged to this was Mafia acknowledgment of his hegemony over the eastern underworld. In this respect, the gathering at Apalachin was practically a replica of the conclave in Chicago that sanctified the 1931 murder of Maranzano and confirmed the rule of Luciano and Genovese over the eastern brotherhood. As before, Genovese dredged up all the unfavorable details available about the departed "mad hatter"; and, given Anastasia's past to work over, there can be little question that Don Vitone had plenty of ammunition.

Indicative of the manner in which the rats deserted the Anastasia ship and scrambled aboard the Genovese dreadnought was Valachi's report on Vincent (Jimmy Jerome) Squillante, the pint-sized hoodlum who dominated the rackets in the garbage collection industry. Long one of Anastasia's closest followers, Squillante reportedly was with Big Al in the Sheraton barbershop on the day of his murder. Some say that he was seated in the next barber chair, and that when the shots began to pop, he crouched down out of sight. In the aftermath, according to Valachi, Squillante came running, practically panting in his eagerness to inform on his departed patron.

"Jimmy Squillante requested, 'If you want me to say more, more things he has done, call on me,' " Valachi testified. "In other words, Albert made Squillante. He made him even a godson. In other words, Squillante was getting all the recognition for being with Albert. Now that he was dead he was kicking that he was willing to testify against him. They told him, 'All right, if we need you we will call you.' Lots of remarks were passed about it. In other words, the punk, now he is looking to hang him."

With this kind of help, Genovese couldn't lose; and it is certain that one accomplishment at Apalachin was the ratification of Anastasia's murder as justified and the recognition of Genovese as the power in eastern gangdom. Another issue settled was that of the Mafia's future role in the narcotics trade.

The Federal Bureau of Narcotics, with skilled agents working undercover in Italy and Sicily and with a relentless drive in this country, had broken a whole series of important narcotics cases. The bureau's campaign made the importation of heroin a much more hazardous adventure than it had been, but it was not this alone that concerned the Mafia. The wave of addiction, with peddlers pushing junk even in schoolyards, had created a wave of public revulsion and indignation in many parts of the country. The gambling rackets that so bountifully bankrolled the underworld, and whose profits often financed large deals in narcotics, carried no such opprobrium. The public would happily patronize the bookie or play the numbers or drop money it couldn't afford in the mob's gambling casinos, and there was no adverse reaction. But with heroin, it was different. The very parents who gambled and financed the underworld and made the narcotics traffic possible somehow became indignant at the calculated and callous debasement of their children. The result on both state and federal levels was the passage of new laws imposing drastic new penalties for narcotics violations.

Assessing all this, the Mafia at Apalachin decided it was time for the organization to retire discreetly into the shadows. So the delegates voted an official ban: all Mafiosi were to get out of the narcotics traffic. "They even set a date, the end of fiscal 1958, for their members to close out their stocks and clean up pending deals," says one federal narcotics expert. "After that, the Mafia was not to get out of the traffic entirely; after all, it was too profitable for them to be willing to give it up altogether. But they were going to fade practically out of sight. They were going to 'franchise' Puerto Rican groups to handle the drug traffic for them. This meant that the Mafia with its overseas contacts and sources of supply would still be supplying the junk, but it wouldn't be taking the risk involved in the actual trafficking; and it would be almost impossible to get evidence against it."

There were other items on the agenda at Apalachin that never did get settled owing to the appearance of Sergeant Croswell and his troopers at the end of Joseph Barbara's drive. One bit of important unfinished business involved the influx of new members, many of whom had not murdered enough to have unquestionably valid credentials.

". . . they were going to talk about eliminating some couple of hundred new members," Valachi testified. ". . . they were going to ask the lieutenants for the list of names of all of soldiers they have under them and to put a cross on everyone that never done anything."

Federal investigators say that much of the dissatisfaction stemmed from the influx of new members from Sicily. The Italian government was beginning a new campaign against the Mafia; and, just as had happened in the days of Il Duce, many of the Mafiosi in the line of fire were fleeing to America. Under the reciprocal system of the international brotherhood, these foreign members automatically were received into the American organization, just as if they were union workers transferring from one local to another.

"This was one of the things the Young Turks were against—guys coming over here who couldn't even speak English and becoming button men," an investigator said.

The intensity of feeling is clear only if one understands the background. According to Valachi, membership in the American Mafia had been frozen after the gang wars of the 1930's, and even such loyal operatives in the criminal vineyard as Johnny Robilotto, with all his close ties to Tony Strollo, hadn't been able to achieve full membership. In the early 1950's, there was a change, and the membership books were thrown open again. Unscrupulous bosses used this as an opportunity to shake down their own troops. Albert Anastasia and Frank Scalise, the Mafia Don of the Bronx, collected as much as $40,000 apiece from eager young applicants who would pay anything for affiliation with the all-powerful brotherhood. It was by paying off Anastasia that Robilotto finally achieved status in the clan, according to Valachi, and such under-the-table shakedowns comprised one of the items cited in Genovese's dossier of justification at Apalachin.

The decisions taken and not taken at Apalachin both tended to foster some disgruntlement among the brethren. The Young Turks for whom Tony Strollo was the spokesman were displeased initially by the failure to purge the ranks of foreign elements, and they were even more distressed by the ukase to get out of the narcotics traffic. The attitude was: "That's fine for you old guys who have made your pile, but not for us. We still have to make ours." Even Joe Valachi, though not a Young Turk, reflected the dissatisfaction that ran through the organization over the ban on narcotics trafficking.

In Chicago, he noted, the Mafia "gave their soldiers two hundred dollars a week to stop selling narcotics, and that is what the soldiers in New York were mumbling about. At least in Chicago they gave you two hundred dollars a week; here they wanted you to stop."

The result, as Valachi acknowledged, was a lot of "sneaking." He went to prison himself when the law caught up with him as a result of his sneaking in violation of the Mafia's narcotics-trafficking ban. Others, especially in the immediate aftermath of Apalachin, were more ruthlessly dealt with.

Shortly after the Apalachin conclave, federal narcotics agents broke a smuggling case and arrested Joe DeMarco, one of the rebellious Young Turks.

"Our stoolie told us DeMarco would be dumped [murdered] within a month after we arrested him," a narcotics agent later recalled. "Actually, it took a little longer than that before they got him, some thirty-one or thirty-two days. His partner, Nick (Bulldog) Martello vanished, too, and is presumed dead." This lesson was supposed to impress upon the troops the seriousness with which the Mafia high command regarded the ban laid down at Apalachin, but the revolt in the ranks was not to be squelched even by murder. The Young Turks were too money-hungry for that, and the results of their insubordination were to be far-reaching.

With the coronation of Vito Genovese, murder ruled the eastern underworld. The system of order that Luciano, Costello, and Adonis had imposed was scrapped, and Vito Genovese's whims, usually put into execution by Tony Bender Strollo, became the only law of the mob. As Joseph Valachi was later to tell the McClellan committee, "You see, Genovese has such a way of it, if he wants to get rid of anybody, he has such a way that he finds a way of legalizing it. In other words, for instance, he will make up stories and there is no one there to dispute him."

Executions technically were still supposed to be carried out only after a vote by "the commission," only after the accused had been condemned in a kangaroo trial; but much evidence seems to indicate that Genovese, as in the cases of Willie Moretti and Albert Anastasia, arranged the murder first and justified it afterwards. The result, vouched for by police records, was that New York began to have more unidentified bodies—and at the same time more mysteriously missing gangsters—than Chicago, the city that had usually led the nation in such lethal statistics. A lot of those who got "dumped" were individuals who simply knew too much about some of the major murders in which the Strollo-Genovese combine had been implicated.

There was, for example, the exceptionally gory Scalise-Squillante sequence. Frank (Sceech) Scalise had been for many years the dominant Capo Mafioso in the Bronx. He was on excellent terms with Lucky Luciano, and whenever he went to Italy, he always visited the deported emperor of the rackets and on at least one occasion had his picture taken with him. Scalise in these visits, according to the narcotics bureau, always went loaded with money and made the return trip much less heavily burdened but content in the knowledge that heroin for which he had paid would soon follow him across the Atlantic.

"God damn it," says one highly placed narcotics agent, "Luciano was in this traffic; we *know* it. The amounts of money delivered to him by big gangsters in the United States were fabulous. Sceech Scalise and others—they all went to him and dealt with him."

In 1957, however, a heroin deal that Scalise had masterminded was blown. Some twenty kilos of heroin were seized, a disaster that represented heavy financial loss for the fellow Mafiosi whom Scalise had brought into the venture. Under such circumstances, the originator of the scheme is always held responsible for its faulty execution, and hence Scalise was expected to reimburse his partners. Scalise promised, but he didn't pay. Repeated warnings had no effect. And so, about noontime on June 17, 1957, when Scalise stopped by a favorite fruit and vegetable stand at 2380 Arthur Avenue in the Bronx, two young men followed him in, whipped out .38's and left him dead among the grapes. The brash young executioners hurried out and escaped—and, of course, no one on the premises had seen anything; no one was able to identify anybody.

According to information that subsequently leaked out, Jimmy Jerome Squillante had been a key go-between in arranging Scalise's murder. Scalise's brother Joseph, in the grief of the moment, shouted loudly and indiscreetly that he would find out who did it and would get revenge. Later, of course, Joseph Scalise quieted down, and when police questioned him, he adhered faithfully to the code of omertà— he knew nothing. Nevertheless, his brotherly grief had been noted, his incautious threat of revenge reported; realizing this, Joseph Scalise decided it would be best if he vanished for a time.

Now began a campaign to lure him back. Jimmy Jerome Squillante began to make overtures. He passed the word through the underworld grapevine that nobody was sore at Joe for Frank's sins. Joe didn't need to run. He could come home and Jimmy Jerome himself would throw a fine party for him, just to show there were no hard feelings.

"Like a fool," says one federal investigator, "Joe Scalise believed it. He came back (this was in September, 1957) and Squillante threw a big party for him at his own house. After the party, they all went to work on Joe Scalise with their knives, and they cut his body up into little, disposable pieces. Then the women of the Mafia took off their party dresses and got down on the floor and scrubbed up the blood."

Squillante, who was only too happy to perform such bloody chores for his Mafia superiors, ran scared after those bullets winged over his crouching head in the Sheraton barbershop to rub out his patron, Big Al Anastasia. In turncoat panic, he was pathetically eager to inform on Big Al's black deeds, a demonstration that disgusted the mob, as Joe Valachi's reaction showed. The truth was obvious: Jimmy Jerome Squillante was not a very stalwart character, not one in whom the Mafia could put full trust should real pressure be applied to him to make him sing. Unfortunately for Squillante, just that kind of pressure was being exercised in his home Nassau County on Long Island. The Nassau County grand jury indicted Squillante for extortion, and he was scheduled to report for trial on October 20, 1960. He never showed up—and for one very good reason. He couldn't. He was dead.

The execution of Squillante was notable for introducing a fiendish new technique in the underworld's Operation Body Disposal. A prominent feature of almost any good-sized auto junkyard is a 12-foot-high hydraulic press. Two powerful rams, each with a striking power of a million pounds, plunge down into a steel-lined pit, smashing to smithereens whatever objects they find in their way. A Cadillac can be placed in the pit, and in 90 seconds it will be hammered into a metal cube 36 inches high, 24 inches long, and 24 inches wide. This cube, with a whole cargo of similar cubes, is then shipped off to a steel mill and plunged into the roaring heat of a blast furnace, where it is melted down to make steel for new cars.

Investigators are positive that Jimmy Jerome Squillante went to his grave in "the crusher." Inveigled out by good friends (it is always one's "friends" in the underworld who do one in), he was shot and his body placed in a car trunk; the car was driven to one of the mob-connected junkyards in the New York area. After being stripped of all disposable equipment, the car was hoisted by a large crane and dumped into the hopper of the hydraulic press. The rams thudded down. If any clues still existed—some strands of hair, teeth, the murder bullets—they vanished in the heat and vapor of the blast furnace. There was no chance that the law could ever establish the first prerequisite of a murder case, the body.

"We *know* this is what happened to Squillante, and we suspect it is what has happened to a number of others who have vanished and been merely reported as 'missing,' " one high federal investigator says.

The elimination of Squillante, who knew too much for his own good, was typical of a new and gory thread of motivation that now ran through the New York underworld. The killers who had killed so well for Strollo and Genovese were themselves killed. With his ingenuity for finding high moral justification for his acts, Genovese naturally always advanced some other and seemingly logical reason for the fate that overtook these key personnel in the ranks; but the sinister fact remains that, in the new carnage that now shook the underworld, the vital operatives who had full knowledge of the murder plots suddenly became the victims of their own art, as practiced by others.

Take the case of Johnny Robilotto, the key figure in the Moretti murder. At 3:35 A.M. Sunday, September 7, 1958, Brooklyn Police Headquarters received a telephone call. "There's a man on the ground," the caller said, adding that the location was Utica Avenue about 100 feet south of a Kings Highway service road. Detectives hurried to the spot and found a body, head on sidewalk, feet in the gutter. It was all that was left of John (The Mortician) Robilotto after someone had drilled his skull with four .38 caliber bullets. Joseph Valachi, who had been a partner with Robilotto in loan-sharking ventures, gave the McClellan committee this rationale for the killing: it had been feared, he said, that Robilotto, a lifelong follower of Tony Strollo, might kick over the traces about the murder of his new patron, Al Anastasia, the man who had taken his money and gotten him his long-deferred membership in the Mafia. Valachi himself had been so concerned that he had made a trip to Brooklyn to warn Robilotto against attempting "a comeback." But he found Robilotto in no vengeful mood. "No, don't worry about it," The Mortician told him. "Tony and Vito already spoke to me." Valachi had grunted, "Good." But it hadn't been good for Johnny Robilotto.

Life suddenly ceased being happy also for Joe Jelly, the Gallo enforcer who had played such a major role in the murder of Anastasia. After Apalachin, the Gallos went to war with the powerful Joseph Profaci, disgruntled, it is said, because Profaci had gobbled all in the redistribution of territories and rackets stemming from the Anastasia rub out and they, who had performed the deed, got nothing. From all the evidence, Tony Bender Strollo played a devious game, unhappy himself at the accretion of power to Profaci and willing from his seat on the New York commission to give covert support to the Gallo power play. The Gallo revolt turned out to be a disaster for the Gallos. Profaci had too many guns. And apparently he was too clever and too ruthless.

In late August, 1961, "friends" lured Joe Jelly on an Atlantic fishing expedition on a private yacht sailing out of Sheepshead Bay. Once the fishing boat was well out, however, the "friends" went to work on the unsuspecting Joe Jelly, encased him in concrete and dumped him in the ocean fathoms deep. A few nights later, a car sped through Joe Jelly's stronghold in the Bath Beach section of Brooklyn. As it passed some of his young hoods, a parcel was dumped at their feet. It was Joe Jelly's coat, wrapped around a dead fish.

Though the execution of Joe Jelly was a backfire from the Gallo-Strollo intrigues, the same could not be said of the murder of Little Augie Pisano. Here the sinister hand of Tony Strollo showed in a fashion much more direct. Little Augie, it will be remembered, was the man who had first succeeded to the Brooklyn prerogatives of Frankie Yale, who, like Frankie, had been the eastern representative of Al Capone, and who had finally yielded place to Joe Adonis. Ever since, Little Augie had been a background figure, dabbling in the rackets, maintaining close ties to the men who mattered—Costello, Adonis, and Strollo. The shooting of Costello outraged Little Augie, as it did Anastasia, and the onetime emperor of the Brooklyn rackets made no secret of his displeasure.

In mid-1957, sometime between the Costello shooting and the Anastasia murder, Vito Genovese called an area meeting of the New York commission in a midtown hotel. His purpose was to explain the past and to tell everyone just what the future was to be. Every major mobster in New York heeded the imperial summons, except Little Augie Pisano. He pointedly abstained. Genovese was furious at the insult. He assigned a couple of his button men to find Little Augie and hale him into the presence. To Tony Bender Strollo, whom he knew to be a good friend of Little Augie, he raged: "If Augie doesn't come in, you'll be wearing a black tie!"

Augie came, since he had no choice, but he made no secret of his feelings. He and Genovese simply did not hit it off, and for Little Augie this was fatal. Don Vitone reacted just the way he had in the case of Willie Moretti; he began to spread stories. Little Augie was weak and not to be trusted, he said; if he was ever nailed by the law, he would be certain to break and reveal all the secrets of the brotherhood. This, naturally, was a thought not to be borne. It seemed obvious to Joseph Valachi, listening to the justification that was being put out in advance of the deed, that the skids were being readied for Little Augie.

Genovese at first assigned a couple of lesser hoods to handle matters, but these operatives encountered difficulties. "We can't get him alone," they bleated to Don Vitone. "He's always with Bender. Should we kill him, too?"

The elimination of his principal lieutenant was not yet part of Genovese's plan. He had relied for most of his career on Tony Bender Strollo as his strong right arm, and the evidence suggests that, having failed to "sneak" the Pisano murder without Strollo's knowledge, he now brought Strollo into the plot to arrange it. Strollo's friendship with Little Augie Pisano might be one thing, but his fealty to Vito Genovese was another.

Friday night, September 25, 1959, was Little Augie's night on the town. He was partying early in the evening at the Copacabana, the nightclub so favored by Frank Costello and other topflight racketeers. There he met Mrs. Janice Drake, the beauty-queen wife of comedian Alan Drake. Little Augie had furthered Alan Drake's nightclub career, and he was considered by both Drake and his wife as a family friend, good old "Uncle Gus." Janice and Uncle Gus had hardly ordered cocktails when, entirely by coincidence of course, they encountered Tony Bender Strollo, also out for a night on the town. Strollo remarked that he was dining at Marino's restaurant about five blocks away. Wouldn't Little Augie and Mrs. Drake like to come along? They would—and they did.

Though Little Augie had had no specific plans for the evening, and so far as he knew this was an entirely chance meeting, someone got word almost the instant Little Augie appeared at Marino's. For a telephone call came for him at the bar from a man who spoke with a deep, heavy voice. Little Augie chatted with the caller, then returned to his dinner. He had arrived at dessert and coffee when a second call came for him. It apparently conveyed exciting news, for when Little Augie returned to the dinner table he was in a sweat to leave Marino's. He threw down a roll of bills, asking those at the table to settle his tab for him, and then, taking Mrs. Drake's arm, he walked out into the night.

Some forty-five minutes later, about 10:30 P.M., along a stretch of road not far from New York's LaGuardia Airport, there was an outburst that sounded like a series of backfires; Little Augie's big black Cadillac leaped the curb; and when police arrived a few minutes later, Little Augie and Janice Drake were slumped on the front seat, both dead, their heads drilled with bullets pumped at them from behind.

In the investigation, one striking circumstance was quickly noted by detectives. Tony Bender Strollo and all his principal henchmen, characters like Vinnie Bruno Mauro and Mike Miranda, had ironclad alibis. All had chosen this night to display themselves conspicuously upon the town; they had been in nightclubs where hundreds of persons could see them—and so it was obvious that none of them could have been near LaGuardia Airport at 10:30 P.M. Defeated almost before they began, detectives went through the weary routine of questioning. Tony Strollo received them politely beside the swimming pool behind his New Jersey mansion, and he took fifteen minutes to tell them how sad he was about what had happened and how he had no idea who could have blasted Little Augie into the beyond.

According to Valachi, the murder of Little Augie had been quite simply arranged once Tony Bender Strollo put his mind to it. It was obvious, of course, that the telephone calls to Marino's must have come from someone Little Augie trusted completely. This "someone," according to Valachi, was Frank Casino, the loyal Costello henchman who apparently had heeded the warning published after the Anastasia assassination. The calls lured Little Augie to the nighttime "business" rendezvous out near LaGuardia Airport, but when he got there, he found the only "business" to be transacted was in the hands of a couple of killers on loan from Vincent (Jimmy Blue Eyes) Alo's Bronx gang.

With the death of Little Augie Pisano, the old order had changed indeed. Joe Adonis had been imprisoned, and then deported. And Willie Moretti, Solly Moretti, Albert Anastasia, Little Augie Pisano all were dead. Only Anthony (Tony Bender) Strollo and Vito Genovese were left to rule the roost in eastern gangdom. In the mobs, they had no competitors for power. There was left only the law.

15

THE DOWNFALL

Vito Genovese lived like a king, and like many a king he had domestic problems. In 1952 his wife, Anna, sued him for separation, and in describing her life with Vito, she put on record details about the high living of a gang lord that, in the Mafia, are almost always buried in a kind of family omertà.

According to Anna, Don Vitone lived on a scale to rival Louis XIV. He spent money as lavishly; he had as many women; and when she protested about the women, he didn't hesitate to strike her with his fists, both in public and in private.

This carnival of high jinks and domestic fisticuffs all began, Anna Genovese testified in her separation suit in Freehold, New Jersey, after Don Vitone thumbed his nose at the law and walked away from the murder charge he had faced when he was brought back from Italy. In 1947 he moved his family from a plush apartment at 29 Washington Square West in Manhattan to a mansion on the Skyline Drive at Atlantic Highlands, New Jersey, a place with a panoramic view over New York harbor with the spires of Manhattan in the background.

According to Anna, the mansion cost Genovese $75,000, another $100,000 for renovations, and some $250,000 for bric-a-brac and furnishings. There were two marble fireplaces and a few life-sized statues imported from Italy, a cream-lacquered grand piano, and two five-foot Oriental vases of the costly Imari pattern.

Anna described for the Monmouth County Court what life was like with Don Vitone:

"We lived very high. We traveled to the best places with a personal maid and chauffeur. We were entertained by very big people. . . . Money was no object.

"Our living room was forty feet long. The dining room was exactly the same size as the living room. Our bedroom was twenty-five feet long.

"A marble staircase led from the living room to the dining room. A very beautiful nude marble statue was at the foot of the staircase. One wall in the living room took an artist six months to paint. He depicted the whole outside of the house—the grounds, the water, the yacht basin—everything.

"The furniture in the bedroom was imported Chinese teakwood. The bed had a swan back made of lucite. All of our furniture was made to order.

"We had twenty-four-carat gold and platinum dishes. Our silverware was the best that money could buy.

"We had parties every weekend. Twenty-five to thirty persons always showed up. Vito insisted that I buy the best champagne—sometimes we even hired entertainers from New York City. We never spent less than five hundred dollars on a party. . . . Vito liked company."

The personal wardrobes of the lord and lady of the mansion did justice to the house. Anna had furs for any occasion—a $4,500 mink coat, a $1,500 Persian lamb coat, a $2,500 ermine coat, an $850 broadtail coat, and mink stoles costing $1,200 and $800. She had more evening gowns than house dresses. There were always, she said, "at least thirty gowns in the closet," and "I paid anywhere from $350 to $900 for a gown." Don Vitone arrayed himself in equally costly garb. "He never paid less than $250 for a suit," his estranged wife testified. "He pays $350 for coats, $35 for shirts and $60 for shoes."

The Genoveses had eliminated one of the most common causes of domestic friction, financial worries; but they had other problems. Foremost in Anna Genovese's recital was Don Vitone's insatiable lust for other women, particularly her own girl friends. He used to like to flaunt her girl friends in her face after successful romps with them, and in 1948, she said, things really got serious for a time when Don Vitone became so infatuated with one of his mistresses that he wanted to shed Anna and marry his paramour.

Anna tried to tell him that he had had other women before, that the mood would pass, "but he wouldn't listen to anything. He would punch me and slap me and use terrible language. He would tell me he was going to find some way to get rid of me; that he would either put me in an insane asylum or have me killed."

At one party, she said, Genovese knocked out two of her front teeth. When one of the women guests tried to intervene, he slugged her, too. Frank Costello tried to mediate the Genovese family problems on one occasion, Anna testified, but not even he could do anything with Don Vitone. No one could. Finally, she became convinced that Genovese might really kill her—and so she moved out and brought her suit seeking $350 a week alimony.

Genovese, of course, blandly denied all. Anna, he intimated, was going through the change of life and wasn't quite herself. He never laid an angry hand upon her. He was just a good father and family man. A Romeo? He laughed. Did he look like one? A millionaire? That was a joke. The only income he had was as manager of the Colonial Trading Company, a paper-scrap firm in Manhattan. The court didn't believe him; it ordered Don Vitone to pay his wife $300 a week alimony and $1,500 in counsel fees.

This public scrap with Anna in the courts and the resulting judicial decision radically altered Don Vitone's way of life. He sold his mansion on the heights and all its costly furnishings, and he moved into a little white-clapboard, five-room bungalow that he rented for $100 a month. Such economies were necessary, he told neighbors in Atlantic Highlands, because he wasn't a wealthy man and he simply had to sell off everything he had to pay Anna her alimony.

Privately, he was worried. The court testimony had triggered a number of inquisitive federal probes into his high scale of living and the sources of his income. Genovese realized that there were penalties attached to gaudy display, and he warned his Mafia lieutenants: "Forget the high living. It'll put you in jail if you're not careful." For himself, he adopted the pose of a poor and humble suburbanite, cooking his own meals, tidying up his own small house, raking leaves off his lawn when they fell in the fall.

Behind the camouflage, he was seething. According to Joe Valachi,

Anna Genovese had reason to be worried that her high-living Don Vitone might have her killed. Valachi recalled that late in May, 1953, shortly after Anna had testified, he received a telephone call from Tony Bender Strollo.

"Stay open late every night until you hear from me," he said Tony told him.

Valachi obeyed instructions and kept his Bronx bar open at all hours. About 3:45 A.M. on June 19, Strollo called again and told him to expect some company. Between the two phone calls, Valachi told the FBI, he had had a chance to talk to Strollo, and Strollo had told him that Stephen Franse, a partner with Anna in the 82 Club at 82 East Fourth Street in Geenwich Village was going to be hit. So Valachi wasn't surprised when, at about 5 A.M., Franse came walking into his bar, accompanied by a couple of Strollo strong arms.

"I welcomed them with open arms," Valachi said. "I offered them drinks, but they turned me down."

Franse said he wanted to examine the appointments of Valachi's kitchen to compare them with his own facilities at the 82 Club, and he walked into the back to make his inspection. The two strong arms followed him. As soon as he passed through the swinging door, they jumped him. One grabbed him from behind in a mugger's hold; the other beat him over the head until he fell to the floor unconscious. The killers grabbed a chain and wrapped it around Franse's neck to strangle him, but they couldn't pull it tight enough. So one of them stood on Franse's neck until it was certain he was dead.

The ghouls then stripped Franse of his rings and watch and gave Valachi his wallet, containing about $90. They whisked the body out to Franse's car, tumbled it in a jackknife position on the back seat, and drove off. Car and body were later found in front of 164 East 37th Street, a long way from Valachi's Bronx bar.

The murder of Franse was a pointed warning to Anna Genovese. When a racket-probing Mercer County grand jury subsequently wanted to subpoena her, they found that her mind had suddenly gone blank. "I don't know anything and I don't want to know anything," she said.

Before the murder of her partner, the angry Anna Genovese, testifying on the witness stand in Freehold, had indicated that she knew quite a lot. She had declared flatly that Vito Genovese was a millionaire many times over (federal officials in 1954 were to estimate he was probably worth some $30 million); and she had itemized the sources of much of his income. He had a controlling hidden interest, she said, in four Greenwich Village nightclubs, a dog track in Virginia, and other legitimate businesses. But his real gold mine was the Italian lottery. "He owns it," Anna testified.

She knew, she insisted to the court, because she had kept the books during all those years that Don Vitone was in Italy, dancing attendance on Il Duce. Genovese's brother, Mike, would make the collections and deliver the money every week. Mike Genovese, Anna said, got $500 a week for his services—and Don Vitone every week of his life cleared upwards of $40,000.

A man clearing $40,000 a week, with no income taxes to amount to anything, can well afford to import marble fireplaces from Italy and spend $500 every weekend on a party. But the $40,000 and the revenue from legitimate businesses were not the only sources of Genovese's income. There was another and an important one—narcotics.

The Apalachin decree against dealing in narcotics came too late to help Vito Genovese. He was already too deeply involved.

In 1957 federal narcotics agents arrested a small and muscular Puerto Rican for selling narcotics on Manhattan's West Side. The prisoner was named Nelson Cantellops, and there was no question about his guilt. Nabbed in the act of making a sale, he had no defense, and so he pleaded guilty and drew a four-to-five-year term. The sentence evidently was stiffer than Cantellops had expected, and after a few weeks in prison, he began to seethe at the injustice of it all. He decided he had been double-crossed because the organization had not provided him with a lawyer who "could fix things," and he turned informer.

This action was one of the greatest breaks law enforcement ever got. Though Nelson Cantellops never achieved the notoriety of Joe Valachi, he had a much greater direct effect on the mob, as single-handedly, by his testimony, he sent to prison for long terms some of the most vicious characters ever to pollute the American scene.

Cantellops, it developed, had been in the narcotics peddling racket for two years, and in those two years he had crossed paths and made contact with most of the major narcotics dealers in the Mafia hierarchy. It all began, he testified, because he owed one of the narcotics importers, Charles Barcellona, some $600. Two of Barcellona's pals,

Joe DiPalermo and Carmine Polizzano, told him he could square the
debt if he would ferry ten pounds of heroin valued at $250,000 out
to Las Vegas, Nevada. Cantellops accepted the assignment, performed
it successfully, and soon became a regular narcotics courier for the
mob, making deliveries or picking up incoming shipments in Chicago,
Cleveland, Philadelphia, Miami, and Los Angeles. For each trip, he
was paid $400 or $500.

On one occasion, he declared, Vincent (The Chin) Gigante, the
Strollo henchman involved in the Costello shooting, drove him to
Cleveland to make a delivery for John (Big John) Ormento, the narcotics kingpin of the East 107th Street mob. Cantellops' reliability in
handling and delivering narcotics shipments worth large fortunes recommended him to the Mafia hierarchy and inevitably brought him
into closer contact with the real powers. Finally, he testified, he met
"the right man," Vito Genovese himself.

The first time he wandered into Genovese's presence was in a bar.
Cantellops was with Ormento and Natale Evola at the time, and though
he did not meet Genovese personally, the Mafia overlord looked him
over and told Ormento that Cantellops "seemed all right." Other
brushing contacts finally led up to the event that was to involve Genovese directly and pack him off for fifteen long years in prison.

Cantellops again was with Big John Ormento and Evola, both of
whom were later to be delegates at Apalachin, when they started out
to drive to the home of Rocco Mazzie in the Bronx for an important
business discussion. Cantellops later testified that he noticed another
car following them, but Evola told him not to worry. A little later,
Evola pulled over to the curb, and both cars stopped. Ormento told
Cantellops to come with him, and they walked back to the trailing
car. Gigante was driving it, and in the back sat Genovese.

"Ormento introduced me to Genovese," Cantellops later testified.
"We got into Gigante's car and Genovese said we were going to a
meeting where territorial control would be discussed."

When they arrived at Mazzie's home, Gigante and Genovese remained sitting in their car outside while he and Ormento went into the
house.

"Evola showed up a few minutes later," Cantellops testified. "The
discussion was about taking over a gambling territory in the East
Bronx that could be used for the distribution of narcotics. Mazzie

said we would have to buy out some gamblers who were already operating in the territory. He figured it would cost $150,000."

The discussion apparently lasted longer than Genovese had figured it would take because he finally left his car and walked into Mazzie's home.

"He wanted to know what we decided," Cantellops testified. "Ormento told him it would cost $150,000 to move into the East Bronx, and said he thought it would be worthwhile. Genovese told him, 'All right, set it up as soon as possible and let me know when I can send the boys in.' "

That was the extent of Cantellops' contact with Genovese, the only time he ever met Genovese personally, and that one sentence he testified Genovese uttered was the only incriminating evidence against the boss of bosses. Admittedly, the case did not look too strong, but Cantellops was an iron-nerved and positive witness. He was unshakable on detail, and Federal prosecutors decided to go ahead with the case.

A Federal grand jury in New York returned an indictment on July 8, 1958, against twenty-four narcotics traffickers whom Cantellops had named in his grand jury testimony. The list was headed by Vito Genovese and it included such names as Big John Ormento, Carmine Galante, Vincent (The Chin) Gigante, and Joseph Valachi. Several of those named vanished for the time being, but Genovese and fourteen others were brought to trial in the Federal Courthouse on Foley Square in the spring of 1959.

When the trial began, little was expected. The prosecutor who had handled the investigation and procured the indictment, U.S. Attorney Paul H. Williams, had resigned in futile pursuit of the Republican nomination for governor, and the task of handling the trial devolved upon his young chief assistant, Arthur H. Christy. Christy was pitted against the best legal counsel money could buy, and admittedly, if these legal slicksters could find one chink in Cantellops' story, the whole house of cards would collapse. But Christy and Cantellops proved equal to the legal battalion arrayed against them. Cantellops testified for a solid week on direct examination, describing in meticulous detail every move and every contact he had made as a narcotics courier for the mob. Then the defense attacked, and for an incredible four weeks, defense attorneys in relays badgered and hounded Cantellops, trying to trip and trap him, trying to get him to contradict himself on some vital point in that maze of detail he had put into the record. Cantellops withstood them all; he emerged from the ordeal with his testimony unshaken. And Genovese and all the rest were doomed.

Though the case against Genovese had been anything but overwhelming, Joseph Valachi was subsequently to put into the record of the McClellan hearings testimony that leaves little doubt about Don Vitone's deep and long involvement in the narcotics traffic. Valachi's testimony involves a complicated sequence of plot and counterplot, spangled with double crosses at virtually every stage of the action. To simplify as much as possible, this is Valachi's version of what happened:

Back in 1952, Valachi discovered that narcotics could be obtained through a Le Havre dealer known to him only as "Dominick." Valachi's henchman, Pasquale Pagano, made contact with Dominick's wife during a visit to New York, and she agreed to arrange for the delivery of fifteen kilograms of heroin for a down payment of $8,000. Not having the $8,000, Valachi went to Tony Bender Strollo. Strollo agreed to put up the money, ignoring the fact that Frank Costello had issued an order in 1948 that none of his Mafia family was to get involved in the narcotics traffic.

The fifteen kilograms of heroin, worth $165,000 on the New York market, were eventually smuggled ashore. Valachi's agreement with Strollo had been that they were to divide the profits evenly, Strollo getting 50 per cent for putting up the money, Valachi 50 per cent for arranging the deal. Once the narcotics had been smuggled ashore through the medium of a Strollo button man named Pasquale Moccio, Valachi suddenly discovered, however, that Tony Strollo had bequeathed him a whole covey of partners. They were: "Vito [Genovese] and Tony Bender, myself, Pasquale Pagano, Sandino Pandolfo, John Stoppelli and Pasquale Moccio, and Vinnie Mauro, and one other I couldn't recall. In other words, I found nine partners."

This was not all that Valachi found. Strollo told him that Genovese owed Frank Costello $20,000—and they were going to take that off the top, paying back Uncle Frank before anybody split any profits. The watering down process went on and on. Valachi was finally given two kilograms of heroin, worth about $20,000, to cover his and Pagano's interest. He and Pagano made arrangements to sell the heroin for this price to a pair of young hoods who would adulterate it and market it. The hitch was that the young hoods could pay only $5,000 down—and that's all they ever did pay.

Had the deal been consummated as originally outlined, with everyone paid for his services, Valachi and Strollo would have split a net profit of about $111,500. Instead, Valachi wound up owing everybody. He owed Strollo the $8,000 he had borrowed. He owed "Dominick" a balance of $29,500 on the delivered heroin. Neither bill was ever paid. As Valachi testified, he just walked away from the whole business in disgust—and his disgust grew the more he learned about what had happened.

Subsequently, Valachi happened to bump into John (The Bug) Stoppelli and asked, "How did you make out?" He quickly saw that Stoppelli didn't know what he was talking about. "You were down as a partner," he told Stoppelli, thinking to jog his memory, and Stoppelli asked in amazement, "I am what, what partner?"

Later, in prison, Valachi was a cell mate of Moccio, the agent who had handled the smuggling arrangements. He had figured that Moccio, who had performed valuable services, certainly would have been paid, but he discovered to his amazement that Moccio hadn't received a dime. "They always used to use the oil," Moccio told him, "they need money, and they need money, and by the time I went to get my money, there was none left." So Valachi figured that the only "partners" he had really had in the deal were Tony Bender Strollo and Vito Genovese; and, since everybody else connected with it had been thoroughly double-crossed, he estimated Tony and Vito must have split about $140,000 between them.

There was one additional fillip to the story. Shortly after this disastrous narcotics transaction, Vito Genovese summoned Valachi to a house in Yonkers. Don Vitone was stern and entirely businesslike.

"Did you ever deal in junk?" he asked Valachi.

Knowing that Genovese had personal reasons to know he had, Valachi responded: "Yes."

"You know you ain't supposed to fool around with junk," Genovese admonished severely.

"Yes," Valachi said.

Genovese's eyes bored right through him.

"Well, don't do it again," he said.

"O.K.," Valachi told him.

A bit bewildered by it all, he later remarked to Tony Strollo that Vito had had him on the carpet over the narcotics deal, the very deal that had made Tony and Vito rich. Tony Strollo just shrugged. "Forget it," he told Valachi. And again Valachi said: "O.K." What else was there to say?

So ran the account of Vito Genovese's involvement with the narcotics traffic. The great wave of prosecutions triggered by Cantellops went on and on, spawning offshoots in several directions. Before examining some of these, it might be well to note one other seemingly significant event. Arthur H. Christy was just thirty-five when he convicted Vito Genovese, the king of crime. He had handled the case so well, against great odds, battling the best lawyers Genovese could hire, that he had secured a sweeping conviction, one that was to stand every test to which it was subjected on appeal. In the judgment of the higher courts, Christy had conducted an exceedingly difficult case without flaw.

Though this final verdict of the appeal courts hadn't been rendered at the time, it seemed logical to expect that the vigorous young prosecutor who had performed so well would be rewarded. The reward that Christy expected and wanted was naturally a permanent appointment as U.S. Attorney, the post he had been filling in an interim capacity for months. But some two months after his greatest courtroom victory, Christy read in *The New York Times* that he wasn't going to get the job. Another was being named in his stead. Christy wasn't fired, of course—just passed over. But the effect was the same. He had no alternative but to get out of government service and turn to the private practice of law. His case was less sensational than some others, but it seemed to prove that the quiet stiletto was as deadly in its effect as the broadsword.

Living in Italy at this time were two awesome powers of the American underworld, Lucky Luciano and Joe Adonis. Though in exile, both still wielded potent influence over the affairs of crime. Of the two, Adonis remained the more enigmatic figure.

Freed from New Jersey State Prison after serving his gambling sentence, he had been hit by an overwhelming barrage of legal actions. He had been indicted for perjury for falsely testifying before a Bergen County grand jury that he had been born in Passaic (at an address that, unfortunately for him, turned out to have been a livery stable on his given birth date in 1901); he faced a contempt sentence for failing to answer some hundred questions before the Kefauver committee; and there were in addition Federal perjury and deportation actions. Recognizing the inevitable, Adonis agreed to deport himself quietly to Italy in exchange for not having to serve any more time in prison.

Despite his misfortunes, he still retained his arrogance. Asked by a woman reporter what his wife thought of the predicaments in which he found himself, Joe A. snapped: "She don't think. I do all the thinking in this family."

So it was that on January 3, 1956, ensconced in a $780 suite aboard the Italian liner *Conte Biancamano,* Joe Adonis prepared to sail back to his native Italy. A battalion of reporters sought a last interview, but Joe A., holed up in his cabin, refused to see them. Finally, he agreed to talk to just one. An Associated Press reporter was selected to represent the press, and when he entered Joe A.'s suite, he found the "gentleman of the mob" all soft contrition and apology.

"I'm sorry to treat you fellows like this," Joe A. said, "but you understand how it is; this is a rather bad day for me. Here—"

He interrupted himself by pulling out a roll of folding money large enough to choke an elephant. Nonchalantly, he peeled off $25.

"Here," he said, extending the money to the astonished reporter, "buy the boys a drink and tell them I'm sorry."

"No, no, no," the reporter said, refusing the money.

The refusal had its ludicrous and significant aspects. Apparently, Joe A. was so used to paying, and so used to having people accept, that he interpreted the refusal in just one way—that the amount wasn't enough. He started to peel off some more bills, and it took considerable persuasion to convince him that his money wasn't wanted. In the interview, of course, Joe A. said nothing of any consequence.

Back in Italy, he established himself at No. 2 Via LaAlvreeci outside Milan. There he puttered around his garden and insisted, on those rare occasions when foreign interviewers managed to catch up with him, that he had discovered new peace of mind just working the soil.

"I told you, I am learning land cultivation," he told one interviewer in the fall of 1956. "I am quite happy. Why should you write anything about me? It causes me more headaches, and I had plenty of them before I came here. I am just learning to cultivate the land, and I wish to be left in peace."

Joe A. was not quite so mild, however, with an Italian newspaperman who pursued him and caught up with him one dark night. The Italian reporter, happening to spot Joe A. driving toward his home, gave chase. It was a furious pursuit up and down mountains and along winding, treacherous Italian roads. Finally, Joe A. stopped his car and jumped out. The Italian newshound was right at his heels.

"Joe," he called, "Joe, wait a minute."

The onetime Field Marshal of the American rackets halted and looked all around at the dark night, assessing the strategic situation. Then he spoke just two words.

"You alone?" he asked.

"Yes," said the reporter.

The minute he spoke, Joe A. hauled off and decked him with a haymaker. Then he jumped into his car and drove away.

The incident suggests that violence still seethed just under the surface of Joe A.'s gentleman-farmer manner. It made him worthy of the continuous attention of the Federal Bureau of Narcotics, which kept a close watch on his contacts and his movements. This vigilance enabled the bureau to scotch one typically adroit Adonis maneuver.

On one occasion in 1959 an underworld informant went to Italian officials, eager to peddle "a straight inside" story. This was to the effect that Joe A. and Charlie Lucky were no longer the great buddies they had once been. Joe A. was positively horrified, the informer said, to discover that his old friend had turned himself into the brains of the international narcotics racket.

"They're real enemies now," the informer assured Italian officials. "They had a real bad falling out. Joe A. doesn't like Lucky because he got implicated in the narcotics traffic, and Joe A. won't have anything to do with him any more."

Learning about this "straight inside story," narcotics agents poked around, hunting the reason it had been so industriously peddled, and they found that, by coincidence, of course, the account of Joe A.'s enmity with Charlie Lucky had been funneled to Italian authorities just when Joe A. was trying to get them to relax restrictions upon him and grant him a visa that would have permitted him to travel widely abroad.

"We scotched that maneuver through our own friends in the Italian government," one narcotics agent said, with a chuckle. "Joe A. never got his passport."

Actually, the secret files of investigative agencies show clearly that a close relationship was maintained between Adonis and Luciano—and that Luciano's influence in the underworld, considering that he was operating from far-off Italy, was all but incredible. Inspector Shanley, of the New York Police Department, put it this way in his testimony before the McClellan committee:

"Well, in relation to Luciano, what would become apparent in these charts is the number of pilgrimages that were made by these various well-situated people to Luciano. Joe Adonis went to see him, and 'Patchie' Evelin went to see him, and Tommy Eboli went to see him, and he apparently—even while he was in Europe—he received this great deal of respect. There is no question that his power was so great that even in Europe he could exercise it."

According to information in the files of the Federal Bureau of Narcotics, Luciano's power was so great that he did not always stay in Europe. He managed at times to give his Italian detective watchdogs the slip. One instance occurred in 1952. The grand council of the Mafia held one of its more important meetings at the Plantation Yacht Harbor not far from Miami. The agenda dealt almost exclusively with the narcotics problem. The entire system of smuggling and distribution was discussed and overhauled; new sources for the supply of heroin were decided upon and new smuggling techniques were devised. According to several informers, the dominant figure at this meeting was Charlie Lucky, who had managed to smuggle himself back into the United States for a brief period to give his fellow Mafiosi the benefit of his advice.

Such surreptitious trips did not satisfy the hunger of Luciano to come back to the States on an open and permanent basis. Quietly, he worked behind the scenes in an effort to refurbish his image and blot out the past. Copious quantities of Luciano cash were spread around, and more than one newspaperman in New York drew a private bounty from the Luciano treasury. "What they can do for him is beyond me," one federal prosecutor commented at the time. "But there isn't any doubt that they're getting it—that he is paying them in the hope that somehow they can make him look good."

Luciano's eagerness to get back to his old American racket haunts

was demonstrated in the summer of 1959. Judge Samuel Leibowitz
and his wife were touring Europe, and in Naples, at their hotel, they
encountered Charlie Lucky. Luciano signified to the judge that he
wanted to talk, and so they sat at a table for two hours while the overlord of the international narcotics racket poured out the story of his
broken heart.

"He had everything," Leibowitz recalls. "Huge apartment build-
ings in Rome and Naples, agencies for the distribution of all kinds of
commercial products, more money than he could ever spend—but
there was one thing he wanted above all others, and this was the thing
he could never have: he wanted to get back to America. He wanted
me to tell him how. I told him it couldn't be done; with all his money
and all his power, that was one thing he couldn't do. He sat there
listening to me and he wept real tears; they coursed in rivers down
his face. It was something to see—this tough, ruthless racketeer sitting
there and blubbering like a baby."

Back in America, the events that would lead to the final chapter
in the Luciano story were now taking place.

Tony Bender Strollo and his Young Turks in the Mafia never had
given more than lip service to the Apalachin ban on narcotics trafficking. But after Vito Genovese was packed away in federal prison, they
became more open in their defiance and began to import heroin from
abroad in huge quantities. Some saw in this signs of a new thrust for
supreme leadership in the Mafia; Strollo had been calling for a long
time for more forceful direction of the affairs of crime, and he may
have figured that, if he could amass a huge bankroll quickly through
narcotics smuggling, he would have the resources to back his grab for
power.

The story of his last fateful caper begins with Joe Valachi. Indicted
on narcotics charges in federal court, Valachi jumped bail in February, 1960, and fled to Toronto, Canada, where he hid out for a
month. While there, he made the acquaintance of Albert Agueci and
John Papallia, who, he learned, had developed absolutely fabulous
sources for the supply of heroin. Returning to New York to face
trial himself, Valachi imparted the knowledge he had gained to Vincent (Vinnie Bruno) Mauro and Frankie (the Bug) Caruso, two of
Strollo's most important henchmen.

Mauro and Caruso got in touch with Agueci and Papallia in Toronto and soon an intricate smuggling scheme was in operation. The Toronto gangsters' contact man in Italy was a travel agent named Salvatore Valenti. Valenti propositioned new immigrants coming to America and arranged for them to include among their baggage a special trunk that he supplied. The trunk, of course, had a false bottom stuffed with heroin. These arrangements made, Valenti would wire to America the name of the immigrant in possession of the trunk, and when the vessel docked in New York, an agent would meet the immigrant with the heroin-hot trunk and bribe crewmen to slip this bit of baggage through customs without inspection.

The price of virtue was so cheap that the bribes at first cost only $10 to $20 a shipment, but as the shipments kept coming, greed gradually stepped up the price to over $100. Still, the cost of this essential cooperation on the pier came cheap. The ring was bringing in from ten to sixteen kilos a shipment, and the standard wholesale price for heroin on the New York market usually ranged from $10,000 to $12,000 a kilo. While it lasted, the racket spelled fortune; but when it ended, it spelled disaster.

On October 21, 1960, Federal Bureau of Narcotics agents tracked a shipment of ten kilos that had just been smuggled ashore from the M. V. *Saturnia* to Mount Vernon in Westchester County, just north of New York City. There they arrested Salvatore Rinaldo and Matteo Palmieri. Palmieri was the man who handled the delicate chore of smuggling the heroin off docking liners; Rinaldo was the go-between who picked up the shipments from Palmieri and handled distribution for Mauro and Caruso.

Caught red-handed with ten kilos in his possession, Rinaldo quickly cracked and spilled the entire story. A sweeping investigation was launched, and Albert Agueci and his brother Vito, Papallia, Mauro, Caruso, and Salvatore Maneri, another Strollo henchman, were swept up in the net. All were indicted on narcotics charges. Mauro and Caruso were held under $50,000 bail each; Maneri, under $10,000. All furnished bonds without apparent difficulty. Only Albert Agueci, whose bail had been set at $25,000, languished in jail, with nobody seeming to care what happened to him.

Agueci had a rough time raising money for his bond. According to narcotics agents, his wife had to sell their home, hock her furs and jewelry, and borrow from friends to raise enough collateral to get Agueci out. By the time liberation came, Agueci was boiling. It seems he had been paying a portion of his profits on each narcotics deal to the Magaddino wing of the Mafia in Buffalo. This commission had been supposed to guarantee Agueci help and protection by the parent organization if he should ever need it; but when trouble came his way, the commissions he had paid did him no good—he became the forgotten man. In fury, according to the underworld grapevine, he went straight to Steve Magaddino, upbraided him as a double-crosser, and threatened to squeal if the brotherhood did not stand by him in his forthcoming legal ordeal. Such a threat in the Mafia can virtually be guaranteed to have one result.

In September, 1961, on the eve of trial, Mauro, Caruso, Maneri, and Agueci jumped bail and vanished. The disappearing act was so skillfully performed that it seemed they had left not a single clue behind them.

Then on November 23, 1961, two hunters out in the northern New York woods near the Canadian border stumbled upon a hideous find. It was the body of a man who had been saturated with gasoline and burned. The horribly decomposed remains were identified as those of Albert Agueci.

The discovery of Agueci's body triggered a new manhunt. Canadian newspapers became interested in the mystery and telephoned George H. Gaffney, then the supervisor of the New York office of the narcotics bureau. Gaffney suggested that, since Agueci had jumped bail at the same time as Mauro, Caruso, and Maneri, there might be some connection with them. He forwarded pictures of Mauro and Caruso to the Canadian press, where they were prominently displayed on the front pages. The results were quick and startling.

A Canadian woman who had just come back from Nassau contacted the Royal Canadian Mounted Police. She recognized the pictures of Mauro and Caruso, she said, as those of two American "businessmen" with whom she had been partying for almost a week. Only, she added, there had been a third man with them, and the names they were using didn't correspond to those in the papers. The three musketeers, the woman said, had gone out deep-sea fishing almost every day, and every night they had spent their time around the nightclubs and chasing every attractive skirt in sight.

The narcotics bureau deduced at once that the three caballeros were probably its missing narcotics peddlers. Agent John E. Enright was dispatched to Nassau to take up the trail. He quickly established that the three fugitives sought by the narcotics bureau had indeed been there, and by checking with airlines servicing the Caribbean area, he learned that on August 3, 1961, three passports had been issued in Ottawa, their numbers in series. A man named Anthony Loschiavo held passport No. 5 280 546; a Gabriel Mattiacci held No. 5 280 547; and a John Pallante had No. 5 280 548. Since the lamsters had had to use their actual photographs on the passports with the phony names, Enright was able to establish that Mauro was traveling as Loschiavo; Maneri, as Mattiacci; and Caruso, as Pallante.

The trail now led Enright and other narcotics agents through the islands of the Caribbean, from Bermuda to Nassau to Jamaica to Venezuela. Everywhere along the route there were the same telltale signs—three loud and party-loving North Americans, scattering money about and trying to make every personable female in sight. At Caracas, this broad spoor ended. The fugitives vanished once more into the unknown. Weeks of frustration followed, during which the bureau obtained not the smallest clue to the whereabouts of the trio.

The scene now shifted to Italy. In mid-January, 1962, Lucky Luciano was having visitors. Since he frequently had visitors, little importance was at first attached to this by surveillant Italian police, but they went through the routine of questioning the newcomers anyway. These turned out to be Henry Rubino and his wife, Therese, of Miami. Rubino explained that he was an American businessman and he had dropped in to see Charlie Lucky because Charlie had given him such excellent advice about the location of a new modern American restaurant he was building in Italy.

After their visit with Luciano, the Rubinos flew to Barcelona in Spain. There Spanish police, who took over the surveillance, found them consorting with three high-living American businessmen. The Rubinos returned to Italy and saw Charlie Lucky once again. Then they took off for Madrid, where they registered at the Palace Hotel and where, as luck would have it, those three American businessmen turned up again. Spanish and Italian police now decided that something peculiar must be going on, and the Spanish police noted down the numbers of the passports on which the three "businessmen" were traveling.

In New York, George Gaffney came into his office about eight thirty one winter morning and began to clear up the clutter on his desk. New York at that time was the focal point for the bureau's overseas operations, and as Gaffney sorted through the pile of routine messages and reports, he came suddenly upon a cablegram from Madrid. And there staring up at him were those familiar passport numbers: 5 280 546, 5 280 547, and 5 280 548. Gaffney grabbed a telephone and put in an overseas call to the bureau's agent in Rome.

The Rome bureau chief hopped the first plane for Madrid and at the Palace Hotel, with the help of Spanish police, he arrested Mauro, Caruso, and Maneri. Illustrative of how hard it is to squander all one's money if one has enough to squander was the discovery that Mauro had in his pockets $11,730 in cash and the key to a safe-deposit box containing $43,759 more.

The arrest of the three fugitives touched off a series of chain reactions. In Rome, Italian police decided it was time to call Luciano in for some stern questioning. They brought him down to headquarters on January 26, 1962, and listened for hours while Charlie Lucky kept repeating that he was just a legitimate businessman who had nothing to do with the world of crime. In the light of the Mauro-Caruso-Maneri episode, however, the old refrain did not sound quite so convincing, and it was evident to Italian detectives that Charlie Lucky sensed he was in trouble. Though dressed in his usual immaculate style, in sharply creased gray flannel slacks and a blue sports jacket, he was not his usual debonaire self. He seemed exceptionally tense, nervous, upset.

Finally, he broke off the questioning, pleading that he had to go to the airport to meet a friend, a motion-picture executive named Martin Gosch. Luciano said police could go with him to the airport if they wished, but he simply had to meet Gosch, who was flying in especially to see him. An English-speaking Italian detective, Cesare Resta, went to the airport with Luciano. While they waited for Gosch's plane to land, Luciano fidgeted nervously, acting like a man under intense pressure. When Gosch arrived, Luciano introduced him to Resta, and the three started to walk out of the airport building. They had taken only a few steps when Luciano staggered, grabbed Gosch by one arm and gasped, "Martin, Martin, Martin." In seconds, he was dead from a heart attack.

The international drama that had resulted from the pursuit of Mauro, Caruso, and Maneri had repercussions throughout the underworld. Stemming from it were a host of pivotal developments.

First, the death of Luciano created a void at the summit of the

Mafia's international operations, and it seemingly left Joe Adonis in a strategic position as the one Mafioso of enormous power, prestige, and demonstrated ability, with ties to the Mafia's operations both abroad and in America.

Second, there were the convictions of Tony Strollo's principal henchmen. Mauro, Caruso, and Maneri were all sent away for long terms. So was Vito Agueci, the brother of the murdered Albert. The narcotics bureau's investigation had involved Vito as well as Albert in the ring's smuggling operations, but Vito was more incensed about his brother's inhuman fate than he was at his own conviction. He was seeking vengeance—and he suspected Joe Valachi of having informed on the ring. It was Vito Agueci's charge against Valachi, credited by Genovese, that was to lead to the squeal heard round the underworld.

And, last, there was the drastically altered status of Tony Strollo. Strollo had defied the Mafia ban on narcotics trafficking; his recklessness in undertaking the steady importation of vast quantities of narcotics had resulted in the arrest and incarceration of his principal lieutenants. He had gambled for high stakes—and lost. For this, in the Mafia, there must be a penalty.

About 10 P.M. on Sunday, April 8, 1962, Tony Bender Strollo told his wife, Edna, that he was going out to buy some cigarettes and he would be "back in a little while." It is not known whether Tony Strollo ever got his cigarettes. What is known is that he never came back.

Mrs. Strollo waited and waited for Tony's return. They had been married for thirty years, she said afterwards, and her Tony had never stayed away without giving her a call to reassure her about his whereabouts. But this time no call came from Tony.

Finally, on Wednesday evening, April 11, Mrs. Strollo could stand it no longer. Clad in leather jacket and toreador pants, she walked into the Fort Lee police station and reported that her husband, for so long a key figure in the eastern rackets, had vanished from their Cliffside home.

The announcement can hardly be said to have touched Bergen County officials to the quick. There had been changes in officialdom since the days when Joe Adonis ran the empire of crime in Bergen County, but one would never have known it from the tepid reactions to Tony Strollo's disappearance. Prosecutor Guy W. Calissi, exhibiting a maximum of unconcern, declared: "I am not doing anything.

I am not going to spend the taxpayers' money looking for him." Fort Lee Police Chief Theodore Grieco said he didn't plan to investigate either since Tony Strollo, during the sixteen years he had resided in Fort Lee, "has always been a good citizen and was never any trouble." One might think that the disappearance of such an estimable citizen would have called for some activity on the part of police, but Chief Grieco didn't see it that way. He finally did bestir himself to send out a missing person alarm.

And that was just about that.

It remained for New York and Federal authorities to discover what had happened to Tony Bender Strollo. Assistant Chief Inspector Raymond V. Martin, who had charge of Brooklyn South detectives during the Profaci-Gallo war, canvassed his underworld sources and came up with this version: a federal investigation of the narcotics traffic had been getting close to Strollo; Tony had created a host of enemies in the Costello-Anastasia-Pisano affairs; he had made others by backing the Gallos against Profaci; and finally he had blundered in his great narcotics gamble. For all of these reasons, it had been decided that he had to go. According to Martin, the underworld version was that the death decree had been cleared with both Joe Adonis and Charlie Lucky in Italy before Lucky's death and with Vito Genovese in federal prison at Atlanta.

Joe Valachi has since confirmed Genovese's role in the murder. Even in prison Genovese received visitors who were able to carry his imperial decisions back to his Mafia underlings; and to one of these, Genovese had passed the word that Tony Strollo, his lifelong right arm, was to be dumped. Valachi learned about it in a chat with Genovese after Tony Strollo's disappearance.

"Vito Genovese told me," Valachi testified, "that it was the best thing that could have happened to Tony, because Tony couldn't take it 'like you and I,' and he is talking to me, and so I looked at him, like I snapped back with my head. I thought maybe he was going to tell me he was an informer or something . . . and I said, 'What do you mean?'

"And he said, 'Well, you know he was a sick guy, and he won't be able to take it like you and I.' Like he couldn't take time, to put it this way, time in prison or a long prison sentence, and so that is the best thing that could have happened."

The significance of Genovese's remark, Valachi said, was simply this:

"It meant that in our language, that he had ordered his death."

Just who were the good "friends" of the unsuspecting Tony Strollo who performed this last charitable service for him is unknown, but underworld rumor persists that Strollo went to his end in "the crusher" as had Jimmy Jerome Squillante before him.

With the murder of Strollo, leadership of the Eastern Mafia, the dominant wing of the brotherhood across the nation, would seem to have been thrown into considerable confusion. There is little doubt that Vito Genovese, even though in prison, remains the all-powerful chief of the tribe, but his sentence is for fifteen years—a long time to wield effective control from behind bars. The affairs of crime are just too complicated for that. Somewhere there must be another Duke's and another field marshal like Joe Adonis to direct the legions of the underworld.

Under the present setup, with murder and the law collaborating to wipe out or deactivate the secret rulers who had for so long dominated the world of crime, Genovese's interests are said to be guarded and protected by Gerry Catena, the New Jersey gang lord who first showed prominently in the days of the Crime Cabinet in Duke's, and by Thomas (Tommy Ryan) Eboli, long a power in Manhattan. Though Catena and Eboli wield great authority, the indications are that the present composition of the Mafia hierarchy can be only temporary. Don Vitone remains behind prison bars, and, for as long as he stays there, there will be room at the top for a leader.

16

THE EVIL AND THE MENACE

A PATHY. Bribery. Corruption. These are the ABC's of lawlessness. Decay is the next stage in the alphabetical progression."

So wrote the General Investigating Committee of the Texas House of Representatives in 1961 following an investigation of organized crime and corruption in the port cities of Beaumont and Port Arthur. The committee in these succinct terms accurately described one of the crucial dilemmas of our time and our society. Apathy. Bribery. Corruption. Decay. These are the four horsemen that today menace the foundations of America, and will continue to do so as long as the worst elements are permitted to dominate the best.

The investigation that led the Texas committee to formulate this dire prognosis had followed the pattern that, by now, is so timeworn and familiar. All the experiences of Nelson Stamler in Bergen County, of Harry Savasten in Youngstown, had been duplicated by the House of Representatives' committee in Texas. The Texas investigators found that the cash boxes of the officers of the law were as heavy in Beaumont and Port Arthur as they had been in Bergen County; the blindness of the law regarding all forms of gambling and vice (there hadn't been a gambling indictment in Jefferson County in thirty years) was just as complete; the alibis for not knowing and not acting were virtually identical; and when the state came in and tried to clean up,

the opposition of constituted local authorities was just as vigorous
and just as vicious.

The state committee's telephone lines were tapped. Its witnesses
were threatened. When it made raids and arrests, the obstructionist
local law made certain no equipment was available to take photographs or fingerprints, and the local District Attorney tried to file
misdemeanor instead of felony charges. When the City Manager of
Port Arthur appeared to testify, he was in a state of terror and denied
he knew of any gambling, any prostitution, any narcotics violations;
later, after the state committee had produced overwhelming evidence
to show that all three were rampant, he confessed that he had received
a threatening phone call before he testified—and that he had been
afraid, if he told the truth, acid would be thrown in the face of his
wife or his daughter.

In such an atmosphere of terror and intimidation, the Texas committee pressed its probe. Describing the difficulties it confronted, it
later wrote:

> Men feared both economic reprisals and threats to their fami-
> lies. Women feared for their children. At least two ladies re-
> ported threatening phone calls within an hour of meeting the
> committee. Grown men would make appointments only at secret
> rendezvous. Some refused to talk over the committee's regular
> phone. A private line was installed. It quickly developed sounds
> of interference.
>
> "I don't want to wind up in the canal" was a common expres-
> sion. Accidental drownings of those who had fallen from favor
> were reported. Some had apparently drowned while swimming
> with their hands tied.
>
> Stories of beatings, brutalities, terror and sadism were told.
> To say that fear hung like a fog over the community sounds
> dramatic. It *is* dramatic when that fear is widespread and gen-
> uine. There was a frightening apathy concerning law enforce-
> ment.
>
> Invariably the committee was told that as soon as it left town,
> business as usual would return. Before the hearings opened not
> one resident held hope of permanent improvement. "This is a
> way of life here—it can't be changed." It is little wonder that
> nonresistance to evil had become a tradition.
>
> In the words of Lowell: "Truth forever on the gallows, Wrong
> forever on the throne."

What were the beagles of the law like under whom such a brazen perversion of the American system had flourished? The committee put a number of them on the stand. There was, for example, Charles H. Meyer, who had been Sheriff of Jefferson County since 1947. His annual income tax returns always showed "campaign contributions" far in excess of his official salary. In 1955, he was paid $9,250 by the county, but his anonymous "campaign contributions" totaled $13,700. In 1959, when he had been rewarded for his services with a boost in official pay to $12,000, the mysterious "campaign contributions" totaled $23,870.

Sheriff Meyer acknowledged that the "campaign contributions" came in infallibly every year whether there was a campaign or not. He got them on years when he didn't have to run for re-election, and he got them one year when he was on the ticket—but had no opponent. The "campaign contributions" always came in plain envelopes. They might be left on his office desk or dropped through the window onto the seat of his parked car; and when he opened the envelopes, he would always find them fat with crisp $100 bills. Sometimes there would be as much as $1,200 in a single envelope. In five years these mysterious "campaign contributions" to the sheriff totaled $85,000.

The sheriff was not the only one who got "campaign contributions." Even lowly constables found they had bashful friends who dropped those mysterious plain envelopes with their crisp $100 bills. According to the state committee, one constable in Beaumont had $7,000 in one bank account, $7,000 more in a second, $6,500 in a third, $2,000 in a credit union, and various other accounts of $500 each in savings and loan and other banks. A Port Arthur constable, making $8,000 a year, paid an income tax on $17,000 in 1960. He conceded that he received about $5,000 in cash that mysteriously appeared in envelopes about the first of every month.

Everyone, of course, insisted that there had been no *quid pro quo* for these gifts from friends too shy to identify themselves. Yet, somehow, none of these stalwarts of the law had ever found any gambling, prostitution, or narcotics trafficking going on in their preserves. The state committee, when it made its raids, found tote boards operating behind windows in full view of passersby on the sidewalks; and when one of its agents just wandered in off the street, "a zealous bookie . . . shoved a daily racing form into his hands and said, 'What'll you have?' before the arresting officer could say, 'You're under arrest.'" Under the circumstances, it should not have been too hard to gather evidence, but District Attorney Ramie Griffin acknowledged that there hadn't been a single felony conviction for bookmaking, gambling, or prostitution during the ten years of his regime.

Summing up, the Texas legislative committee wrote:

> Ordinarily, unless jolted by some personal experience, citizens don't think much about the existence and influence of organized crime. They don't realize that organized crime can flourish only in a climate of police protection. They don't grasp the full import of what rottenness in public life can do.
>
> By the time the phenomenon of politico-criminal corruption is comprehended, their community is debauched, their jobs are jeopardized, their property and their very lives are affected.

The extent to which property and lives are affected was dramatically demonstrated by the New York State Commission of Investigation in its 1964-65 probe into loan-sharking. The committee found that the limitless millions of dollars put into the hands of gangsters by gambling, narcotics peddling, and other rackets are channeled into trade through the medium of the loan shark and are used to terrorize, corrupt, and eventually take over legitimate businesses. With the loan shark acting as the go-between for top racketeers, even brokerage houses and banks have been infiltrated and destroyed.

The career of one New York business executive, whom the committee identified only as "L," ran the gamut from gambling to corruption. A short, well-dressed, soft-spoken man, the executive had worked for many years in the garment industry and had risen to the vice presidency of a leading sportswear firm. His salary was in the $20,000–$25,000-a-year range; he had the complete trust of his employers; and he seemed like the very model of the rising American businessman.

But L had a secret vice—gambling. The urge to bet on anything and everything became a compulsive habit with him. He lost and lost and lost. Deluding himself that he could make a lucky killing, he borrowed from the loan sharks, plunged for ever-heavier wagers and so hurried the day of disaster. At the end, he was betting $1,000 a day—and losing it.

Long before this, of course, he was in hock up to his eyebrows. The loan shark puts out money in small amounts at the typical rate of six for five; in others words, you borrow $5 this Friday, you must pay back $6 next Friday—a 20 per cent fee for one week's use of the money. On larger loans the standard charge is 5 per cent a week, which figures out to a mere 260 per cent a year. A little arithmetic shows that, if a borrower keeps borrowing and his loan stretches over a period of months, it is perfectly possible to pay back two or three times the amount of money originally borrowed, and still owe the entire principal.

L was in just this kind of a predicament. His favorite loan shark was Milton Kaufman, one of the largest peddlers of blood money in New York and a man whose connections were evidenced by his use of prominent Syndicate strong arms as collection agents. L got in so deep that his weekly obligations to Kaufman and other money lenders came to almost $2,500, a tariff his yearly $20,000 salary wouldn't begin to support. There was no way out, so L started to steal his company's checks. In the period of a year, he purloined some 2,000 checks sent in to his company to pay for goods. The embezzlement totaled more than $200,000.

The harassed vice president told Kaufman the checks had come to him in private deals, apart from his company; but, as he testified, Kaufman must have had good reason to doubt this. How, for example, did Kaufman cash the checks after they were turned over to him? Very simply. He had corrupted a bank. The loan shark took L around to his favorite banking institution and introduced him to the bank officers and key personnel. Kaufman would endorse the checks L gave him, slip them to his favorite teller and get immediate cash. He would deduct 10 per cent for his services in handling the deal (not applying this to L's loan or "vigorish," as the loan shark's tariff is called); he would then turn the balance over to L, get L to deposit it in his own account and make out checks to fictitious individuals. Kaufman would receive these fictitious checks, endorse them and deposit them in his own account. This intricate larceny was made possible by slipping cooperative bank personnel $10 or $15. In the course of a year, L testified, he paid out some $2,000 in bank bribes. Eventually, the crushing burden of the whole conspiracy became too much for him; he turned himself in to the police and sought refuge from the loan sharks in prison.

L's experience, though it touched many bases in the racket-corruption chain, was really only a mild illustration of the enormous leverage on our whole society that the underworld has obtained through their unlimited millions of dollars. This racket money undermines, corrupts, and subverts in infinite ways. As one Genovese-connected loan shark bragged to an associate, "he had a clientele that couldn't be beat, going into doctors, stockbrokers, the highest people that you want to meet." One New York builder needed a million dollars to finance a large construction project. Through a friend, he contacted a loan shark who was the chief lieutenant of one of the underworld syndicates. When the builder began to talk about credentials and collateral, the loan shark cut him short. He didn't want to see any credentials, he wasn't concerned about collateral.

"Your body is your collateral," he told the builder.

The amount of "black money" (racket money) which funnels through loan sharks into legitimate business is literally staggering. The New York commission estimated that across the nation $1 billion a year is working for the rackets in this manner. Assistant District Attorney Rogers, one of Hogan's staff, told the committee that "reliable information" showed one gang leader in 1959 or 1960 spread out $500,000 among his subordinates to be invested in loan-sharking. The money came back to him in such copious quantities that, by 1964, it was estimated he had turned the $500,000 into $7.5 million. Rogers added that there were, in New York City alone, "at least ten men who are comparable to him. A loan shark that we know of lent a million dollars in the morning and a million dollars in the afternoon."

Once so deeply involved with a loan shark, there is almost no way the victim can free himself. His weekly vigorish on such huge loans is back-breaking, and almost before the borrower knows it, he has acquired chiefs of the criminal syndicate for his partners. The record of the New York hearings was studded with instances in which the rackets, with loan sharks acting as go-betweens for the black money of syndicate bosses, muscled in and took over legitimate businesses from their original owners. Bar and restaurant owners, often operating on thin margins, borrow from the loan sharks; garment district firms, engaged in a highly competitive, unstable, and cyclical industry, run short of cash and go to the loan shark. All wind up being devoured. So do brokerage houses—and even banks.

The evil worked by black money operating behind the facade of a brokerage house was illustrated in the activities of Arthur Tortorello, also known as Joseph Grasso and Artie Todd. A convicted felon, Tortorello was a longtime associate of Carmine Lombardozzi, one of the lieutenants of Mafia chieftain Carlo Gambino. Tortorello, combining money and violence in his methods, came to dominate a whole group of securities houses—Carlton Securities, Provincial American Securities, Philip Newman Associates Inc., Harwyn Securities, Hilton Securities, and J. C. Gray and Company.

Tortorello's methods were described to the New York commission by a witness identified only as "M." On one occasion, this witness said, he did a favor for a friend. His friend had borrowed "a substantial sum of money" from Tortorello to keep his Long Island plant running, and M, who was going into the city, took two checks with him to deliver to Tortorello. When he presented the checks, Tortorello flew into a rage because there were only two instead of three. M testified:

"Well, he started yelling about the third check . . . and he got up there and he started beating me, and —— got in between us and he said . . . he is holding me . . . I don't know why he held me instead of Artie . . . that he could kill me.

"And I started to go out, he gave me a terrific kick in the backside that I really . . . I thought I was going to pass out. . . ."

The New York commission concluded that "this vicious and demeaning assault was intended as a message to the borrower—as a sample of what he would receive if he was again short in his payments."

M himself had been involved with Tortorello. He had borrowed $1,400 from the loan shark on one occasion and had been obligated to pay Tortorello back at the rate of $200 a week for ten weeks. He found he couldn't meet the payments, and Tortorello sent him over to Jersey City to work as a shill in the over-the-counter firm of Carlton Securities until the loan was paid off. The witness quickly discovered that Carlton Securities was only a front for Tortorello, whose favorite strong arm brought its weekly payroll across from New York. Inevitably, with this kind of hidden ownership, the firm was a bucket shop, peddling worthless stocks to the public. At the time M joined the staff, the brokerage firm was concentrating on two dogs, C. & F. Electronics and Belmont Oil. Tortorello and his associates disposed of 750,000 shares of worthless Belmont Oil stock, hawking all the way from New York to California. The cost to mulcted customers was nearly $1 million. The C. & F. Electronics deal was even better. Carlton Securities flooded the market with more than one million shares of this clunker at an average price of $1.25 a share.

How had Tortorello managed to get control of such securities firms? One way was discovered by M when he went to work for Provincial American Securities at 170 Broadway in Manhattan. The ostensible boss of the firm was Stanley Younger, but M soon discovered that Tortorello was constantly on the premises and the real authority. He inquired of veterans in the firm how this had come about:

"I found out that he [Tortorello] made a loan to Stanley Younger because Stanley Younger got involved in gambling in Las Vegas and he needed money to operate, and he was introduced to Arthur Tortorello and Arthur Tortorello put up all the money he needed. I understand it was around $75,000."

The result was that Provincial American Securities and another Tortorello bucket shop, Philip Newman Associates Inc., began to collaborate on the widespread distribution of another fraudulent stock called Monarch Asbestos. The New York Attorney General's office stepped in to stop this swindle in mid-career. It estimated that, at the rate the stock was selling in October, 1958, the public would have been bilked for another $1.5 million in a year.

Not only brokerage houses, but even banks, have fallen prey to the corruptive influence and the unscrupulous raiding of the underworld. A wave of bank failures in 1964-65 has been attributed by Federal officials directly to systematic looting by underworld combines infiltrating the executive suite.

In its New York probe, the state investigation commission developed detailed testimony about the various kinds of chicanery practiced by the underworld in its raids on bank vaults. One caper involved the corruption of bank officials and looting the till for literally millions of dollars in unsupported "loans." A past master of this particular swindle was John (Gentleman Johnny) Massiello, a loan shark believed by authorities to have close connections with the Genovese family.

Massiello, the New York commission found, had managed to bribe the loan officer of a New York bank. Once he had corrupted this key official, the rest was easy. A businessman unable to obtain credit from any other source came to Massiello, needing a $6,000 loan. Massiello had him execute a promissory note for $8,000, took the note to the bank and discounted it through the corrupt loan officer at the standard rate of 6 per cent—and pocketed $2,000 vigorish for his trouble.

The note, of course, was as worthless as the paper on which it was written.

Not content with using the bank's resources for such loans to needy businessmen, Massiello developed the practice of obtaining loans in the names of a number of dummy corporations created out of nothing more substantial than his own imagination. Massiello in these transactions paid the bank its normal interest rate of 6 per cent—and obtained thousands of dollars that he could put to work at the loan shark's vigorish rate of 260 per cent. The records would seem to indicate that Massiello didn't even pay the 6 per cent out of his loan-sharking profits; he simply pyramided the whole deal with fresh "borrowings," defraying the costs of old loans with proceeds from the new.

In 1962, the bank became aware of these transactions—and fired its corrupted loan officer. An investigation established that between May, 1959, and January, 1962, Massiello and his associates had obtained close to $1.5 million in "loans." By December, 1964, the bank had been able to recover only about half of this amount.

The New York bank could weather this loss, but not all institutions have been so fortunate. Take, for example, the Crown Savings Bank of Newport News, Virginia.

This story opens with the activities of a New York loan shark named Julio (Julie Peters) Gazia, who was related by marriage to Vito and Mike Genovese. Gazia headed a Fifth Avenue outfit known as the First National Service and Discount Corporation; and First National, as witnesses testified, obtained its money for loan-sharking operations from such sources as Thomas (Tommy Ryan) Eboli and Mike Genovese, the brother of Vito and known in mob circles as "the wise man."

In 1962, the president of a light bulb manufacturing concern, already in hock to Julie Peters Gazia, sought a second loan shark to help him pay off the first. He landed in the clutches of Peter D'Agostino, who operated a money-lending business known as Norwalk Investors Inc. in Mineola, L.I., D'Agostino negotiated two loans for the manufacturer, one for $50,000 with a Long Island bank and a second for $30,000 with the Crown Savings Bank of Newport News, Virginia. D'Agostino took $10,000 of the proceeds as a "finder's fee." On another occasion, D'Agostino got Gazia's firm a $25,000 loan from the Long Island bank, boosting the resources on which it could collect its 260 per cent vigorish.

D'Agostino was able to work such miracles, as he and his staff later admitted to investigators, only because he had found the Long Island bank president and his employees susceptible to the receipt of cash and expensive presents. The commission reported that the president of the bank was given an envelope containing $400 in cash "just a few weeks before he was to appear as a witness before the commission."

The experience of Crown Savings in Newport News was more extensive and disastrous than that of the Long Island bank. D'Agostino's Norwalk Investors did a flourishing business with Crown Savings, discounting with it third-party notes that usually turned out to be worthless. D'Agostino, however, was not the only one who had got his hooks into Crown Savings. In December, 1964, a federal grand jury in Atlanta indicted the cashier of Crown Savings and five officers of money-order firms in Atlanta for conspiring in a kiting operation. The Federal Deposit Insurance Corporation discovered in addition that Crown Savings was carrying on its books more than $1.5 million in high-risk loans. The bank, indeed, had been looted to the point where it was insolvent, and the FDIC closed its doors.

Similar disasters were overtaking other banks across the nation. Over a span of twenty years, no more than two or three federally insured banks failed in any given year; but in 1964, in the midst of the most sustained boom in the nation's history, seven banks collapsed and in the first months of 1965 four more went under.

Federal officials on every level hold that gangland mobs, entering the banking field, are mainly responsible. Courtney A. Evans, Assistant Director of the FBI, told a bankers' group in New York that the bureau had learned of "situations where notorious hoodlums and racketeers have invested, either directly or through individuals 'fronting' for them, in banks and other financial institutions. Thereafter, funds are made available to the criminals' friends and associates with little or no collateral required." Federal banking officials told the McClellan committee that the looting and collapse of the Brighton (Colorado) National Bank evidently had been the handiwork of Chicago gangland figures.

Rep. Wright Patman (Democrat, Texas), chairman of the House Banking Committee, has been outspoken in his denunciation of racket infiltration into the sacred purlieus of banking. He has charged "hoodlum connections with some of the biggest banks in the country," and he adds: "Criminal control of banks is widespread. It reaches from

New York to Miami to Chicago, and even to some small towns. I would say that there are dozens of banks influenced or owned by hoodlums."

Apathy. Bribery. Corruption. Decay.

The brokerage-house and banking scandals emphasize that the Texas legislative committee's maxim is working its evil in some of the most respected circles of American society. The significance of the underworld and its secret rulers is to be found not just in its own multimillion-dollar rackets, but in the corruptive influence of its great wealth, spreading out in ever-expanding rings.

Why should this be? Why, under the present system, *must* it be?

The answer is in the virtually complete immunity that the underworld and its political and police collaborators have managed to achieve. The enormous bankroll of the rackets has corrupted law enforcement and politics on many levels—corrupted them to such an extent that it has become almost axiomatic that no investigation can be allowed to go "all the way" because the disclosures would be too sweeping and too calamitous for too many highly placed individuals. Hence we have the disgraceful sequence, repeated over and over, known as busting the rackets-buster. The rare and honest prosecutor who refuses to play ball is discredited by every known unscrupulous tactic. Abe Reles said the mobs were out to "get America by the pocketbook." Joe Valachi told the McClellan committee: "We have an expression, you have money, you have weight. Weight works men's strength." The underworld's philosophy that only money counts has become increasingly the philosophy of respectable America.

The result is cynicism—and apathy. How could it be otherwise? There is no longer any *belief* in the integrity of law enforcement, any *faith* in the probity of prosecutors and the courts. The politico-judicial system has collapsed so often, so abjectly, that it has in effect underwritten with its sanction regimes of brutality, rape, and murder. The grossest provocations bring only minimal punishment—and sometimes not even that. Typical were the closing chapters of the Bergen County saga.

The post-Stamler scorecard in Bergen County—typical of exposés across the nation—furnishes one of the most vivid examples of the manner in which high officialdom bands together for self-protection.

Harold John Adonis, the governor's clerk who had built a mansion with cash, became virtually the only sacrificial offering on the altar of virtue. There was no doubt that he had had an enormous volume of cash on which he had not paid income taxes, and the federal government put him away for five years. After serving this sentence, he went on trial in Bergen County Court on the charge of conspiracy to protect the Bergen rackets. Adonis' defense was that he had received part of his unexplained cash from a wealthy Venezuelan divorcée and the rest, an even larger amount, from John Dickerson for services he had performed for the Republican party. Dickerson roared a loud and angry denial that Adonis had ever received a cent from him. The jury deliberated an hour and thirty-five minutes—and acquitted Adonis, a verdict that was hailed by former Governor Driscoll, who had become a wealthy business executive, as demonstrating that his administration had been snow-white in its purity.

Michael Orecchio, the county detective chief who had never been able to find Costa's Barn, even with a road map provided by New York authorities, was indicted for misconduct in office and perjury. He went to trial in April, 1952, and was convicted on three misconduct charges. The conviction was set aside on appeal, and a new trial ordered. It was never held.

Frank Borell, the Cliffside Park police chief who had dined in the mob hangout of Duke's until the food began to disagree with him, was indicted for misconduct in office and false swearing. He was convicted on the false swearing count and was sentenced to nine months in prison. An appeal from this conviction was pending when he died.

Prosecutor Winne, indicted for misconduct, waged a series of legal battles. One judge obligingly threw out the entire indictment, but the State appealed and managed to get it reinstated. With the case already shadowed by this judicially imposed handicap, the trial opened in the spring of 1954 and lasted for fifty-three days. The courtroom was always packed with spectators, a heavy percentage of them members of Bergen's official family, there to wish Winne well. The defense made every possible appeal to local prejudice. The impact of Hogan's evidence was softened by the wily stratagem of building Hogan up as one of the nation's greatest prosecutors, operating with a large, expensive, and highly trained staff. Winne was pictured as the staff-poor, handicapped rural boy who couldn't possibly have known what was going on when it took even the Great Hogan two years to perfect his case. The jury deliberated five hours and thirty minutes—and acquitted Winne. The Courthouse claque almost lifted the roof with their cheers.

Stamler had brought a whole series of other indictments against police and local officials in the almost totally corrupt Bergen County. It is axiomatic that, in cases of this kind, convictions and heavy sentences imposed on lower-echelon bribe-takers are most important. A stern law that convinces everyone it means business can elicit from the bottom the squeals that lead to the top. And so it is significant to see what happened in Bergen County. The pattern read monotonously the same in case after case: misconduct in office, not guilty; misconduct in office and conspiracy to obstruct justice, not guilty; misconduct in office, convicted, decision reversed on appeal, new trial, not guilty; misconduct in office, perjury and subornation of witnesses, convicted of misconduct, conviction reversed on appeal, new trial, not guilty. On and on ran the unvarying record. In Bergen County nobody was guilty of anything.

Both local and federal grand juries, composed for the most part of high-class citizens, were frustrated by the wall that was suddenly and mysteriously erected, blocking their paths the moment they tried to probe too hard into the Bergen rackets. Stamler's last grand jury— the jury that had felt it was getting "close to home" and was going to make "people squirm"—closed its work with the frustration of a presentment, an angry and bitter indictment, it is true, but then harsh words never hurt anybody.

The jury lashed out at the system under which the criminal, "flanked by expensive attorneys and advisers," was "able to cut deeper into our social structure by corrupting weak officials than he ever did by open defiance and violation." The jury was sharply critical of the legal profession for its representation of the mob. "It is our belief that such conduct casts a baneful reflection on the bar of the community and in our opinion is entirely unwarranted," the jury wrote. It added that it had been "appalled by the fact that a number of individuals who testified before it in this investigation could commit perjury or false swearing with apparent unconcern," and it said "it considers it unpardonable that public officials should continue to hold office after refusing to answer a question under oath on the grounds of self-incrimination."

A Federal grand jury that sat in Trenton for eighteen months and went out of office in June, 1953, was even more frustrated than the

Bergen County panel, if that is possible. The Federal jury had tried to probe the Moretti murder case, but had been blocked because murder fell outside its jurisdiction. Its members then switched their attention to a field in which their authority would seem to be unquestioned —the income-tax angle. Oddly enough, however, almost the instant that the jurors touched this sensitive nerve, they found that impenetrable wall of official inertia blocking their way. This jury, too, was reduced to the frustration of returning a presentment indicting "the system" that weds crime and politics.

The jury reported that it had wanted to probe the income and the tax returns of certain high public officials in New Jersey. But U.S. Attorney Grover Richman, who was directing its activities, had informed it that it could not initiate investigation of specific cases; it could act only on cases prepared and presented to it by the criminal division of Internal Revenue. The jury swallowed this limitation with the greatest reluctance, and its presentment showed why. It charged that *more than a million dollars in taxes* had gone unpaid through the failure of public officials to report their full incomes. ". . . the fact stands out," the jury wrote, "that a substantial part of more than $1,000,000 unpaid by this group of tax dodgers will never be collected." The jury was prescient. As soon as its term ended, all thought of harassing Jersey officials died.

In disclosing that more than one million dollars in taxes had gone unpaid by Jersey officialdom, this federal grand jury made a recommendation that, of course, was ignored. It urged that Internal Revenue "be required to make periodic checks" of the income-tax returns "of all public officials, particularly with respect to their private sources of income. . . . We believe that this recommendation is of vital importance because of the obvious detrimental effect upon the morals of the tax-paying public when it appears that its own officials have been able wholly to escape their share of the tax burden."

Such was the picture in Bergen County, and such has remained the picture throughout the nation. Time and again prosecutors who have tried to prosecute have found their best efforts thwarted by superiors or the courts. The most important accomplishments of Milton Wessel's short-lived Group on Organized Crime were vitiated on appeal. The conviction of Chicago gang lord Tony Accardo in an income-tax case was thrown out by an appeals court that ruled he had not had a fair trial because he had had such an unfair press, a contention often advanced by unlucky defendants but rarely ratified by the courts as valid. Wessel's own conviction of twenty of the Apalachin conferees on a conspiracy charge was also kicked out by a federal appeals court whose bias perhaps was shown by the action of one judge who could not resist writing a separate opinion traducing Sergeant Croswell by comparing him with Victor Hugo's scoundrelly Inspector Javert. When a judge on one of the nation's higher courts can so mistreat a hero of the law and turn him into villain, we have come close to the end of the trail marked by those signposts of apathy, bribery, corruption, and decay.

If we are ever to get off this disastrous road, to change the trend of the times, there will have to be sweeping changes on every level of American life.

The two-dollar bettor and the thousand-dollar bettor must be made to realize that the money they feed the bookie bankrolls every evil on the calendar from narcotics peddling to murder—and not just the murders of the Morettis and Anastasias, but of the Tommy Cavallaros, the Arnold Schusters, and the Charles Ferris.

We are going to have to discard a heavy cargo of old myths—that the gamblers of the mob are gentlemen sportsmen instead of a bunch of vicious pack rats; that mob murders don't matter as long as the mobsters knock each other off; that "campaign contributions" to "the party" don't influence the man; that there is such a thing as "honest graft," the ridiculous conception that bribes taken from gamblers don't count and don't corrupt. These conceptions, peddled by the mob and their police and political protectors, have been accepted in great degree by an unthinking public, and each has played its part in fostering the climate of indifference and apathy in which the mob's bankroll, its power, its terror have become superior to the law.

Finally, we are going to have to revise the priorities we assign to many crimes. We are going to have to recognize that bribery is a crime equal to murder. Since it is a crime that makes murder and all else possible, the time must come when the man who accepts a bribe is condemned and punished with the severity we reserve today only for the most hardened criminals. As it is, there is no statute of limitations on murder, but the bribe-taker, if he can get away with his taking for a limited number of years, is free and clear and can never be prosecuted. In a society increasingly influenced by the bankroll of the underworld, there should be no statute of limitations on bribery, and compulsory provisions like the regular tax checkup on officials recommended by the Trenton federal grand jury should be instituted.

Perhaps most important of all, we must give more attention to the control of campaign expenditures and to the financing of campaigns by ethical procedures. Nelson Stamler, who survived the Bergen County experience and was elected to the State Assembly and later to the Senate, was astounded to find himself ridiculed when he filed meticulous expense accounts in his first campaign. "But the law says I must file this schedule," Stamler told a courthouse attaché. "Yes," the man answered, "but did you ever look to see what penalty the law provides if you don't?" Stamler looked. He was shocked to find that the campaign-expenditure provision had been born without teeth; the law contained absolutely no penalty for its violation. With the cost of state-wide political campaigns running into astronomical figures, such loopholes are wide-open invitations for the limitless bankroll of the mob to purchase influence on some of the highest levels in the land. There can be little argument that the entire system of campaign financing has to be revised if we are ever to stop the corruptive thrust and influence of the mob.

Either we are going to change in these drastic but necessary ways, or we are going to see further and disastrous forays by the four horsemen of apathy, bribery, corruption, and decay. They are at full gallop now, and if not stopped, will trample virtually the whole of legitimate society. Then, indeed, will the underworld rule the world. And the people will know it.